Despite the great wave of publications on European cities and towns in the pre-industrial period, little has been written about the thousands of small towns which played a key role in the economic, social and cultural life of early modern Europe. This collection, written by leading experts, redresses that imbalance. It provides the first comparative overview of European small towns from the fifteenth to the early nineteenth centuries, examining their position in the urban hierarchy, demographic structures, economic trends, relations with the countryside, and political and cultural developments. Case studies discuss networks in all the major European countries, as well as looking at the distinctive world of small towns in the more 'peripheral' countries of Scandinavia and central Europe. A wide-ranging editorial introduction puts individual chapters in historical perspective.

Themes in International Urban History

Small towns in early modern Europe

Themes in International Urban History

Series Editors
PETER CLARK
DAVID REEDER

The Centre for Urban History, University of Leicester

This series examines from an international perspective key themes in the historic development of cities and societies. The series is principally, although not exclusively, concerned with the European city, with an emphasis on the early modern and modern periods, and it will consider urban systems, structures and processes. Individual volumes will bring together and present in an accessible form the best work of the wide variety of scholars from different disciplines and nations currently engaged in research on urban history. The series is published by Cambridge University Press and Editions de la Maison des Sciences de l'Homme in association with the Centre for Urban History, University of Leicester. The first volumes in the series include collections of commissioned pieces organized around certain key themes that lend themselves to comparative analysis. They have a substantive introduction by the volume editor/s, making explicit linkages between individual essays and setting out the overall significance and context of the work.

Themes in International Urban History will interest scholars and students in a variety of sub-disciplines within social and economic history, geography, sociology and urban planning. It rides on the wave of important and exciting new developments in the study of cities and their history, and reflects the growing internationalization of the area of study.

Titles already published

1 Edited by Ronald K. Goodenow & William E. Marsden *The City and Education in Four Nations*
2 Bernard Lepetit *The Pre-industrial Urban System: France 1740–1840*
3 Edited by Peter Clark *Small Towns in Early Modern Europe*

Small towns in early modern Europe

Edited by

Peter Clark

University of Leicester

CAMBRIDGE
UNIVERSITY PRESS

EDITIONS DE LA MAISON DES SCIENCES DE L'HOMME

Published by the Press Syndicate of the University of Cambridge
The Pitt Building, Trumpington Street, Cambridge CB2 1RP
40 West 20th Street, New York, NY 10011-4211, USA
10 Stamford Road, Oakleigh, Melbourne 3166, Australia
and Editions de la Maison des Sciences de l'Homme
54 Boulevard Raspail, 75270 Paris Cedex 06

First published 1995

Printed in Great Britain at the University Press, Cambridge

A catalogue record for this book is available from the British Library

Library of Congress cataloguing in publication data

Small towns in early modern Europe / edited by Peter Clark.
  p. cm. – (Themes in international urban history)
  Includes bibliographical references.
  ISBN 0 521 46463 3 (hard)
  1. Cities and towns – Europe – History. 2. Europe–History, Local.
I. Clark, Peter, 1944– . II. Series.
D210.S623 1995
940.2–dc20   94–10674 CIP

ISBN 0 521 46463 3 hardback
ISBN 2 7351 0610 1 hardback (France only)

CE

Contents

Figures

Tables

Notes on contributors

VERA BÁCSKAI is Professor and head of the Department of Economic and Social History at Eötvös Lóránd University, Budapest. She is president of the association of Hungarian social historians and has undertaken extensive research on early modern and modern urban and social history. Her publications include: *Towns and Urban Society in Early 19th century Hungary* (Budapest, 1989), (editor), *Bürgertum und Bürgerliche Entwicklung in Mittel- und Osteuropa* (Budapest, 1986), and many works in Hungarian.

BRUNO BLONDÉ is a research officer at the University of Antwerp-UFSIA. He is currently completing his doctoral thesis on the urban network of Brabant in the eighteenth century as well as a study about living patterns in Antwerp during the sixteenth to the eighteenth century. He has published a study of the social structure and economy of 's-Hertogenbosch (Tilburg, 1987) and is the co-editor (with R. Baetens) of *New Approaches to Living Patterns* (Turnhout, 1991).

PETER CLARK is Professor of Economic and Social History and Director of the Centre for Urban History, University of Leicester. He has written or edited a number of books on urban history including *The Transformation of English Provincial Towns 1600–1800* (1984). Since 1985 he has directed a major project with ESRC and European Commission funding on English Small Towns. He is at present finishing a book on British clubs and societies in the eighteenth century.

FINN-EINAR ELIASSEN was educated at the University of Oslo and has carried out extensive research on small towns in Norway. He has recently received a major grant from the Norwegian government to undertake a project on early modern towns in that country.

JUAN GELABERT studied modern history at the University of Santiago de Compostela, the Instituto Internazionale di Storia Economica 'Francesco Datini', Prato and at the Johns Hopkins University. He is now professor at the University of Cantabria, Santander. His current field of research is

Castilian society in the sixteenth and seventeenth centuries. His publications include *Santiago y la Tierra de Santiago de 1500 a 1640* (Coruna, 1982).

RAYMOND GILLESPIE teaches in the History Department, Maynooth College, Ireland. He has done research on many aspects of sixteenth- and seventeenth-century Irish society. Among his publications are *Colonial Ulster: the settlement of east-Ulster 1600–41* (Cork, 1985), and with Ciaran Brady, editors, *Natives and Newcomers* (Dublin, 1986).

HOLGER GRÄF is assistant at the Historical Institute, Humboldt-Universität, Berlin. His main research interests are small towns and pre-industrial urbanisation, the international system in the early modern period, and the social and ecclesiastical history of Berlin. Publications include 'Kleinstädte in Hessen 1500–1800', *Mitteilungen des Oberhessischen Geschichtsverein*, 76 (1991) and *Konfession und internationales System. Die Aussenpolitik Hessen-Kassels im konfessionellen Zeitalter* (Darmstadt and Marburg, 1993).

BERNARD LEPETIT is a researcher and teacher at the Ecole des Hautes Etudes en Sciences Sociales, Paris where he directs the Centre de Recherches Historiques. His current research is on the history of economic space. His publications include (with J. Hoock) *La ville et l'innovation en Europe 14e–19e siècles* (Paris, 1987); *Les villes dans la France moderne 1740–1840* (Paris 1988), published in translation as *The pre-industrial urban system: France 1740–1840* (Cambridge, 1994); and (with D. Pumain), *Temporalités urbaines* (Paris, 1993). He is one of the co-directors of *Annales ESC*.

SVEN LILJA is a research officer at the Institute of Urban and Municipal History at the University of Stockholm. His particular fields of interest are urban and local history and historiography and he has published (in Swedish) two books and several articles in this area. He is currently completing a major research project on the urbanisation process in early modern Sweden and Finland.

PETER MUSGRAVE is a Lecturer in the Economic and Social History Department, University of Leicester. He has undertaken extensive research on northern Italy and has recently published *Land and Economy in Baroque Italy: Valpolicella 1630–1790* (Leicester, 1992).

MICHAEL REED is Professor of Topography at Loughborough University. His research interests include English small towns, especially their social and cultural history, and he is also working on a study of the pictorial representation of English towns before 1830. His publications include

The Buckinghamshire Landscape (1979) and *The Landscape of Britain* (1990). He has also recently edited a special issue of *Storia Urbana* devoted to the English town.

PETER STABEL is research assistant at the University of Gent and is working on a major project on the social history of late medieval towns in Flanders. Among his publications are articles in: H. van der Wee, ed., *Growth and Stagnation in the Urban Network of the Low Countries (14th–16th centuries)* (Leuven, 1990); M. Boone and W. Prevenier, eds, *Drapery production in the late medieval Low Countries: markets and strategies for survival (14th–16th centuries)* (Leuven, 1993); and *Le réseau urbain en Belgique dans une perspective historique* (Brussels, 1992).

Series editorial preface

Themes in International Urban History is a series which is principally, though by no means exclusively, concerned with urban structures and processes in Europe. It embraces studies by individual authors as well as collections of essays organised around key themes in the history of urban development, bringing together scholars from different disciplines and countries. Underpinning the series is the belief that a comparative, international approach to urban history may help diversify the study of the city and its past, opening up new perspectives for research. In the process we hope to raise if not resolve some of the major epistemological issues of disciplinary scope and definition, while exposing the distinctive nature of particular national methodologies. The theme of the present volume is particularly appropriate in this context.

The study of European small towns is very much an invention of the last two decades and is only now starting to find its feet. There are many difficulties of definition and also great variations in the structure and development of small towns on the ground, as between different parts of Europe, regions and localities. Again there are quite specific historiographical approaches in different countries, related at least in part to the highly variable quality of the documentation. Nevertheless, through its survey of small towns from the Hungarian plain to county Galway, from Sweden to Spain, the present collection provides the first attempt at establishing a framework of definition and comparative analysis of European small towns in the early modern period.

The book originated in a lively international conference on European small towns organised by the Centre for Urban History at Leicester University in July 1990 with the financial support of the Nuffield Foundation. With the burgeoning interest in the subject in previous years, the conference sought to bring together some of the leading research scholars in the field from across the continent. One of the fortuitous benefits of the ending of the Cold War was the presence of a number of excellent colleagues from central Europe. The book is the child of the conference – smaller and hopefully neater. Contributions have been extensively revised in the light of conference debates and ongoing research findings. Regrettably, for reasons of space it was not possible to include papers by Michael Lynch on Scotland, Luigi Piccioni on southern Italy, Gyula Benda on Hungary, Adrian Wilson on English aggregative trends, and Kathleen Devroe on Belgium, though some of these are referred to in the footnotes.

The plan of the volume is broadly geographical. After the introduction, chapters 2–4 focus on a number of countries of the so-called European periphery with lower levels of urbanisation (Norway, Sweden, Hungary and Poland). Chapters 5–7 examine small town developments in the British Isles, a region which was generally moving away from peripheral to more developed urban status by the eighteenth century. Finally chapters 8–12 examine the changing condition of small towns in some of the most developed urban countries in the early modern period – France, western Germany, the southern Netherlands, northern Italy and Castile.

There is no orchestrated, strict tempo consensus of views among the contributors about the character, structure and trends of small towns in this period. The reader will find considerable differences in approach reflecting different perceptions and urban realities, though there is a common recognition of the essential importance of such communities in the urban landscape of pre-industrial Europe. In the European periphery including Scandinavia and central and eastern Europe what is striking is not the absence of towns but the plenitude of very small towns. In Norway, as Finn-Einar Eliassen argues with great clarity in chapter 2, the early modern era saw the creation by the Crown of numerous new towns both to control trade and to confirm its authority. Competition between towns was fierce and many centres were of a marginal size; nonetheless they had a distinctive profile of their own, social and economic, as well as political and cultural. Sven Lilja's wide-ranging study of Sweden and Finland (chapter 3) is also concerned to vindicate the significance of small towns, despite their low population, limited occupations and financial weakness. He suggests that during the eighteenth century some of the smallest micro-towns were growing faster and more consistently than bigger communities. In central Europe the precise pattern of small towns varied greatly, as Vera Bácskai ably demonstrates in chapter 4. But here small towns – both chartered and seigneurial – were widespread and numerous and during the later part of the period enjoyed substantial growth, particularly in Hungary. Among key factors were the growing trade in specialist agrarian products and the acquisition of new urban amenities such as schools, clubs and coffee-houses. Certainly the periphery was not condemned to urban backwardness.

For the British Isles Peter Clark in chapter 5 uses demographic data to describe the growth pattern of English small towns from the sixteenth to the mid-nineteenth century. Expansion in the late seventeenth and eighteenth centuries was particularly notable, keeping pace with that of the bigger provincial cities. This performance was linked with increasing urban specialisation (including the efflorescence of industrial, leisure and marketing centres) and distinguished by growing regionality with clear differences emerging between East Anglia, the South-West and more dynamic, mainly industrialising regions. Also on England, Michael Reed (chapter 6) articulates with vivid detail the diffusion of new cultural activities and images – from concerts and clubs to classical-style town houses and town halls – across the network of small towns during the seventeenth and eighteenth centuries; he likewise shows the marked local variations in the cultural kaleidoscope. The final chapter on the British Isles by Raymond Gillespie (chapter 7) charts the emergence of a small-town network in Ireland by the seventeenth century, with older towns being supplemented by a host of new colonial centres. He further demonstrates how the period after the Restoration saw increasing prosperity and industrialisation, particularly in the small towns of Ulster.

Turning to the more developed and earlier urbanised regions of Europe, Bernard Lepetit's dissection of small towns in France (chapter 8) is a methodological tour de force, questioning the real specificity of small-town functions in an economic and social landscape crowded with big cities, bourgs (or marketplaces) and large villages. By the eighteenth century, however, it is evident that small towns were officially identified as a distinct urban class, though one whose contours remained problematical. Interestingly, small towns retain this special recognition in contemporary France with President Mitterrand recently summoning a meeting with the mayors of French small towns. Another dimension of urban development is explained by Holger Gräf's study of Hesse small towns in western Germany (chapter 9), which offers valuable insight into the complicated hierarchy of small towns, and the divergent experiences of different types of community. By the eighteenth century those centres (including new towns) linked in some way to the state, as princely residential towns or under state industrial patronage, flourished, while other centres without such ties stagnated and turned in on themselves. More advanced, the southern Netherlands was for much of our period one of the most urbanised areas of Northern Europe and the changing role of small towns in the urban system is explored in this collection from two angles. Peter Stabel (chapter 10) looks at the demographic processes – high mortality, fertility and migration – which influenced the variegated pattern of growth in Flemish towns in the sixteenth century. This is a pioneering paper exploiting a range of difficult sources. On the later period Bruno Blondé (chapter 11) shows that small towns in Brabant did better than their larger counterparts for much of the eighteenth century and investigates in turn the possible explanations – foreign trade, transport improvements and domestic demand. In the Mediterannean the greater cities which had overshadowed the urban system were in growing difficulty by the end of the sixteenth century. In his discussion of Northern Italy (chapter 12) Peter Musgrave shows that important beneficiaries of the decline of cities like Verona were many small centres which became prosperous foci for industrial and agricultural trades – at least until the mid-eighteenth century when the process started to go into reverse. In Castile, according to Juan Gelabert (chapter 13), small towns contributed to the growing crisis of cities by rushing to buy their autonomy from an indigent Crown and developing steadily as rival centres for agricultural distribution and crafts.

Three general points emerge from the chapters. First is the great difficulty any historian has in dealing with so many towns with such inadequate documentation. In many instances the student of the small town has no chance to raise the questions and issues which scholars of big cities take for granted as part of their basic programme of investigation. But necessity is the mother of invention and the study of small towns is forcing historians to think more imaginatively about the available sources and ways of utilising them. Secondly, despite these studies there is a great deal more new work to be done and one hopes this book will provide a springboard for further research over the next decades. Thirdly, the extraordinary variety of small town experiences across Europe provides us with important evidence for understanding the rich complexity of regional and local conditions in the early modern period (more so perhaps than the study of the great cities where national and international trends are increasingly seen as in the ascendant). These points however do not obviate the need for attempting to view the diversity of European small towns in an overall framework, a task undertaken in the first, introductory chapter.

PETER CLARK
DAVID A. REEDER

1   Introduction

Peter Clark

Throughout the medieval and early modern period the small town, with a few hundred or thousand people, often clustered behind stone or earthen ramparts, with farms and orchards in its midst, and a handful of public buildings around the marketplace, was a constant and quintessential feature of the European landscape. In the high Middle Ages small towns with fewer than 2,000 inhabitants may have comprised over 90 per cent of all urban communities in northern Europe, housing more than half the urban population. By the seventeenth century England had more than 700 small towns; France over 2,000 and the Holy Roman Empire over 3,000; further east Poland had above 800 small towns.[1] Across Europe, there were five or more times as many small towns as all other kinds of urban community put together. The density of settlements was particularly high in southern and western Germany with one small town for every 6 or 7 square kilometres; in England the average was nearer one for every 110 square kilometres, though with much higher densities in the south; in central and eastern Europe the pattern was more diffuse with a settlement for every 322 square kilometres in Lithuania.[2] Despite the growth of bigger commercial and metropolitan centres small towns frequently dominated regional hierarchies, particularly where there were few middle-rank or larger centres. In France Gersoise Gascony was said to be 'a country of very small towns with narrow hori-

Preliminary ideas for this survey were presented at the Leicester conference in July 1990 and I am grateful to the participants for their comments. I am also indebted to Bernard Lepetit, Jonathan Barry, Penelope Corfield and Nicholas Davidson for their suggestions on an early draft.

[1] P. Hohenberg and L. Lees, *The Making of Urban Europe 1000–1950* (1985), p. 53; P. Clark and J. Hosking, *Population Estimates of English Small Towns 1550–1851: Revised Edition* (Leicester, 1993); ex information Prof. J-P. Poussou; see below, p. 186; M. Bogucka, 'The network and functions of small towns in Poland in early modern times', in A. Maczak and C. Smout, eds, *Gründung und Bedeutung kleinerer Städte im nördlichen Europa der frühen Neuzeit* (Wiesbaden, 1991), pp. 222–3, 229.

[2] M. Terao, 'Rural small towns and market-towns of Sachsen, Central Germany at the beginning of the modern age', *Keio Economic Studies*, vol. 2 (1964), 51; A. Everitt, 'The market towns', in P. Clark, ed., *The Early Modern Town* (1976), pp. 191–4; A. Wyrobisz, 'Townships in the Grand Duchy of Lithuania during the agrarian and urban reform . . .', in Maczak and Smout, eds, *Gründung*, p. 195.

zons'; and the same was true of several other provinces of France.[3] In peripheral regions of Europe such as Scandinavia, there were hardly any centres above the level of small towns. In early modern Spain, as Juan Gelabert shows (chapter 13), the urban system saw a marked shift away from bigger cities towards new smaller communities. In Germany about 1500, 14 per cent of the national population may have lived in towns with fewer than 2,000 inhabitants; in England there was a similar figure in 1700 for towns with under 5,000 people; in France by the end of our period 4 per cent of the national population resided in smaller towns, but this represented 29 per cent of the urban population; in the United Provinces in 1795, 18 per cent of townspeople lived in towns under 5,000, maybe 8 per cent of the total population.[4] Whether or not they lived there, for most Europeans the small town was their most direct and important contact with the urban world.

At the same time, the role and significance of small towns varied widely across Europe. Taking Europe as a whole, one needs to recognise the division between the northern periphery – Scandinavia, central and eastern Europe, and the British Isles (at least until the eighteenth century), where localised small towns played a major role; and the more developed, core regions of western Europe, especially the Low Countries and northern Italy, where in the fifteenth and sixteenth centuries small towns were more closely integrated (and subordinated) within national and regional hierarchies of towns.[5] But regional differences were also marked. In the British Isles there were marked differences in the pattern and structures of small communities between England, Scotland and Ireland; and, as we see in chapter 5, regionality became accentuated in England during the eighteenth century.[6] Across Europe regional differences were shaped by geophysical factors, along with the antiquity (or otherwise) of the urban system. In Germany the eastern areas had fewer and bigger small towns, mainly under seigneurial control; in the west and south not only was the density higher,

[3] F. Beriac, 'Petites villes ou bourgs? Le cas du Gers', in J-P. Poussou and P. Loupès, eds, *Les petites villes du Moyen Age à nos jours* (Paris, 1987), p. 39; R. Favier, 'Les petites villes dauphinoises face à leur environnement rural au XVIIIe siècle', in Poussou and Loupès, eds, *Petites villes*, p. 323; C. Nières, 'Les villes en Bretagne: 12, 40 ou 80', *Revue du Nord*, vol. 70 (1988), 681; M. Gresset, 'Les institutions municipales des petites villes comtoises au XVIIIe siècle' (Mamers Conference on Small Towns, Sept. 1991).

[4] See below, pp. 90, 186, 271–93; J. Meyer, *Etudes sur les villes en Europe occidentale*, vol. I (Paris, 1983), pp. 122–3; J-P. Poussou *et al.*, *Etudes sur les villes en Europe occidentale*, vol. II (Paris, 1983), pp. 328–9.

[5] For integration in the southern Netherlands see below, pp. 213, 215; for a good study of the subordination of a small Northern Italian town to a major city see Judith C. Brown, *In the Shadow of Florence: Provincial Society in Renaissance Pescia* (Oxford, 1982).

[6] See below, chapters 5, 7; for Scottish small towns see I. D. Whyte, 'The function and social structure of Scottish burghs of barony in the 17th and 18th centuries', in Maczak and Smout, eds, *Gründung*, pp. 11–30; see below, pp. 102–18.

but the towns were smaller and more of them were organic centres, developing out of the needs of the rural economy. No less important, each German territorial state developed its own complex mosaic of communities. In south-west France the proportion of the population living in small towns ranged from 12 to 31 per cent according to province. Finally there were differences between individual towns encouraged by local rivalries and a strong sense of urban particularism. In England the bigger and more successful small towns tended to be those established in the Anglo-Saxon period.[7]

Until recent times the number, importance and complexity of European small towns have been largely ignored by urban historians. Thus small towns have been striking by their absence from the survey literature. This is evident in one of the most important studies of European urbanisation during the early modern period by Jan de Vries (1984). De Vries looks primarily at the demographic trend of cities of more than 10,000 inhabitants to argue that while the sixteenth and early seventeenth centuries saw a sustained and fairly general urban growth across Europe, the next hundred years witnessed a concentration of growth in the biggest cities – particularly capital cities and Atlantic ports; in turn the late eighteenth century saw a deceleration of growth among the leading centres and the expansion of middle-rank cities, linked with industrialisation and population renewal. Unfortunately, de Vries' parameters exclude not only smaller towns but virtually all the towns of 'peripheral' Europe. How far were the trends he describes for the seventeenth century true for smaller places as well as the middle-rank losers? Or were there balancing flows of population into the market towns as well as the capital cities? And to what extent did small towns participate in and sustain the general urban revival of the late eighteenth century? Paul Bairoch's *La population des villes européennes* (1988) employs a lower urban threshold (5,000), but one still too high to catch more than a tiny minority of Europe's smaller centres. Paul Hohenberg and Lyn Lees in their valuable survey *The Making of Urban Europe* (1985) recognise the importance of small towns as part of a central place system of traditional towns closely identified with regional hinterlands and rural economies – in contrast to the outward-looking international trade network of major cities. But there is little detailed discussion of small-town developments and small centres are generally perceived as dependents of larger cities in the urban hierarchy.[8] There is insufficient awareness of the

---

[7] See below, pp. 187–8; Terao, 'Rural small towns', pp. 51–9; J-P. Poussou, *Bordeaux et le Sud-Ouest au XVIIIe siècle* (Paris, 1983), p. 211; A. Everitt, 'The Banburys of England', *Urban History Yearbook 1974* (Leicester, 1974), pp. 28–38.

[8] J. de Vries, *European Urbanisation 1500–1800* (1984), esp. pp. 95–101; de Vries has a brief discussion of smaller towns on pp. 58–66; P. Bairoch, *La population des villes européennes* (Geneva, 1988); Hohenberg and Lees, *Making of Urban Europe*, pp. 51, 101, 106.

distinctive role of small towns interfacing between the urban system and rural Europe, forging demographic, industrial, commercial and cultural linkages. National surveys of urbanisation in the Low Countries have been equally reticent about the large numbers of small towns in those areas.[9]

Part of the problem until the past few years has been the general absence of detailed research. The study of urban society in early modern Europe has made big strides since the 1960s. A great amount of important work has been published on the larger and middle-rank cities – the Antwerps and Amsterdams, the Leicesters and Lilles. By contrast small towns, for various reasons (some related to academic politics) have failed to attract the attention they deserved. This picture is changing rapidly, however, and the aim of this volume is to bring together some of the new wave of research to shed systematic light on the subject from a comparative perspective. In the following chapters we shall be looking at urban structures, functions and trends across a wide spectrum of European countries. The studies deploy a range of different approaches and examine a variety of demographic, economic, cultural and political issues.

A serious obstacle to understanding and comparing European small towns stems from problems of definition. How can we distinguish such centres, small in size and often highly ruralised, from the villages of their hinterland? And when this becomes somewhat clearer in the eighteenth century, how are we to draw a meaningful functional distinction with the bigger towns? This is not just a historiographical conundrum. Contemporaries were almost equally bemused at the status and actual role of pre-industrial small towns. An early official attempt at clarification for the Pontifical territories of northern Italy, the Constitutiones Aegidianae of about 1357, combined recognition of urban functional reality with an ideal order for each level of community.[10] Elsewhere terminological confusion ran riot. In eighteenth-century Denmark one hears how in this world of small towns, 'the peasant becomes a burgher and the burgher a peasant'. As late as the 1790s the Duke of Rutland could dismiss Saltash in Cornwall as 'a little village', though another writer shortly after spoke of it as 'a market town with a market house and above an assembly room'. The inferiority complex of some small towns may have contributed to the uncertainty, as when the officials of a Burgundian community apologised for the 'pettiness of a town which people nowadays barely deign to look at'.[11]

---

[9] H. Klompmaker, 'Les villes Néerlandaises au XVIIe siècle', *Recueils de la Societé Jean Bodin*, vol. 7 (1955), 577–601; Poussou *et al.*, *Etudes sur les villes*, vol. II, pp. 227–230.

[10] P. Jansen, 'Qu'est-ce qu'une petite ville en Italie à l'époque médiévale?' in Poussou and Loupès, eds, *Petites villes*, pp. 15–28.

[11] J. M. Bizière, 'Petites villes et micro-ports, l'exemple du Danemark', in Poussou and Loupès, eds, *Petites villes*, p. 423; I. Moreau, 'Les petites villes du sud de l'Angleterre à travers les récits de voyage' (Mamers Conference, 1991); C. Lamarre-Tainturier, 'Admin-

Early on there seems to have been very little direct comment about small towns as such except in so far as they had civic privileges. By the eighteenth century, however, growing demographic interest (along with the increasing activity of the state) led to a new awareness of small towns as a category of urban population. Such categorisation, however, was not always in accord with their ancient political status. Medieval municipalities, as in Brittany, sometimes had tiny populations by the close of the *ancien régime*.[12] Population size, moreover, was no infallible proxy for economic activity. In France in particular definition was complicated by the need to distinguish between towns, bourgs (market centres), and villages. As Bernard Lepetit demonstrates (chapter 8), any attempt at simple demographic (or economic) classification founders in a morass of regional and local exceptions. In areas of southern Italy and eastern Hungary there were populous agro-towns with only minimal urban economic functions.[13]

Political definition hardly works any better. In a few countries such as England all but a minority of small towns lacked royal charters; by the eighteenth century some of these unincorporated towns, especially in the industrialising districts of the West Midlands and southern Lancashire, were increasingly dynamic and expansive.[14] Elsewhere, as we have noted, civic privileges were much more important for urban status and ranking. The loss of administrative privilege could be disastrous. But towns differed enormously in their confection of rights and the precise permutation of privilege was vital in establishing contemporary perceptions of ranking. Molinier has written of France: 'there exist no two towns having the same privileges in the whole kingdom'.[15] In this context civic rights were an index not to urban ranking but to communal particularism.

These problems of definition underline the uncertainty and ambiguity at the heart of the economic and social world of small towns in pre-industrial Europe. For much of our period small towns lacked a secure, defined

istrations et petites villes en Bourgogne à la fin du XVIIIe siècle', in Poussou et Loupès, eds, *Petites villes*, p. 321.

[12] See below, pp. 173–4; also F. de Dainville, 'Grandeur et population des villes au XVIIIe siècle', *Population*, vol. 13 (1958), 459–78; Nières, 'Villes en Bretagne', pp. 679–83.

[13] See below, pp. 167, 170–3; also P. Benedict, ed., *Cities and Social Change in Early Modern France* (1989), p. 10; R. King and A. Strachan, 'Sicilian agro-towns', *Erdkunde*, vol. 32 (1978), 110–22; T. Hofer, 'Agro-town regions of peripheral Europe: the case of the Great Hungarian Plain', *Ethnologia Europaea*, vol. 17 (1987), 69–95; see also below, p. 86.

[14] M. B. Rowlands, *Masters and Men in the West Midland Metalware Trades before the Industrial Revolution* (Manchester, 1975); L. Weatherill, *The Pottery Trade and North Staffordshire 1660–1760* (Manchester, 1971), chapters 8–9; J. Langton, *Geographical Change and Industrial Revolution: Coalmining in South West Lancashire 1590–1799* (Cambridge 1979), pp. 95–110.

[15] R. Plessix, 'Les petites villes de l'Anjou, du Maine et du Perche', in Poussou and Loupès, eds, *Petites villes*, p. 127; A. Molinier, 'Villes languedociennes (XVe–XVIe siècles)' in Poussou and Loupès, eds, *Petites villes*, p. 149.

position in the European urban system. They were frequently manufactured by landowners or rulers in bouts of speculation. Thus 270 new baronial burghs were founded in Scotland after 1500, mostly during the sixteenth and early seventeenth centuries, to try and profit from the expansion of internal trade. In Lithuania in the late sixteenth century 394 seigneurial towns were created to exploit agricultural commercialisation; there was a similar development in Poland.[16] In Sweden the central government tried to extend its control over inland areas of economic importance by granting 30 new charters between 1580 and 1680. In seventeenth-century Ireland, as Raymond Gillespie indicates (chapter 7), new chartered towns were part of the game plan of English colonisation and commercialisation. In Spain a host of new centres were created about this time to bail out the royal treasury.[17]

New seigneurial or royal towns established from the late Middle Ages were frequently superimposed on an existing network of urban centres. As Raymond van Uytven has shown, Northern Brabant saw a spate of new towns inserted during the late Middle Ages into a web of established centres. In Germany new seigneurial centres were matched by an upsurge of organic towns. The result in many areas was an excess of urban settlements, with far too many towns chasing too little business. Across much of Europe the problems created by the relatively high numbers of small towns were considerable, even if muted by the fragmentation of space. Where specialisation among towns was limited, competition was intense. In early modern Norway, according to one authority, 'the history of the towns . . . [was] characterised by struggle', towns fighting with ports of shipment to stifle their development as new urban centres. The picture was similar elsewhere in Europe, with the challenge coming not only from other small towns but also from bigger cities.[18] Quite often newly founded towns never achieved urban take-off. In seventeenth-century Cumbria, for instance, a number of new market towns like Ambleside and Shap ended in failure. In Scotland

---

[16] Whyte, 'Scottish burghs', pp. 13–14; Wyrobisz, 'Townships in Lithuania', p. 196; Bogucka, 'Small towns in Poland', p. 229.

[17] B. Ericsson, 'The foundation and function of small towns in Sweden in the early modern period', in Maczak and Smout, eds, *Gründung*, p. 103; see below, pp. 270ff.

[18] R. van Uytven, 'Les moyennes et petites villes dans le Brabant Septentrional avant 1400', in *Les petites villes en Lotharingie: Die Kleinen Städte in Lotharingien* (publications de la Section Historique de l'Institut G.-D. de Luxembourg, vol. CVIII, 1992), p. 80; Terao, 'Rural small towns', pp. 54–7, 87; Meyer, *Etudes sur les villes*, vol. I, pp. 35–6; R. Fladby, 'The urbanisation of Norway in the early modern period', in Maczak and Smout, eds, *Gründung*, p. 130; K. Markalf *et al.*, 'Town and countryside in early modern Hungary – the case of Sopron c. 1500–1800' (Conference on Town and Countryside, Leuven University, April 1991); J. J. Chevalier, 'Permanences et mutations dans l'appareil productif d'une petite ville des Manges, Chemillé' (Mamers Conference, 1991); see also in Northern Italy, below pp. 255–8.

about three quarters of new baronial burghs after 1500 were unsuccessful. In Norway several newly chartered towns became 'shadow towns'. Even where they passed the urban threshold, many small towns limped along, enjoying a precarious existence. In more central or core regions where the network of small towns was more entrenched and integrated, such as parts of the Low Countries and Italy, there may have been greater stability, aided by economic specialisation.[19] But across much of the continent the instability of the small town was striking.

For many small centres a serious weakness was the absence of a viable urban infrastructure. This was most evident in England where the great majority of small towns lacked walls or gates and before the eighteenth century had no more than a market house or cross to consecrate their urbanity. Continental small towns were often better equipped, but even so the investment in physical plant, in local roads and bridges, paved streets and civic buildings was well behind that of major towns. Infrastructure was part of the urban patrimony and heritage, along with civic myths, ceremonies and pageants. There are indications that these too were less developed in European small towns, undermining a coherent sense of urban identity.[20] Vital here was finance: the promotion of the cultural and physical image of the town was expensive and, as we shall see, most small towns were poor.

Another factor contributing to the urban fragility of small towns was their over-dependence on their hinterlands and the local market system. The founding aim of most European small towns was to serve as a marketing outlet for the agricultural surplus of the adjoining countryside, selling in exchange a limited variety of goods and services. The umbilical link with the countryside was emphasised by the residence in many towns of substantial numbers of farmers and people following agricultural-linked trades – in some French centres over 60 per cent of the inhabitants, rising to 70 per cent in Poland.[21] Towns of this type met a strong demand in the rural economy. In Denmark attempts by the government to suppress smaller centres provoked a peasant outcry for their maintenance or restoration. However traditional hinterland trade was generally unsophisticated and unspecialised. Given the crowded urban network, marketing centres found them-

---

[19] R. Millward, 'The Cumbrian town between 1600 and 1800', in C. Chalklin and M. A. Havinden, eds, *Rural Change and Urban Growth 1500–1800* (1974), pp. 210–15; Whyte, 'Scottish burghs', p. 18; see below, pp. 31ff; Brown, *In the Shadow of Florence*, esp. ch. 3.

[20] O. Degn, 'Small towns in Denmark in the 16th and 17th centuries', in Maczak and Smout, eds, *Gründung*, p. 157.

[21] M. Couturier, *Recherches sur les structures sociales de Châteaudun* (Paris, 1969), p. 121; M. Vovelle *De la Cave à Grenier* (Quebec, 1980), pp. 34–5; M. Bogucka, 'Le réseau urbain et les campagnes en Pologne (1500–1800)', *Storia della Città*, vol. 36 (1986), 78.

selves under pressure from neighbouring towns and unable to grow.[22] The alternative was to try and develop a niche economic role, linking the town into a regional and maybe national network of more specialist urban centres. There was a constant need to add new economic strings to the urban bow: as more specialist industrial centres, as service towns attracting local gentry, as administrative or religious foci. In the Low Countries and other more advanced regions, specialisation was achieved earlier, though it was often difficult to sustain. But before the eighteenth century many small communities tended to acquire only a random scattering of minor or half-developed economic activities. This lack of functional coherence was one of the obvious aspects of traditional small-town economies.[23]

For small towns, then, the bread and butter of local trade originated in the countryside. The latter was also usually the operational base of those landowners who founded, protected and patronised small towns. But the relationship with rural society was highly complex, often shaped by the nature of the agrarian economy. In the less densely populated, pastoral areas of Europe, small towns were often less numerous but may have had a stronger economic position as the centre of most local trade. By contrast, in more populous arable regions one finds a wider range of commercial outlets for agricultural sales – not all of them located in town.

Dependence on the hinterland was certainly no bowl of cherries. It carried many potential challenges to small-town communities. Bad harvests might not only curb local demand for urban goods and services, but open the floodgates to a torrent of poorer villagers seeking food and work in local towns. Rural industry was a continuing threat to urban artisans through most of the period. Local landowners frequently encouraged rival industries on their own estates, or tried to set up new markets to divert trade away from established centres.[24] With their limited resources small towns were especially vulnerable to disaster such as fire, and the worst of man-made afflictions – war. In the Dauphiné small communities like Saint-Antoine were overwhelmed during the French Wars of Religion by 'terribles afflictions de famine, peste et guerre'. Military conflict also had a devastating

---

[22] Degn, 'Small towns in Denmark', p. 157; A-L. Head, 'Contrastes ruraux et urbains en Suisse de 1600 au début du XIXe siècle,' in L. Mottu-Weber and D. Zumkeller, eds, *Mélanges d'histoire économique offerts au Professeur A-M. Piuz* (Geneva, 1989), p. 130.

[23] Cf. J. P. Jourdan, 'Petites villes et bourgs des Basses Pyrénées au milieu du XIXe siècle', in Poussou et Loupès, eds, *Petites villes*, pp. 228–34.

[24] C. Dyer, 'The consumer and the market in the later Middle Ages', *Economic History Review*, 2nd series, vol. 42 (1989), 323–4; J. Jorgensen, 'The economic condition of Zealand provincial towns in the 18th century', *Scandinavian Economic History Review*, vol. 19 (1971), 2–5.

effect on the smaller towns of the southern Netherlands and Germany in the late sixteenth and seventeenth centuries.[25]

This concatenation of pressures and uncertainties meant that the failure rate among small towns was relatively high. In late medieval England several hundred small towns declined to villages. In seventeenth-century Poland many small towns went the same way. Even where the system proved more stable, small towns sometimes experienced general de-urbanisation as the rural population grew, eroding distinctions of status.[26] Larger urban communities waxed and waned according to their economic and political fortunes but they rarely fell out of the urban system: they had permanency. The propensity to disappear – to become villages – seems to have been a special feature of European small towns, particularly the lesser ones.

The identification of the role and functioning of small towns in pre-industrial Europe is clearly a complex and difficult exercise. Bernard Lepetit goes as far as suggesting that the problems are so great in France that the pursuit of the small town as a separate category may be impossible.[27] His stimulating approach exposes the danger of trying to impose a standardised and over-rigid concept on the immensely varied reality of small towns on the ground. Single definitional criteria are clearly useless. On the other hand, if we assemble a flexible matrix of demographic, economic, social, political and other attributes we start to get an idea of the profile of the great multitude of small communities.

Predictably small-town populations were relatively low. In France communities below the level of middle-rank towns usually had between 1,500 and 5,000 inhabitants. In peripheral regions the thresholds were considerably less. In Denmark the average size of a small town was about 1,200; in Poland 88 per cent of the towns had fewer than 2,000 inhabitants and nearly half 500–600; in Ireland 60 per cent of the small towns had fewer than 200 taxable persons. In the more advanced European regions, however, such as the southern Netherlands with higher levels of urbanisation and numbers of

---

[25] For the impact of fire on English country towns see D. Underdown, *Fire from Heaven: The Life of an English Town in the Seventeenth Century* (1992), pp. 2–5; and E. L. Jones *et al.*, *A Gazetteer of English Urban Fire Disasters 1500–1900* (Historical Geography Research Series, no. 13 1984); M. Greengrass, 'The later wars of religion in the French Midi', in P. Clark, ed., *The European Crisis of the 1590s* (1985), esp. pp. 106–14, quotation at p. 106; see below, pp. 196–7, 216–17; also C. Friedrichs, *Urban Society in an Age of War: Nördlingen 1580–1720* (Princeton, NJ, 1979).

[26] Everitt, 'Market towns', pp. 168–9; Bogucka, 'Small towns in Poland', p. 228; Head, 'Contrastes ruraux', pp. 134–6.

[27] See below, pp. 166–83.

large cities, the lesser towns were relatively bigger – with up to 10,000 inhabitants.[28]

Yet population parameters *tout court* are of limited significance. They may indicate the differential between bigger and lesser centres, but they are far from reliable in distinguishing town and countryside, where some villages were often larger than their urban cousins. More interesting are the demographic dynamics. Mortality appears to have been greater often in small towns than the countryside, but small towns did not usually suffer the large demographic deficits of bigger cities and some even enjoyed surpluses. However, as Peter Stabel (chapter 10) suggests, industrial small towns in Flanders were more likely to have deficits than marketing centres; in England growing urban and economic integration caused higher levels of mortality in small towns.[29] Whatever the internal demographic balance, many small towns, like larger centres, had high levels of physical mobility. At Mamers in France 54 per cent of marriage partners between 1740 and 1789 were immigrants; at Meulan there was a similar figure, though in Provence the proportion was nearer 20 per cent. At Nyköping in Sweden in the early seventeenth century 53 per cent of inhabitants were newcomers. In Norway too we find very high levels of population turnover. But recruitment tended to be more localised than for the cities, exploiting and underpinning the essential link with a restricted hinterland. In Provence the small town of Cadenet had inflows of migrants from 75 different places with a fairly dense network of contact up to 30 kilometres. The picture of localised immigration was also apparent at Thonon in Savoy. At the small centres of Faversham and Maidstone in Kent newcomers had travelled less than half the distance of movers to the middle-rank city of Canterbury. The smaller the town the more localised the recruitment pattern. In Flanders half of the migrants to bigger small towns had come from less than 20 kilometres, but the proportion was between two thirds and three quarters for some of the smaller places.[30]

[28] Favier, 'Les petites villes dauphinoises', p. 324; Bizière, 'Petites villes du Danemark', p. 422; Bogucka, 'Small towns in Poland', pp. 222–3; see below, p. 154; also for Sweden and Norway below, pp. 23, 25, 54. See below for the southern Netherlands, p. 207.

[29] R. Leboutte, 'A propos de la taille des villes . . . à l'aube du XIXe siècle', *Le réseau urbain en Belgique dans une perspective historique (1350–1850). Une approche statistique et dynamique* (Brussels, 1992), pp. 498–503; B. Ericsson, 'Town and hinterland ca. 1350–1800. Recent trends in Swedish urban history', *Storia della Città*, vol. 36 (1986), 14; Couturier, *Châteaudun*, ch. 2; Friedrichs, *Nördlingen*, p. 46; see below, pp. 223–4; A. Wilson, 'Population developments of early modern English small towns; the parish register evidence for four regions' (paper at the European Small Towns Conference, Leicester, 1990).

[30] Plessix, 'Les petites villes de l'Anjou, du Maine et du Perche', pp. 119–20; M. Lachiver, *La population de Meulan du XVIIe au XIXe siècle* (Paris, 1969), p. 100; Vovelle, *De la Cave*, pp. 60–1, 63; Ericsson, 'Town and hinterland', p. 14; see below, p. 39; R. Tinthoin, 'Essai de géographie urbaine historique: une petite ville: Thonon dans la première moitié du

We have already stressed the traditional function of small towns as centres for the agrarian economy. As well as having substantial numbers of their population directly involved in farming or related trades, virtually all small towns had markets and fairs, serving the local hinterland. But these were by no means exclusive to towns. In France markets and fairs were also found in bourgs and villages. Indeed in the late eighteenth century the majority of markets and fairs were not held in towns, though there were significant regional variations. But towns, including small centres, supported the most frequent and important markets and fairs, helped by bans on outside merchants trading directly with the peasantry.[31] As the period progressed, urban markets tended to become increasingly specialist, particularly in the bigger centres. A town like Mamers in western France with 4,000 inhabitants had a very large livestock market selling 23,000 cattle, 2,500 pigs and 26,000 sheep annually.[32] Throughout Europe markets not only provided the principal economic channel between small town and countryside but dictated the topography and built environment of towns. As is still often the case to the present day, the marketplace lay at the physical heart of the community, everything growing out of it.

No less crucial for small-town economies was the presence of a range of artisanal trades. In the villages of eighteenth-century Dauphiné it was unusual to find more than six or eight different trades, but in the region's small towns there might be up to 40 artisanal occupations. Swiss small towns, frequently with fewer than 500 inhabitants, had on occasion over 50 different occupations including trades and services. In sixteenth-century East Anglia small towns had a score or more non-agricultural trades compared with fewer than ten in the villages.[33] Nonetheless, the industrial or craft economy of small towns was often basic. Many inhabitants had limited capital and expertise and their output was largely directed at local and hinterland consumers. Tailoring, shoemaking and agricultural tools were often the leading trades. At the same time, industrial activity in European small towns tended to be less constrained by guild structures and regula-

XVIIIe siecle', *Revue de Géographie Alpine*, vol. 60 (1972), 349–50; P. Clark, 'The migrant in Kentish towns 1580–1640', in P. Clark and P. Slack, eds, *Crisis and Order in English Towns 1500–1700* (1972), p. 126; D. Terrier, 'Capacité d'attraction et hiérarchie des petites villes de Flandre Maritime', *Revue du Nord*, vol. 70 (1988), 766.

[31] D. Margairaz, *Foires et marchés dans la France préindustrielle* (Paris, 1988), esp. ch. 2; Terrier, 'Petites villes de Flandre Maritime', p. 758; Terao, 'Rural small towns', pp. 77–80.

[32] Plessix, 'Les petites villes de l'Anjou, du Maine et du Perche', p. 121; for market specialisation in England see Everitt, 'Market towns', pp. 187–91.

[33] R. Favier, 'Les artisans dans les petites villes dauphinoises au XVIIIe siècle' (Mamers Conference); also A-M. Cocula-Vaillières, 'Un critère qualitatif et quantitatif au XVIII siècle', in Poussou and Loupès, eds, *Petites villes*, pp. 162–3; Head, 'Les contrastes ruraux', pp. 127–8; J. Patten, 'Village and town: an occupational study', *Agricultural History Review*, 20 (1972), 9–10.

tions than was the case in the big cities. Small towns may thus have had greater flexibility and cheaper costs, helping them to cope with the recurrent problem of rural competition.[34]

For many small towns certainly by the eighteenth century there was another strand of economic activity: the provision of a growing range of services to the adjoining countryside. England saw an important growth of retail shops in small towns by the early eighteenth century, steadily eclipsing the markets and fairs; as Peter Musgrave shows in chapter 12, permanent shops were also found in the small towns of Northern Italy.[35] Elsewhere in Europe retailing developed more slowly, but there was a general growth of the professions. By the eighteenth century many French towns had clusters of professional men – in one Provençal town we find six doctors, fourteen lawyers and notaries, and four teachers. In the Austrian Netherlands the town of St Niklaas had a number of lawyers, a college and several secondary schools and was also active in money-lending to country farmers. In Spain tertiary activities, particularly professional services, were vital in defining the urban status of small towns.[36]

Professional ranks were also reinforced in continental small towns by growing numbers of officials. At Nyköping in Sweden ducal officials were as numerous as town burgesses. At Cadenet in France there were a dozen administrators of different kinds, while at Châteaudun officials comprised about 10 per cent of tax payers in 1694. At Nördlingen in Germany the proportion of professional men and officials rose to about 10 per cent of male citizens in the late seventeenth century and, no less important, they had trebled their taxable wealth since the late sixteenth century.[37]

The professional and official classes along with merchants and traders formed the core of the elite in European small towns. But in terms of social structure, one can see that most towns lacked the socially polarised arrangements of the major cities. There was no heavily entrenched patrician class: elite groups were often narrow, in Danish small towns comprising fewer than two dozen people. In Norway, as Finn-Einar Eliassen shows in chapter

---

[34] Patten, 'Village and town', p. 12; Wyrobisz, 'Townships in Lithuania', p. 200.

[35] I. Mitchell, 'The development of urban retailing 1700–1815', in P. Clark, ed., *The Transformation of English Provincial Towns* (1984), pp. 259–78; also H-C. Mui and L. H. Mui, *Shops and Shopkeeping in 18th-century England* (1989), esp. ch. 2 (this underestimates the role of market towns); for Northern Italy see below, p. 260; shops are also found in Dutch small towns: J. A. Faber, *Drie Eeuwen Friesland*, vol. I (Wageningen, 1972), p. 400.

[36] Vovelle, *De la Cave*, p. 34; P. van Duyse, 'The development of small towns in the 18th century. The case of the Waasland' (Conference on Urban Hierarchies, Leicester University, April 1989); M-C. Huetz de Lemps-Emine, 'Villes et petites villes en Nouvelle Castille à la fin du XVIIIe siècle et au début du XIXe siècle', in Poussou and Loupès eds, *Petites villes*, pp. 102–3.

[37] Ericsson, 'Town and hinterland', p. 12; Vovelle, *De la Cave*, p. 34; Couturier, *Châteaudun*, p. 122; Friedrichs, *Nördlingen*, p. 136.

2, one or two people might control the town; the loss of a key player could threaten economic and political disaster for a small community.[38] Spatially, one finds more social mixing than in bigger cities. There were no overwhelming numbers of poor crowded into slum or shanty-town areas. Even so, the social configurations often displayed marked differences from the countryside. At Nördlingen in Germany a quarter of the citizens paid the lowest rate of tax, while seven citizens controlled 10 per cent of the town's taxable wealth. In some French towns up to a quarter of the residents were day labourers compared with much lower numbers in rural settlements. The small German town of Uelzen had 35 per cent of its inhabitants living on or under the subsistence line. Rural problems of poverty and destitution frequently migrated into local towns and became more concentrated there. Though social pressures and social segregation were undeniably less acute than in the biggest cities, small towns were by no means urban arcadias.[39]

On the political role of small towns it is difficult to generalise. As already noted, civic privileges varied greatly from one community to another. Small towns frequently devised an idiosyncratic superstructure of governing bodies whose structural diversity was an important buttress of their autonomy. At the same time, one needs to distinguish between urban pretension and real power. The smallness and weakness of elite groups was compounded by the civic indigence of many small towns. A small town of the Zwin had a civic income at the end of the Middle Ages equivalent to less than half a per cent of that enjoyed by nearby Bruges. In Sweden the poverty of civic treasuries meant that small towns could afford only a few civic officials.[40] By the eighteenth century the civic significance of many small centres was on the decline and what political influence they wielded increasingly derived from operating as the local base for state administrative agencies. Thus Mamers was the centre of a royal bailliage extending over 44 parishes, housed a sousdélégué for the area, and was the headquarters for forest officials with jurisdiction over nearly 150 places.[41]

As in the political sphere, traditionally small towns sought to create their own individual cultural world. In most parts of Europe they had their walls and gates and a scattering of public buildings – though, as we have said,

---

[38] L. Coste, 'Les élites municipales des petites villes du sud de la Gironde (fin XVIIIe–début XIXe siècle)' Mamers Conference, 1991); A. Contis, 'Graulhet au XVIIIe siècle' (Mamers Conference, 1991); Jorgensen, 'Zealand provincial towns', pp. 6–8; see below, pp. 41–2.

[39] Friedrichs, *Nördlingen*, pp. 104–5; H. Schilling, 'The European crisis of the 1590s: the situation in German towns', in P. Clark, ed., *The European Crisis of the 1590s* (1985), p. 143.

[40] M. Walker, *German Home Towns: Community, State and General Estate 1648–1871* (1971), pp. 18–19 and *passim*; B. Fossion, 'Bruges et les petites villes du Zwin', *Le réseau urbain en Belgique dans une perspective historique*, pp. 330–1; see below, p. 70.

[41] Plessix, 'Les petites villes de l'Anjou, du Maine et du Perche', p. 120; also Nières, 'Les villes en Bretagne', pp. 684–9.

often a pale reflection of the splendid works in big cities. In Northern Brabant the bigger small towns had an early béguinage, hospitals and secular chapters – unlike their smaller counterparts. As in the great cities, religious activity played a vital part in helping shape the urban image and identity. In France bigger small towns usually had one or more religious houses, particularly friaries. After the Counter-Reformation religious orders like the Capuchins created a network of convents in small towns and the ecclesiastical importance of small centres in France continued into the nineteenth century. From the later eighteenth century nonconformist chapels were an important part of the cultural vocabulary of small towns in England. No less important, civic myths, ceremonies, plays and pageants helped sustain the special meaning of the small town's identity. In England before the Reformation fraternities played a vital social and cultural role linking market towns to their hinterlands. After the Reformation schools became an important and distinctive aspect of small-town society, leading to notably higher literacy levels than in the countryside, the spread of book-ownership, and later the arrival of booksellers and libraries.[42]

This then was the world of the European small town, particularly in the sixteenth and seventeenth centuries. They were anchored in and permeated by rural society – in Norway we even discover some form of urban feudalism. Economically unsophisticated, they faced competition not only from bigger rivals but also from a host of similar small towns. Politically and culturally limited, their local autonomy was accompanied by a notable vulnerability to structural change in both the urban and agrarian worlds. Up to a point, this model of the traditional small town is a caricature. Three qualifications must be made. Firstly, as we shall see below, small towns in the core regions of Europe, including the Low Countries, parts of France, and Northern Italy, were more closely integrated into the urban system, economically, socially and culturally, by the end of the Middle Ages; they were linked through specialist trades to wider national and international networks. These linkages were not without risks, however; early special-isation was often difficult to sustain and might lead into an economic

---

[42] Van Uytven, 'Les moyennes et petites villes', pp. 78–9; J. Le Goff, ed., *La ville médiévale des Carolingiens à la Renaissance* (Paris, 1980), pp. 234–9; R. Darricau, 'Les Capucins dans le Midi de la France de 1582 à 1880', in Poussou and Loupès, eds, *Petites villes*, pp. 373ff; P. Loupès, 'La Dimension religieuse de la petite ville au XIXe et XXe siècles', in Poussou and Loupès, eds, *Petites villes*, pp. 355ff; Lamarre-Tainturier, 'Petites villes en Bourgogne', in Poussou and Loupès, eds, *Petites villes*, p. 318; R. W. Unwin, 'Tradition and transition: market towns of the Vale of York 1660–1830', *Northern History*, vol. 17 (1981), 86–113; G. Rosser, 'Communities of parish and guild in the late Middle Ages', in S. Wright, ed., *Parish, Church and People* (1988), pp. 29–46; B. Simon, ed., *Education in Leicestershire 1540–1940* (Leicester, 1968), esp. chs 1–2; P. Clark, 'The ownership of books in England, 1560–1640: the example of some Kentish townsfolk', in L. Stone, ed., *Schooling and Society* (Baltimore, 1976), pp. 97–109; see below, pp. 140–2.

cul-de-sac. Secondly, there were considerable differences in institutional structures between towns in different countries. On the one hand, we have the tightly regulated, fiercely autonomous and individualistic ancient Home Towns of Germany; and, on the other, the mainly open small towns of England, without walls, corporations or guilds, where controls were mostly of the informal variety, though effective nonetheless.[43] Thirdly and most important, within the small-town universe, it is evident there was a range, even a hierarchy of communities. In his study of Norway, Finn-Einar Eliassen speaks of chartered towns, export towns, micro-towns, even shadow towns. In Hesse, Holger Gräf (chapter 9) identifies four levels of urban community under the demographic ceiling of 2,000 people. Peter Musgrave identifies tiny rur-towns below the level of small centres. Those communities at the bottom end of the hierarchy usually had only a few hundred inhabitants and a very limited non-agrarian economy. They were often new towns or ones on the economic periphery, lacking the functions of more developed communities with their wider array of economic, social and cultural activities. As we have already noted, they may have been most vulnerable to failure or disappearance, at least in the earlier period. By the eighteenth century, however, there are signs that at least some of them were enjoying considerable growth.[44]

Yet despite their differences, European small towns shared many common features and developments. They also experienced in some measure common challenges, challenges which became progressively intrusive by the seventeenth century, helping to transform the universe of the small town. One challenge came from the growth of economic integration, particularly through the development of new industries, both in town and countryside, linked to national and international markets. Stabel shows that, in the fifteenth and sixteenth centuries, a number of the Flemish small towns developed new industries and specialist trades in response to the demands of the Antwerp market, the commercial metropolis of Northern Europe. There was a similar pattern elsewhere in the Low Countries (for instance, the growth of a long-distance cattle market at Lier) and also in parts of

---

[43] See below, p. 48; Brown, *In the Shadow of Florence*, pp. 124–5; see below, p. 213; also J. P. Peeters, 'De-industrialization in the small and medium-sized towns in Brabant at the end of the Middle Ages', in H. van der Wee, ed., *The Rise and Decline of Urban Industries in Italy and in the Low Countries* (Leuven, 1988), pp. 165–79; Walker, *German Home Towns*, pp. 34–7; P. Clark and P. Slack, *English Towns in Transition 1500–1700* (1976), pp. 17–23.

[44] See below, pp. 30–1, 190, 252; for the growth of micro-towns in Sweden see pp. 71–3; for the rapid, if fluctuating, growth of small towns with between 500 and 2,000 people see M. Noble, 'Growth and development in a regional urban system: the country towns of eastern Yorkshire, 1700–1850', *Urban History Yearbook 1987* (Leicester, 1987), p. 5.

Northern Italy. But not all small centres in these regions benefited and by the later sixteenth century even the specialist centres were suffering decline as the pattern of European trade changed. From the seventeenth century the growth of the Atlantic economy and rising domestic demand had an accelerating general impact across Europe. Growing outside competition threatened inefficient craft industries with destruction, but there were also new opportunities to serve as a conduit between urban capitalism and new rural industries or as the local focus of so-called proto-industrialisation.[45] A second challenge stemmed from the growing power of the state. Throughout Europe governments were increasingly intervening in the political and economic life of towns, and small towns were particularly vulnerable to this kind of pressure. In France state intervention became pervasive in the early eighteenth century. Not that the intervention was always negative in its effect. Danish small towns benefited from additional civic privileges granted under the absolutist kings of the eighteenth century and in Spain small communities profited from the heavy fiscal pressure imposed on the big cities by the Habsburg monarchy. As Sven Lilja notes for Sweden (chapter 3), military expenditure in small towns (on barracks, fortifications, provisions) might also be beneficial. Quite often the European state located new administrative organisations, judicial, police or medical, in small towns, albeit mainly in the bigger centres.[46]

Related to the growing power of the early modern state was the massive expansion of capital cities. According to de Vries nearly half the fastest-growing cities in Europe between 1650 and 1750 were capital cities; equally striking was the great continuity and persistence in their growth performance.[47] Fuelled by the rise of government bureaucracy, state finance and the influx of landowners to Court, great cities like London, Paris and Madrid not only trebled or quadrupled their population, but had an increasingly extensive economic and cultural impact on provincial society.[48] There was also a major effect on the urban system, though the significance

[45] See below, p. 215; H. van der Wee and E. Aerts, 'The Lier livestock market and the livestock trade in the Low Countries from the 14th to the 18th century', in E. Westermann, ed., *Internationalier Ochsenhandel (1350–1750)* (Stuttgart, 1979), p. 241; see below, pp. 255ff. For the problems of Bayeux industry see O. Hufton, *Bayeux in the Late 18th Century* (Oxford, 1967), pp. 15–18; for the difficulties in the south-west of France see Poussou, *Bordeaux et le Sud-Ouest*, pp. 252ff.

[46] M. Bordes, *L'administration provinciale et municipale en France au XVIII siècle* (Paris, 1972), esp. ch. 10; Gresset, 'Les institutions municipales des petites villes comtoises'; T. Riis, 'Les villes et les campagnes au Danemark ca. 1350–1800', *Storia della Città*, vol. 36 (1986), 33. For Spain see below, pp. 271ff; for military expenditure in small towns see below, pp. 68–9. Nières, 'Les villes en Bretagne', pp. 684–6.

[47] De Vries, *European Urbanization*, pp. 136–42.

[48] E. A. Wrigley, 'A simple model of London's importance in changing English society and economy 1650–1750', *Past and Present*, no. 37 (1967), 44–70; Meyer, *Etudes sur les villes*, vol. I, p. 93 and *passim*; D. R. Ringrose, *Madrid and the Spanish Economy 1560–1850* (1983).

for small towns seems to have varied according to the precise shape of the urban network. In France the growth of Paris seems to have caused serious problems for small towns in the region. In England the enormous increase of the capital appears to have provided numerous market towns in the Home Counties with new industrial and commercial opportunities at least into the eighteenth century (see chapter 5). In Spain the rise of Madrid was a disaster for bigger provincial cities but more advantageous for lesser towns.[49] How far small towns were able to exploit the economic changes in the later part of the period depended increasingly on communications. Accelerating improvements in roads, river navigation, canal construction and, later, railways had a highly selective and often indirect impact on urban fortunes. St Niklaas in the Waasland was a prime beneficiary from the road and canal improvement in the area in the late eighteenth century, but other centres bypassed by the new communication links faced isolation and decay. In the nineteenth century French small towns with mainline rail connections achieved nearly the same rate of growth as bigger cities; those without trailed far behind. Whether transport innovation generated economic dynamism or the other way round is not always clear. Bruno Blondé argues in chapter 11 that improvements of this type were a sufficient but not a necessary explanation of economic growth in the Austrian Netherlands.[50]

Finally, local landowners, always influential in the development of small towns, began increasingly to take up residence there by the eighteenth century. This was particularly the case in England, France, Germany and the Austrian Netherlands.[51] Landed newcomers not only enlarged and reinforced the urban elite but brought badly needed purchasing power to the urban economy, stimulating the growth of the building and service trades. Arguably, they also contributed to the declining political and cultural autonomy of small communities, helping to integrate them into regional and national society.

All these changes led to the clarification and consolidation of the urban functions of many European small towns, strengthening their position in the urban system. During the eighteenth century in many parts of Europe, including Sweden, England, Ireland, the Austrian Netherlands, Germany, Spain, Hungary and France (between 1740 and 1790), small towns grew strongly in population terms,[52] and came to play a significant role in the

---

[49] J-M. Moriceau, 'Le contrecoup de la Révolution française dans le réseau urbain autour de Paris' (Mamers Conference 1991); M. Reed, ed., *English Towns in Decline 1350–1800* (Leicester, 1986), ch. 4; Ringrose, *Madrid*, chs. 11–12; see below, pp. 282ff.

[50] Van Duyse, 'Small towns in the Waasland'; B. Leaute, 'Le chemin de fer et le développement des petites villes' (Mamers Conference 1991). For sceptical views on the impact of transport changes see B. Lepetit, *Les villes dans la France moderne (1740–1840)* (Paris, 1988), pp. 320–2; also see below, pp. 234–8.

[51] See below, pp. 100–1, 122, 176, 203, 246–7.

[52] See below, pp. 72–3, 99–100, 164 et passim; for France see Meyer, *Etudes sur les villes*, vol. I, pp. 74–5.

economic and cultural processes of urbanisation. Linked with this was the growth of urban specialisation.

In continental countries the spread of new rural industries, so-called proto-industrialisation, depended crucially on the dynamic role of small towns, as sources of capital, as production, marketing and distribution centres, benefiting from the cheaper labour and less rigid economic structures found there compared with big cities. Indeed, in eighteenth-century Europe proto-industrialisation might be re-styled small-town industrialisation. In the Dutch Republic when the textile industries migrated from major urban centres such as Leiden, the small towns like Eindhoven, Enschede and Helmond en Brabant were significant beneficiaries serving as manufacturing points but also as intermediaries between big-city entrepreneurs and rural producers. In the Waasland, St Niklaas became a substantial textile hub with four linen printing factories and numerous looms producing mixed fabrics, while in France important developments include the emergence of industrialising textile centres near Lille, along with new proto-urban mining centres in the Valenciennois.[53] In eighteenth-century Catalonia the wool textile industry moved to small towns with looser guild structures and easy access to large rural markets, while Portuguese small centres developed silk and cloth trades. In the British Isles, Scottish small towns became centres for the saltmaking, textile and coal-mining industries, and specialisation transformed the network of English small towns with the growth of new consumer industries, the manufacture of components for producers in bigger towns, and the influx into small centres of crafts from the countryside – thus lace-making in Buckinghamshire and hosiery in Leicestershire. During the eighteenth century Ulster saw the growth of the linen industry largely based on small towns.[54] In industrialising regions small towns were a major reservoir of skills and entrepreneurial expertise.

But it was not just a case of industrial specialisms. Throughout Europe small towns developed as successful centres for agricultural processing and specialist trade outside their local hinterland. One can see this in Hungary, Spain and also Northern Italy. In Hungary agricultural commodity pro-

[53] J-C. Boyer, 'Petites villes, réseaux urbains et protoindustrialisation dans les Provinces Unies' (Lille Conference on Small Towns, 1987); van Duyse, 'Small towns in the Waasland'; A. Lottin, 'Un chantier de recherche – les petites villes du Nord/ Pas de Calais (1750–1850)', Revue du Nord, vol. 70 (1988), 675; P. Guignet, 'La genèse des petites villes du bassin minier du Valenciennois au XVIIIe siècle', Revue du Nord, vol. 70 (1988), 629ff.

[54] J. Torras, 'The old and the new marketing networks and textile growth in 18th-century Spain', in M. Berg, ed., Markets and Manufacture in Early Industrial Europe (1991), pp. 96–100.; J. Gaspar, 'Le réseau urbain et la campagne au Portugal (XIIe–XVIIIe siècles)', Storia della Città, vol. 36 (1986), 116; Whyte, 'Scottish burghs', p. 24; Corfield, 'Small towns', p. 96; see below, pp. 164–5; also W. H. Crawford, 'The evolution of Ulster towns, 1750–1850', in P. Roebuck, ed., Plantation to Partition (Belfast, 1981), pp. 143–5.

duction and long-distance trade in agrarian produce led to the massive growth of towns on the Hungarian Plain; in Andalusia production of wine, oil and other agricultural products was vital to the prosperity of the region's small towns during the eighteenth century.[55] Elsewhere small towns developed alternative specialist functions. Increasingly eclipsed in overseas trade by the rise of the great ports, small havens concentrated on coastal shipping and, in Britain at least, prospered. A growing number developed as spa or later seaside resorts. These had their first major impact in England with an upsurge from the late seventeenth century of small centres like Epsom, Tunbridge Wells, Cheltenham, Scarborough, Weymouth, Margate and Brighton.[56] But by the end of the *ancien régime* similar types of town were appearing in France, Belgium and elsewhere.[57]

Another related type of specialist centre was the landed or residential town. Often these places had a growing administrative function linked with the state or a princely ruler. Local landowners flocked there because of the increasing unfashionability during the Enlightenment of the countryside, which came to be regarded by the upper classes as primitive, dirty and dark. Moreover, as Michael Reed argues for eighteenth-century England (chapter 6), the more progressive small towns were increasingly able to offer many new public improvements: paved streets, new public buildings, street lighting, public walks; by the end of the eighteenth century even the old town fortifications were being demolished.[58] Major landowners quite often promoted this physical transformation. The new improved town served as an amphitheatre for a host of new fashionable social activities beloved by the landed and professional classes: cafes and coffee-houses, libraries, theatres, assemblies, concerts, clubs, masonic lodges and learned societies.[59] In both France and England freemasonry recruited extensively at the level of small towns. In Hesse, residential towns were important centres for the Enlightenment, and there were similar developments in central Europe, as Vera Bácskai indicates in chapter 4. Public sociability of this kind created and structured the image of the successful small town as the focus of an

---

[55] See below, pp. 86, 290–1, 260ff.
[56] See below, pp. 112–13; J. Walton, *The English Seaside Resort: a Social History 1750–1914* (Leicester, 1983), chs 2–3; J. Barrett, 'Spas and seaside resorts', in J. Stevenson *et al.*, *The Rise of the New Urban Society* (Milton Keynes, 1977), pp. 43–69.
[57] L. W. B. Brockliss, 'The development of the spa in 17th-century France', in R. Porter, ed., *The Medical History of Waters and Spas* (*Medical History*, Supplement No. 10, 1990), pp. 23–30; M. Cassou-Mounat, 'Le rôle du tourisme dans la création des petites villes balnéaires au XIXe siècle', in Poussou and Loupès, eds, *Petites villes*, pp. 435–6; J. P. de Limbourg, *Les amusements de Spa* (1782–3).
[58] See below, pp. 129–33, also p. 198.
[59] See below, pp. 120ff., 176, 263–4; Huetz de Lemps-Emine, 'Villes et petites villes en Nouvelle Castille', pp. 108–9; Poussou *et al.*, *Etudes sur les villes*, vol. II, pp. 289–96, 455–61; N. Bulst and J. Hoock, 'Structure territoriale et réseau urbain. Le cas du Comté de Lippe', *Revue du Nord*, vol. 70 (1988), 750–1; R. Favier in Benedict, *Cities and Social Change*, pp. 238–9.

urbane social world, drawing for its inspiration on the effervescent cultural scene of the metropolis, but patterning its precise configuration of activities according to local needs. Bigger small towns were in the forefront of the urban conquest of the vernacular rusticities of the countryside.[60]

All this would indicate that the conventional view of small towns as bystanders in the powerful processes of urbanisation which affected early modern Europe is misguided. The surge of urbanisation which occurred in the sixteenth century was accompanied by a proliferation of new small towns, particularly in the European periphery, and in some regions a significant growth of specialisation and integration of small towns into the urban hierarchy. By the seventeenth century the rise of state capitals and the problems of middle-rank cities created multiple opportunities for small towns as marketing and increasingly as craft centres. In the last part of the period the role of small towns was transformed by economic, political and cultural changes. Not only did they acquire more specialist industrial, agrarian, residential and distributive functions, but quite often with their greater flexibility and openness they served to short-circuit larger cities in the established urban hierarchy. They played a key role in the shaping of new regional patterns. With their expanding populations, they were a vital component in the re-making of urban Europe.

By the start of the nineteenth century many of Europe's small towns had crossed the Rubicon. No longer did they straddle the fence uncomfortably between urban and rural society. They belonged definitively to the urban system. When William Cowper observed in the 1780s that 'God made the Country, and Man made the Town', he might well have applied the critique to his own small town of Olney in Buckinghamshire with its bustling lace-makers, its scientific lectures, reading circles and other accoutrements of late Georgian urbanity.[61] The traditional model of the small town – in some measure autonomous but insecure – was replaced by a new one in which the successful small town was more securely integrated into an urban system which was increasingly dominated by international trading relationships. Economic specialisation and integration, communication advances, the influx of landowners, public improvement and new cultural fashions eroded the urban–rural duality of many older small towns and gave them a new identity.

It was not a homogeneous process: there were time lags and regional variations. The so-called peripheral regions, particularly Scandinavia and

[60] R. Halevi, *les loges maçonniques dans la France d'ancien régime* (Paris, 1984), pp. 67ff; see also M. Agulhon, *Pénitents et Francs-Maçons de l'ancienne Provence* (Paris, 1968), esp. part 2; for England see below, pp. 120ff. See pp. 165, 176.

[61] J. King and C. Ryskamp, eds, *The Letters and Prose Writings of William Cowper*, vol. II (Oxford 1981), pp. 27–8, 54 and *passim*; T. Wright, ed., *The Diary of Samuel Teedon* (1902), p. 39 and *passim*.

southern Italy, were much slower to experience this kind of transformation – often not until the late nineteenth century. Nor was it without casualties. Weaker centres, sometimes but not invariably towards the bottom of the small-town hierarchy, which failed to develop a specialist function or missed the bus of transport improvements, found survival increasingly difficult. Alongside mounting urban competition they faced growing pressure from the spread of new tertiary activities, particularly retailing, into the countryside. The eighteenth century saw the start of the rationalisation of the old overcrowded world of small towns with the weakest centres going to the wall, subsiding into village status, conflated with rural society. The following century saw a further second wave of reorganisation in England with the consolidation of industrialising regions. Moreover, there were no simple options even for the successful small towns. They may have enjoyed new urban success, but they steadily lost their own distinctive image and role within the urban system.[62] By the late nineteenth century they were increasingly variations on an urban theme orchestrated by the great cities. Even so it would be wrong to write them off prematurely. In the post-war period smaller urban centres have been important beneficiaries of the funding largesse of the European Community, while in a number of more dynamic regions they have flourished as centres of new industry and technology and as commuter centres, complementing and frequently outcompeting their big urban neighbours. The small town remains an essential building block of European society.

[62] See below, pp. 173ff.

2   The mainstays of the urban fringe: Norwegian small towns 1500–1800

Finn-Einar Eliassen

Mandal, Norway's southernmost town, was a fairly representative town in early modern Norway. A marketplace with no permanent settlement in the early sixteenth century, it grew into a small town during the early 1700s, its economic backbone the export trades in timber and fish, combined with shipping. Mandal grew irregularly in three different locations near the mouth of the Mandal river. Practically all its houses were made of timber, large merchants' houses rising above the smaller houses and simple huts of the middle and lower classes. David Inglis, one of the first foreign tourists to visit Mandal, in the 1820s, was 'struck with the singular appearance of this first-seen Norwegian town. I found the houses painted all different colours, – red, yellow, blue, in all their various shades; but the first seemed the favourite colour.'[1] Mandal had not changed much since the late eighteenth century, and Inglis found it 'the chief town (though little better than a village) of a district of the same name . . . situated at the bottom of a very small bay, flanked on each side by ledges of high rocks, and backed by a rugged rocky country'.[2]

From the late seventeenth century and well into the nineteenth, Mandal's economic, social and political life was dominated by a single family. Having no privileges of its own until the last decades of the eighteenth century, the town was formally dependent on Kristiansand, the nearest chartered town, some 20 miles to the east. Functionally, Mandal was nevertheless a town in its own right, like many other unprivileged or underprivileged towns in early modern Norway. Many of them share Mandal's main characteristics not least the 'small town feudalism' which places these small

An earlier, shorter version of this paper was presented at a seminar at the Centre for Urban History, Leicester University, in October 1990. The present version has benefited from the discussion there, and from suggestions made by Prof. Peter Clark.
[1] D. H. Inglis, *A Personal Narrative of a Journey through Norway, Part of Sweden, and the Islands and States of Denmark* (Edinburgh 1829) (written under the name of Derwent Conway), p. 7.
[2] D. H. Inglis, *A Personal Narrative*, p. 14.

Table 2.1. *Norwegian urbanisation, 1500–1800*

Year	Number of towns	Total urban population	Urban population as per cent of total population
1500	c. 10	5–10,000 (?)	c. 3% (??)
1600	c. 10		
1665	c. 12	20–25,000	c. 5%
1700	c. 15		
1800	c. 30	c. 90,000	10–12%

early modern towns in their proper European, as well as Norwegian, context.[3]

1   The urban fringe

In early modern Europe, Norway belonged to the periphery in more than one sense. Geographically, economically and culturally, the country was far removed from the centre of the continent, and even within the kingdom of Denmark/Norway, Norway was secondary to Denmark itself, and far removed from the capital, Copenhagen. Its population was much smaller than that of Denmark, its economy less developed, its inhabitants generally poorer, and its towns fewer and smaller than in the main part of the kingdom.

Even with a liberal definition of the term 'town', Norway had within its present borders only eight towns at the end of the Middle Ages. A further three small medieval towns – Marstrand, Oddevold (Uddevalla) and Konghelle (Kungälv) – were lost to Sweden in 1658. By 1700, the number of towns had increased to 15, and a century later, in 1801, Norway had some 30 towns (see table 2.1 and Fig. 2.1). Denmark then had twice as many, and Sweden nearly three times as many towns as Norway.[4] In addition, most Norwegian towns were small. Around 1530, only three towns had as many as 1,000 inhabitants: Bergen (6–7,000), Trondheim and Oslo (about 1,000 each). None of the others had a population of more than 500, and two thirds

---

[3] F-E. Eliassen, 'Den førindustrielle byen, c. 1500–1850' in *Mandal Bys Historie*, vol. I (Mandal 1994).

[4] F-E. Eliassen, 'Norske byer, 1500–1800: identifikasjon, avgrensning, funksjoner', *Heimen* 24 (1987), 139–151; O. Degn, 'De nyanlagte byer og byudviklingen i Danmark 1600–1800', in G. Authén Blom, ed., *Urbaniseringsprosessen i Norden*, vol. II (1977), pp. 9–11 and 42; S. Lilja, 'Small towns in the periphery' (in this volume); see also the articles by B. Ericsson, R. Fladby, H. C. Johansen and O. Degn in A. Maczak and C. Smout, eds, *Gründung und Bedeutung kleinerer Städte im nördlichen Europa der frühen Neuzeit* (Wiesbaden 1991), pp. 103–169; see also notes 5, 6 and 7, below.

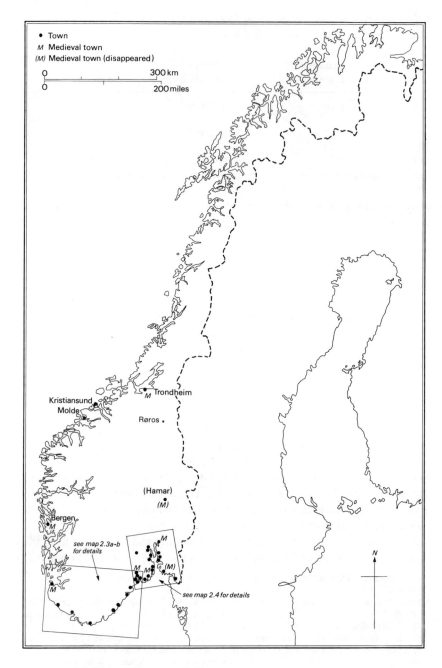

2.1 Norwegian towns 1801

of all Norwegian towns must thus be termed small at the time of the Reformation. Two medieval towns – the episcopal and cathedral towns of Hamar and Stavanger – suffered decay after 1537, Hamar disappearing completely before 1600, Stavanger just surviving, with only 200 inhabitants in 1567.[5]

By the 1660s, Norway's population had more than trebled since 1500, and the urban population had increased even more than that. Nevertheless, only seven out of some 12 towns had more than 1,000 inhabitants, and four of these had only about 1,500 each.[6] Even as late as 1801, when the population of Norway had doubled again, and more than 10 per cent of all Norwegians were town-dwellers, only 11 of the 30 towns then existing had more than 2,000 inhabitants, and only six had populations of more than 3,000[7] (see tables 2.1, 2.2 and 2.3). Also, large parts of the country had no towns at all until very late in the eighteenth century, or even well into the nineteenth. Northern Norway – north of Trondheim – was completely devoid of towns until the late 1780s. And after the demise of Hamar, the whole of inland Norway had only a couple of mining towns, which both originated in the mid-seventeenth century (see Fig. 2.1).

The Norwegian urban population was probably less than 10,000 in 1500, less than 25,000 in 1660, and less than 100,000 in 1801, when the total population of Norway was some 900,000 (see table 2.1). The most heavily urbanised region was the Oslo Fjord area, with some 18 towns and nearly half of Norway's urban population in 1801 (see Fig. 2.4). But the country's only town of a European format remained Bergen, then with 18,000 inhabitants, the third largest Nordic town throughout the early modern period.

In a Nordic context, Norway as a whole belonged to the urban periphery, alongside Finland and Northern Sweden. Denmark and Southern Sweden had more developed urban networks in the seventeenth and eighteenth centuries, reflecting more favourable geographical and economic conditions in those regions. Norway, Northern Sweden and Finland all developed a system of coastal towns, but had no – or practically no – inland towns. And Northern Norway, like Iceland and the extreme north of Sweden and Finland, was beyond even the urban fringe until the end of the eighteenth century. Only in the nineteenth century did towns in any real sense emerge in those outlying regions, as well as in inland Norway and Finland[8] (see Fig. 2.2).

[5] R. Fladby, 'Samfunn i vekst – under fremmed styre 1536–1660', Handbok i Norges historie, vol. V (1986), p. 133.
[6] R. Fladby, 'Samfunn i vekst', p. 134.
[7] Folketeljinga 1801. Ny bearbeiding, NOS B 134 (1980), pp. 86–91.
[8] G. Authén Blom, ed., Urbaniseringsprosessen i Norden, vol. II, pp. 90, 138.

Table 2.2. *Norwegian towns by population size c. 1530–1801*

	c. 1530		c. 1660		1801	
	Population size	Number of towns	Population size	Number of towns	Population size	Number of towns
Large towns	2,000 and over	1	2,500 and over	3	4,000 and over	6
Medium-sized towns	c. 1,000	2	1,200–2,499	4	1,500–3,999	12
Small towns	200–500	5	200–1,199	5	400–1,499	13
Total number of towns		8		12		31

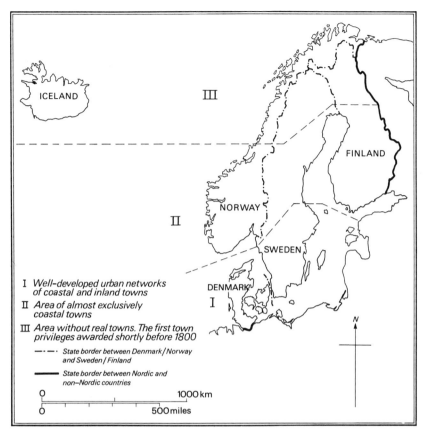

2.2 The Nordic countries: zones of urbanisation c. 1800

Within the map:

ICELAND

III

FINLAND

NORWAY

II

SWEDEN

DENMARK

I

I *Well-developed urban networks of coastal and inland towns*
II *Area of almost exclusively coastal towns*
III *Area without real towns. The first town privileges awarded shortly before 1800*

—·—· *State border between Denmark / Norway and Sweden / Finland*

——— *State border between Nordic and non–Nordic countries*

0   1000 km
0   500 miles

N

2   Size, status and origin

With the enormous population growth in Norway between 1500 and 1800 –
from some 150,000 inhabitants to nearly 900,000 – it seems highly reasonable to use a sliding scale to distinguish between small, medium-sized and
large towns through the early modern period. In the Norwegian context, a
town of about 1,000 inhabitants must be considered medium-sized in 1500,
with small towns ranging from some 200 to 500 inhabitants, and Bergen the
country's only large town. Three hundred years later, a small town would
have had a population of 400 to 1,500, a medium-sized town between 1,500
and 4,000 inhabitants, and a large town more than 4,000. That would give
Norway 15 small towns out of a total of 27 towns in 1769, and 12 small towns

out of 30 towns, as well as nearly 10 'micro-towns' and 'shadow towns' (of which more will be said later) in 1801[9] (see table 2.3).

These urban settlements were divided into four formal categories, defined by their royal privileges, or lack of them. A *kjøpstad* (literally a trading town) was a town with full urban rights and privileges, including its own governing bodies and officials, full trading rights, comprising the import and export of all legal merchandise, as well as exclusive trading rights within a defined circumference, usually with a radius of 30 or 40 kilometres. All this was laid down in the town's charter, and we shall henceforth call these settlements *chartered towns*. A *ladested* (loading place) was a port – and not necessarily a town – with limited exporting rights, of timber, fish, iron or copper, and with the right to import grain from Denmark, but no merchandise from foreign countries. We shall refer to such a place as an *export port*. Its burghers – merchants, shipmasters and some craftsmen – were subject to the jurisdiction of a neighbouring chartered town, through which foreign goods had to be imported.

However, the distinction between *kjøpstad* and *ladested* became blurred as the eighteenth century wore on. New urban privileges were more limited than the old ones; new chartered towns did not obtain exclusive trading areas, but had to compete with their neighbours. Their administrative structures were made less complex than those of older chartered towns; the number of councillors was reduced, new towns had only one mayor, and many newly chartered towns were governed only by a town bailiff during the first 10 to 15 years of their privileged status, having a so-called 'minimum administration'. Similarly, urban privileges tended to be granted piecemeal to new chartered towns after 1662, creating different degrees of formal urban status.[10] On the other hand, export ports might be granted quite extensive privileges concerning trade, the rights of burghers to reside in these port towns, and so on. Around 1780, several export ports – notably Mandal and Flekkefjord on the south coast (see Fig. 2.3a–b) – received the same trading rights (including imports from foreign countries) as most chartered towns, making the distinction – in this field at least – largely meaningless. In general, the so-called 'liberalization' of the late eighteenth century did much to undermine the whole system of urban privileges, by granting them to a large number of towns, whether these held urban

---

[9] *Norges første folketelling 1769*, NOS B 106 (1980), p. 46. See also notes 4–7, above, and 10–12, below.

[10] B. Sogner, 'De "anlagte" byer i Norge' in G. Authén Blom, ed., *Urbaniseringsprosessen i Norden*, vol. II, pp. 49–84; S. Supphellen, 'Byadministrasjon i Noreg på 17.h.talet', in B. Ericsson, ed., *Stadsadministration i Norden på 1700-talet* (1982), pp. 117–22 and 135–6; see also the various town monographs.

Table 2.3. *Norwegian towns 1769 and 1801*

		Number of towns	
Category	Population	1769	1801
Large towns	10,000 and over	1 ⎫	1 ⎫
	4,000–9,999	3 ⎬ 4	5 ⎬ 6
Medium-sized towns	3,000–3,999	2 ⎫	0 ⎫
	2,000–2,999	4 ⎬ 8	5 ⎬ 12
	1,500–1,999	2 ⎭	7 ⎭
Small towns	1,000–1,499	5 ⎫	6 ⎫
	400–999	10 ⎬ 15	7 ⎬ 12
'Micro-towns'	c. 200–399	?	5

charters or not.[11] So although the distinction between *kjøpstad* and *ladested* still had some meaning in late early modern Norway, we must not lay undue emphasis on it.

A *strandsted* (*coastal village*) had no trading rights whatever, but was simply a cluster of houses on the coast. Only the concentration of houses and people distinguished it from the rural settlements around. Most coastal villages cannot be considered as towns, or even 'micro-towns' (see below), but some of them had both the size and certain of the functions of a small town.

Finally, a *bergstad* (mountain town) was a *mining town*, in which the mine-owners enjoyed extensive privileges. A mining town might have its own governing bodies and public officials, and usually held trading rights for the provision of miners, officials and farmers delivering items such as firewood to the mines. The circumference of a mining town was established for the benefit of the mining company, which might be state-owned (as at Kongsberg, the silver-mining town) or private (as at copper-mining Røros for most of its history).[12] However, this category was also less clear-cut than it seems, for Kongsberg received some *kjøpstad* rights as early as 1717, and became a regular chartered town in 1802. Røros, on the other hand, was a unique combination of a rural and urban settlement, the miners owning

[11] F-E. Eliassen, 'Den førindustrielle byen', ch. 6; S. Dyrvik *et al.*, *Norsk økonomisk historie 1500–1970*, vol. I (1979), p. 227; K. Mykland, 'Kampen om Norge 1784–1814', *Norges Historie*, vol. 9 (1978), 99–104.

[12] K. Mykland, 'Gjennom nødsår og krig 1648–1720', *Norges Historie*, vol. 7 (1977), 265–74; B. Sogner, 'De "anlagte" byer', pp. 57–58; J. Simensen, 'Røros som historisk eksempel på sentrum-periferi-relasjoner', in 'Periferi og sentrum i historien', *Studier i historisk metode*, vol. 10 (1975), 60–81. K. Mykland *et al.*, 'Norge under eneveldet 1660–1720' in *Handbok i Norges historie*, vol. III, part ii (1972), pp. 116–17.

small fields close to the built-up area. Kongsberg was Norway's second largest town in 1769, Røros a small town in 1801.

All the surviving medieval towns were chartered towns in the early modern period, and they held their own against their younger rivals. Norway's three largest towns in 1801 – Bergen, Christiania (Oslo)[13] and Trondheim – had also been the country's three leading towns in the High Middle Ages as well as in the Reformation era and in the mid-seventeenth century. And no medieval town was less than medium-sized in 1801. As elsewhere in Europe, the continuity of urban settlements in Norway from the medieval through the early modern period is notable.

But the main feature of urbanisation in early modern Norway was undoubtedly the emergence of new towns. Some of these were established as early as the sixteenth century, but their numbers and population increased markedly in the seventeenth and particularly in the eighteenth century. Most of the new towns grew gradually (albeit unevenly) over a long period, typically becoming first an export port, later a chartered town. Of the eight new towns which emerged between 1500 and 1665, six had become chartered towns by the end of the seventeenth century. Another six new towns were given charters in the eighteenth century, followed by two more in 1802 and 1807. Of some 23 new towns which sprang up between 1500 and 1800, 14 had attained *kjøpstad* status before 1810. In addition, three places in Northern Norway – Tromsø, Hammerfest and Vardø – were made chartered towns shortly before 1800, long before they became towns in any real sense.[14]

Government policy concerning the granting of town charters had two aspects. Before 1660 and in Northern Norway, the government's intention was to *create* new towns in order to control and centralise trade in a particular region. Christiansand on the south coast, which was granted full urban privileges in 1641, is a case in point. After 1660, however, the absolutist state normally awarded town charters as recognition of urban status to settlements which were already functional towns. Some of these were medium-sized, but most of them were small towns with fewer than 1,000 inhabitants at the time of receiving their town charters: Larvik (1671) c. 600, Risør (1723) c. 700, Molde (1742) c. 600, Christiansund (1742) c. 400, Holmestrand (1752) 5–600, and so on.[15]

---

[13] In 1624, after a devastating fire, the medieval town of Oslo was rebuilt on a new site, under the walls of Akershus castle, and renamed Christiania (later spelled Kristiania) after the king, Christian IV. In 1925, the town was given its old name, and has since then been known as Oslo.

[14] K. Mykland, 'Kampen om Norge', pp. 101–3; B. Sogner, 'De "anlagte" byer', pp. 83–4.

[15] Sadly, no comprehensive study of the Danish/Norwegian government's policy towards Norwegian towns has been undertaken. Urban historians have tended to concentrate on individual towns, specific events (particularly the urban privileges of 1662), or the economic

In 1801, Norway had 23 chartered towns, more than two thirds of which had emerged since the Reformation. In addition, eight export ports and a couple of coastal villages were large enough to be considered as towns (see table 2.3). All of these un-chartered towns were of recent origin, the great majority becoming towns only in the late eighteenth century.[16] Some densely populated places, which by their status or size might appear to have been towns, still did not qualify as such. The three chartered towns of Northern Norway may be regarded as 'shadow towns', having the legal trappings but not the substance of real towns, their populations ranging from 79 (Hammerfest) to 151 inhabitants (Tromsø) in 1801.[17] In Southern Norway, a number of places on the coast may be considered as 'micro-towns', with populations ranging from 200 to nearly 400, and having at least some of the functions of real towns, particularly as trading centres. They were settlements like Grimstad on the south coast (which was given its town charter as early as 1816), Sandefjord, Åsgårdstrand and Stathelle on the western side of the Oslo Fjord, and the twin settlements of Son and Hølen on the eastern side of the same fjord (which the Dutch called 'Zoon (i.e. Son) Water') (see Figs. 2.3, 2.4). Son and Hølen, lying only a couple of miles apart, might legitimately be considered as one small town, with a combined population of 550 in 1801. Hølen, on the river of the same name, had sawmills and watermills, and was where the leading merchants resided. Son, at the mouth of the river, had a good harbour and two thirds of the inhabitants, including skippers and sailors.[18]

A special problem is posed by mining communities and large pre-industrial works. Whereas Kongsberg was definitely a town, and Røros may be considered a small town in 1801 (see above), several works settlements – e.g. Vallø salt works by Tønsberg (500 inhabitants in 1801) or Bærum iron works west of Christiania/Oslo – were obviously not towns in any real sense of the term.

Finally, the coastal village of Stavern appears to have become a small town at the end of the eighteenth century, with 590 inhabitants in 1769 and 1,090 in 1801. Interestingly, in this period the village population actually declined, and the increase was concentrated on the naval base and shipyard of Frederiksvern, which had been established in 1750. But closer study reveals that the naval base developed a symbiosis with the civilian village, the officers and garrison of Frederiksvern providing a growing market for

---

privileges of the burghers. But see B. Sogner, 'Om bygrunninger i Norge i 16–1700-årene', *Historisk Tidsskrift*, vol. 53 (1974), 215–42; and S. Supphellen, 'Byadministrasjon i Noreg', plus various town monographs and local studies.
[16] See notes 7 and 14.   [17] See note 7.
[18] F-E. Eliassen, 'Ladested, omland og utland. Son og Hølen 1645–1720' (unpublished Ms).

Table 2.4. *Status and size of Norwegian towns 1801*

Status	Size				Total
	Large	Medium	Small	'Micro-towns'	
Kjøpsteder (privileged towns)	5[a]	10[b]	4	3	22
Ladesteder (export ports)	0	2	6	5	13
Strandsteder (coastal villages)	0	0	2	0	2
Bergstader (mining towns)	1	0	1	0	2
Total	6	12	13	8	39

Notes:
[a] 6 if Bragernes and Strömsö are counted as one town.
[b] 8 if Bragernes and Strömsö are counted as one town. (They were united in 1811, under the name of Drammen.)

the traders and innkeepers of Stavern, preferring a local source of supply to the privileged town of Larvik, some 5 miles away. This stimulus was crucial to the declining trade of Stavern, which was under heavy attack from Larvik during most of the eighteenth century.[19] The combined settlement of Stavern and Frederiksvern may thus be regarded as a small town when considered as a whole (see Fig. 2.4).

If we combine formal status and population size in a matrix, based on the population census of 1801, an interesting pattern emerges (see table 2.4). Even at this late point in time, one third of the chartered towns were small, and more than half of them had fewer than 2,000 inhabitants. Nearly all the export ports were small towns, and the only two which by our definition were medium-sized, Mandal and Porsgrunn, only just qualify as such, both having fewer than 1,700 inhabitants in 1801. Two coastal villages – Stavern and Svelvik – make up the rest of the small towns category, which comprised 13 towns in 1801 – over 40 per cent of the total number of towns. We have also seen that in the seventeenth and eighteenth centuries, a small town was almost always a new town, and normally did not have full urban privileges. Although modified by the government's policy of granting town charters to quite a few small towns, this pattern was still apparent at the turn of the nineteenth century.

[19] Ø. Rian, *Vestfolds Historie Grevskapstiden, 1671–1821* (1980), pp. 326 and 343.

3 Foreign trade and urbanisation

We have already noted that the Norwegian early modern town was almost without exception a coastal town, and the reason is obvious: their economic backbone was the export trade in timber, fish and metals. The new towns as well as the surviving medieval ones were all – apart from the mining towns – situated with their hinterland on one side, the sea on the other, and a good harbour in or close by the town. Many of the new towns of south-eastern Norway and on the south coast were built at the mouth of a major river, which connected a large, timber-producing hinterland to the town. Many towns were built on a fjord – an inlet of the sea, which gave access to the sea at the same time as providing a sheltered harbour. (Mandal, situated at the point where the Mandal river meets the Manne Fjord, exemplifies both these points.) All towns – even the smallest 'micro-towns' – also provided their hinterland with merchandise from abroad, from Denmark, and from other parts of Norway, directly or via a chartered town.

A new town often began its life as a market without any permanent settlement, or it replaced a nearby market which was less favourably situated. Mandal belonged to the former category, Molde to the latter. The urban embryo was usually a resident merchant, who inserted himself as a middleman between the rural population and the skippers and merchants from other countries or other towns, who came in the summer to buy timber or fish and sell foreign goods and grain. Alongside the newly resident merchant, craftsmen and workers established themselves, making barrels, planks and tools, salting and packing fish, loading and unloading ships. Several inns would spring up, catering for residents and visitors alike, and eventually the trading community would arouse the interest of the government in Copenhagen, often resulting in the arrival of customs officials to supervise the trade and secure His Majesty's dues. Within a few decades of the first merchant setting up shop, the settlement might have a couple of hundred inhabitants and be well on its way to becoming a small town. Arendal reached that stage early in the sixteenth century, Mandal in the middle of the seventeenth, and Molde by the turn of the eighteenth century.[20]

However, at that stage of their development, such settlements were rather unstable, often fluctuating between one hundred and two hundred inhabitants for many decades, highly vulnerable to economic and demographic fluctuations. However, once their population had reached the 400 mark, which was often passed in a surge of rapid growth over a decade or two, they became stable, if small, towns, never dropping below that level of popu-

[20] C. Poppe, 'Før Arendal ble kjøbstad', *Aust-Agder-Arv 1975–76* (1977), 11–13; F-E. Eliassen, 'Den førindustrielle byen', ch. 1; N. de Seve, *Molde bys historie*, vol. I (1962).

lation again.[21] So there is good reason for regarding 400 inhabitants as the threshold size for a Norwegian town in the seventeenth and eighteenth centuries. Four hundred was also the population size of the smallest community to gain a town charter in the early modern period, except for the 'shadow towns' of Northern Norway.

4   Urban networks?

Norwegian towns were situated far from the capital, Copenhagen, and suffered none of the depressing effects felt by Danish towns, which were seen as competitors and carefully held in check by the capital.[22] On the other hand, there was considerable rivalry and competition between Norwegian towns, the larger, chartered, often older towns trying to dominate or even eliminate the younger, smaller and un-chartered towns within their region.

Government policy, prompted by the established, chartered towns, was to concentrate trade – and particularly foreign trade – in a few, large towns with full urban privileges. Within its region, such a large, chartered town might have several dependent export ports, whose trade was meant to be controlled by the merchants of the chartered towns. Thus, urban networks grew up, or were established, consisting of a dominant, fairly large, fully privileged central town and several smaller towns with limited trading rights around it. Such a network was established by royal decrees in the mid-seventeenth century, on the south coast of Norway (see Fig. 2.3a). Here, a new town, Christiansand, was founded by royal command in 1641, on the site of an old market. The new town was given full urban rights and privileges, two major rivers connected it with a huge hinterland, and four small settlements were subordinated to Christiansand as export ports: Arendal and Øster-Risør in the east, Mandal and Flekkefjord in the west. None of these places had more than 200 inhabitants at the time. The purpose of this arrangement was to make Christiansand the urban centre for the whole south coast (Agder or 'Sørlandet') region, and eventually to concentrate the region's entire trade and all its burghers there.

The reality proved to be different. Although Christiansand grew rapidly, to more than 1,500 inhabitants in 1665 and more than 3,000 in 1720, its smaller neighbours fought successfully for their own interests. The eastern ones broke free of Christiansand to become chartered towns themselves in 1723, and the western ones managed to stay economically independent of their big neighbour, growing into quite successful small towns, and even

[21] F-E. Eliassen, 'Norske byer, 1500–1800', pp. 140–1.
[22] H. Becker-Christensen, 'De danske købstæders økonomiske udvikling og regeringens erhvervspolitik 1660–1750', *Erhvervshistorisk Årbog 1979* (Århus, 1980), pp. 41–97.

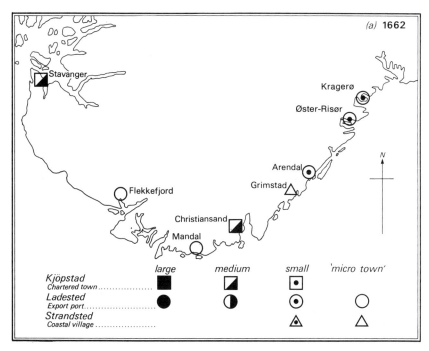

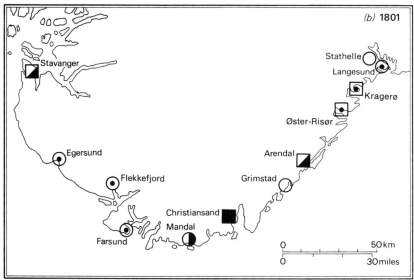

2.3a Norway: south coast towns 1662
2.3b Norway: south coast towns 1801

gaining the right to import from abroad all lawful merchandise in 1779/80.[23] In 1801, Mandal and Arendal were medium-sized towns – albeit *small* medium-sized towns – and the south-coast region presented a pattern of independent urban development in several centres along the coast (see Fig. 2.3b).

The main reason why small towns like Mandal managed to survive quite fierce and persistent onslaughts from the merchants and magistrates of Christiansand lay in the topography of the region. The landscape consists of a rocky coastal zone, a narrow belt of fertile soil just inside it, and long river valleys extending into the forests and mountains of the interior. Thus each town's hinterland was effectively protected from intrusion by the merchants of another by land barriers. As export goods – notably timber in various forms – were bulky but of low value in relation to bulk, the cost of transport overland across the valleys prohibited the merchants of Christiansand from taking over another town's trade, or substantial parts of its hinterland.[24]

Another – similar, but more complex – pattern is presented by the Oslo Fjord region (Fig. 2.4). This was the most heavily urbanised region in early modern Norway, as is still the case today, and several of the towns had medieval origins. The area also had more chartered towns than any other part of Norway around 1800, and most of the Oslo Fjord towns were large or medium-sized by that time. Even so, many small towns existed in this region as well, and many of the medium-sized towns of 1801 had been small only a decade or two earlier – for instance Tønsberg, Fredrikstad and Porsgrunn.

Compared to the south-coast towns, the small towns on the Oslo Fjord had more restricted and less well protected hinterlands. For instance, Fredrikshald's hinterland was restricted by its western neighbour, Fredrikstad. Son, Hølen and Drøbak were hemmed in by their big neighbours, Christiania in the north, Moss in the south, and Fredrikstad, which controlled the river valley of the Glomma, in the east.[25] On the western side of the Oslo Fjord, the towns between Bragernes/Strømsø in the north and Skien in the south were situated so close to each other that competition was fierce. The only successful town in this area was Tønsberg (Norway's oldest

---

23 S. Steen, *Kristiansands historie*, vol. I, *1641–1814*, ch. 15; Eliassen, 'Den førindustrielle byen', ch. 6.

24 One exception to the rule was the parish of Øyslebø, in the middle of the Mandal valley, at the mouth of which Mandal was situated. From Øyslebø church, a road cut across the north–south lines of the main valleys, following minor valleys south-eastwards to Christiansand. Most of the planks from the Øyslebø sawmills were transported overland to Christiansand in the mid-eighteenth century, whereas timber and planks from the valley to the north and south of Øyslebø followed the Mandal river and valley down to Mandal town.

25 F-E. Eliassen, 'By og omland på 1600- og 1700-tallet', in R. Fladby and H. Winge, eds, *By og bygd, stad og omland* (1981), pp. 122–38.

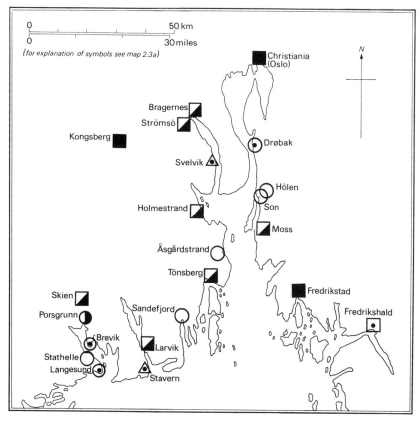

2.4 Towns around the Oslo Fjord 1801

town), which had secured a niche of its own as one of the country's foremost shipping towns.[26] The small towns on the Oslo Fjord typically depended on relatively small hinterlands, which they served as market towns and exploited for timber and agricultural produce. Some of them were able to take advantage of favourable situations or market corners which might give them an edge over a bigger rival in some particular field. A closer look at one set of towns will reveal this.

The four towns on the Frier Fjord – Porsgrunn, Brevik, Stathelle and Langesund – all emerged in the early modern period. Skien, the medieval town of the area, was situated, not on the fjord itself, but some 5 miles upstream, on the river that bears the town's name. Porsgrunn, at the mouth

---

[26] Ø. Rian, 'Vestfolds Historie', pp. 339–42; A. O. Johnsen, *Tønsberg gjennom tidene* (1971), pp. 127–30.

of the Skien river, began its life as Skien's deepwater port. In the 1580s, the Frier Fjord was Norway's major outlet of timber products, and early in the seventeenth century, Porsgrunn had become the greatest timber port in the area. The customs house was moved from Skien to Porsgrunn in 1653, in acknowledgement of this fact.[27] Throughout the early modern period, Skien remained the larger of the two towns, but Porsgrunn grew faster, and in 1801, both can be classified as small medium-sized towns, with populations of 1,812 and 1,529, respectively. Skien was still the social and administrative centre, and Porsgrunn remained an export port under Skien – but only until 1807, when it, too, became a chartered town.[28]

Brevik and Langesund also served as ports under Skien, but to a much lesser degree than Porsgrunn. Brevik was built on the first good harbour inside the mouth of the fjord where it could also command a reasonably large hinterland. Indeed, in the seventeenth century, Brevik appears to have been slightly larger than Porsgrunn.[29] But due to its more restricted hinterland – unlike Porsgrunn, Brevik has no river – it had only half the population size of Porsgrunn in 1801. Across the Frier Fjord from Brevik, the small settlement of Stathelle emerged only very slowly as a purely local centre in the eighteenth century, and was still too small to be considered a real town in 1801. Langesund, in the mouth of the Frier Fjord, was badly situated in relation to the inland trading routes, and had no great hinterland of its own. However, this small town specialized in fisheries and the export of fish, besides being an important harbour of refuge on a difficult part of the coast. It was also a staging point on the main road from Christiania (Oslo) to Christiansand and Stavanger.[30]

5   The significance of small towns

As we have seen, small towns played different parts and filled various niches in different regions – and even in different areas within a region. Small towns – and towns with less than full urban privileges – also shared many of the characteristics of larger and chartered towns. Their economic basis was roughly the same: the export trades, shipping, and the so-called 'bonde-handel' ('peasant trade'), supplying their hinterland with various goods from abroad, or from other Norwegian and Danish towns. Even if they were not administrative towns, they normally had *some* administrative bodies of their own, or at least acquired them in the course of the eighteenth century:

[27] K. Svalastoga, *Byer i emning. Porsgrunn, Brevik og Langesund 1660–1740* (1943), pp. 11–18 and 22–3.
[28] J. Tønnessen, *Porsgrunns historie*, vol. I: *Fra lasteplass til kjøpstad 1576–1807* (1956). See also notes 7 and 9.
[29] K. Svalastoga, 'Byer i emning', pp. 17–20 and 194–5.
[30] K. Svalastoga, 'Byer i emning', pp. 18–20 and 215.

harbourmaster and harbour commission, health commission, police and fire brigade, and so on.[31] As we have seen, young chartered towns often had only a skeleton administration. And many small towns, like their larger counterparts, were administrative centres of a wider region, with residing government officials like bailiffs, judges and county governors.

So what was the significance of small towns? Did they have any special functions or characteristics, which would make it reasonable to treat them as a special category? In other words, did small towns really exist? Or were there just *towns* – of various sizes? Starting with the demographic data, it has long been a truism that early modern towns – in Norway as elsewhere in Europe – had an almost constant surplus of deaths over births, which prevented natural population growth and made net immigration vital to the very survival of the town. Furthermore, in eighteenth-century Norway, there was a steady net movement of people from the inland areas, which produced a fairly regular population surplus, to the coast, where mortality was high, mainly because of greater contact with the outside world.[32] And that was where nearly every town was situated. However, it appears that most, if not all, small and medium-sized towns did produce a regular surplus of births over deaths through most of the eighteenth century. In Mandal, for instance, there was not one five-year period between 1750 and 1800 in which the number of burials exceeded the number of baptisms. There were demographic crises, of course, particularly in the early 1770s, but they were short and sharp rather than long and devastating.[33]

Turning to migration, the net migration pattern was the one just mentioned, from inland to coastal areas, from countryside to town, and also from small towns to large towns, or abroad. In the case of Mandal, the direction of net migration was normally from its hinterland into the town, and from the small town of Mandal to the much larger chartered town of Christiansand, to other Norwegian and Danish towns, and abroad. But net migration was only the crest of the wave, or more accurately, the crest of the stronger wave. The total migration into and out of Mandal amounted to *ten times* the net migration figures. And over a period of 18 months in 1762–4 (which is exceptionally well covered by sources), a number of people equalling 10 per cent of the town's population moved into or out of Mandal. (Since servants, apprentices, and young people in general moved much more frequently than others, this of course did not imply a complete turnover of the population

---

[31] K. Svalastoga, 'Byer i emning', pp. 189–220; F-E. Eliassen, 'Den førindustrielle byen', ch. 9.
[32] S. Dyrvik *et al.*, *Norsk økonomisk historie 1500–1970*, vol. I, p. 130; S. Sogner, *Folkevekst og flytting* (1979), pp. 90–103.
[33] F-E. Eliassen, 'Den førindustrielle byen', ch. 5.

within a decade.)[34] Thus there was an enormous flow of population into and out of Norwegian towns, and particularly between a town and its immediate hinterland. This extremely mobile section of the population was particularly sensitive to the changing economic fortunes of towns and rural districts, settling in or moving on from a town according to the expansion or contraction of its main branches of trade and production. Although this phenomenon occurred in and affected the development of every town, its impact was greater in small towns, exactly because of the small size of the resident population. Moreover, for the migrants themselves, moving from a rural community to a small town – or vice versa – was a less dramatic change than moving to or from a large town, a point we shall return to shortly.

Turning to the economic life of towns, we have already noted that practically all Norwegian towns fulfilled many of the same functions as centres of export, shipping and local market trading. But most of the export ports lacked the right to import merchandise directly from abroad, and the rest only obtained that privilege at the end of the eighteenth century. Also, the imports of a large town differed not only in quantity, but also in the range of imported products, from those of a small town. Both in terms of its population size and the wealth of the inhabitants, as well as the population and purchasing power of its hinterland, a small town served a much more restricted market than a large town did. This market also tended to be less sensitive to new trends and fashions than the elite of a large town and its hinterland – at least before the end of the eighteenth century, when there was a small 'consumer revolution' in large and small towns alike.[35]

On the whole, local trade tended to be relatively more important in a small town, whereas regional trade played a greater role in the economic life of a medium-sized or large town. But on this point, there were great differences of scale between Western Norway, where towns were scarce and all of them served quite large hinterlands, and the Oslo Fjord area, whose many towns had hinterlands varying between the minuscule and the simply enormous, mostly corresponding to the size of the town – or vice versa.

In general, economic, and therefore social, diversification and specialisation were much greater in large towns than in small towns. This can also be observed as a trend in many expanding small towns of the eighteenth century: new trades, firms and modes of production were established, a greater variety of services was offered, and a greater diversity of occupations

---

[34] F-E. Eliassen, 'Den førindustrielle byen', ch. 5. The basis for this calculation is a series of poll-tax lists, compiled and revised monthly between September 1762 and April 1764, listing all inhabitants aged 12 and above, and recording not only movements across parish borders and in and out of towns, but also between houses in a small town like Mandal. The population census of 1769 (see note 9) gives total population figures.

[35] See note 37.

appeared in tax rolls and census lists.[36] The causes of this development were at least threefold. In the first place, economic expansion, due, for instance, to increasing demand for fish, timber or copper, enabled a number of persons who previously had to combine various jobs and trades to make a living through the year, to work full-time in one trade, become more skilful, and perhaps eventually take up a more specialised craft or trade.

The second cause was the stimulus provided by the growth of the town itself. A larger population generated greater demand locally, and the greater the local market, the more likely it was to provide a living for craftsmen and professionals catering for special demands and interests. This development also went hand in hand with a third trend in the late eighteenth century: the rise in the standard of living of the majority of the urban population, followed by a greater degree of commercialisation and 'consumerism'.

On all these points, the small towns were generally deficient. Chronic underemployment and various combinations of trades and odd jobs were common features of their labour markets. A small urban society provided only a limited demand for specialised services and products. Finally, the smaller the town, the slower the development of a 'consumer society'. The most spectacular 'consumer boom' can be observed in those towns which experienced the most rapid growth in the late eighteenth century, particularly small chartered towns which within a few decades grew into medium-sized or even large towns: Moss, Fredrikstad, Tønsberg.[37]

The structure of urban society also varied between towns of different sizes. All towns, large and small, had an urban elite, a patriciate of families and individuals whose background, status and, most obvious, wealth raised them far above other members of the upper classes, not to mention the great mass of the urban population. However, in a small town, the elite was much smaller than in a medium-sized or large one, and its members tended to dominate the life of the town to an even greater extent than was the case in the larger towns. In a small town, two or three families – and sometimes only one – might control all or most of the large-scale economic activity in and

---

[36] F-E. Eliassen, 'Den førindustrielle byen', ch. 8. See also various other town monographs. However, one source of error must be taken into consideration: information on people's trades and occupations became more detailed as the eighteenth century wore on, culminating in the population census of 1801. Part of the economic differentiation may thus reflect the improvements in registration.

[37] N. J. Ringdal, *Moss bys historie*, vol. II, *1700–1880* (1989); Eliassen, 'Den førindustrielle byen', ch. 8; C. Hopstock, 'Livet i byene', in *Norges Kulturhistorie*, vol. III (1980), pp. 47–74. The 'consumer boom' was based on a combination of increasing real incomes and the availability of relatively cheap imported consumer goods like cotton textiles, tobacco and coffee, which percolated rapidly down through the social strata after having been introduced by the upper classes.

around the town, often owning the very ground upon which the town was built. They also usually kept a firm grip on local politics, for example representing the 'interests of the town' (which tended to coincide with their own) to government officials and the king himself.

In Mandal in 1789, three men, two merchants and the local judge, who was also a landowner and shipowner, together owned more than 80 per cent of the combined taxable wealth of the town, which had then some 1,200 inhabitants. Among other things, the judge owned the ground upon which three quarters of the town was built. These three men – Fredrik Gjertsen Nedenes, Johan Fredrik Knutzen and Fredrik Fredriksen – were brothers-in-law, the two last-mentioned having married into the Nedenes family, which dominated the town and hinterland of Mandal over four generations – from the late seventeenth century to the 1820s.[38] In neighbouring Farsund, the Lund family owned and ran a large fishery firm, which was the basis of that town's emergence and existence in the latter half of the eighteenth century and into the nineteenth.[39] Around 1700, the Solgaard family played much the same role in Son and Hølen as the Nedenes family in Mandal.[40]

Small towns lacked the broader upper and middle classes of the larger towns, where there were more government and local officials, more professional men, and – as we have noted – a wider range of trades. The evidence is ambiguous, but it seems that small towns generally had a higher proportion of poor inhabitants than their larger counterparts. Between one fourth and one third of the population of Mandal in the eighteenth century could be reckoned as poor in at least some sense of the term, and roughly 10 per cent of the town's inhabitants received poor relief. The corresponding figure for Bergen was 5 per cent.[41]

But life in a small town had more agreeable aspects as well. Although the relative gap between the very rich and the poor was great, in absolute terms it was narrower than in a large town. In towns like Christiania (Oslo), Christiansand, Bergen and Trondheim, the very rich were a great deal more affluent than small-town patricians. At the same time, the cost of living –

---

[38] Eliassen, 'Den førindustrielle byen', particularly ch. 8.
[39] J. Seland, *En by og en bank. Farsunds historie og Farsund sparebanks 125 års historie* (1967); B. Dannevig, *Farsunds sjøfarts historie* (1967).
[40] Eliassen, 'Ladested, omland og utland'.
[41] Eliassen, 'Den førindustrielle byen', ch. 8; A. B. Fossen, *Bergen bys historie*, vol. II, *Borgerskapets by, 1536–1800* (1979), pp. 772 and 788–94. However, the extent of the poor relief depended more on supply (how much the upper and middle classes were prepared to pay) than on demand, so such figures should be treated with great caution.

housing and food prices – was higher in a large town, tending to make conditions worse for the poor.[42]

There was also much less social segregation in small towns than in large ones.[43] Of course, the wealthiest merchants tended to concentrate in the central parts of the town (see Figs. 2.5 and 2.6, below), and day labourers, along with the poorer craftsmen, fishermen and so on, on the outskirts. But small houses belonging to mariners, small traders, craftsmen and lesser officials were scattered among the big ones, filling in gaps in the lines of houses as building space grew scarce, or surviving from the earliest days of the settlement. Conversely, merchants and prominent officials moving into a small town often had to build their residences on the outskirts, where there was more space for major buildings than in the central area. Indeed, at the outset, the embryonic town was often just such a mixed settlement of merchants, craftsmen and labourers, living close to each other. Large houses and small huts mingled together in what became the nucleus of the town.

This mingling together of social groups and classes within a small area of a small town had profound social and cultural consequences. People of highly different backgrounds would meet daily in the streets and know each other by sight and often by name. And even if they had no private contact, they would often meet again as employer and employee, creditor and debtor. As long as a town remained very small, people would know each other by their first names, often supplemented by their places of residence within the town, their occupations, or any other distinctive designation. In the mid-seventeenth century, Son and Hølen had a number of inhabitants known as 'Svend Skipper', 'Torbjørn Tailor', 'Nils in the Cellar', 'Halvor in the Castle', 'Laurids Shoemaker' and the like. In early eighteenth-century Mandal, we find people like 'Andor on Malmø', 'Torkild on the Sand', 'Jacob Sexton', 'Ole Blacksmith', 'Govert in Kleven' and 'Jens Christian from Jutland'. (Malmø, the Sand and Kleven were three of the main parts of the town, see Fig. 2.6.) Mandal had fewer than 800 inhabitants at the time. Even leading merchants of the town were known by their first names, like 'Jørgen Otto' (Tönnesen Dedekam) and 'Sr. Tørres' (Christensen Nedenes, Mandal's dominant figure in the first decades of the century).[44] The fact

---

[42] Thus, at the turn of the nineteenth century, several carpenters from Mandal declined an offer to work in Christiansand for better wages, pointing out that the costs of living were considerably higher in the large town than in Mandal.

[43] J. H. Munksgaard, 'Kristiansands kvadratur', *Agder Historielags Årsskrift*, Vol. 58 (1982), 8–37; K-O. Masdalen, 'Yrkes- og bosetningsstruktur i Arendal omkring år 1800'. *Aust-Agder-Arv* 1979–1980 (1981), 101–31; J. A. Wikander, *Gamle tomter i Grimstad. Grunneiere og huseiere* (1973); F-E. Eliassen, 'Den førindustrielle byen', chs. 1, 2, 3, 10 and 18.

[44] Eliassen, 'Den førindustrielle byen', ch. 8; Eliassen, 'Ladested, omland og utland'.

that such names were used even in official documents – church registers, court registers and tax-lists – points to small and close communities where everybody *knew of* almost everybody else, even if they all did not know each other personally.

However, as Mandal expanded into a medium-sized town by the end of the eighteenth century, the use of surnames became necessary in all official dealings, bearing witness to a tendency towards increasingly impersonal relations. Other facts point in the same direction: Törres Christensen Nedenes' paternalistic attitude around the year 1700 was replaced by a hard, impersonal exploitation of the town's workforce by his descendants, accompanied by the establishment of public social relief for the poorer inhabitants of the town. Social control was (and has remained) close in Norwegian small towns. People living close to each other in small communities kept their neighbours under observation, and privacy was scarce. Slander and rumours were a corollary of this social control, serving to keep a person in his (or her) place.

The Norwegian small town of the early modern period was deeply rooted in its hinterland. We have already noted the economic ties between town and countryside, and the flow of people between a town and its immediate hinterland. This meant that many town-dwellers had a rural background, and many more still had relatives and friends in the rural areas surrounding a town. In a small town, these relationships forged strong cultural ties between the middle and lower classes of the urban society and the rural population outside the town. Throughout most of the early modern period, the majority of the inhabitants of a small town dressed, talked, built their houses and celebrated their weddings in the same manner as people in the surrounding countryside. The vernacular architecture of the hinterland permeated the town, fiddlers from neighbouring farms were invited to play at weddings and parties in the town, and to this day there is normally little or no difference between the dialect spoken in a small town and in the countryside around it.

Thus, a small town must be studied and understood within its local context. To a much greater degree than large towns and cities, small towns were 'towns in local communities' – each of them an integral part of a wider local society. At the same time, small towns illustrate the urban–rural continuum of early modern Norwegian society. 'Town' and 'countryside' were not distinct and opposite social categories, but should rather be seen as theoretical extremes of a sliding scale on which most local communities can be placed closer to one end or the other, according to its density of settlement, economic functions and social characteristics.[45]

45 F-E. Eliassen, 'Norske byer, 1500–1800', p. 140.

As we have seen, the differences between small and large towns were to a great extent differences of degree rather than kind. But the sum of all the differences tended to give small towns a distinctive 'profile' of its own – socially, economically, culturally, topographically, and even politically. In addition, there is one further aspect of small-town society which merits attention. The relationships of power and dependence within a small town throw light on a central feature of early modern Norwegian society, at the same time putting Norwegian small towns into their proper European context.

6   Power and dependence in a small town

A small, unprivileged or underprivileged town lacked most of the governing bodies and officials with which the larger, fully-privileged towns were so well endowed. The ground on which the town was built would be privately owned, and the small-town society was dominated by a few families. As we have noted, this provided a wide scope for the exercise of private power.

A new town in the early modern period was normally built on outlying and agriculturally unproductive parts of one or – usually – several farms: on sand, rocks, islands and river banks. Grimstad (Fig. 2.5) emerged by a natural harbour, between cliffs, at a site where three farmers owned land: Skaregrøm, Berge and Ytre Bie. Mandal (Fig. 2.6) grew in three or four separate locations, on sand, cliffs, river banks and on an island, under two farms: Halshaug and Skinsnes.[46] The shape of each town was largely dictated by the physiognomy of its site or sites, and in the absence of government regulation, such towns have been termed 'selvgrodde' ('self-grown' or organic). In reality, however, the landowners decided where town houses might be built, so there was no 'wild urban growth'. Only towards the end of the eighteenth century was private development tempered by any measure of public regulation, mostly aimed at preventing fire and keeping the streets open to traffic.[47] In chartered towns, public planning control was much stricter, and the town itself, through its public bodies, would normally own, or at least have wide powers over, the site of the town.

In Grimstad and Mandal, as well as in many other small towns, the owners of the farms on which the urban settlements were located were in a position to control and benefit from the growth of the towns, and their economic activities. This made the ownership of such farms highly attractive to men who wished to control the towns in question. Among the owners

---

[46] J. A. Wikander, 'Gamle tomter', pp. 13–21 and 24–5; F-E. Eliassen, 'Den førindustrielle byen', ch. 1.

[47] The bodies and officials appointed for these purposes included police, fire brigade, night-watchmen, chimney sweeps and harbour commission. The former four in particular worked closely together. See F-E. Eliassen, 'Den førindustrielle byen', ch. 10.

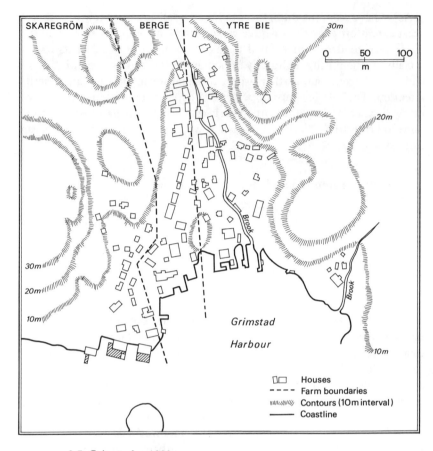

SKAREGRÖM   BERGE   YTRE BIE   *30m*

Houses
Farm boundaries
Contours (10m interval)
Coastline

Grimstad

Harbour

2.5 Grimstad c. 1800

of the farms on whose soil Grimstad was built, we find merchants, local
government officials, and the owner of Froland iron works, which Grimstad
served as export port from 1791.[48]

As urban landowners, merchants and other entrepreneurs had a number
of advantages. Leasing out plots of land for a yearly rent, they were assured
a steady and growing income as the town expanded. As part of the rent was
paid in kind, as two or three days' labour per house per year, the landowners
also had a ready supply of labour available whenever the need arose,
amounting to several hundred days' work a year. A merchant-landowner
like Tørres Christensen Nedenes in Mandal or Søren Lauridsen Solgaard in

[48] J. A. Wikander, 'Gamle tomter', pp. 13–17.

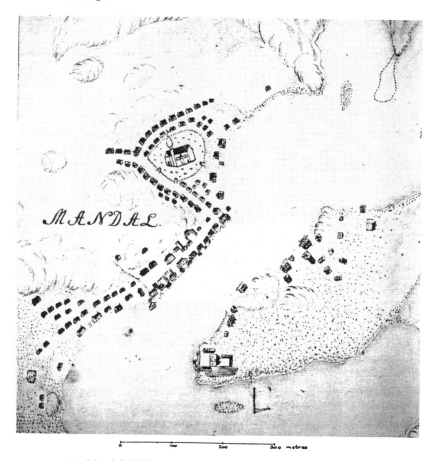

2.6 Mandal 1766

Hølen would even help people buy or build their own houses, by lending a great part of the money required or selling building materials on credit. The householder would then mortgage the house in question as a security for the loan, so that often, in a very real sense, the urban landowner *owned* the town. It is particularly interesting to note that householders in Mandal were not pressed for payment of such mortgage loans, particularly if it would force them to give up their houses and leave the town. Indeed, on the death of a householder, his or her heirs were often allowed to keep the mortgaged house, even if it meant postponing the payment of the debt for another generation. In the end, the house might fall into decay and the debt be written off altogether. Still, there was a clear logic behind such seemingly senseless economic dispositions.

A man like Törres Christensen Nedenes managed Mandal town like a firm. His main interest in developing the settlement, which had fewer than 150 inhabitants in 1700, into a small town with a population of more than 400 at his death in 1721, was to keep at his disposal a workforce to be employed when business was brisk. He needed sailors for his many ships, longshoremen to load and unload the ships, shipwrights, blacksmiths and carpenters to build and repair ships, day labourers for a multitude of odd jobs, carriers, coopers and so on, for his many lines of business: timber and fish trade, retail trade, shipping, building and repairing ships, and so on. An early modern entrepreneur, Törres Christensen needed a large and flexible workforce. But economic fluctuations made employment irregular, and in times of low activity, people would tend to leave the town to seek employment elsewhere. To avoid this and to keep a stable supply of labour to be employed at short notice when the need arose, it made economic sense to provide people with houses and to refrain from pressing them for payment when times were difficult, in order to have a ready workforce at hand when economic recovery occurred.[49]

We thus find in Mandal, in the twin towns of Son and Hølen, and no doubt in many other small towns of early modern Norway, a kind of 'urban feudalism', under which the town was seen and treated as a firm or part of a shipping and trading enterprise.[50] It resembled the cottar ('husmann') system in many rural areas, whereby a farmer would provide a house and often a small plot of land in return for the cottar's labour in field or forest (and often that of his family as well, and an annual rent in money or kind). In fact, the lease of a plot in a small town was modelled on a typical cottar's contract in the early eighteenth century.[51]

But the closest parallel to the urban feudalism described above is to be found in various works communities, notably iron works and copper mills, of the early modern period.[52] In such communities, we find the owners of the works providing workers with simple houses, which belonged to the factory, and which served to tie the workers to the works. The rent was normally deducted from the worker's wages, or added to his debts, which also was an insurance against his seeking work elsewhere. At Røros, the copper-mining community, the mine-owners even provided the miners with small plots of land to ensure them a living of sorts when work was not plentiful in the mines, making sure that they remained in Røros to be re-employed when the demand for copper increased again.

---

[49] F-E. Eliassen, 'Den førindustrielle byen', ch. 3.

[50] I am currently running a three-year research project on 'Landowners, householders and lodgers in Norwegian small towns of the early modern period', to investigate the extent of 'small-town feudalism' and related phenomena in Norway, c. 1650–1800.

[51] S. Sogner, 'Freeholder and Cottar', *Scandinavian Journal of History*, vol. 1 (1976), 181–99.

[52] L. Marthinsen and H. Winge, *Asker og Bærum til 1840* (1983), pp. 253–78.

In all these cases, as in many small towns, employers – landowners, merchants, entrepreneurs – provided houses for their employees to ensure a stable supply of labour in their various forms of production. This production of goods, made from timber, fish and metals, and services like shipping, was more often than not directed at an international market: iron for Denmark (where Norwegian producers held a formal monopoly from 1735), timber products mostly for north-western Europe, copper for Amsterdam, and fish for Catholic southern Europe, much of it carried in Norwegian ships. Norway, economically as well as geographically on the outskirts of Europe, was mainly an exporter of raw materials. As such, Norway was connected to the trading system of western – particularly north-western – Europe, and within this system, Norwegian small towns played a part, which was also the *raison d'être* of the 'urban feudalism' that characterised many of them. We have thus come full circle, back to Norway's position on the European periphery, which is the context within which the country's early modern small towns must be seen and understood.

3 Small towns in the periphery: population and economy of small towns in Sweden and Finland during the early modern period

Sven Lilja

Introduction

Writing in the early 1920s the late Professor Eli Heckscher delivered his judgement on Swedish towns in the early modern period. They were, he said, the products of medieval social and economic ideas that were unrealistic for and inappropriate to the Swedish reality: imported from the economically more fertile ground of the European continent, such ideas could not be expected to flourish in the poor soil of Sweden's autarkic, agrarian society. Only a handful of Swedish towns achieved any degree of prominence. With the exception of the metropolis, Stockholm, just a few medium-sized towns, such as Gothenburg, Karlskrona and Norrköping, could be counted as urban by international standards.

Professor Heckscher's severe judgement was well argumented: 'It can hardly be denied that the strange and uniform picture that emerges from our sources and studies is of the creation of societies which, though they undoubtedly had their strengths, possessed very few of the functions for which towns were intended and therefore few of the economic characteristics those functions created.'[1] This was for a long time the verdict on the Swedish pre-industrial town, both before and after Heckscher. Support for his view could be found in disparaging comments by the leaders of the Swedish seventeenth-century state. The king himself, Gustavus Adolphus II, had found his towns 'lacking in trade, rotten and broken down', and the Chancellor Axel Oxenstierna referred to them as 'insignificant market-places', and 'thieves' dens'.[2]

Evidence for such views was not lacking. Many Swedish towns were in fact merely agglomerated villages endowed with a few 'urban' functions. Most bore the physical imprint of agrarian structures. They were sur-

---

[1] E. Heckscher, 'Den ekonomiska innebörden av 1500- och 1600-talens svenska stadsgrundningar', *Historisk tidskrift* (1923). Quotation on p. 344.
[2] E. Heckscher, *Sveriges ekonomiska historia från Gustav Vasa. Del 1:2* (Stockholm, 1936). Quotation on p. 393. See also C. T. Odhner, *Bidrag till Svenska Städernas och Borgareståndets Historia före 1633* (Uppsala, 1860), pp. 1 and 9.

rounded by fields and meadows for agriculture and cattle breeding, and the urban landscape itself was dotted with vegetable gardens. Cow-sheds and stables were standard features of urban architecture, and residential and other buildings were often topped by grassed roofs that served as pasture for smaller livestock.

Contemporary testimony from as late as the eighteenth century provides the modern scholar with colourful images of the early modern Swedish town. The great Swedish naturalist Carl von Linné was a man with a fine eye for the domestic virtues of the Swedish landscape and in the course of his extensive travels through the country he recorded many picturesque details about urban husbandry and cultivation. In Simrishhamn (c. 650 inhabitants in 1750), for instance, he noted that sheep, of disparate quality, grazed in the fields in 'unbelievable multitude', and at Köping (c. 1,250 inhabitants by 1750) he could report that the goslings had already hatched.[3] In Lund, a Swedish university town (c. 2,000 inhabitants by 1750), the mayor imported snails or 'cochlea nemorum . . . in all kinds of colours' and planted them on his apple trees to protect the garden from moss and lichen. Another mayor, of the medium-sized town Kristianstad (c. 3,000 inhabitants in the 1770s), was an enthusiastic advocate of the Chinese pigs which, as he explained, were less hairy, cleaner and had flatter backs than the Swedish specimen, though the crossbred variety were the best, being the fattest.[4]

In spite of his sharp eye for Swedish urban 'ruralities', Linné was less observant when it came to more properly urban qualities. Visiting Gränna, a micro-town on the shores of Lake Vättern with approximately 500 inhabitants by the middle of the eighteenth century, he made the methodological mistake of comparing like and unlike entities. 'The main street', he said,

is divided in the middle by a small canal in the Dutch manner, and beside this canal large deciduous trees are planted, which, likewise in the Dutch manner, lend the town no small summer beauty. Thus one can, as in Amsterdam, drive in the shade on both sides of the canal. The square is like a garden parterre covered by good green turf and similar in beauty to the stone-paved exchange of Amsterdam . . .[5]

Beauty, of course, is in the eye of the beholder, and while this vision can seem somewhat disproportionate, von Linné was clearly undeterred by the small size of his subject. He reports that: 'The town of Gränna is generally considered one of the smallest in Sweden, but that is not quite true, for the town possesses things that no other town can boast of.' Continuing with his

---

[3] *Linné i Skåne. Carl Linnaeus dagboksmanuskript från Skåneresan 1749, utdrag ur den publicerade reseberättelsen 1751 – huvudsakligen där dagboksark är försvunna – samt ur andra tryckta arbeten.* En antologi sammanställd av B. Gullander (Stockholm, 1975), pp. 23 and 126.
[4] *Linné i Skåne*, pp. 71f and 248.   [5] *Linné i Skåne*, p. 368.

comparative approach, von Linné established that townspeople 'in Europe mostly enjoy the delights of the evenings, but in contrast do not care for the mornings, when the burning sun tortures their eyes. But here the sun does not trouble anyone until late in the day, and in wintertime she doesn't peek into the town before 10 or 11 o'clock.' If the early modern small town in Sweden is apt to appear a pastoral idyll to modern eyes, much clearly depends on the perspective of the observer.[6]

A change of perspective occurring in modern Swedish urban history has led to a revision of the earlier negative view of the pre-industrial town. Modern Swedish scholars have drawn attention to the fiscal and military rationale that underpinned urban economic policy, a policy that was not as irrational and unsuitable for Swedish economic conditions as Professor Heckscher maintained. In an age of mercantilism, the towns, be they old or new, facilitated greater government control, and the export towns were significant sources of fiscal revenues. They were also important focal points of an embryonic monetary economy. It was in the towns that surplus goods could be transformed from 'use value' to 'exchange value', something of special interest to the Crown and the leading aristocracy. Small size notwithstanding, the towns also stimulated social mobility, created employment, and contributed to the diffusion of ideas and innovations.[7]

Many of these urban functions defy measurement, of course, and the debate can never be free of value judgements. What is known for certain is that with few exceptions early modern towns in Sweden were small. Equally certain is that these small towns fulfilled their 'urban functions' within the contemporary economic framework. Crown policy was influenced by a mixture of rational and irrational motives in much the same manner as economic policy is today. What distinguished the early modern period from the present day is the power of the political instruments available to implement policy, and the structure of knowledge which informed political decision-making at this time. Both real power and real knowledge were limited in the early modern period and it was this that set limits to the effectiveness of urban policy.

Evaluating the importance of Swedish small towns requires an appropriate scale of reference. What exactly do we mean when we speak of early

---

[6] *Linné i Skåne*, pp. 367f.
[7] L-A. Norborg, 'Krona och stad i Sverige under äldre vasatid. Några synpunkter', *Historisk tidskrift* (1963); B. Ericsson, *De anlagda städerna i Sverige (ca. 1580–1800) (Urbaniserings-prosessen i Norden. Del 2. De anlagte steder på 1600–1700 tallet)* (Trondheim, 1977); J. Lindegren, *Den svenska militärstaten 1560–1720*, Magtstaten i Norden i 1600-tallet og de sociale konsekvenser. Rapporter til den XIX nordiske historikerkongres. Bind I, (Odense, 1984), pp. 104f; S. Lundkvist, *Centralmakten och de norrländska stadsgrundningarna*, Landsarkivet i Härnösand 50 år 1935–1985. Symposiet 'Städers uppkomst och liv', 17–19 September 1985, I. Arkiv i Norrland 7 (Härnösand, 1986).

modern Swedish towns as being 'small'? The scale of reference to use is not that of present-day Sweden, nor the German and Dutch towns of the seventeenth century, but rather early modern Sweden. Only with this scale can we hope to grasp the social and economic relevance of the urban system in early modern Sweden.

This chapter will try to survey the demographic, economic and political significance of Swedish small towns. Where can we draw a reasonable demarcation line between 'small' and 'large' centres? What was the demographic role of small towns in the urban network and in the urbanisation process? What were the main patterns of economic structure? How did town-dwellers earn their living? How successful were small towns in meeting the judicial, administrative and political standards imposed by the bureaucratised early modern Swedish state?

The chapter is in four parts, beginning with a general description of the urban network. The second section outlines the economic structure of small towns, sketching the main patterns of production, trade, credit relations and socio-economic distribution. Section three examines the inability of small towns to meet the bureaucratic demands of the state authorities. In the fourth section small-town growth is used to shed light on the main trends in the early modern urban system in Sweden. The conclusion argues for the significance of the specifically 'small-town dimension' in the urbanisation process in peripheral regions of early modern Europe.

The urban network

It has become standard international practice to consider European towns of fewer than 5,000 inhabitants as 'small' towns.[8] In the developed urban regions of continental Europe, this demarcation line between small and large may be useful. In the more peripheral parts of the European 'world economy', however, 5,000 inhabitants is not a convincing threshold. Sweden (including the Finnish part of the kingdom) offers a fairly typical example of what happens if we treat all towns with fewer than 5,000 inhabitants as small towns. Before the latter part of the seventeenth century only one town (Stockholm) could be characterised as *larger* than 'small' on this scale, while the remaining one hundred-odd towns would all be classified as small. The place of the 'small towns' in the total urban system was not greatly modified by the end of the eighteenth century; in the 1770s 93 per cent (96 out of 103) of the towns had fewer than 5,000 inhabitants.

---

[8] Two recent databases concerning European towns set the lower limits at respectively 10,000 and 5,000 inhabitants. J. de Vries, *European Urbanization 1500–1800* (1984), and P. Bairoch, J. Batou and P. Chèvre, *La population des villes européennes de 800 à 1850* (Centre d'histoire économique internationale, Université de Genève, 1988).

Table 3.1. *Swedish and Finnish towns 1570–1850, distributed by size category*

Town type	Size category	Decade							
		1570s	1610s	1650s	1690s	1730s	1770s	1810s	1850s
(a) *Number of towns*									
Metropolis	15,000 <	–	–	1	1	1	1	1	3
Large towns	5,000–15,000	1	1	–	4	3	6	6	13
Large medium towns	2,000–5,000	1	2	10	7	10	20	25	29
Small medium towns	1,000–2,000	12	15	15	24	26	28	32	38
Small towns	500–1,000	15	20	33	30	35	38	33	26
Micro-towns	>500	40	38	43	35	26	10	13	7
Total		69	76	102	101	101	103	110	116
UP (thousands)		48	59	118	154	151	237	269	352
AG %			0.52	1.75	0.67	−0.05	1.13	0.32	0.67
UG %			4					10	8	9

Town type	Size category	Decade							
		1570s	1610s	1650s	1690s	1730s	1770s	1810s	1850s
(b) *Percentage distribution*									
Metropolis	15,000 <	–	–	1	1	1	1	1	3
Large towns	5,000–15,000	1	1	–	4	3	6	5	11
Large medium towns	2,000–5,000	1	3	10	7	10	19	23	25
Small medium towns	1,000–2,000	17	20	15	24	26	27	29	33
Small towns	500–1,000	22	26	32	30	35	37	30	22
Micro-towns	>500	58	50	42	35	26	10	12	6
Total		100	100	100	100	100	100	100	100

Abbreviations:
UP = approximate urban population
AG % = percentual annual growth of aggregated UP
UG % = approximate degree of urbanisation
Sources:
1. All *urban data before the 1770s* comes from a database in my research project 'Swedish urbanization c. 1570–1770: structure–chronology–causes'. The data derives from household figures in tax registers. In the calculation of urban population sizes I have used the coefficient 4.0, which is close to the mean household size of urban populations which can be established at the middle of the eighteenth century.
2. *Urban data between the 1770s and the 1850s* comes from the following sources:
   Finland: Oiva Turpeinen, *De finländska städernas folkmängd 1727–1810* (Finsk historisk tidskrift, 1977), and *Suomen tilastollinen vuosikirja* (Statistical yearbook of Finland) (1989).
   Sweden: Yngve Fritzell, *Yrkesfördelningen 1753–1805 enligt Tabellverket: de särkilda städerna* (Statistisk tidskrift, 1983:4), and *Historisk statistik för Sverige. Del 1. Befolkning.* (Statistiska centralbyrån, 1969).
3. The calculation of *the urbanization rate in the 1610s* is based on Sigurd Sundquist, *Sveriges folkmängd på Gustaf II Adolfs tid. En demografisk studie* (Lund 1938), and by the same author, *Finlands folkmängd och bebyggelse i början av 1600-talet*, Tabellavdelning III (Generalstabens krigshistoriska avdelning, Stockholm, 1929). This calculation is, of course, only a very rough estimate.

Quite clearly this is not a meaningful analysis of the Swedish urban system. But which towns, then, should we classify as 'small' within the Swedish urban framework? In table 3.1 the towns are classified in size categories in order to show the quantitative dimensions of the Swedish urban system from the middle of the sixteenth to the middle of the nineteenth centuries. The size categories distinguish between what I refer to as 'micro-towns' with fewer than 500 inhabitants, 'small towns' with between 500 and 1,000 inhabitants, 'small medium-sized towns' with between 1,000 and 2,000, 'large medium-sized towns' with between 2,000 and 5,000, 'large towns' with between 5,000 and 15,000, and lastly the 'metropolis' (only Stockholm before 1850) with more than 15,000 inhabitants.

Under this system of classification Swedish 'small' towns (fewer than 1,000 inhabitants) form the majority of all urban settlements up to the middle of the eighteenth century, a result which appears to bear out the Heckscher thesis. However, the urban system as a whole actually grew throughout the early modern period, thereby indicating an underlying increase in the economic potential for urbanisation. During the early seventeenth and at the middle of the eighteenth century, in particular, growth rates reached relatively high levels. The seventeenth century in fact stands out in the early modern era as a key phase of urban change, with the rate of urbanisation more than doubling from around 4 per cent to approximately 10 per cent in the next century. During the late sixteenth and early seventeenth centuries the urban system expanded from fewer than seventy towns to more than one hundred, and the aggregated urban population rose from approximately 50,000 to 120,000. A situation of primacy developed in the urban hierarchy, with Stockholm consolidating its position as by far the single most important urban centre. The population of the capital rose from around 10,000 in 1610 to 55,000 in 1690.[9]

This rapid transformation process nevertheless came to a rather abrupt end. In the early part of the eighteenth century, the Swedish urban system experienced what might be described as an 'urban crisis', in the course of which the aggregate urban population seems to have stagnated or even slightly diminished. Stockholm was particularly hard hit, but recession affected the entire urban network. There are indications that almost 40 per cent of all towns experienced negative growth between the 1690s and 1730s. Three quarters of all towns had an annual growth rate below 0.5 per cent.

---

[9] G. Utterström, *Stockholms folkmängd 1663–1763*, Historiska studier tillägnade N. Ahnlund 23/8/1949 (Stockholm, 1949), p. 252; B. Lager, *Stockholms befolkning på Johan III:s tid* (Stadshistoriska institutet, Stockholm, 1962), pp. 29, 157f; G. Lundgren, *Stockholms befolkning under Gustav II Adolfs tid*, Stockholms stad. Kommunstyrelsens utlåtanden. Bihang 1987: 33. Arkivnämndens verksamhetsberättelse med bokslut för 1986. Bilaga 7 (Stockholm, 1987), pp. 38f.

Several reasons can be given for this urban downturn, including famine, disease and military pressure. However, the demographic, economic and social pressures arising from Sweden's demise as a European great power, combined with unfavourable international economic trends, are the most likely causes of this urban crisis.

In the 1730s the recession gave way to a brief period of expansion, which had some similarities to the expansion of the previous century. This was particularly the case for Stockholm, which in the space of a few decades made up its earlier population losses. Between 1720 and 1760 the capital city grew from approximately 45,000 to 69,000 inhabitants.[10]

Urban growth during the late eighteenth and early nineteenth centuries was in line with national increase, and corresponded to the growth of the Swedish/Finnish population as a whole. It is possible to speak of a balanced urban growth; the urbanisation rate was more or less stable during the period. Fairly reliable figures point to an urbanisation rate of around 10 per cent at the middle of the eighteenth century, and a similar rate also seems to have been registered at the beginning of the nineteenth century. Within the urban hierarchy, meanwhile, the relation between the metropolis and the lower ranks reversed once again in favour of smaller and medium-sized towns. From around 1760 up to the middle of the nineteenth century, Stockholm experienced a relatively low growth rate.[11] The modern 'urban transition' in Sweden began modestly in the 1830s but gained momentum during the latter part of the nineteenth century. By 1900 urbanisation had begun to approach the 20–25 per cent levels characteristic of industrialising societies.[12]

What then was the role of small towns in the urban process? Grounds exist for distinguishing between several types of small town, notably according to differences in their age and geographical location. Generally speaking, older towns were larger than more recent towns, while coastal towns were larger than inland towns. But this pattern is far from absolute, and other factors also played a vital role in urban development.

The geographical distribution of the Swedish urban system comes close to what Hohenberg and Lees have described as a network system, in which major cities function as 'gateways and originators of regional systems' and as nodal points connecting the international economy to the regional economy in the city's hinterland.[13] As Figure 3.1 shows, the Swedish urban network

---

[10] Utterström, *Stockholms*, pp. 252f.

[11] J. Söderberg, 'Den stagnerande staden. Stockholms tillväxtproblem 1760–1850 i ett jämförande perspektiv', *Historisk tidskrift*, vol. 2 (1985), 155–86.

[12] L. Nilsson, *Den urbana transitionen. Tätorterna i svensk samhällsomvandling 1800–1980*, Studier i stads- och kommunhistoria 5 (Stockholm, 1989), pp. 128ff.

[13] P. M. Hohenberg and L. H. Lees, *The Making of Urban Europe 1000–1950* (1985), pp. 62ff.

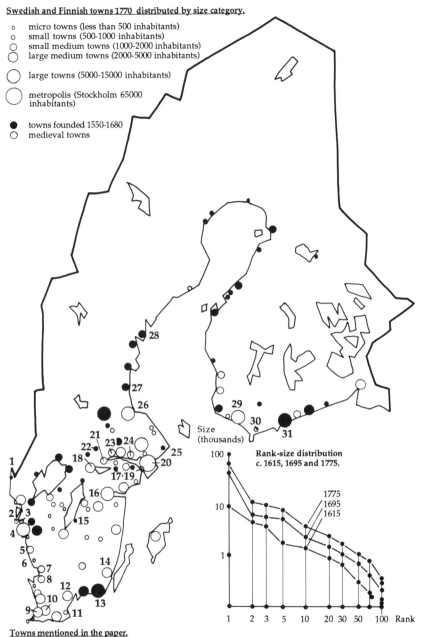

Swedish and Finnish towns 1770 distributed by size category.

o   micro towns (less than 500 inhabitants)
o   small towns (500-1000 inhabitants)
○   small medium towns (1000-2000 inhabitants)
◯   large medium towns (2000-5000 inhabitants)

◯   large towns (5000-15000 inhabitants)

◯   metropolis (Stockholm 65000 inhabitants)

●   towns founded 1550-1680
○   medieval towns

Size (thousands)

Rank-size distribution c. 1615, 1695 and 1775.

1775
1695
1615

100

10

1

1   2   3   5   10   20 30 50   100 Rank

Towns mentioned in the paper.
1. Strömstad 2. Marstrand 3. Kungälv 4. Göteborg/Nya Lödöse 5. Varberg 6. Falkenberg 7. Halmstad
8. Laholm 9. Malmö 10. Lund 11. Simrishamn 12. Kristianstad 13. Karlskrona 14. Kalmar 15. Gränna
16. Norrköping 17. Eskilstuna 18. Örebro 19. Södertälje 20. Stockholm 21. Arboga 22.Lindesberg 23. Köping
24. Enköping 25. Norrtälje 26. Gävle 27. Söderhamn 28. Härnösand 29. Åbo 30. Ekenäs 31. Helsingfors

3.1 Swedish and Finnish towns 1770 distributed by size category

was strongly oriented towards the sea; but it also displayed a tendency towards a loosely organised central place system, which gradually became more integrated during the early modern period. Regional centres tended to be located on the coast, and were distributed evenly over the more densely populated parts of the kingdom. Urban regions can be identified as oriented towards Malmö in southern Sweden, Kalmar/Karlskrona in the south-east, Gothenburg in western Sweden, Norrköping in the east, and Åbo in southern Finland. The vast and sparsely populated northern areas of Sweden and Finland were oriented towards Stockholm, as were also the central parts of Sweden in the Mälar basin.

Small towns performed a variety of functions within this framework. Consistent with a central place model, some occupied intermediate positions between larger towns. This was the case, for instance, with Falkenberg, a diminutive town on the west coast in the county of Halland. Falkenberg was situated between the larger third-rank towns of Varberg and Halmstad, and on the border line between the urban regions of Gothenburg in the north and Malmö in the south. Similar examples abound. This intermediate location of small towns was not a phenomenon confined to the coastal regions. A number of small inland towns had similar functions, and this hierarchical distribution of towns was accentuated as the Swedish urban system became more integrated.

Another feature of the geographical pattern is a centre–periphery relationship in which town size tends to fall the greater the distance from the metropolis. This is especially clear in the northern parts of the kingdom. With few exceptions the towns were smaller in the inner part of the Gulf of Bothnia than they were further south, closer to Stockholm. The vast area of northern Sweden and Finland was sparsely populated, and farming here was tightly clustered around the coast and the major river basins. In the inland areas, the economy was based mainly on small-scale mining, hunting, fishing, reindeer and forestry. The population of these inland regions was too small and the economy too primitive to support a more developed urban system; instead the coastal towns functioned as the trade nodes of vast hinterland regions, stretching from the coast to the borders of Norway and Russia, respectively.

A third feature of the Swedish urban system was the uneven balance between different *already urbanised* regions. As can be seen from Fig. 3.1, almost all of the new towns founded between 1580 and 1680 were located along the coastline of the Gulf of Bothnia and in the western parts of Bergslagen, the Swedish mining district in the inner part of central Sweden. Other regions were already more or less fully urbanised at the start of the early modern period.

A particularly distinctive 'small towns area' can be identified in these fully urbanised regions. In the county of Skaraborg, between Vänern and Vättern, Sweden's two largest lakes, the towns were considerably smaller than in other urbanised areas of the realm, and were to remain so throughout the early modern period. This was an inland agrarian district occupying a somewhat peripheral position in relation to the more centrally located regions of southern and central Sweden. Urbanisation was relatively late here.[14] Most of its towns had been founded during the late medieval period, when Sweden in common with other areas of Europe experienced a long-lasting agrarian crisis. The fact that the national boundary between Sweden and Denmark before 1658 separated the Danish coastland from the Swedish interior tended to accentuate the peripheral character of the region. Prior to 1658 the only connection between this inland area and the western sea was by a narrow corridor between the west coast counties of Bohuslän and Halland. Gothenburg and its predecessor Nya Lödöse functioned here as a 'gateway' to the markets of north-west Europe.

The small-town economy

Production

The economic structure of the Swedish small town was simple and firmly rooted in the immediate hinterland. Images like that of untethered swine rooting in the middle of the town square of Härnösand seem to bear out the negative views of Eli Heckscher.[15] According to Heckscher, Swedish small towns were nothing but villages adorned with town charters. That a large share of production in these towns was directed towards fulfilling subsistence needs is not in doubt. Cattle-breeding and farming were very important activities, and in some cases output was sufficient to meet a large part of the needs of the entire population. Generally speaking, however, urban production was too small to satisfy total demand. The level of grain production necessary for self-sufficiency in Swedish and Finnish towns in the middle of the eighteenth century has been calculated by Arthur Imhof, who concludes that most towns were far from fulfilling their own needs. Fifty six out of the 76 towns he examined fell below the 20 per cent self-sufficiency level, and in this respect there was no marked difference between large and small towns. Sixteen out of 22 micro-towns, and 18 out of 28 small towns, fell below the same threshold.[16]

---

[14] H. Andersson, 'Städer i öst och väst – regional stadsutveckling under medeltiden', *Bebyggelsehistorisk tidskrift* (1982).

[15] Heckscher, *Sveriges*, p. 393.

[16] A. Imhof, *Aspekte der Bevölkerungsentwicklung in den nordischen Ländern 1720–1750*, teil II. (Berne, 1976), pp. 859ff. The same conclusion, concerning Linköping, was drawn by

In addition to arable farming, cattle-breeding stands out as an important 'rural' activity in Swedish and Finnish towns. All Swedish and Finnish towns possessed large quantities of livestock. The 14 burghers of the town of Ekenäs on the southern Finnish coast, for instance, between them owned 39 cows, 11 calves, 32 swine, 35 sheep and one horse. Only the two poorest burghers owned just a single cow; all the others had several, and the richest of them, Lasse Olsson, was the proud owner of seven cows.[17] Conditions at Ekenäs were typical. According to livestock registers from the 1620s, 22 Swedish and Finnish towns had a total of 2,238 horses, 5,475 swine, 3,656 sheep and goats, and 5,960 head of cattle (4,759 cows). This livestock population was distributed over a human population of approximately 7,000 households, giving an average of 2.5 animals per household. Although such calculations naturally have wide margins of error, they give an unmistakable indication of the importance of cattle-breeding in the Swedish urban economy during the early modern era.

This was not unique to small towns. Indeed, the majority of towns were dependent on some kind of 'rural' economic activity. The most important difference between small and large towns was not their degree of dependence on domestic production, but rather the role in the urban economy of secondary economic activities, notably trade. This can be illustrated using data from a property tax collected by the Swedish Crown in 1571 to pay off a war indemnity to the Danes. Table 3.2 shows the relative importance of cattle compared to trade assets (money, goods) and silver. As can be seen, cattle-breeding was relatively more important in smaller than in larger towns.

Another essentially 'rural' activity of some significance in the urban economy was fishing. It was of major importance in the Finnish town of Ekenäs during the seventeenth century.[18] The same was true in most of the coastal towns. Smaller towns, like Ekenäs, were often heavily dependent on fishing, and it was not unknown for this branch of economic activity to grow to considerable proportions. The fishing fleets of the Western sea had experienced veritable herring booms during the high medieval period, and another such boom occurred in the late eighteenth century. On both occasions the fortunes of the fishing industry had a direct effect on the urbanisation process. Thus in the latter part of the eighteenth century small west-coast towns like Strömstad, Marstrand and Kungälv underwent a

---

F. Lindberg in his *Linköpings historia. 2. 1567–1862. Näringsliv och förvaltning*, 2nd edn (Linköping, 1975), pp. 138f. In Imhof's table data are missing from approximately a quarter of the towns in eighteenth-century Sweden and Finland.

[17] A. Takolander, *Ekenäs stads historia*, I (Ekenäs, 1930), p. 59.
[18] Takolander, *Ekenäs*, pp. 60f.

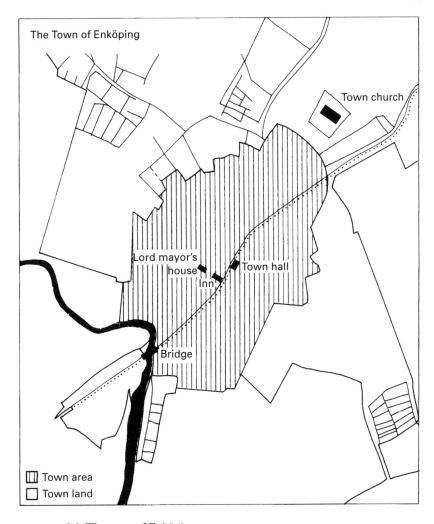

3.2 The town of Enköping

spectacular demographic growth that was directly linked to the upsurge of fishing.[19]

These more or less 'agrarian' economic activities were not geared exclusively to an urban subsistence economy: a part of production was destined for market consumption. In a few instances small towns specialised in commer-

[19] Y. Fritzell, 'Yrkesfördelningen 1753–1805 enligt Tabellverket: de särskilda städerna', *Statistisk tidskrift*, vol. 4 (1983), 307f, 320f; S. Högberg, *Utrikeshandel och sjöfart på 1700-talet. Stapelvaror i svensk export och import 1738–1808* (Lund, 1969), pp. 165–83.

Table 3.2. *Property distribution in Swedish towns 1571 (index)*

Town category	Number of towns	Large cattle index	Small cattle index	Silver index	Merchant-goods, money index
100< hld	6	100	100	100	100
50–100 hld	4	161	159	106	65
>50 hld	7	200	174	36	19

Abbreviations: hld = households
Sources: Hans Forssell, *Sverige 1571* (Stockholm, 1872).

cialised 'agrarian' production. Proximity to a large town was a key consideration here, as for instance in eighteenth-century Enköping, a town of some 1,000 inhabitants in 1750, on the shore of Lake Mälar not far from Stockholm. The existence of easy communications encouraged the town burghers to develop commercial horticulture for the flour markets of the metropolis.[20] What became a key sector of the local economy was practised on an extensive tract of surrounding common land (see Fig. 3.2) with arable surface split up into a multitude of small plots. Most households had their share and it was unusual for one household to hold more than one plot, though privately owned plots were less equally distributed, ranging in size from the 8 acres owned by alderman Enbom to plots of under one acre owned by a number of handicraft masters. The distribution of land around Enköping clearly indicates that a large proportion of the town burghers were dependent on horticulture, agriculture or cattle-breeding for their main source of income. The importance of this rural economic structure is further attested to by the fact that until the later part of the eighteenth century Enköping had almost no merchants. In 1750 there were only three tradesmen in the town and none of them was a wholesaler.[21]

The basic dependence of the smaller towns on agricultural production was well known and recognised by the Crown. All town foundations of the sixteenth and seventeenth centuries were accompanied by land donations. The prevailing belief among the ruling classes, however, was that town burghers should develop their community through trade and handicraft industry. As part of this utopian view, Crown policy was designed to try to

[20] G. Carlsson, *Enköping under frihetstiden. Social struktur och lokal politik*, Studia Historica Upsaliensia 89 (Uppsala, 1977), pp. 25ff.
[21] *Enköpings stads historia. II – Från 1718 till 1950* (Ed S. Dahlgren. Published by the town of Enköping, 1979), pp. 21–51, map on p. 34. The map is a simplified version of Olof Gerdes' map of Enköping in 1736.

Table 3.3. *Handicraft structure of Swedish towns 1650, 1750 and 1790*

Town category (population)	Number of towns	Trades per town	Workshops per town	Employees per workshop
1650				
>500	27	5	8	–
501–1,000	22	11	27	–
1,001–2,000	10	18	49	–
2,001<	10	25	101	–
1750				
>500	19	9	16	0.4
501–1,000	27	17	33	0.8
1,001–2,000	14	23	52	1.2
2,001<	18	32	115	1.4
1790				
>500	9	14	32	0.5
501–1,000	22	19	38	0.7
1,001–2,000	22	25	60	0.9
2,001<	22	34	120	1.5

Sources: E. Söderlund, *Hantverkarna. Andra delen. Stormaktstiden, frihetstiden och gustavianska tiden,* (Stockholm, 1949), tables 1–3, pp. 469ff.

force particular trades out of the countryside and into the towns. In a vast, sparsely populated country like early modern Sweden this was scarcely realistic, and trade and handicraft production both persisted as important rural activities.

Handicraft industry was nonetheless an important sector of small-town production. Most of it was for local needs, but some trades served a wider market area. Among 65 trades in the 1650s only five were represented in more than half of 66 provincial towns. The most common trades were shoemakers (61 towns), tailors (60), blacksmiths (50), carpenters (40) and goldsmiths (40). In the course of the next 100–150 years the situation altered somewhat. By the 1750s 19 trades were represented in 79 provincial towns, and by the 1790s 24 trades in 75 towns. The new trades included several of a more specialist nature, such as dyers, glovers, hatters and wig-makers. Behind this expansion of handicraft industries lay a combination of general urban population growth and changes in taste and fashion.[22] The structure of production was simple. In many cases the master was the only worker in his workshop; in smaller towns the average number of employees was less

[22] E. Söderlund, *Hantverkarna. Andra delen. Stormaktstiden, frihetstiden och gustavianska tiden* (Stockholm, 1949), pp. 52ff.

than one per workshop. Production units tended to be larger in the larger towns, but even in towns with more than 2,000 inhabitants the average number of employees did not exceed 1.5 (see table 3.3).

The number of trades and workshops was limited. In towns with fewer than 1,000 inhabitants the average number of trades never exceeded 25, and even in the larger towns the number stayed below 35. The degree of specialisation was necessarily low. Furthermore, in smaller towns the majority of trades were represented by only one or two masters, which gives a good indication of the essentially local character of handicraft production. Where larger production units did exist in the early modern urban economy of Sweden and Finland they were primarily concentrated in larger towns, and their economic importance is hard to measure. One writer estimates that the handicraft workers comprised 'only a few per cent' of the population of smaller towns in the eighteenth century. Large-scale industrial production in Sweden was associated chiefly with the mining industry, and that was a predominantly non-urban activity. Large-scale industry in towns (mainly textiles and some leather, sugar, metal and tobacco production) was located in regional and national centres like Stockholm, Norrköping, Gothenburg and Malmö. It was in these larger towns that demand was greatest.[23]

A few small towns did have larger industrial plants, however. Towns like Söderhamn and Norrtälje were centres of arms manufacturing, a sector encouraged and supported by the Crown.[24] A more spectacular example is Eskilstuna, which was founded in the 1650s and whose development was inextricably linked with that of an iron-manufacturing plant. This plant in fact became a town within the town, having its own name (Carl Gustafs stad), its own town plan, and its own judicial status. From the outset, therefore, Eskilstuna was characterised by a dual economic and social structure.[25] In the eighteenth century the duality of Eskilstuna became even more strongly pronounced, when the manufacturing town acquired so-called 'free town' (fristad) status. After 1771 the handicraft production of the old town of Eskilstuna continued to be regulated and organised within a traditional guild system. In the 'free town' of Eskilstuna, on the other hand, artisans and craftsmen could set up and produce unhindered by guild

---

[23] Heckscher, Sveriges, p. 513; P. Nyström, Stadsindustriens arbetare före 1800-talet. Bidrag till kännedomen om den svenska manufakturindustrien och dess sociala förhållanden (Stockholm, 1955), pp. 90ff, 138ff.

[24] Heckscher, Sveriges, p. 395; C. M. Kjellberg, Norrtälje stad. Dess historiska utveckling 1622–1922 (Norrtälje, 1922), pp. 33ff.

[25] M. Thunander, Carl Gustafs stad. Manufakturverkets tillkomst och utveckling, Carl Gustafs stad. Reinhold Rademachers manufakturverk och Eskilstuna. Utg av Eskilstuna stad vid 300-årsjubiléet 1959. Historiska skrifter utgivna av Eskilstuna stad I, pp. 43ff; Ericsson, De anlagda, p. 123.

restrictions. This was something almost without precedent in Swedish economic policy, a result of the new, anti-mercantilist ideas which began to manifest themselves in several economic areas during the middle and latter part of the eighteenth century. But *ancien régime* restrictions were not finally swept away until a hundred years later. The 'free town' of Eskilstuna certainly contributed to strong demographic growth, but the total population of the town remained below 1,400 inhabitants at the beginning of the nineteenth century.[26]

Trade

During the early part of the seventeenth century the mercantilist policy of the Swedish Crown sought to allocate urban trade between different categories of towns. By three great decrees (1614, 1617, 1636) towns were divided between 'staple towns' (*stapelstäder*), with rights to passive and active foreign trade, and 'hinterland towns' (*uppstäder*). In principle the 'hinterland towns' were to be responsible for inland trade, but since the staple towns soon recovered their right of access to the markets of the smaller hinterland towns the latter's control over inland trade in fact became illusory.

The practical consequence of this policy was to exclude small towns from important large-scale trading activities. When the staple system was completed in the 1630s all towns north of Stockholm and Åbo had more or less lost their right to foreign trade. Furthermore, all inland towns, and some of the smaller coastal towns in southern Sweden and Finland, were totally or partially isolated from direct contact with foreign merchants.[27] In some cases the loss of rights in foreign trade created acute economic and demographic problems. Stagnation or retardation in towns like Södertälje, Arboga and Gävle, for example, was seen as a direct result of this mercantilist policy.[28]

---

[26] B-E. Ohlsson, *Eskilstuna fristad. Fristadsinrättningen i Eskilstuna före sammanslagningen med Gamla staden 1771–1833*, Utg. av Eskilstuna kommun vid 200-årsjubiléet 1971. Historiska skrifter utgivna av Eskilstuna kommun III, pp. 24ff, 50ff; A. Hörsell, *Borgare, smeder och änkor. Ekonomi och befolkning i Eskilstuna gamla stad och Fristad 1750–1850*, Studia Historica Upsaliensia 131 (Uppsala, 1983), pp. 28ff, 40ff; L. Nilsson, *Privilegiesystem under upplösning. Administrativt tätortsbildande i Sverige 1620–1865*, Stadshistoriska institutet. Studier i stads – och kommunhistoria 4 (Stockholm, 1989), pp. 19ff; Söderlund, *Hantverkarna*, pp. 221ff.

[27] H. G. F. Sundberg, *Den svenska stapelstadsrätten. En undersökning av institutets utveckling och nuvarande innehåll* (Stockholm, 1927), pp. 41ff; *Stadsväsendets historia i Finland*, P. Tommila, ed., published by Finlands stadsförbund (Kunnallispaino Vanda, 1987), pp. 57ff; Heckscher, *Sveriges*, pp. 673ff.

[28] C-F. Corin, *Arboga stads historia. Andra delen. Från 1500– talets mitt till 1718* (Arboga, 1978), pp. 154ff, 177, 353ff; T. Karlström, *Gävle stadsbild. Bebyggelsehistoria och samhäll-*

Much of provincial trade was focused upon local and regional centres. To attract rural production and distribute salt, grain, cloth and other necessities to the local peasant population, most towns held a fair at least once a year. The fairs were nodes of a regional commercial network necessary to maintain the distribution channels to the large coastal 'gateways'. For merchants from the staple towns the fairs provided an occasion to meet and make credit arrangements and establish new contacts. In addition, some fairs also functioned as regional political assemblies, being used by the Crown for declarations and negotiations.[29]

Annual fairs linked economically disparate inland regions with each other and with the larger international market. But the small towns also functioned as centres for purely local exchange. On marketday each week the neighbouring local population assembled in the town square to trade their eggs, butter, meat, fish, vegetables and rough homespun cloth in return for various handicraft products, simple luxuries, salt and the like.[30]

In spite of constant efforts by the Crown to direct trade into the towns and eliminate it from the countryside, rural trade continued to exist. The main reason for this was the often very great distance between peripheral rural settlements and the nearest town. Another factor was the tendency of the peasant population to bypass the smaller towns, and instead deliver their merchandise directly to the larger staple towns, where demand was stronger and prices better.[31] The credit system accentuated this tendency. The large merchants of the staple towns enjoyed a competitive advantage thanks to their larger stocks of capital, and by means of credit ties they were able to bind the peasants directly to themselves and effectively eliminate the intermediate role of the smaller hinterland town burghers.[32] Very close relationships could develop between debtor and creditor. Particularly in southern Finnish towns, but in other parts of the kingdom also, a credit system based on a more or less paternalistic relationship became an important economic mechanism. Over-generous advances bound the peasant to his particular creditor/burgher. It was at the house of his creditor, moreover, that the peasant would typically receive board and lodging when visiting the town, thereby tying him still tighter to the burgher. This long-established and traditional system did not find favour with the seventeenth-century

---

sutveckling till 1900-talets början (Gävle, 1974), pp. 29, 33; S. I. Olofsson, *Medeltiden och nya tiden till 1860*, Södertälje stads historia 1 (Stockholm, 1968), pp. 247ff, 314ff.

[29] N. Staf, *Marknad och möte. Studier rörande politiska underhandlingar med folkmenigheter i Sverige och Finland intill Gustaf II Adolfs tid* (Stockholm, 1935); L. Linge, *Gränshandeln i svensk politik*, Bibliotheca Historica Lundensis XXIII (Lund, 1969), pp. 37f.

[30] G. Rystad, *Den borgerliga staden under 1500- och 1600-talen*, Skara I. Före 1700. Staden i stiftet (Skara, 1986), p. 753; F. Lindberg, *Linköpings historia. 2. 1567–1862 Näringsliv och förvaltning* (Linköping, 1975), p. 71.

[31] Heckscher, *Sveriges*, p. 533.   [32] Lindberg, *Linköpings*, p. 63.

Table 3.4. *Economic structure of adult male population in Swedish towns c. 1751; percentage distribution*

Economic structure	Town class					
	>500	500–1,000	1,000–2,000	2,000–5,000	5,000–15,000	Stockholm
Persons of rank	6	5	6	5	7	11
Merchants	8	6	6	1	3	3
Manufacturers	0	1	1	1	1	1
Soldiers	3	3	3	6	24	17
Seamen	5	2	3	5	2	5
Artisans	20	13	16	12	7	6
Free workers	26	26	20	18	10	13
Public servants	4	4	5	5	3	4
Servants/employees	27	38	40	44	41	38
Poor and crippled	1	1	1	2	2	1
Total	100	100	100	100	100	100
Number of individuals	1,897	3,874	3,926	7,169	10,574	21,149
Number of towns	15	17	10	10	4	1

Source: Yngve Frizell, *Yrkesfördelningen 1753–1805 enligt Tabellverket: de särskilda städerna* (Statistisk tidskrift, 1983:4, pp. 279ff.)

Swedish Crown, which saw it as undermining the trade rights of the open market and strengthening the position of the rich merchants.[33] Credit relations played a vital role in the economic connections between burghers and peasants. Long and complex chains of credit could in effect link rural producers to great international metropolises such as Lübeck, Hamburg or Amsterdam.[34]

Economic structure

The relatively simple economy of the Swedish small town was mirrored in the socio-economic structure of its population. Absence of published sources and research makes it impossible to present data on an aggregated basis prior to the middle of the eighteenth century. By that time, however, published data clearly shows the relative importance of artisans and free workers among the adult male population in the smaller towns. These two categories account for more than 35 per cent of adult male inhabitants in towns with fewer than 1,000 inhabitants (see table 3.4). For larger towns,

[33] Heckscher, *Sveriges*, p. 570; Ranta, *Stadsväsendet*, p. 61.
[34] P. Jansson, *Kalmar under 1600-talet. Omland, handel och krediter* (Uppsala, 1982), pp. 16f.

Table 3.5. *Percentage share of burghers in Swedish and Finnish towns 1747*

Town class (households)	Number of towns	Average % share of burghers
> 124	43	70
125–249	32	67
250–499	16	59
500 <	12	33

Source: D. Almqvist, *Tillståndet i Sveriges städer 1747* (Historisk tidskrift, 1949).

the proportion then tends to fall as population increases, until in towns of above 5,000 inhabitants it is below 20 per cent.

A similar decrease is observed in the merchant category, which falls from 8 per cent in 'micro-towns' to 3 per cent in 'large towns'. This fall in the proportion of merchants and artisans is indicative of the lesser role played by traditional 'burgher occupations' in the larger towns. It is also, of course, a reflection of the more complex economy that had developed in the larger towns during the seventeenth century. As a result of this change the burghers had been reduced to a small minority in many of the larger Swedish and Finnish towns, although during Sweden's so-called Age of Liberty they continued to play a vital political role at both the local and national level.[35] In most of the smaller towns they remained in the majority (see table 3.5).

In contrast to the declining share of traditional occupations in the large as opposed to small centres was the rising share of such categories as 'persons of rank' and 'soldiers' (including military seamen). These figures are evidence of a more differentiated economic structure and greater range of public office in the larger towns. The main state institutions were localised in such towns, something which in turn forced noble and non-noble officials in the higher echelons of the administration to take up residence here. As a result the market for labour and goods expanded. Unlike small towns, the larger centres could feed and support a relatively wide range of trades and services. The figures also reflect the strategic military importance of some of the large towns. In fact, large-scale military investment had the potential to raise a town from 'small' to 'medium' or even 'large' status in the space of just a few years. The most spectacular example of this kind of state-aided urban development concerns the town of Karlskrona, founded in 1680 as Sweden's main naval base; within 50 years it had grown to be the country's

---

[35] G. Carlsson, *Enköping under frihetstiden. Social struktur och lokal politik* (Uppsala, 1977), pp. 14f.

second or third largest town, with a population of approximately 10,000 inhabitants in the 1750s. In Finland the future capital city, Helsingfors (Helsinki in Finnish), became a military stronghold against the Russians following the treaty of Åbo in 1743. Within a few decades – from the 1730s to the 1770s – this small town of roughly 1,000 inhabitants grew into a large centre of 6,000 inhabitants. State officials, soldiers, seamen and other groups associated with the military formed the majority of the total population in both Karlskrona and Helsingfors.[36]

Small-town political structure

The cycle of urban growth during the early modern era was indissociable from developments in the political sphere. Urban growth in the seventeenth century paralleled the expansionist phase of the Swedish imperial experiment. By the end of the century, however, the financial and military resources of the Swedish state were no longer adequate to its status as a European great power, and the tide began to turn. In the early eighteenth century Sweden lost its role as a major power on the European political stage, a development that was in turn reflected in a slackening of the urbanisation process.

This cycle of historical development had a direct bearing on the political organisation of towns. Expansion of the state in the seventeenth century impinged on local politics and local government. Between the 1630s and the 1680s most town administrations were reorganised in a manner that strengthened the interests of the Crown at the expense of the traditional local mercantile interests. Starting at the top of the urban hierarchy the Crown gradually managed to replace locally appointed 'merchant' mayors by legally trained 'royal' mayors, a policy that was subsequently extended to the entire city council. The state demand for local authorities with a legal training led to the appointment of so-called 'literate' magistrates to counterbalance the merchant interests traditionally dominant in the town councils.

Although this extension of state control often aroused serious local opposition, such resistance had little real chance of success, not least because the legally trained mayors were full-time professionals with a greater mastery of administrative and judicial matters. The attack on local interests was underlined by the new powerful regional administration set up during the 1630s.

[36] Ericsson, *De anlagda*, p. 124; S-E. Åström, *Anlagda städer och centralortssystemet i Finland 1550–1785*, Urbaniseringsprosessen i Norden, Del 2. De anlagte steder på 1600–1700-tallet, Det XVII, nordiske historikermöte (Trondheim, 1977), pp. 164, 173; Fritzell, *Statistisk tidskrift* (1983), p. 304; *Mantalslängder* (tax registers), *Nylands och Tavastehus län 1773–1776*, The Public Record Office of Finland, Helsinki. The figures for Helsinki include the garrison at the nearby fortress of Sveaborg.

The provincial governors now became key actors mediating between the local authorities and the king. The seventeenth century was thus characterised by a far-reaching effort by the central power to organise and regulate Swedish society, a policy whose key aspects were bureaucratisation and professionalisation.[37]

During the following century the centralising trend weakened and local authorities were able to regain some of their political power. The system put in place during the seventeenth century actually survived until the latter half of the nineteenth century, but the strong tendency towards control and organisational regulation waned and, as far as small-town administration was concerned, gave way to more realistic objectives. The simple economic structure and lack of municipal resources of such towns proved an effective barrier to a highly professionalised and bureaucratised administration.

One result of this was that the degree of administrative complexity varied considerably between towns of different sizes. The salaries paid to officials were limited by the financial strength of the local budget. In the medium-sized town of Örebro (c. 2,200 inhabitants by 1750) the major earned 600 dsmt[38] in 1750, whereas in the small town of Lindesberg (c. 600 inhabitants by the 1730s) the same official earned only 240 dsmt. The magistrates were paid 100 and 25 dsmt, respectively. The more complex administrative structure of Örebro required 15–20 officials compared to about ten in Lindesberg, and at every level of officialdom the salaries were higher at Örebro than at Lindesberg.[39]

The general increase in administrative costs posed special problems for small towns. Their inability to pay competitive salaries to professional mayors made it difficult for them to recruit competent personnel. Indeed, the willingness of the Crown to cover the cost of employing a qualified mayor was one of the levers used by the state in the seventeenth century to gain control over local authorities. Central policy in the eighteenth century, however, was directed towards an acceptance of simpler forms of local government. During the latter part of the century the Swedish Board of Commerce took initiatives in this direction, suggesting that town councils in small towns should be abolished and their judicial affairs be subordinated to the law and judges of neighbouring regions. This attempt at large-

---

[37] L. Ericson, *Borgare och byråkrater. Omvandlingen av Stockholms stadsförvaltning 1599–1637*, Stockholmsmonografier utgivna av Stockholms stad, 84 (Stockholm, 1988), pp. 49ff; *Stadsväsendets historia i Finland*, pp. 62ff, 67ff, 74, 112ff.

[38] dsmt = daler silvermynt – silver rix-dollars.

[39] B. Ericsson *et al.*, *Stadsadministration i Norden på 1700-talet*, Det nordiska forsknings-projektet Centralmakt och lokalsamhälle – beslutsprocess på 1700-talet. Publikation 1 (Oslo–Bergen–Tromsö, 1982), pp. 185ff, 192.

Table 3.6. *Average growth rates of Swedish and Finnish towns distributed by size category, c. 1570–1770*★

Town category	Yearly growth rates					
	1610–1650	1650–1690	1690–1730	1730–1770	1770–1810	1810–1850
P < c. 500 inh						
Average growth rate	1	0.8	0.7	0.8	0.6	1.2
Number of towns	26	32	29	25	11	11
P < c. 1,000 inh						
Average growth rate	0.8	0.7	0.4	0.9	0.4	1.1
Number of towns	36	53	51	47	47	44
P > c. 1,000 inh						
Average growth rate	0.8	0.1	0.2	0.9	0.4	1.3
Number of towns	12	16	19	24	53	62
P > c. 2,000 inh						
Average growth rate	1	0.0	−0.2	1.2	0.4	1.4
Number of towns	3	9	7	8	24	32
All towns						
Average growth rate	0.8	0.5	0.3	0.9	0.4	1.2
Number of towns	48	69	70	71	100	106

★ Due to lack of data the table does not include all existing towns before 1770.
Abbreviations: inh = inhabitants
Sources: see Table 3.1.

scale reform ran into heavy opposition, however, and was pushed through in only a few newly-founded towns at the end of the century.[40]

Broadly speaking, the long-term tendency was towards a reduction of municipal administration. This was already visible for town councils in the seventeenth century. Thus the average size of council meetings in the Finnish towns fell from seven members in the 1630s to five in the 1690s. At the time the state authorities did not approve of this development, though since it was a reflection of local financial constraints they were powerless to prevent it.[41]

Small-town growth

Swedish small towns have not yet been the subject of general quantitative

[40] Ericsson *et al.*, *Stadsadministration*, p. 213; *Stadsväsendets historia i Finland*, pp. 192f.
[41] *Stadsväsendets historia i Finland*, pp. 68ff.

studies and it is difficult to reach any firm conclusions about their overall economic development. Examination of the demographic growth figures, however, gives some idea of their experiences. Table 3.6 indicates that the small towns, and in particular the very small 'micro-towns', had a good growth potential throughout the early modern period. Average annual growth for these towns was usually above, and sometimes well above, the national average. Their annual growth figures never fell below the 0.6 per cent threshold, compared with national figures of 0.3 per cent, 0.4 per cent and 0.5 per cent, or the virtually nonexistent growth of the larger towns in the late seventeenth and early eighteenth centuries.

In statistical terms, of course, it was easier for micro-towns than for larger towns to lose or gain in *relative* size, and this is a possible explanation for their persistently higher growth rates. Having said this, the fact that decline would also produce the same kind of over-representation makes it likely that the difference in growth rates is real and not just a reflection of statistical phenomena. The evidence in Table 3.6 suggests that micro-towns, *as well as* larger towns, both participated in the general expansion of the early modern Swedish urban system, and that these small towns performed relatively well.

The table also points to a significant difference in growth over time between micro- and larger towns. Generally the average urban growth followed the growth cycle of the aggregate urban population.[42] But the average growth of small towns fluctuated considerably less than that of larger towns. This contrast was particularly marked during the period of relatively slow growth in the late seventeenth and early eighteenth centuries. One probable explanation was the wave of crown-initiated town foundations that occurred between the 1580s and the 1680s. Very few of these new towns were established completely from scratch; most were situated in older market centres, or in locations with some other kind of central-place function, such as manufacturing or a politico-administrative role. With only a few exceptions, these new settlements became permanent and survived as chartered towns throughout the early modern era. In the seventeenth century they participated in the process of embryonic urban development, as a result of which they registered necessarily high initial growth rates. In spite of this head start, however, many of them remained small towns even by Swedish standards.

The growing disparity between micro-towns and larger towns was further accentuated by the 'urban crisis' of the early eighteenth century. The micro-towns were in fact the only category of town to continue to experience any significant growth. Their average annual growth rate was as high as

---

[42] See Table 3.1, p. 54 above.

0.7 per cent between 1690 and 1730, an impressive performance in comparison to other size groups. Towns with more than 1,000 inhabitants, for example, registered a growth rate close to zero. During the recovery period of the mid-eighteenth century a more even growth-rate distribution prevailed. None of the size categories deviated significantly from the national average. Only the large and large-medium towns showed any positive deviation from the main trend, and that was a reversal of the situation in the previous century. One factor here was the recovery boom in the larger towns that had been hardest hit during the period of crisis.

In the late eighteenth and early nineteenth centuries the situation of more balanced urban growth persisted. The late eighteenth century was a period of slow overall growth, but also a period when the micro-towns maintained some of their demographic momentum within the national urban context. This is the period of early modern urbanisation in Sweden that comes closest to the 'new urbanisation' or 'urban growth from below' identified for Europe as a whole by de Vries.[43] In part it may be an indication of rural expansion heralding the industrial breakthrough of the late nineteenth century. This idea is supported by the contemporaneous stagnation in the overall rate of urbanisation. The rural population during this period expanded at the same pace, if not more quickly, than the urban population.

The early nineteenth century witnessed a noticeable acceleration of the growth process. The high rates registered between 1810 and 1850 reflect the fact that Sweden had embarked on the path towards the modern urban world. At this early stage, however, the broad growth process seems to have continued in a relatively unbroken manner from the eighteenth century. The weak tendency towards higher growth rates among larger towns did not disrupt the general picture of balanced urban growth.

In conclusion, it is reasonable to take the persistent growth of the very small towns as an indication of a continuous growth potential from below in the Swedish and Finnish urban system as a whole. The conjunctural differences that characterised the overall urbanisation process during the early modern period seem to have affected mainly the higher reaches of the urban hierarchy.

Conclusion

The conventional picture of the Swedish early modern town presented by Heckscher and others was that of a 'small' town, and one that had precious little potential for growth, that was rural in type and function, and that was the fruit of an ideologically misguided urban policy. Proof for the thesis was

---

[43] de Vries, *European Urbanization*, pp. 258ff.

found in the extremely underdeveloped character – into the early nineteenth century – of most towns founded after 1500.

That the Swedish urban system was underdeveloped is not in doubt. Equally clear is that throughout the early modern period most towns in the country have to be classified as 'small' when compared to the towns of Renaissance Italy or early modern Holland. Yet as I have tried to argue in this paper such comparisons are meaningless, since it was not just Swedish towns but Swedish society as a whole that was less developed than the economically more advanced regions of Western Europe. The general contours of the Swedish urban system were more comparable to urban structures in central and eastern Europe or possibly those of Scotland and Ireland. According to Vera Bácskai, in 1500 91 per cent of Austrian towns and 98 per cent of urban settlements had fewer than 5,000 inhabitants. The situation seems to have been much the same in Hungary.[44] In Sweden (with Finland) only one late medieval town, Stockholm, out of almost 70 towns, had more than 5,000 inhabitants. In the eighteenth century six towns out of 103 had population figures above 5,000 inhabitants.

Raymond Gillespie's definition of Irish small towns as having between 120 and 500 taxable urban dwellers uses limits comparable to the Swedish scale. The same is true of the seventeenth-century urban system in Scotland. The Scottish metropolis, Edinburgh, was of comparable size to Stockholm, and the lower strata of the urban hierarchy had clear affinities with small towns in Sweden. The main difference between the urban hierarchies in the two countries seems to lie in the smaller size of Swedish second-rank towns. The Swedish hierarchy was, at least in the middle of the seventeenth century, closer to a primacy distribution than its Scottish counterpart, a difference that suggests stronger forces of political centralisation at work behind Swedish developments.[45]

An interesting parallel also exists between the Swedish urban process and that in Ireland. According to Raymond Gillespie, a series of town and market foundations occurred in Ireland in the sixteenth and early seventeenth centuries. These new urban or semi-urban creations proved somewhat unstable and not all survived into the nineteenth century; but many did, thus creating urban networks in formerly non-urbanised regions. This movement was part of a reform programme designed to tighten political control and promote economic development. State-led urban development

---

[44] For East Central Europe see V. Bácskai, chapter 4, below.

[45] For seventeenth-century Ireland, see R. Gillespie, chapter 7, below; for Scotland see M. Lynch, 'Urban Networks in Seventeenth Century Scotland', Paper delivered to the European Small Towns Conference, Leicester 1990, pp. 3f. For the analytical contrast between economic forces of concentration and political/administrative forces of centralisation see S. N. Eisenstadt and A. Shachar, *Society, Culture, and Urbanization* (Newbury Park, 1987), especially chapter 2.

in Ireland had clear parallels in contemporary Sweden, where an analogous wave of town foundations expanded Swedish state control in peripheral areas around the Gulf of Bothnia and in the northern and western inland regions with the aim of stimulating economic growth and, in the long run, directing surplus resources towards the political centre.

The fact is that the Swedish urban system in the early modern period experienced many of the same developments as in other parts of Europe. Among these was a tendency in the seventeenth century towards primacy in the rank-size distribution of towns, followed by a slower but more balanced urban growth during the eighteenth and early nineteenth centuries, and a gradual integration of the urban system as a whole. To this could be added a tendency towards increasing state control and bureaucratic developments within urban administration during the seventeenth century. In Sweden, as elsewhere, the early modern nation-state can be seen as a powerful agent in the pattern of urban development.

As we have seen, within this urban context the towns of lower rank had a very simple economic structure. 'Rural' activities played a vital economic role and the structures of production and trade were designed primarily to fulfill local needs. Moreover, small-town administrations had to guard against too ambitious central organisational demands. However, even the smaller towns fulfilled some functions in the larger economy, often acting as nodal points for seasonal trade between different economic regions within the Swedish realm. Although denied access to the international market between the 1630s and 1770s, they nonetheless had a vital role in the transportation of staple goods from the hinterland to the large coastally located export towns. In spite of unfavourable urban policy, they often constituted an important link in the long chain which integrated the Swedish producer to the international market.

Small towns thus had vital economic functions to fulfill, albeit within an underdeveloped urban context. As far as can be judged from the tax registers, many towns, particulary the smallest micro-towns, enjoyed uninterrupted demographic growth. Under no circumstances, however, can the Swedish urban system of the early modern period, handicapped as it was by factors such as low population density and an economically peripheral status, be compared to that in the developed parts of Europe. The real comparison should instead be drawn with other countries of the Euroepan periphery or semi-periphery, such as Ireland, Scotland and Hungary.

The parallels, not to stress the obvious differences, between Irish and Swedish urbanisation highlight the importance of the forces of political centralisation in the urban process in early modern Europe, particularly in the sixteenth and seventeenth centuries. De Vries identified this as an era of stagnation in the lower strata of the urban hierarchy. In contrast to the 'urban growth from below' characteristic of the eighteenth century, the sixteenth and seventeenth centuries appear as an era of polarisation in the urban hierarchy, when large cities grew at the expense of lesser centres.[46] This is certainly the case if the European small town is left out of the picture. In Sweden as in Ireland, however, politically driven small-town growth seems to have been a significant component of the urbanisation process of the 'long sixteenth century'. Political centralisation is thus seen to have a small-town dimension worthy of further exploration in a broader European context.[47]

[46] De Vries, *European Urbanization*, pp. 95ff, 255ff.

[47] The research for this article has been carried out as part of a project on 'Swedish Urbanization c. 1550–1750/1800: Chronology, Structure, Causes', financed by the Swedish Board for the Humanities and the Social Sciences. I would like to thank Professor Peter Clark, the members of the European Small Towns Conference at the University of Leicester in July 1990, and Professor Per Thullberg, Stockholm for valuable comments on the paper. Any remaining errors are entirely my responsibility. The figures were drawn by Kerstin Kåverud and Embla Ritbyrå, and my English has been corrected by Marie-Louise Rodén and Godfrey Rogers. My thanks to all of them.

4   Small towns in eastern central Europe

Vera Bácskai

The study of small towns is of particular importance for eastern central Europe, because in the pre-industrial period this area was dominated by small towns. Small towns were characteristic of the region not merely in the sense that the great majority of towns were small – for that was the case all across Europe – but because the top categories were missing from the hierarchy of towns. Not only were large cities with more than 10,000 inhabitants few and far between, but there were not too many middling towns of 5–10,000 people either. Furthermore, the urban function of most of the towns – even of the relatively larger ones – was typically small-townish, limited and underdeveloped. Some historians see their semi-urban character exemplified by agricultural production which tended to continue in these small towns and sometimes even dominated their economy. However, in most instances one finds not self-sufficient production of foodstuffs, but rather a specialised, market-oriented agrarian economy including viniculture, cattle-breeding, and so on.

Since studies of European urbanisation usually say very little about the multitude of small towns and their significance, historians of central Europe, too, have tended to compare the region's urban development with large and middle-sized European cities and have concentrated on the history of the few major cities in the region. The approach has led to the not unwarranted conclusion that the urban development of central Europe lagged behind that of the rest of the continent. The weakness of the cities in both economic and political terms and the lack of a significant urban bourgeoisie has meant that urban history in east and central Europe has remained a rather neglected field, together with the study of domestic trade, which, of course, cannot be done without proper attention to the smaller towns and the entire urban network. The study of the lesser towns has remained the domain of local history, which, naturally, tends to investigate towns individually, rarely considering their place in the wider picture of town and countryside.

A more general study of urbanisation in this region raises first of all a theoretical issue, namely, whether only cities with full-blown privileges should be considered members of the urban network, or whether towns without full urban status, in seigneurial dependence (*oppida, Märkte, miasteczko*), might also be included, at least in part. There is still no consensus on these matters among students of urban history in any of the countries under review, even less in the region as a whole.

In Hungary for instance some students of urban history have discarded definitions based on legal status and have been striving to formulate a concept of towns applicable to the specific development of the country, namely that the number of industrial-commercial *civitates* with wide-ranging autonomy and urban liberties had been very low since the Middle Ages. Their development came to a halt in the fifteenth century, when a rather different type of agrarian-urban settlement called *oppidum* became the leading market centre. These *oppida* were of a very heterogeneous social and legal character, ranging from populous and important towns with wide-ranging autonomy to small villages without any privileges except the right of holding markets. The urban functions of the late medieval and early modern market towns are generally recognised but assessed in different ways. One school of opinion considers the *oppidum* to be a transitional form between town and village which had reached deadlock in its urban development. The growth of craft industries is seen as an indicator of their urban character. Other urban historians regard some *oppida* as examples of a special type of town, characterised by specialised market-oriented agriculture (viticulture, husbandry) coupled with handicrafts. The intertwining of the two types of production over centuries was seen as a sign of adjustment to a particular economic structure of Hungary. Besides the overwhelming role of agriculture, is the heterogeneity of the legal status of the *oppida* (and the lack of urban liberties for a great – albeit in the different countries variable – part of the market towns) which has led many historians to regard the legal criteria as decisive. However, other historians tend to include non-privileged towns if they seem to (or can be proven to) fulfil central-place functions.[1]

[1] E. Mályusz, 'Geschichte der Bürgertums in Ungarn', *Vierteljahrschrift für Sozial und Wirtschaftsgeschichte*, vol. 20 (1927–8), 356–407; I. Szabó, *Tanulmányok a magyar parasztság történetéből* (Budapest, 1948); I. Szabó, *A középkori magyar falu* (Budapest, 1969), p. 236 *et passim*; F. Erdei, *Magyar város*, 2nd edn. (Budapest, 1974); F. Erdei, *Településpolitika, közigazgatás, urbanizáció* (Budapest, 1977), pp. 68–106; J. Szücs, 'Das Städtewesen in Ungarn im 15–17. Jr.', *Studia Historica*, vol. 52 (1963); L. Makkai, 'A magyar városfejlödés történetének vázlata', in J. Borsos, ed., *Vidéki városaink* (Budapest, 1961), pp. 27–75; Z. Dávid, 'A városi népesség nagysága Magyarországon', *Történeti Statisztikai Közlemé-nyek*, 1963–4, pp. 110–27; J. Major, 'A magyar városhálózatról', *Településtudományi Köz-lemények*, vol. 16 (1964), pp. 32–65; A. Kubinyi, 'A XV–XVI, századi magyarországi városi fejlödés kérdéséhez', *Századok*, 1965; V. Bácskai, *Magyar mezövárosok a XV. században* (Budapest, 1965); S. Gyimesi, *A városok a feudalizmusból a kapitalizmusba való átmenet időszakában* (Budapest, 1975); Gy. Granasztói, *A középkori magyar város* (Budapest, 1980);

This debate explains the many theoretical and empirical studies, especially for the seventeenth to nineteenth centuries, which focus on the question of the urban character of one or other settlement.[2] These divergent opinions are not mere theoretical quibbles, because positions in the debate determine the enumeration and assessment of the role of small towns as well as the overall view of urbanisation in central Europe. Personally I see urbanness defined not by legal constitutional criteria but on the basis of urban central functions. However, it is difficult to select truly urban centres from among the many hundred non-privileged towns – including a number of semi-urban settlements which may differ from a village only by their market rights – because the sources are virtually nonexistent. It is necessary to study separately, wherever possible, cities with full urban status and various types of other towns and their places in the urban network.

My chapter here concentrates on towns within the Habsburg Empire, because for these we have fairly reliable, and more or less uniform and simultaneous, data, which, after the partition of Poland, also include information on towns in part of the former Polish Kingdom. For the earlier period I shall utilise occasional information for Polish towns. To put later developments in perspective I want to start with a survey of the urban network of the region at the end of the Middle Ages.

The late medieval context

According to the databank of Prof. Bairoch,[3] around 1500 the countries of the later Habsburg Empire had ten cities with more than 5,000, and eight with over 10,000 inhabitants; the corresponding figures in 1700 were fourteen and eight, i.e. there was no significant change over 200 years. The number of larger cities in Poland during the same period is estimated at three and six, and two and six, respectively. These estimates – for that is what they are, since we have very few reliable population figures – are to my mind too high and incomplete.

V. Bácskai and L. Nagy, *Piackörzetek, piacközpontok és városok Magyarországon 1828-ban* (Budapest, 1984).

[2] H. Samsonowicz, 'Das polnische Bürgertum in der Renaissancezeit', in *La Renaissance et la Réformation en Pologne et en Hongrie* (Budapest, 1963); M. Malowist, 'Die Problematik der sozial-wirtschaftlichen Geschichte Polens vom 15. bis um 17. Jh.', in *La Renaissance*, pp. 23–4; A. Wyrobisz, 'Typy fukcyonalne miast polskich XVI–XVIII.w', *Preglad Historyczny* (1981); J. Wiesiolowski, 'Le réseau urbain en Grande Pologne aux XIIIe–XVIe siècles', *Acta Poloniae Historica* (1981); Mitterauer, 'Das Problem der zentralen Orte als sozial- und wirtschaftshistorische Forschungsaufgabe', *Vierteljahrschrift für Wirtschafts und Sozialgeschichte*, vol. 58 (1971), 443–67; A. Spiesz, 'O kriteriách mestkosti na Slovensku v obdobi neskového feudalizmu', *Historicky Casopis* (1972), 503–34.

[3] P. Bairoch, J. Babou and P. Chèvre, *La population des villes européenes de 800 à 1850* (Geneva, 1988).

We have more reliable data for the region of present-day Austria. Here there were (around 1500) 87 cities and 344 *Märkte*, of which two had more than 10,000, and four had 5,000 or more inhabitants. Thus small towns, housing fewer than 5,000 people, constituted 91 per cent of the cities and 98 per cent of all urban settlements. The number of towns with full urban status grew only slowly between 1300 and 1600 from 71 to 86 – and this growth was essentially achieved between 1300 and 1400 – while that of the *Märkte* tripled from 131 to 409. Lacking population figures, we can make comparisons only on the basis of the number of houses. In the period 1300 to 1660 there was a decline of cities versus the *Märkte*, with the percentage of houses in the cities (as a share of all urban dwellings) falling from 38–9 per cent to 36 per cent; this suggests a more rapid urbanisation in the non-privileged towns. In subsequent centuries the proliferation of both types of settlement slowed down. Around 1850 the area had 119 cities and 520 *Märkte*: the number of cities had increased by one third, the market towns by a quarter.[4]

A similar trend can be observed in detail in Hungary. In the late Middle Ages the kingdom (including Croatia and Transylvania) had some 30–5 free royal cities and about 800 to 850 seigneurially dependent towns (*oppida*). In Bairoch's tables two cities are listed with over 10,000 inhabitants and eight above 5,000. In fact only Buda's population was around 10,000, six or seven other cities may have reached or surpassed the 5,000 mark but none of the *oppida* had such a size.[5] Thus the percentage of small towns among the privileged cities was approximately 75 per cent and in the entire urban network some 99 per cent. At the same time, it would be an overstatement to regard all the 800-plus Hungarian *oppida* or the 344 Austrian *Märkte* as real towns: only a small fraction fulfilled any kind of urban or central-place function. Perhaps 50–60 of the Hungarian towns can be counted on this basis, which reduces the ratio of small towns in the total urban system to 90 per cent.[6]

The number of cities and urban-type settlements in Hungary did not change much until the mid-nineteenth century owing, among other factors, to the reluctance of landlords to confirm the new royal charters granted to their towns which deprived landlords of important income and curtailed

---

4 E. Bruckmüller, *Sozialgeschichte Österreichs* (Vienna, 1985), p. 146; cf H. Knitler, 'Österreichs Städte in der früheren Neuzeit', in E. Zöllner, ed., *Österreichs Städte und Märkte in der Geschichte* (Vienna, 1985).
5 J. Szücs, *Városok és kézmüvesség* (Budapest), pp. 42–4; A. Kubinyi, 'Budapest története a késöbbi középkorban Buda elestéig (1541-ig)', in L. Gerevich and D. Kosáry, eds, *Budapest Története*, vol. II (Budapest, 1973), p. 134; I. Szabó, *La répartition de la population de Hongrie entre les bourgades et les villages dans les années 1449–1526* (Budapest, 1960); V. Bácskai, *Magyar mezövárosok*, pp. 23–8.
6 V. Bácskai, 'A mezövárosok kialakulásának történeti folyamata', *Városépítés* (1973).

their power. From the early seventeenth century several acts were passed by the Diets to prevent the elevation of seigneurial towns to the rank of free royal towns without the agreement of their landlords. Royal charters had to be confirmed by the Diet which often delayed recognition for decades.[7] Nevertheless, the ratio between privileged cities and non-privileged towns shifted somewhat. In the sixteenth century two towns acquired royal free status, in the seventeenth century ten, in the eighteenth century nine, and in the early nineteenth century three, raising the total to 65 towns, as against about 850 *oppida*. Many lesser towns vanished during the Ottoman occupation and the Turkish wars, yet two thirds of the market towns were medieval in origin. The 30 new cities chartered before 1850 were mostly long-standing *oppida*. All told, the urban network did not change qualitatively before c. 1850.

As far as Poland is concerned, our data are regionally very uneven. Lacking population figures, different kinds of estimates suggest very divergent pictures. Thus Wiesolowski counts small towns as comprising 63 per cent of all urban settlements in the late sixteenth century; Wyrobisz, in contrast, gives a figure of 90 per cent. At any rate, even though the seigneurially dependent towns dominated the urban network in Poland as well, they were less overwhelming than in Hungary; according to J. Senkowski, they amounted only to 60 per cent of the network in the seventeenth century.[8] Since the literature on Bohemia does not contain data on the late Middle Ages, comparisons can be made only for the eighteenth and nineteenth centuries.

Overall, the late sixteenth and the seventeenth centuries are seen by most authors as an age of urban decline in central Europe. This view is reinforced by the fact that the spectacular expansion of medieval urbanisation proceeding in this region from the twelfth to fifteenth centuries had ceased with the emergence of only a few new towns. The population of the large and medium-size towns was stagnant or declined: the striking decrease in their tax yields suggests an impoverishment of urban dwellers. The small towns, serving as centres of local exchange, managed to survive this period, but they did not expand or develop to any significant extent either. With the exception of a few important trading centres such as Gdansk, Prague and Vienna, the urban economy preserved its medieval character; the system of guild craft and restricted local trade remained intact; agriculture – especially in Hungary and Poland – became an increasingly important source of income for townspeople.

---

[7] A. Csizmadia, *A magyar városi jog* (Kolozsvàr, 1941); E. Deák, *Das Städtewesen der Länder ungarischen Krone (1780–1918)* (Vienna, 1979), vol. I, pp. 73–88.

[8] A. Wyrobisz, 'Typy funkcyonalne miast', p. 37; J. Wiesiolowski, 'Le réseau urbain', p. 20; J. Senkowski, 'Der Staat und die Städte in Polen des 14.–17. Jahrhunderts' (manuscript).

Table 4.1. *Number of towns in eastern central Europe 1780s–1851*

	1780s			1828			1851		
Province	Cities	Market towns	Total	Cities	Market towns	Total	Cities	Market towns	Total
L.A.	35	213	248	35	239	274	35	240	275
U.A.	14	152	166	17	114	131	17	118	135
S.	20	97	117	20	96	116	20	94	114
C.C.	27	49	76	25	42	67	25	42	67
T.V.	17	14	31	22	33	55	22	28	50
Bohemia	548	431	979	278	259	537	318	237	555
Moravia	122	171	293	118	178	296	117	186	303
Galicia	123	192	315	95	194	289	95	193	288
Hungary	61	431	492	61	775	836	61	657	718
Transylv.	8	70	78	34	37	71	25	65	90
Dalmatia	–	–	–	17	35	52	15	32	47
Total	975	1,820	2,795	722	2,002	2,724	750	1,892	2,642

L.A. = Lower Austria; U.A. = Upper Austria; S. = Styria; C.C. = Carinthia and Carniola;
T.V. = Tyrol and Vorarlberg; Transylv. = Transylvania.
Galician data include Bukovina; Hungarian data include Croatia and Slavonia.

In several countries stagnation had been worsened by the shocks caused by the ravages of wars, which led to the destruction and depopulation of many towns. Bohemia did not recover from the devastation of the Thirty Years War for decades, and Hungary needed half a century or more to repopulate its many towns and villages after their liberation from Ottoman rule at the end of the seventeenth century.

The number and ratio of small towns in the late eighteenth and early nineteenth centuries

The earliest reasonably accurate data about towns in the region can be found in the government censuses of the 1780s. These have been compared to the information contained in the tables of the first Austrian statistical survey of 1828 and that for 1851[9] (Table 4.1).

[9] A. Gürtler, *Die Volkszählungen Maria Theresias und Joseph II. 1753–1790* (Innsbruck, 1909); D. Dányi and Z. Dávid, *Az elsö magyarországi népszámlalás (1784–87)* (Budapest, 1960); *Tafeln zur Statistik der österreichischen Monarchie* (Vienna, 1828–1951); L. Nagy, *Notitiae politico-geographico-statisticae Inclyti Regni Hungariae* . . . (Pest, 1828); F. Dvoracek, 'Soupisy obyvatelstava v Cechách na Morave a ve Slezsku v letech 1754–1921', *Cesko-slovensky Statisticky vestnik*, vols 5–7 (1923–6).

Table 4.2. *Number of towns in eastern central Europe by size category 1828–1851*

Province	1828			1851		
	Under 2,000	2,000 to 4,999	5,000 or over	Under 2,000	2,000 to 4,999	5,000 or over
L.A.	26	7	2	20	10	5
U.A.	8	6	3	8	6	3
S.	18	1	1	13	5	2
C.C.	21	2	2	21	2	2
T.V.	12	6	4	11	7	4
Bohemia	170	97	11	169	124	25
Moravia	71	37	10	34	65	18
Galicia	36	40	19	26	43	26
Hungary	5	19	37	6	18	37
Transylv.	26	1	7	15	2	8
Dalmatia	9	7	1	9	2	4
Total	402	223	97	332	284	134

For abbreviations see Table 4.1.

Table 4.3. *Urban population in eastern central Europe by size category 1828–1851 (excluding market towns)*

Province	1828		1851	
	2,000 to 4,999	5,000 or over	2,000 to 4,999	5,000 or over
L.A.	12,405	313,496	28,726	460,364
U.A.	19,710	39,586	23,125	36,828
S.	4,570	42,145	14,147	62,271
C.C.	6,634	19,460	6,150	29,357
T.V.	17,415	36,956	20,914	38,498
Bohemia	281,781	152,055	484,575	191,916
Moravia	108,285	103,977	137,737	189,555
Galicia	125,452	196,775	134,600	340,129
Hungary	67,680	573,113	63,573	692,847
Transylv.	4,235	89,800	6,908	87,599
Dalmatia	19,555	5,896	10,648	28,609

For abbreviations see Table 4.1.

The total number of urban settlements did not change significantly between the 1780s and 1828, but the ratio between cities with full urban status and seigneurial towns did – in favour of the former. Significant changes can be noted in the Bohemian and Galician data; but the decline in the total number and especially the privileged cities may be caused more by uncertainties concerning categorisation than by actual losses in the level of urbanisation.[10] This assumption is supported by the fact that only in these regions did the number of cities grow significantly between 1828 and 1851. In the first half of the nineteenth century selective development took place in Bohemia with a 6 per cent decrease in the number of market towns and a 3 per cent increase in cities and a relative fall in the number of all urban places. Yet, in general it seems that there was no major change in the total number of towns in this period, though there may very well have been some changes in the composition of the urban network.

Since we have no late eighteenth-century population data for individual cities (save for Hungary), the ratio of smaller and larger towns cannot be studied except for the nineteenth century. Even then, this can be done only partially, for initially the statistics relate only to the privileged cities with over 2,000 souls. Thus developments covering the whole period from 1828 to 1851 can be studied only for the cities with full urban status (see Table 4.2).

Small towns below 2,000 inhabitants amounted in 1828 to 86 per cent of the cities and to 83 per cent in 1851; the proportion of their population as a share of all urban dwellers grew from 29.8 per cent to 32.6 per cent (see Table 4.3). In 1851 82 per cent of all cities and market towns in the region were small towns and housed 40 per cent of the inhabitants of all towns above 2,000 inhabitants. All in all, at the beginning of the nineteenth century in eastern central Europe about one third of urban dwellers lived in small towns. This is a ratio in line with most other regions of Europe (with the exception of the highly industrialised areas). That population growth was higher in towns than the average is also a general feature: in our region the proportion of urban dwellers (in towns over 2,000) grew from 8.1 per cent to 13.7 per cent. Generally speaking, population growth in small towns was faster than in big cities.

There are, however, considerable differences within the areas under review. The ratio of small towns to large cities was very different from region to region: highest in the industrialised regions of Austria and

---

[10] The inconsistency of the statistical categories is obvious in the 1851 table of Hungarian towns. Earlier statistics counted seven episcopal towns among the privileged (free royal) cities. In 1851 a number of partly privileged *oppida* were also included while two episcopal cities were relegated to the 'market town' category and two royal cities totally omitted, although no legal changes had been introduced in the urban status. These errors are corrected in my table, but I was unable to scrutinise the statistics for other parts of the monarchy.

Bohemia-Moravia, lowest in the more agrarian part of Hungary and, to a small extent, Galicia. The same phenomenon can also be observed within the hereditary Habsburg provinces (Upper and Lower Austria, Styria, Carinthia, Carniola, Tyrol and Vorarlberg): the proportion of small towns was higher in the industrialised ones. While the overall pattern was characteristic of the area both in 1828 and in 1851, there were some differences in urban development in the western and eastern parts of the empire.

In the Austrian, Bohemian and Moravian lands the dominance of small towns continued well into the mid-nineteenth century in spite of the industrialisation boom of the 1830s, but the 1828 level (with over 90 per cent of urban settlements in the small-town category) declined: in Austria to 86.5 per cent and in Moravia to 81 per cent, remaining at over 90 per cent only in Bohemia. Yet the development of the urban network and of the role of small towns varied considerably in these industrialised provinces. Although the number of larger cities increased most in Bohemia, the population of small towns grew from two thirds of city dwellers (in 1818) to almost three quarters by 1851, clearly, because the ratio of towns with fewer than 2,000 inhabitants was still very high. In Austria the number of cities did not change much, the number of small-town-dwellers also grew a little, yet their share of the urban population remained small – about 12–13 per cent (even if Vienna is excluded from the total the porportion was still only 30 per cent). In Moravia, however, the small-town-dwellers decreased from 51 per cent to 42 per cent of the total urban population, because here the major towns grew faster. Nevertheless, the small towns grew too, so that towns with fewer than 2,000 inhabitants decreased from two thirds to one third of all towns. An explanation for this particular process will be possible when new detailed research is done on Moravian towns.

In contrast to the western part of the empire the number of small towns and their population share was smaller and decreasing in Galicia and Bukovina. During the second quarter of the nineteenth century the proportion of small towns fell from 80 to 72 per cent, and their urban population share from 39 to 28 per cent. Here, too, the larger cities grew faster, though industrialisation was minimal.

The proportion of small towns at this time was lowest in Hungary. They constituted about one third of the urban network and their inhabitants numbered only 10.6 per cent of the urban population in 1828 and only 8.4 per cent in 1851. While the number of really small towns (below 2,000) decreased everywhere west of the River Leitha, this process took place in Hungary in the 1800s.[11] They began to grow again after that time (by some

---

[11] G. Thirring, 'Városaink népességének alakulása 1787–1910-ig', *Városi Szemle IV* (1911), 465–92; G. Thirring, 'Az 1804. évi népösszeírás', *Magyar Statisztikai Szemle* (1936), 1–21.

20 per cent in the first half of the nineteenth century) when decline was more visible in towns with 2–10,000 inhabitants. At the same time Hungary had the highest number of larger cities.

The growth of Hungarian large towns was not the result of industrialisation – in the early nineteenth century this was still in its infancy. The major factor was agricultural commodity production and trade in agrarian products. Huge agrarian towns developed on the Hungarian Plain, supported first by extensive cattle-breeding on their vast pasturelands and later by corn producing creating a peculiar settlement pattern of the *tanya*-type, with scattered homesteads in the midst of arable lands. These towns marketed their produce in faraway places and were not connected to any city, while the surrounding populous settlements did not depend upon their services either. Their industries and commerce served above all the local population, but the concentration of people triggered the growth of urban-type commercial, administrative and educational institutions. Their urban character is beyond doubt, in spite of the absence of central-place functions. But whether they should be called, in *functional terms*, small, middling or large towns, remains so far an unresolved issue.[12]

All this does not question the validity of arguments about general trends in European urbanisation, but rather the problem of defining cities in general, and urban growth in particular, by reference to population figures. Above all, it seems questionable whether it is possible to establish 'critical values' in terms of population figures for towns in regions with different socio-economic development and differing economic and settlement patterns. The divergent ratio of small towns in the western and eastern part of the Habsburg Empire was clearly connected with the average population figures of the settlements. In the western provinces the market towns and villages usually had small populations, hardly any of them surpassing the 5,000 mark; Hungary, on the other hand, had, besides the 37 cities with more than 5,000 inhabitants, 96 market towns and 25 villages of similar size in 1828, and 102 towns and 25 villages with more than 5,000 inhabitants in 1851. Mere population level, without consideration of functional criteria, of the population size and economy of the surrounding settlements and the features of the whole urban network, fails to provide an adequate explanation of the role of small towns in eastern central Europe.

The function and role of Hungarian small towns

An investigation of the Hungarian urban network according to functional

---

[12] V. Bácskai, *Towns and Urban Society in Early Nineteenth Century Hungary* (Budapest, 1989), p. 49.

criteria[13] yields the following results. In agriculturally backward regions, where the majority of people lived in small settlements below 1,000 people, small towns and market towns with fewer than 5,000 inhabitants could play the role of craft and commercial centres for quite considerable regions. So for instance the economic pull of Balassagyarmat, a county seat populated with 3,700 inhabitants, affected an area with about 100,000 people. In 1828 91 merchants were active in business in the town, 9 of them as wholesalers.[14] The episcopal town of Szombathely with an equal population, situated near the western border, was the only marketplace in the area, with 36,000 people, and another 100,000 lived in its secondary hinterland. The town was a county seat and episcopal see and housed a seminary, an academy and a secondary school. Máramarossziget, another county seat lying in the under-developed eastern part of the country, had 3,800 inhabitants, and influenced a hinterland of about 100,000 inhabitants. In this apparently rustic small town 15 wholesalers and 44 shopkeepers were recorded in 1828.[15]

So these and several other similar settlements were, despite their small size, not typical small towns with local market-centre functions, but had the same role as middle-rank towns with developed central-place functions. These functions and activities were clearly influential for the professional, social and mental world of these towns. Their society was more stratified and complex than that of the neighbouring villages with equal populations. In such towns farmers lived together with a considerable number of artisans and merchants, carriers, carters and a variety of wage earners. Conditions for entrepreneurial activity were sometimes more favourable in seigneurial small towns than in the larger royal free towns. In the latter the guilds hindered the establishment and activity of Greek Orthodox and Jewish merchants doing business in new ways,[16] whereas seigneurial centres welcomed them as creditors, tenants and traders of produce. Paradoxically perhaps, small towns under seigneurial jurisdiction often offered more favourable conditions for the rise of a modern middle class than free towns. It is symptomatic that a considerable part of the merchants, bankers and entrepreneurs of Pest came from the Jewish communities of the Transdanubian small towns.[17]

Towns that served as centres for county, ecclesiastical or manorial

---

[13] V. Bácskai and L. Nagy, *Piackörzetek.*

[14] MOL (Hungarian National Archives) Archivum Regnicolaris No. 26; Conscriptio Regnicolaris art. VII. 1827 ordinatae (1828–1832); Conscriptio oppidi Balassagyarmat.

[15] MOL, Conscriptio oppidi Máramarossziget.

[16] G. Eperjessy, *A szabad királyi városok kézmüvesipara a reformkori Magyarországon* (Budapest, 1988), pp. 150–73; P. Balázs, *Györ a feudalizmus bomlása és a polgári forradalom idején* (Budapest, 1980), pp. 106–9; L. Nagy, 'Budapest története 1790–1848', in D. Kosáry, ed., *Budapest története III* (Budapest, 1975), pp. 386–7.

[17] V. Bácskai, *A vállalkozók elöfutárai* (Budapest, 1989), pp. 19–20.

administration had growing numbers of professional men and clerks, while noblemen increasingly kept permanent residences there. Despite the social detachment of the landowners, their consumer habits and cultural demands, their lifestyle and behaviour, had an important impact on small-town society.[18]

Because agriculture remained an important sector of the urban economy (even in larger cities) most small towns did not have an urbanised image. Foreign travellers, like the Englishmen Townson and Bright visiting Hungary in the 1790s and 1810s, did not find them worthy of attention. Passing through them they mention at best their inns (often critically). If they stopped in county, episcopal or seigneurial centres they were usually guests at an aristocratic mansion, and these were generally the only buildings in the place which engaged their attention.[19]

Nevertheless, as well as the fine city centres of several declining small free towns, civic improvements were in process in Transdanubian seigneurial towns as well, especially in the administrative centres inhabited by noblemen and professional men, and above all in the episcopal towns, where new county houses, churches, palaces, monasteries, prebendal houses and schools were built. They were joined by new or rebuilt civic houses at least around the marketplace or on the High Street. Townscapes in a modest provincial Baroque style did not impress foreign travellers accustomed to western towns but the improvements were praised by native travellers. Their reports published in contemporary newspapers put special emphasis on the social intercourse and social events in these towns: the opening of clubs and coffee-houses, the foundation and activities of various societies and associations, balls and promenades, theatres and dramatic performances. These were institutions and places usually established by the citizens' own initiative, where the different layers of town society could meet together.[20]

In this way Hungarian small towns, even though somewhat rural in character, prepared their inhabitants for a more differentiated economy, stratified society, and ideas of urban liberty and educational as well as cultural enlightenment. In their markets not only were goods exchanged, but information and knowledge about the outside world as well. In the early nineteenth century the flow of goods and information was not confined to fairs: both were distributed by merchants picking up news on their business

[18] G. Benda, ed., *A keszthelyi uradalom 1850 elötti hagyatéki és vagyonösszeírásai I. Keszthely 1711–1820* (Budapest, 1988), pp. XXIX *et passim*.

[19] R. Bright, *Travels from Vienna through Lower Hungary* (Edinburgh, 1818); R. Townson, *Travels in Hungary* (1797).

[20] Reports on improvements and on social life in small towns in the contemporary newspapers and literary periodicals (*Pester Zeitung*, *Életképek*, *Regélö Pesti Divatlap*, *Vaterland* etc.).

trips or from commercial correspondence with their partners. A case in point is a contemporary comedy in which a merchant's clerk was entertaining the customers with the latest news of the Napoleonic wars.[21] Thus these semi-rural, semi-urban small towns created an increasingly urban population, an important source of men and ideas for the otherwise rather limited bourgeoisie of the country.

Conclusion

As far as population data and the number of small towns are concerned, the eastern central region of Europe experienced during the early modern period and above all from the eighteenth century many of the same developments as other parts of the continent. Advances in agriculture and growth of inland trade in the Habsburg Empire led to a relatively rapid population growth of small towns but in contrast to the north-western European countries this process was not followed by the expansion of large and middle-sized towns. So the urban system was in comparison with the main areas of Europe undeveloped, or, in the context of the European periphery at least, unbalanced: a network of small towns under the strong primacy of Vienna, with very few large or middle-sized towns. The shape of this urban system was determined by economic and social factors, especially the slow place of industrialisation and the insignificant role of long-distance trade as well as the anti-urban policy of the landlords.

It is likely that given this urban context the role and functions of Hungarian small towns must have been different from those of small towns in the more developed European regions. There may have been regional differences of this kind in the empire as well, though comparison is not feasible because of the lack of detailed research. At the same time the Hungarian experience shows distinct variations: small towns fulfilling the functions of regional market centres or serving as seats of county and ecclesiastical administration, together with very populous agrarian towns with less diversified societies and very limited central functions. Thus population level and urban functions were less interrelated in an underdeveloped urban context. Despite several similarities the small towns of the European periphery belonged to a rather different world than the small towns of the European centre.

---

[21] V. M. Csokonai, 'Az özvegy Karnyóné és a két szeleburdiak' (1799) összes Müvei, Budapest, p. 1397.

5 Small towns in England 1550–1850: national and regional population trends

Peter Clark

Between the sixteenth and nineteenth centuries England was transformed from being one of the less urbanised regions of Europe to the most urbanised nation in the world. For much of that period England remained a country dominated by its small towns. Notwithstanding the spectacular rise of London and the explosive expansion of specialist industrial towns from the reign of George III, the hundreds of small towns with a few thousand inhabitants continued to play an influential role in English economic, social and cultural life until the early nineteenth century. Though figures are almost impossible to calculate, about 1700 approximately 54 per cent of English townspeople may have lived in settlements of fewer than 5,000 inhabitants, approximately 14 per cent of the national population; in 1801 the comparable figures were in the region of 31 per cent and 12 per cent.[1] As we shall see, many English small towns responded positively to the challenge of economic and social change affecting the country in the eighteenth century. The number of small towns (excluding Middlesex) declined from just over 700 in the late seventeenth century to somewhat under 600 in 1811. There was a significant turnover of urban settlements with numbers of small towns facing problems and the loss of their urban identity, while others grew rapidly and became major urban centres. At the same time, some new settlements emerged, particularly in the later eighteenth century, as a consequence of industrial and metropolitan growth. Regional variations were increasingly marked.

Research for this study, part of the Leicester project on Small Towns in England 1600–1850, has been generously supported by the Economic and Social Research Council, the Nuffield Foundation and the European Commission. I am also grateful to Dr K. Gaskin, Dr A. Wilson, Mr E. Sullivan, Mr A. Milne and Mr R. Weedon for their research advice and assistance.
[1] The 1700 figures are estimated from Gregory King's calculations (with revised population figures for London and England) in D. V. Glass and D. E. C. Eversley, eds, *Population in History* (1965), p. 178; the 1801 figures are based on Dr Corfield's figures for towns in England and Wales recalculated to include towns under 2,500 inhabitants (P. Corfield, 'Small Towns, Large Implications: Social and Cultural Roles of Small Towns in 18th-century England and Wales', *British Journal for Eighteenth-Century Studies*, vol. 10 (1987), 134).

I

In spite of their number and significance, English small towns have never, until recently, received due attention. In part this reflects the flimsy and difficult nature of much of the documentation for towns of this type, many of which were not incorporated and so did not generate their own civic archives. But the neglect is long-standing, rooted in the attitudes of contemporary commentators. During the sixteenth and seventeenth centuries writers about towns were mostly local gentry who were hostile to urban privileges. Richard Carew, for instance, an Elizabethan landowner, declared of the small boroughs in Cornwall that their 'large exemptions and jurisdictions [were] a garment . . . over-rich and wide for many of their wearish [withered] and ill-disposed bodies'. Generally, however, early topographers and observers said relatively little about small towns, though Thomas Baskerville, writing after the Restoration, was more complimentary.[2] During the eighteenth century visitors to small towns were Londoners or landowners with experience of the great metropolis. Almost invariably they measured life in the small towns by the yardstick of London improvement and prosperity and usually found it wanting. In the 1730s Lord Oxford dismissed a number of the East Anglian market towns as poor and mean, describing Diss as the 'worst town and . . . the worst inn I ever was at in Britain'. Some years later Lord Grimston decried Newport Pagnell in Buckinghamshire as 'very dirty, ill-paved, and not worth observation', and Chesterfield as 'a very disagreeable, ill-built town'. The historian Edward Gibbon remarked of Shaftesbury in 1762, 'a pleasant town in summer, bleak in winter, and old and ruinous at all times'.[3] But with the diffusion of urban prosperity and improvement, there was growing recognition of the economic and cultural achievements of the bigger small towns such as Lewes in Sussex, praised as a pretty town, well inhabited, with assemblies where many gentry came once a week. Lord Grimston confessed that Tetbury was 'no despicable county town. The houses in general are built with stone and I think remarkable for their neatness. Here is a market kept and a good woollen manufactory carried on.'[4] In the early nineteenth century local antiquarians continued to note the modest successes of small country towns. David Elisha Davy, for instance, remarked on Mendlesham in Suffolk that 'for such an out of the way place I found [it] a much more

---

[2] R. Carew, *Richard Carew of Antony: The Survey of Cornwall etc.* (ed. F. E. Halliday, 1953), pp. 137, 157–8. Small towns are barely mentioned in Robert Reyce's survey of Suffolk in 1618; cf. F. Hervey, ed., *Suffolk in the 17th Century* (1902). *Historical Manuscripts Commission* (hereafter *HMC*), Portland MSS., vol. 2, 264 *et passim*.

[3] *HMC*, Portland MSS., vol. 6, 156, 170; *HMC*, Verulam, MSS., pp. 299, 240; D. M. Low, ed., *Gibbon's Journal* (1929), p. 47.

[4] *HMC*, Portland MSS., vol. 6, 68; *HMC*, Verulam, p. 248.

respectable place than I had expected; the season was no doubt much in its favour but it appeared neat and clean'. Trade directories, anxious for local sales, also tended to be flattering. From the late eighteenth century there were even some town histories singing urban praises.[5] But interest in small towns was increasingly overwhelmed by the heavily publicised attractions of the great Victorian cities. By the later nineteenth century small towns, growing relatively slowly, if at all, were increasingly dismissed as the detritus of an outmoded agrarian economy. When there was a reaction to the massive social problems of the Victorian city at the end of the century, the revived interest in rural society and rustic urbanity (the Garden City movement) displayed minimal interest in England's heritage of small towns.

Only since the second world war has there been any serious historical work on the evolution of small towns – coinciding perhaps with their revived prosperity, especially in southern England. The turning point probably was Alan Everitt's seminal study of market towns between 1500 and 1640 which appeared in the *Agrarian History of England and Wales*, volume IV, in 1967. Though primarily concerned there with what he saw as the major expansion of market centres in the sixteenth century linked with advances in agricultural and the growth of inland trade, Everitt published further work on the history of small towns which put them firmly on the historical agenda.[6] In turn his research inspired a number of doctoral theses on small towns in the sixteenth and seventeenth centuries, including the Leicestershire towns of Ashby de la Zouch, Melton Mowbray and Lutterworth.[7] Though these studies provide valuable analysis of the distinctive economic, administrative and socio-cultural development of the towns, most failed to set them in a wider, comparative context.

Another surge of interest in small towns in these years came from historical geographers. Notable here were the publications of Harold Carter on Welsh towns in the 1960s and John Patten on East Anglian towns in the 1970s. Their lead encouraged a series of other studies including Stephen Royle on nineteenth-century Leicestershire market towns and Margaret

[5] J. Blatchly, ed., *A Journal of Excursions Through the County of Suffolk* (Suffolk Records Soc., vol. 24, 1982), 169; R. W. Unwin, 'Tradition and Transition: Market Towns of the Vale of York, 1660–1830', *Northern History*, vol. 17 (1981), 83–4.

[6] A. Everitt, 'The Marketing of Agricultural Produce', in J. Thirsk, ed., *The Agrarian History of England and Wales*, vol. IV (Cambridge, 1967), pp. 466–592; *idem*, 'The Banburys of England', *Urban History Yearbook 1974* (Leicester, 1974), pp. 28–38; *idem*, 'Town and Country in Victorian Leicestershire: the Role of the Village Carrier' in *idem*, ed., *Perspectives in English Urban History* (1973), pp. 213–36.

[7] C. J. M. Moxon, 'Ashby-de-la-Zouch: a social and economic survey of a market town', (unpublished D.Phil. thesis, Oxford Univ., 1971); D. Fleming, 'A Local Market System: Melton Mowbray and the Wreake Valley 1549–1720' (unpubl. Ph.D. thesis, Leicester Univ., 1980); J. Goodacre, 'Lutterworth in the 16th and 17th centuries' (unpubl. Ph.D. thesis, Leicester Univ., 1977).

Noble on country towns in Eastern Yorkshire 1700–1850.[8] Such work was important for opening up discussion of the spatial relationships of small towns, but it had serious limitations. Heavily influenced by central-place theories, the approach, at its worst, tended to be static in focus and mechanistic in style.

From the late 1970s general work on urbanisation during the early modern period stimulated increasing interest by historians in small towns. In 1976 Paul Slack and I argued, in line with Everitt, for the expansion of small towns in the sixteenth and early seventeenth centuries and for their subsequent contraction. John Chartres in a number of pieces also maintained a negative view about the fortunes of English market towns in the late seventeenth and early eighteenth centuries, suggesting from the evidence of market listings that substantial numbers disappeared. Alan Dyer in an important article in 1979 criticised this scenario, emphasising instead the variety of experience of small towns, particularly in southern England.[9] In 1982 Penelope Corfield drew attention to the rationalisation of the market town network in the eighteenth century with the apparently inexorable decay of minor centres. But in a subsequent article on small towns she argued for a more positive view of the social and cultural role of smaller communities in Georgian England, pointing to their significance as the arena of local enlightenment.[10] Parallel to the growth of academic attention, there has been escalating research by local history groups on places like Ludlow, Tetbury, Woodstock, Marlow, Thame, Faversham and St Albans.[11]

---

[8] H. Carter, *The Towns of Wales: A Study in Urban Geography* (Cambridge, 1966); *idem, The Growth of the Welsh City System* (Aberystwyth, 1968); *idem*, 'The growth and decline of Welsh towns', in D. Moore, ed., *Wales in the 18th Century* (Swansea, 1976), pp. 47–62; J. Patten, *English Towns 1500–1700* (1978), esp. ch. 6; S. Royle, 'Aspects of the Social Geography of Leicestershire Towns 1837–1871' (unpublished Ph.D. thesis, Leicester Univ., 1976); *idem, Functional Divergence: Urban Development in 18th and 19th century Leicestershire* (Leicester, 1981); M. Noble, 'Growth and development in a regional urban system: the country towns of eastern Yorkshire 1700–1850', *Urban History Yearbook 1987* (Leicester, 1987), pp. 1–21; also *idem*, 'Growth and development of country towns: the case of eastern Yorkshire' (unpublished Ph.D. thesis, Hull Univ., 1982). For a more sensitive treatment see S. A. Lewis, 'An historical and geographical study of the small towns of Shropshire 1600–1830' (unpublished Ph.D. thesis, Leicester Univ., 1990).

[9] P. Clark and P. Slack, *English Towns in Transition 1500–1700* (1976), pp. 17–25; J. Chartres, 'The Marketing of Agricultural Produce in Metropolitan Western England in the late 17th and 18th centuries', in *Exeter Papers in Economic History*, vol. 8 (1973), 63–74; *idem*, contribution in J. Thirsk, ed., *Agrarian History of England and Wales*, vol. V(2) (Cambridge, 1985), pp. 409–20; A. Dyer, 'The Market Towns of southern England 1500–1700', *Southern History*, vol. 1 (1979), 123–4.

[10] P. J. Corfield, *The Impact of English Towns 1700–1800* (Oxford, 1982), pp. 20–1; *idem*, 'Small Towns, Large Implications', pp. 127–35.

[11] Among various publications see D. Lloyd and P. Klein, *Ludlow: a Historic Town in Words and Pictures* (Chichester, 1984); J. M. Cook, ed., *Great Marlow: Parish and People in the 19th Century* (Marlow, 1991); S. Smyth, *The Faversham Poor in the 18th and early 19th centuries* (Faversham, 1987).

Since 1985 the Economic and Social Research Council, Nuffield Foundation, European Commission and other bodies have funded the Small Towns project at the Centre for Urban History, Leicester University which has sought to provide a national quantitative framework for research in England from the sixteenth to the mid-nineteenth century. The research has focused, firstly, on devising population estimates at specific points in time for our sample of small towns, in order to plot demographic trends. Secondly we have been collecting parish register aggregative data to try and understand the dynamics of population change. A third part of the project relates to the creation of a database of occupational evidence to help identify economic trends, and we are also starting to gather material on the social and cultural characteristics of small towns.[12]

II

The remainder of this chapter will concentrate on the first concern of the Leicester project, the analysis of the demographic trends of English small towns from population estimates. In all countries defining what one means by a small town is always a difficult if not jesuitical exercise. For England not only is there the problem that many small towns lack corporate recognition before 1835 and so are barely distinguishable politically and administratively from villages, but there is also the difficulty caused in the eighteenth century by the emergence, protoplasmically, of new towns as a result of industrial and metropolitan growth; many of these settlements only slowly acquire a range of urban functions. Our primary sample of small towns includes all settlements with fewer than approximately 2,500 people in the 1660s and 1670s which were classed as towns in contemporary listings. At the same time, because of rapid growth in the eighteenth century, we have also included all towns with under 5,000 inhabitants in 1811 which were listed as urban centres in contemporary directories. Our sample covers all English counties with the exception of Middlesex, where rapid metropolitan growth meant that numerous small towns were transformed into very large quasi-suburban centres whose inclusion into the database would have severely distorted our findings. Most of the small towns of

---

[12] For preliminary discussion of the aggregative data see A. Wilson, 'Population developments of early modern English small towns: the parish register evidence for four regions' (paper at the European Small Towns Conference, Leicester 1990). For initial analysis of occupational material for the 1790s see P. Clark, 'Entrepreneurs, Elites and English Small Towns during the Industrial Revolution', in E. van Cauwenberghe and P. Klep, eds, *Liber Amicorum for Herman van der Wee* (forthcoming).

Cheshire and Lancashire have also been excluded from the following analysis because of the problems of the parish data.[13]

As far as early population data are concerned, we have derived our estimates for small towns principally from national ecclesiastical surveys or fiscal returns of varying quality. For 1563 there is the diocesan survey of communicants with extant returns for about a third of the country (216 small towns). Another similar if less complete survey was made in 1603 (212 small towns). After the Restoration of Charles II, Parliament approved the introduction of a tax on hearths to finance royal government. This was essentially a household tax though with complicated categories of exemption for poor families, industrial hearths, etc. The tax was levied a number of times and one or more returns survive for most parts of the country (we have parish data on 310 and 106 small towns at different periods).[14] In 1676 there was a further diocesan survey of communicants – the Compton Census (497 small towns). The parish returns have been tabulated and exhaustively analysed in Anne Whiteman's *The Compton Census of 1676*. Even so there remain various uncertainties with estimating population figures from this source.[15] After the Revolution of 1688 government policy shifted away from

[13] The maps and statistics in this chapter are based mostly on data originally published in P. Clark, K. Gaskin and A. Wilson, *Population Estimates of English Small Towns, 1550–1851* (Leicester, 1989). This contains preliminary estimates of population size, based on various ecclesiastical and taxation listings for 1563, 1603, post-1660 and 1676, plus early nineteenth-century census enumerations. The data base is in the process of revision and some account of those changes was taken in the preparation of the final text of this chapter. A revised edition of *Population Estimates of English Small Towns, 1550–1851* (Leicester, 1993) by P. Clark and J. Hosking was published while this book was in the press. Towns were selected for analysis here if meaningful estimates were available on a parish basis, with township estimates excluded. For the statistics on which Figs 5.2–3 were based, all small towns with a suitable estimate from one or both of the diocesan surveys (1563 and 1603), plus c. 1670, were included. For those from which Figs 5.4–7 were derived, towns were included if they had a suitable parish estimate for c. 1670, 1811 and 1851. Unfortunately, the North-Western region (Lancashire and Cheshire) is represented by only two towns, c. 1670–1811, because parish areas there are especially large and include numerous townships; the region is therefore generally excluded from the analysis.

It is difficult to specify a range of accuracy for the estimates, but erring on the side of caution, the upper demographic limit for the definition of a seventeenth-century small town was raised by 15 per cent, from 2,500 to 2,875. This proxies variations seen when generating the estimates. The ceiling ensures that no small town defined as such c. 1670 would be excluded by a strict adherence of the 2,500 upper limit, when other sources would not warrant such action, while it is set at a sufficiently low level to distinguish the larger towns.

[14] For the problems of using the Hearth Tax see N. Alldridge, ed., *The Hearth Tax: Problems and Possibilities* (Hull, 1983), esp. the chapters by Arkell and Husbands. To generate a single estimate for each town in c. 1670, a simple average was taken of available estimates, excluding the least reliable (based on exemption lists from the Hearth Tax). Given the nature of the original sources, and the averaging process, these estimates for c. 1670 represent an approximate centre for a range of possible estimates.

[15] A. Whiteman, ed., *The Compton Census of 1676: A Critical Edition* (1986).

general direct taxes towards a selective land tax and heavy indirect taxation, while the state ceased to maintain an interventionist role in provincial administration. In consequence, there are no national enumerations or sets of fiscal data available for assessing town populations in the eighteenth century. The most we have is a scattering of local population returns. Though the first national Census was taken in 1801 we have preferred the more reliable second enumeration in 1811 (583 small towns with parish data), together with the 1851 Census (583 small towns with parish data).[16]

Needless to say, one is confronted with a multiplicity of problems in trying to estimate small-town populations during the early modern period. As well as the particular difficulties of individual sources, there are marked variations in the comprehensiveness of returns and complex questions about the correct multipliers. A further question relates to the distinction between parish and township. In most cases the extant data are for the parish: in this analysis we have deployed only parish data. If the parish is small in area or the town extensive the difference is likely to be minimal. But in many instances the parish embraced a quite large, though not necessarily populous, rural hinterland. This is a serious and in many ways intractable problem.

Studying small towns as an isolated category would be of limited value. It is essential to draw comparisons with general urbanisation trends in the provinces. Unfortunately the demographic documentation for bigger provincial towns is if anything worse than for small towns. Data for this study are based on a systematic analysis and collation of recent estimates from the secondary literature for a number of bigger towns from the sixteenth to the eighteenth centuries; after 1811 census figures are used.[17] One final point needs to be stressed. It is clearly dangerous to use demographic data on its own as a proxy for economic change. In this chapter we have tried, wherever possible, to correlate and qualify the evidence for population with other material. Any student of population has to be a natural born sceptic.

Table 5.1 indicates estimated annual population growth rates for small town parishes derived from a comparison of national returns in 1563, 1603 and at the Restoration (collating the Hearth Tax and Compton Census

---

[16] *Population Abstract 1811* (1812); *Census of Great Britain, 1851* (1852).

[17] For comparative purposes we used a small sample of larger centres, where appropriate population estimates were available for c. 1550, c. 1600 or c. 1670: data were drawn from P. Bairoch, *La population des villes européennes de 800 à 1850* (Geneva, 1988); Patten, *English Towns*; C. Chalklin, *The Provincial Towns of Georgian England* (1974); Corfield, *Impact*; Clark and Slack, *English Towns*, etc. The sample includes Birmingham, Bristol, Bury St Edmunds, Colchester, Coventry, Exeter, Gloucester, Great Yarmouth, Ipswich, King's Lynn, Leicester, Newcastle-upon-Tyne, Northampton, Norwich, Nottingham and York. For the 1811–51 period data on all towns over 5,000 inhabitants were abstracted from B. R. Mitchell, *Abstract of British Historical Statistics* (Cambridge, 1962), pp. 24–7.

Table 5.1. *Demographic trends in English provincial towns 1563–1670*

	n	Annual per cent growth: mean	Standard deviation[18]
Small towns 1563–c. 1670	216	0.27	0.525
Larger towns 1563–c. 1670	10	0.43	0.470
Small towns 1603–c. 1670	212	0.17	0.586
Larger towns 1603–c. 1670	17	0.68	0.614

returns). The data for bigger towns are limited, drawn from available secondary sources. It would be naive to be complacent about the secureness of the evidence. Nonetheless Table 5.1 does raise questions about the development of English small towns in the period. The picture seems to be at odds with Everitt's scenario of buoyant economic conditions for market towns in the sixteenth and early seventeenth centuries with growing agricultural trade benefiting the smaller centres, new markets being established and old ones resuscitated. Everitt's evidence, however, is rather impressionistic and it is not clear how much of the new trade was actually channelled through the market towns rather than into private marketing.[19] It may also be the case that the proliferation of new market centres in the sixteenth century spread the cream of commercial expansion rather thinly. By contrast, Table 5.1 would seem to indicate that bigger provincial towns were doing better in the late sixteenth and early seventeenth centuries, though one must remember that our sample of bigger towns is strictly limited.

Case studies of small towns in the sixteenth century suggest mixed fortunes. At the small port of Rye on the Sussex coast the Elizabethan

---

[18] The standrd deviation gives an indication of the range of distribution of values around a mean. In a normal distribution, for example, 68% of observations would fall between ± one standard deviation of the mean. Standard deviations are given in Table 5.1, since the mean growth rates represent the simple average of the annual growth rates seen for the individual towns. In Tables 5.2–6, the growth rate is calculated by summing the total population seen for each category for each point in time, and projecting a trend at the beginning and end points of each table.

[19] Everitt, 'The Marketing of Agricultural Produce', esp. p. 502 *et passim*; for the importance of private marketing already in the fifteenth century see C. Dyer, 'The Consumer and the Market in the later Middle Ages', *Economic History Review*, 2nd series, vol. 42 (1989), 323–4.

period witnessed a major decline in population with an exodus of inhabitants from the town, partly but not wholly caused by the growing problems of the town's haven. At Warwick, towards the top end of the small-town rankings, the economy stagnated badly in the sixteenth century leading to very high levels of poverty. On a smaller scale, Lutterworth in Leicestershire enjoyed considerable population increase as a result of the growth of food processing trades in the town. In East Anglia, according to John Patten, the overall performance of the smaller towns was static though with a mixture of declining and growth centres. In Cumbria the textile town of Kendal suffered from growing rural competition, with the most serious problems emerging in the early seventeenth century.[20] The signs are that there may have been a good deal of regional and local variation in the experiences of small towns, a point we shall return to shortly.

According to Table 5.1 the divergence between small and bigger towns actually increased between 1603 and the Restoration. It must be pointed out, however, that because of documentary coverage the sample of towns is not identical for 1603 and 1563. It is also problematical whether this reduced rate of growth affected the whole period. The main culprit here may have been the upheavals and high epidemics associated with the Civil War. Recent work would suggest that the impact on towns of the conflict of the 1640s was more severe than was once thought. Small unfortified towns may have been particularly vulnerable to military incursions with all the attendant demographic and economic disruption.[21] Some support for this view comes from limited demographic data available for the period 1642–c. 70, which points to a significant fall in small-town populations. On firmer ground Wrigley and Schofield's national estimates show that the high mortality of the 1640s inaugurated a period of contraction as the population declined from 5.2 million in 1651 to 4.9 million in 1691.[22]

If there was a demographic recession in the mid-seventeenth century, blighting small towns, it was short-lived. By the time of the Compton Census in 1676 everything would point to the start of an urban recovery which continued through the eighteenth century. The quickening pace of urbanisation after the late seventeenth century is well known. In general,

20 G. Mayhew, *Tudor Rye* (Falmer, 1987), pp. 233–69; A. L. Beier, 'The social problems of an Elizabethan country town: Warwick, 1580–90', in P. Clark, ed., *Country Towns in Pre-industrial England* (Leicester, 1981), pp. 48–53; Goodacre, 'Lutterworth', ch. 4; Patten, *English Towns*, pp. 266–9; C. B. Phillips, 'Town and Country: economic change in Kendal c. 1550–1700', in P. Clark, ed., *The Transformation of English Provincial Towns 1600–1800* (1984), p. 113–15.
21 I. Roy, 'England turned Germany? The aftermath of the Civil War in its European Context', *Transactions of the Royal Historical Society*, 5th series, vol. 28 (1978), 127–44; also J. Morrill, ed., *Reactions to the English Civil War 1642–1649* (1982), pp. 77–82.
22 E. A. Wrigley and R. S. Schofield, *The Population History of England 1541–1871: a Reconstruction* (1981), p. 528.

Table 5.2. *Demographic trends in English provincial towns*
c. 1670–1811

	n	Annual per cent growth
All small towns	583	0.70
All larger towns	30	0.75
All towns	613	0.72

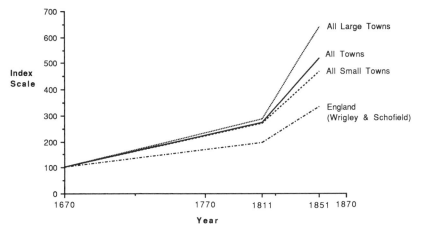

5.1 English towns: comparative growth trends 1670–1851

however, there has been a tendency to see the post-Restoration expansion focused on the bigger cities. Most obvious was London where the population soared from 400,000 in 1650 to 675,000 in 1750, but the major regional centres like Bristol, Newcastle and Norwich also flourished.[23] Until recently, however, as noted earlier, most writers have suggested that small towns were faltering after the Restoration as a result of greater competition from the bigger and more successful towns.

Figure 5.1 offers graphic support for a more optimistic interpretation of the performance of small towns from the late seventeenth century. Up to 1811 it looks as though the small towns of the Restoration era expanded at a similar or faster pace than the national population.[24] Predictably, the rate of

[23] Corfield, *Impact*, esp. ch. 1; Clark, *Transformation*, ch. 1; P. Borsay, *The English Urban Renaissance; Culture and Society in the Provincial Town 1660–1770* (Oxford, 1989), esp. ch. 1.

[24] National population estimates from Wrigley and Schofield, *Population History*, pp. 528–9.

growth was behind the quick march of the larger provincial cities, boosted by accelerating industrialisation and commercial differentiation. But their performance was probably not vastly different from that of the provincial urban system as a whole, as one can judge from Table 5.2.

Clearly small towns as a whole were not excluded from the urban prosperity of Hanoverian England. As in the case of larger cities, economic specialisation played a decisive role. Numerous small centres developed industrial or craft specialisms, sometimes in dynamic relationship with major towns. Thus one discovers the rise of the hosiery industry at Tewkesbury and Hinckley, blanket-making at Witney, hats at Luton and Dunstable, straw tankards at St Albans, chairs at High Wycombe, saddles at Burford, scissors at Woodstock, lace-making at Olney and Wellingborough, cutlery at Sheffield and so on. As well as housing specialist crafts, small towns frequently served as the distributive and entrepreneurial hub for allied industries in the adjoining countryside. Other small towns became leisure, spa or seaside resorts including Lichfield, Stamford, Chichester, Cheltenham, Buxton, Weymouth, Scarborough and Bangor. Yet more became specialist marketing towns, for instance in the horse-trade, while several others (such as Lechlade and Stourport) were embryonic transport nodes.[25]

A substantial majority of English small towns undoubtedly prospered in the Georgian period. There are indications that they became distinctly urban at this time. Firstly one sees the increasing sophistication of their economies with the marked decline of agricultural trades (except in the smallest centres) and the substantial growth of retailing and professional activity. Secondly, small towns, particularly those engaged in longer-distance trade, were often affected from the late seventeenth century by the high levels of mortality associated with bigger cities. Thirdly, small towns acquired a new urbane cultural identity. A key factor here was the growing influx of minor gentry from the adjoining countryside. In East Anglia by George III's reign the majority of small market towns had an array of assemblies, benefit concerts, and later music clubs, to entertain genteel visitors as well as town worthies. Freemason lodges were increasingly found in some of the bigger small towns – for instance in 1740 at Spalding, Banbury, Tewkesbury, Braintree and Shepton Mallet. Twenty years later about 38 per cent of Modern lodges in the English provinces held meetings in small centres.[26]

---

[25] For a contemporary list of industrial and other specialisms see *HMC*, Portland MSS., II, 274–5. Clark, *Country Towns*, pp. 17–18; D. Hey, *The Rural Metalworkers of the Sheffield Region* (Leicester, 1972); Corfield, *Impact*, chs 2–4; Borsay, *English Urban Renaissance*, ch. 1.

[26] Unwin, 'Tradition and Transition', pp. 80–4; Clark, 'Entrepreneurs. Elites and English Small Towns'; Wilson, 'Population Developments'; *A List of Regular Lodges* (1740); *A List of Regular Lodges* (1760).

Table 5.3. *Demographic trends in English provincial towns 1811–1851*

	n	Annual per cent growth
Small towns (pre-1811 sample)	583	1.40
Small towns (1811 sample)	525	1.08
Larger towns (pre-1811 sample)	30	2.02
Larger towns (1811 sample)	88	2.00

But for many small towns horse-racing marked the high point of the social calendar with a variety of associated events – dinners, cockfights, cricket matches and balls. Before 1740 there were over 130 race courses in England and two thirds of those which survived the legislation that year were located in or close to country towns.[27] Even lesser towns enjoyed quite extensive if piecemeal rebuilding or refronting of houses on their main streets with classical brick-built façades replacing vernacular architecture. All this is discussed at greater length in Michael Reed's chapter below.[28]

Nonetheless, not all towns flourished. There were a number of casualties. As we shall see in a later section, sizeable numbers of towns under-performed in demographic terms and in some instances were eventually declassified as towns. About 18.8 per cent of our seventeenth-century small towns had populations below 1,000 in 1811 and a substantial number were not listed in directories at the time: they had 'disappeared'. Once again there were marked regional variations in this picture.

By 1811 England was on the eve of large-scale industrial transformation. Over the next 40 years a large proportion of small towns, though expanding at a historically high rate of population growth, became marginalised from the accelerating juggernaut of urbanisation. By 1851 the majority of English people lived in towns, but probably only 20–25 per cent in towns under 5,000 (about 8 per cent of the national population).[29] The general problems for small towns are visible from Fig. 5.1 and Table 5.3.

Clearly the mean rate of growth of small towns lags far behind that of the bigger cities. The discrepancy is less marked if we use the original (pre-1811) sample because this includes small towns which had reached

[27] J. Weatherby, *Racing Calendar* (1781).   [28] See below, pp. 129–47.
[29] Calculations based on Small Towns Populations database, Leicester.

over 5,000 inhabitants in 1811. The 1811 sample is narrower, excluding dynamic places which had leapt the 5,000 threshold and also lesser centres which had failed to achieve 1,000 inhabitants, increasingly the bottom line of urbanity. Overall, however, it is evident that small towns in many regions were increasingly affected by the loss of industrial specialisms due to competition from the more mechanised and centralised production centres in the Midlands and the North. At the same time, the agricultural crisis after the Napoleonic wars with falling prices curtailed local rural demand for the goods and services of the country towns. Here the situation was aggravated by the penetration of basic service and other trades, including retailing and some professional activity, into the villages, competing with urban suppliers. Finally, the landed classes, such an important mainstay of small-town economies, began after the 1790s to migrate back to their country houses. Country life, aided by improvements in transport and domestic amenities, was becoming more congenial again, coinciding with the increased fashionability of the romantic, picturesque vision of the countryside. This was the Golden Age of the English Country House.[30] In contrast only London and certain leisure towns, older inland spas and the growing number of seaside resorts, maintained, indeed enhanced, their allure as urban social centres. A particular crisis for many smaller towns occurred in the 1820s and 1830s as secular pressures coincided with short-term financial instability and the collapse of small country banks.[31]

Some of these problems are evident in the North Riding of Yorkshire whose small towns enjoyed substantial population growth between the 1670s and 1811, more than doubling their population on average. In the early nineteenth century, however, a number of these centres suffered difficulty. At Helmsley for instance the town's inhabitants, 1,415 in 1811, were supported up to the 1810s by a successful manufacturing sector, with a considerable trade in cottons and linens, flax being brought by pack-horse from Hull. But the crisis in the textile trades in 1821–3 knocked the stuffing out of the local economy and by 1840 it was said that the introduction of machinery had destroyed the local linen industry, rendering the inhabitants almost exclusively dependent upon agriculture. Occupational evidence suggests that not only industrial trades but marketing and dealing activities stagnated. The problem was that as a market centre Helmsley faced stiff competition from Whitby, Richmond, York, New Malton and other places.

---

[30] See below, pp. 114–15; E. A. Wrigley, 'Men on the Land and in the Countryside: Employment in Agriculture in Early-Nineteenth-Century England', in L. Bonfield *et al.*, eds, *The World We Have Gained: History of Population and Social Structure* (Oxford, 1986), pp. 298–303; M. Girouard, *Life in the English Country House* (1980), pp. 218ff.

[31] L. S. Presnell, *Country Banking in the Industrial Revolution* (Oxford, 1956), esp. pp. 477–500, 509, 538.

With the retreat of the genteel classes the town's professional class became almost invisible with no attorneys listed in 1840. Little wonder the town's population fell from 1,520 in 1821 to 1,465 in 1841. Guisborough was another small North Riding town whose specialist industries succumbed in the early nineteenth century. From the 1830s the town's cloth-making industry fell victim to factory production in the West Riding and cheap imports from Ireland and Scotland. The population which stood at 1,988 in 1831 fell to 1,776 in 1841 and the town's economy only revived with the discovery of iron mines in the area in the 1840s. By contrast, the larger town of Northallerton (2,332 in 1811) did somewhat better. Though the town's important linen industry faded from the 1820s due to competition, the leather trade survived because of the town's importance as a cattle market. Even more important, Northallerton's administrative function, as the head town of the North Riding, strengthened its public service and professional sector, with a sizeable number of attorneys. By 1851 the population had risen to 3,086.[32] Thus the early nineteenth century posed a serious challenge to many small towns, but some places responded much more effectively than others.

III

National aggregates always hide more than they tell and this is the case even in England's relatively integrated and (by the eighteenth century) modernising society and economy. In the next sections the focus will shift to an examination of the regional variations to the national scenario previously outlined. In the process it may be possible to explore some of the key determinants in the contours of urban growth.

In Tables 5.4–6 the demographic performance of small towns after the Restoration is analysed and displayed in terms of seven regional configurations: the North (mostly the border counties), Yorkshire, East Anglia (including Cambridgeshire and Huntingdonshire), the East Midlands, West Midlands, South-East (excluding Middlesex) and South-West.[33] The

---

[32] N. Raven, 'De-Industrialisation and the Urban Response: the Small Towns of the North Riding of Yorkshire c. 1790–1850', in R. Weedon and A. Milne, eds, *Aspects of English Small Towns in the 18th and 19th centuries* (Leicester, 1993), pp. 48–67.

[33] The counties in the regional groups are as follows: North: Cumberland, Durham, Northumberland and Westmorland; Yorkshire: East, North and West Ridings; East Anglia: Cambridgeshire, Huntingdonshire, Norfolk, Suffolk; East Midlands: Derbyshire, Leicestershire, Lincolnshire, Northamptonshire, Nottinghamshire, Rutland; West Midlands: Herefordshire, Shropshire, Staffordshire, Warwickshire, Worcestershire; South-East: Bedfordshire, Berkshire, Buckinghamshire, Essex, Hampshire, Hertfordshire, Kent, Oxfordshire, Surrey, Sussex; South-West: Cornwall, Devon, Dorset, Gloucestershire, Somerset; Wiltshire. The North-West (Lancashire and Cheshire) has been omitted from the analysis; see above, p. 95n.

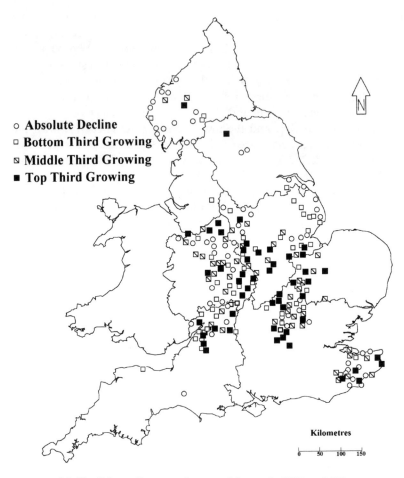

○ **Absolute Decline**
□ **Bottom Third Growing**
▨ **Middle Third Growing**
■ **Top Third Growing**

Kilometres

5.2 English small towns: demographic trends 1563–c. 1670

tables use the same data sets as in Tables 5.1–3. Unfortunately, because the regional coverage is spotty for both 1563 and 1603, it is not possible to present meaningful regional statistics for the early period. For the later period the tables help to illuminate broad regional variations in small-town development, which will figure in the following discussion. At the same time, it is arguable that for most of our period distinct regional divisions had only limited significance on the ground for the urban network. Relatively little work has been done on the pattern and development of English regions in the early modern period but there are signs that coherent regions of a sub-national variety only began to emerge in the eighteenth and nineteenth

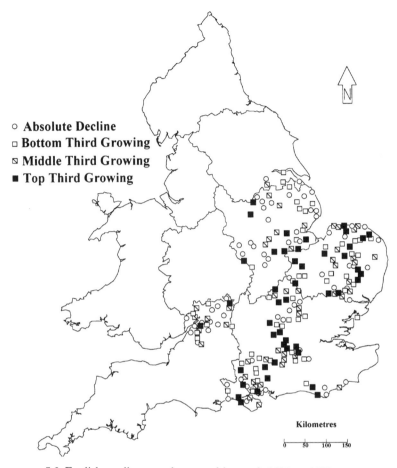

- ○ **Absolute Decline**
- ▢ **Bottom Third Growing**
- ◨ **Middle Third Growing**
- ■ **Top Third Growing**

5.3 English small towns: demographic trends 1603–c. 1670

centuries.[34] A less arbitrary and more sensitive guide to local and regional trends may be provided by mapping urban growth rates.

Figures 5.2–7 cover the main periods of study and categorise small towns according to their annual rate of growth. Figure 5.2 covers the period from the late sixteenth century to the Restoration and is based on a comparison of

[34] See A. Kussmaul, *A General View of the Rural Economy of England 1538–1840* (Cambridge, 1990), esp. ch. 4 *et seq*. For the rise of provincial politics in the eighteenth century see D. Read, *The English Provinces c. 1760–1960* (1964). For a disastrous attempt to identify a system of regions in seventeenth-century England see D. H. Fischer, *Albion's Seed: Four British Folkways in America* (Oxford, 1989).

data in 1563 and c. 1670 (Hearth Tax and Compton Census figures conflated). Figure 5.3 compares data for 1603 and c. 1670. Figures 5.4–5 highlight growth between c. 1670 and the 1811 Census. The final sequence (Fig. 5.6–7) compares data from the 1811 and 1851 Censuses, using the pre-1811 sample. The map sets are thus directly comparable between periods and in conjunction with Tables 5.4–6 they afford an opportunity of studying the complexities of English urban growth during an important period of transition.[35]

As we have said, because of documentary gaps, regional data for the late sixteenth and early seventeenth centuries are patchy and incomplete. Even so, from Figs 5.2–3 it may be possible to identify certain local trends. Among the areas whose small towns were apparently doing less well, Lincolnshire is particularly noteworthy, with a high number of low-growth lesser towns and very few larger high-growth places. Lincoln, the county town, was in the doldrums due to the collapse of the wool trade in the late Middle Ages. The port of Boston was also in trouble with its haven affected by silting and its population falling from about 2,378 to about 2,250 between 1563 and 1603. Elsewhere in the county small towns may have suffered from the sluggish expansion of agriculture, with improvement, especially in the fens, retarded by weak manorial control and the opposition of a large population of small peasants. Though water transport was potentially good, overland communication was poor and the area something of a backwater. One sign of this is that few Lincolnshire people appear as migrants in other parts of the kingdom. The area's remoteness from London was also a disadvantage: the small ports may have failed to exploit the expansion of metropolitan trade.[36]

In the North, in Cumbria, a similar picture is obtained from Fig. 5.2, with a disproportionately large incidence of stagnant or declining towns. Large-scale subsistence crises in the 1590s and 1620s dealt a major blow to the population in this area, but it was not just a demographic problem. As already noted, Kendal suffered commercial difficulty at this time with the

---

[35] The maps were generated by calculating the annual percentage growth rate between the start and end point of each period, and then ranking the towns according to this. Those showing growth were divided equally into thirds (top, middle and bottom growers), while those experiencing absolute decline were identified separately. The maps thus show the demographic trends of town parishes defined as small in the late seventeenth century, relative to the whole sample.

[36] J. W. F. Hill, *Tudor and Stuart Lincoln* (Cambridge, 1956), pp. 19–23, 66–8, 85; P. Clark and J. Clark, eds, *The Boston Assembly Minutes 1545–1575* (Lincoln Record Soc., vol. 77, 1987), x–xiv; Thirsk, *Agrarian History of England and Wales*, vol. IV, pp. 38–40; G. A. Hodgett, *Tudor Lincolnshire* (Lincoln, 1975), pp. 132–7; P. A. Slack, 'Vagrants and Vagrancy in England 1598–1664', *Economic History Review*, 2nd series, vol. 27 (1974), 379; N. J. Williams, *The Maritime Trade of the East Anglian Ports 1550–1590* (Oxford, 1988), pp. 58–9.

loss of its traditional textile industry and increased competition from lesser centres. A flurry of new markets appeared in the early seventeenth century including Ambleside, Hawkshead and Whitehaven. Most had a rather exiguous life until the end of the century but the challenge of the newcomers may have added to the pressure on the existing network of towns. In the short run the Anglo-Scottish union (1603) does not seem to have boosted local urban economies. One of the main structural constraints was poor communications, with most transport in the North confined to pack-horses before the late seventeenth century.[37]

Elsewhere there are more signs of urban expansion. In Buckinghamshire, to the north-west of London, one can identify from Figs 5.2–3 a significant cluster of faster growth centres, both big and small. Michael Reed's work has already suggested a range of factors at play.[38] The county's proximity to the capital meant that its landowners and farmers were quick to respond to increasing metropolitan demand for foodstuffs, with the spread of enclosure from the fifteenth century and the growth of specialist livestock farming. Important here were good communications to London: the county is crossed in the south by the Thames and in the north by the Roman Watling Street, seconded by numerous drove roads. Also supporting growth among the Buckinghamshire small towns was the early advent of craft specialities, including lace, brick, furniture and paper manufacture. With farmers and gentry doing well from high food prices, local demand by the mid-seventeenth century was buoyant, shopkeepers carrying large stocks of wares. The county's small towns were also aided by the absence of any major urban competitor in the vicinity: Buckinghamshire had no town with more than 2,000 inhabitants at the start of the seventeenth century.

In the West Midlands the overall picture is rather mixed but the concentration of bigger-growth towns in Warwickshire and North Worcestershire is evident from Fig. 5.2, almost certainly linked with the spread of the metal-working industry around Birmingham.[39] At the same time, one should be wary of trying to draw a rigid regional diagnosis from these maps. Taking both Figs 5.2 and 5.3, one is struck by the almost random distribution of different types of small town. In many areas, for instance East Anglia, there is a goulash of high-, medium- and low-growth settlements.

[37] A. Appleby, *Famine in Tudor and Stuart England* (Liverpool, 1978), esp. ch. 8; Phillips, 'Town and Country', pp. 107–15; R. Millward, 'The Cumbrian Towns between 1600 and 1800', in C. Chalklin and M. Havinden, eds, *Rural Change and Urban Growth 1500–1800* (1974), pp. 206–14; D. Hey, *Packmen, Carriers and Packhorse Roads* (Leicester, 1980), pp. 94, 96.

[38] M. Reed, 'Decline and recovery in a provincial urban network: Buckinghamshire towns 1350–1800', in M. Reed, ed., *English Towns in Decline 1350–1800* (Leicester, 1986), ch. 4.

[39] R. Holt, *The Early History of the Town of Birmingham 1166 to 1600* (Dugdale Soc., Occasional Papers, No. 30, 1985), pp. 13–22.

Table 5.4. *Regional trends in small-town growth c. 1670–1811*

	n	Annual per cent growth
North	19	0.72
Yorkshire	41	0.96
East Anglia	82	0.47
East Midlands	59	0.71
West Midlands	67	0.88
South-East	176	0.66
South-West	138	0.56

This may in part reflect the considerable instability of the English urban system at this time. Population increase, coinciding with a decline of real wages in town and countryside, left domestic demand uncertain. Moves towards improved agriculture, better transport, new industries and a more integrated economy were slow to have an effect. The Civil War may also have had a disruptive impact.

IV

The evidence for the late seventeenth and eighteenth centuries suggests a different ball game, with the emergence of more marked regional trends. Crude data are provided by Table 5.4.

According to this, it would seem that northern areas (the North, Yorkshire) and the Midlands, especially the West Midlands, were particularly dynamic, with growth rates above the national mean. Such a scenario matches closely with what we know about the development and impact of industrialisation in those areas. More striking perhaps are the low growth rates recorded for East Anglia and also to some extent the South-West. In contrast the South-East appears to have been doing significantly better, though below the national average.

More precise evidence for local and regional variations is provided by Figs 5.4–5, plotting different rates of small-town growth. In the North Cumberland clearly experienced accelerating expansion, with substantial numbers of high-growth centres. Some small towns did tremendously well from the coal industry. Whitehaven, for instance, became one of the kingdom's leading provincial ports in the early eighteenth century, shipping coal from the easily mined field of West Cumberland; Workington and Maryport also prospered. Other Cumbrian towns acquired new specialisms. Kendal became a major hosiery-making town, while Cockermouth had great markets and fairs for cattle and horses, reaping the dividend of growing

Anglo-Scottish trade.[40] In the East Midlands Lincolnshire saw the earlier miasma of decline evaporate with the bigger centres in particular benefiting from the piecemeal improvement of farming. This may have been helped by the revival of ports like Boston, which serviced the growth of coastal trade, especially with London.[41] In other regions burgeoning prosperity before the Civil War was confirmed, extended and amplified.

Most obvious from Fig. 5.5 is the heavy density of high- and medium-growth towns in the West Midlands, not only in Warwickshire and Worcestershire but also now in adjoining Staffordshire. In this county virtually all of the small towns advanced, even the minor or marginal ones. Three of Staffordshire's seventeenth-century towns had demographic growth rates well above 300 per cent and by 1811 six of the county's towns had more than 5,000 people. Critical here was rapid industrialisation: the spread of metal-working and iron-making in south Staffordshire and the growth of the potteries in the north of the county. Also influential was heavy investment in infrastructure. By 1770 the county was the fifth most heavily turnpiked area of the kingdom with 569 miles of turnpike road; it was also crossed by five canals with access to Liverpool and Birmingham.[42] In Yorkshire, another expanding region, Figs 5.3–4 make plain that the engine of growth was the West Riding, its small towns, both big and little, boosted by rising textile and metal-ware production; the North and East Ridings were also reasonably buoyant.[43]

In the South-East, likewise, the regional rate of growth masked significant local variations. Figures 5.4–5 demonstrate that the growth centres were mainly in the Home County areas close to London, but with a penumbra of less dynamic centres in outer districts, particularly in Hamp-

---

[40] S. Collier and S. Pearson, *Whitehaven 1600–1800* (1991); J. E. Williams, 'Whitehaven in the 18th century', *Economic History Review*, 2nd series, vol. 8 (1955–6), 393–404; Phillips, 'Town and Country', pp. 104, 115–16; Millward, 'Cumbrian Town', pp. 208–21; also J. Marshall, 'The rise and transformation of the Cumbrian market town 1660–1900', *Northern History*, vol. 19 (1983), 137–69.

[41] J. Thirsk, *English Peasant Farming* (1957), pp. 192–204; G. S. Bagley, *Boston: its Story and its People* (Boston, 1986), pp. 113–27.

[42] L. Weatherill, *The Pottery Trade and North Staffordshire 1660–1760* (Manchester, 1971), esp. pp. 109–44; P. Large, 'Urban Growth and agricultural change in the West Midlands during the 17th and 18th centuries', in Clark, *Transformation*, pp. 169–86; M. B. Rowlands, *Masters and Men in the West Midland Metalware Trades before the Industrial Revolution* (Manchester, 1975); E. Pawson, *Transport and Economy: The Turnpike Roads of 18th century Britain* (1977), p. 155; C. Hadfield, *British Canals* (1984), esp. ch. 5; for stress on the impact of canals on regional concentration and differentiation see G. Turnbull, 'Canals, coal and regional growth during the industrial revolution', *Economic History Review*, 2nd series, vol. 40 (1987), 540–58.

[43] R. G. Wilson, 'The Supremacy of the Yorkshire Cloth Industry in the 18th century', in N. B. Harte and K. G. Ponting, eds, *Textile History and Economic History* (Manchester, 1973), pp. 225–46; D. T. Jenkins, 'Early Factory Development in the West Riding of Yorkshire 1770–1800', *ibid.*, pp. 247–66; Hey, *The Rural Metalworkers*; Noble, 'Growth and development of Country Towns', pp. 136ff; see above, p. 102.

○ **Absolute Decline**
■ **Bottom Third Growing**

5.4 English small towns: absolute decline and low growth c. 1670–1811

shire and Sussex. Buckinghamshire's small towns, already quite prosperous by the time of the English Revolution, enjoyed a golden era of expansion. London continued to provide an almost insatiable market for the county's agricultural produce. Buckinghamshire developed a sophisticated role in fattening Welsh and Northern cattle for the metropolis. The southern market towns on the Thames developed food-processing functions, malting barley for the London brewers. But agriculture itself had only a minor role in the county's small towns, where manufacturing and distribution were the main functions. Lace, paper, furniture and shoemaking were increasingly concentrated in and around Buckinghamshire towns by the late eighteenth century, though still on a workshop basis. Last but not least, the

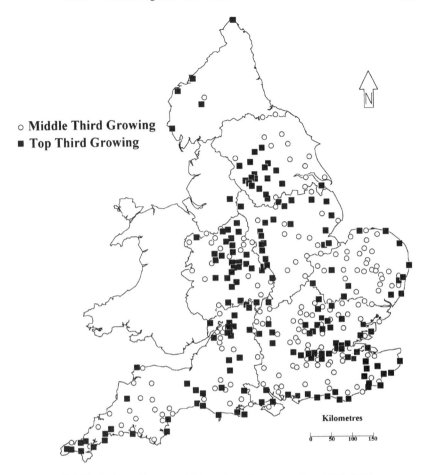

o **Middle Third Growing**

■ **Top Third Growing**

5.5 English small towns: high and medium growth c. 1670–1811

rapid increase of coaching traffic, especially on the Watling Street, brought economic success to Towcester and Stony Stratford with their large numbers of inns and coaching establishments.[44]

But small towns in other Home Counties also prospered. Kentish small towns, which had showed a rather patchy performance in the preceding period, now moved smartly ahead. The principal source of expansion appears to have been agricultural production for the London market. Transport was also a strong point; by 1770 the county had 514 miles of turnpiked road, in the top tier of improved counties. Along the Watling Street towns like Rochester, Sittingbourne and Gravesend throve on metro-

[44] Reed, 'Decline and recovery'.

politan food trade and the growing volume of fashionable traffic between London and the Continent. But Kent's numerous small ports also played an important part in the expanding coastal trade with the capital; one or two (such as Margate) started to add a second string to their bow by becoming seaside resorts. The only losers were the former textile and iron-making towns in the Weald, close to the border with Sussex, whose industries suffered adversely from the metropolitan effect on wages and profitability.[45]

Although Figs 5.4–5 highlight several of the main areas of urban growth, they also confirm the regions of recession so far as small towns are concerned. As already suggested by Table 5.4, one depressed area was East Anglia. In Suffolk six of the county's small towns failed to reach 1,000 inhabitants by 1811 and not a single one breached the 5,000 ceiling. Part of the explanation was the growing weakness of the textile industry due to competition from Yorkshire and the West Country. Only Norwich retained a clothing sector and even this was under acute pressure by the later eighteenth century. Linen production was increasingly concentrated in a few centres and by the end of the century was also in decline. The textile towns in North Essex were also badly affected. Near the Suffolk coast dairy farming developed for London consumers and one or two places like Woodbridge benefited. But corn prices were falling for much of the late seventeenth and early eighteenth centuries and when they began to recover in later decades agricultural improvement undermined the position of small farmers. Poor rates were especially high in the region at the end of the eighteenth century. Compared with the Home Counties there was little investment in transport. Suffolk had virtually no canals or navigation schemes and only 136 miles of turnpiked road by 1770, ranking thirty-second in the county league table.[46]

Figures 5.4–5 make a final point which is not at all evident from Table 5.4. It is often stressed that small ports suffered in the eighteenth century, excluded from overseas trade, their commerce cannibalised by the great

[45] J. Thirsk, ed., *The Agrarian History of England and Wales*, vol. V(1) (Cambridge, 1984), p. 273 *et passim*; D. C. Coleman, 'The Economy of Kent under the Later Stuarts' (unpublished Ph.D. thesis, London University, 1951), pp. 115, 139, 146, 228ff; Pawson, *Transport and Economy*, p. 155; J. Whyman, 'A Hanoverian Watering Place: Margate before the Railway', in Everitt, *Perspectives*, pp. 138–54; B. Short, 'The de-industrialisation process: a case study of the Weald 1600–1850', in P. Hudson, ed., *Regions and Industries: a Perspective on the Industrial Revolution in Britain* (Cambridge, 1989), pp. 156–74; also H. Cleere and D. Crosley, *The Iron Industry of the Weald* (Leicester, 1985), pp. 187–216.

[46] Thirsk, ed., *Agrarian History of England and Wales*, vol. V(1), pp. 215–17, 231–4; N. Evans, *The East Anglian Linen Industry: Rural Industry and Local Economy 1500–1850* (Aldershot, 1985), ch. 5; N. Raven, 'A Study of the Changes in the Occupational Structure of Four North Essex Towns 1700–1830' (Certificate dissertation, Centre for Urban History, Leicester Univ., 1990); Mr Raven is currently undertaking doctoral research on these Essex towns and I am grateful for his advice. Kussmaul, *General Views*, p. 128; Pawson, *Transport and Economy*, *ibid.*; Hadfield, *British Canals*, pp. 83, 205.

Table 5.5. *Regional trends in small town growth 1811–1851 (pre-1811 sample)*

	n	Annual per cent growth
North	19	0.68
Yorkshire	41	1.61
East Anglia	82	1.09
East Midlands	59	1.48
West Midlands	67	1.61
South-East	176	1.38
South-West	138	1.15

overseas ports such as Liverpool, Bristol and Hull. Dr Corfield has wisely urged the case for caution, suggesting that any decline was relative rather than absolute. And this view is clearly supported by the maps. Larger and lesser small ports were expanding considerably in this period. One factor here was the tremendous volume of coastal trade, particularly with London, compensating for the loss of overseas traffic. But as already noted, numerous ports, from the east coast to the south-west, were also starting to diversify as smart seaside resorts for the genteel classes.[47]

V

As we saw above, in the early nineteenth century English small towns started to lose ground compared to bigger centres, albeit maintaining quite high levels of growth. Tables 5.5–6 display some of the regional dimensions to these changes.

Table 5.5 presents data using our original (pre-1811) sample of small towns. In some measure the pattern confirms trends evident before 1811. Both Yorkshire and the West Midlands saw their small towns expanding at an above-average rate. Those in the South-West and East Anglia did less well, but the main casualty appears to be the North (the border counties), where the small towns appear to have experienced a major setback, marginalised from the main industrial growth area within the region – Tyneside – and from the industrialising areas outside – the West Riding and southern and central Lancashire. The problems seem to be similar to those affecting

[47] Cf. the problems of the small ports in E. A. G. Clark, *The Ports of the Exe Estuary 1660–1860* (Exeter 1960); Corfield, *Impact*, pp. 43–4; also T. S. Willan, *The English Coasting Trade 1600–1750* (Manchester, 1938), esp. pp. 220–2. See above, p. 100; e.g. S. Farrant and J. Farrant, 'Brighton 1580–1820: from Tudor Town to Regency Resort', *Sussex Archaeological Collections*, vol. 118 (1980), 331–50.

Table 5.6. *Regional trends in small town growth 1811–1851 (1811 sample)*

	n	Annual per cent growth
North	12	0.80
Yorkshire	22	0.71
East Anglia	56	1.09
East Midlands	33	1.43
West Midlands	44	0.88
South-East	141	1.20
South-West	106	0.97

the North Riding discussed earlier. Thus Cumbria experienced considerable out-migration in this period, associated with the decline of older textile trades in small towns, as well as leadmining.[48]

But as we indicated above in the national analysis, our pre-1811 sample of small towns is hardly ideal for the early nineteenth century. By then it includes a substantial number of fast-growth centres which have graduated into the ranks of bigger towns. It also includes some minor places with small populations which have essentially de-urbanised. The 1811 sample of small towns (used in Table 5.6) takes account of these changes, concentrating on towns with populations of between 1,000 and 5,000 in 1811.

The omission of faster-growth and de-urbanising centres from the 1811 sample causes not only a significant decline in regional growth rates compared with Table 5.5, but some surprising changes in regional rankings. Both Yorkshire and the West Midlands tumble down the growth ladder, suggesting that the early nineteenth-century small towns lacked the dynamism evident earlier, or, to be more precise, that growth was increasingly concentrated on the bigger towns, many of them transformed from small centres. By comparison East Anglia fared rather better. There is some supplementary support for this apparent improvement in Figs 5.6–7. But we should be cautious. In part the improved picture for East Anglian small towns simply reflects the exclusion of the region's very small loser towns from the new sample. The signs of growth in the early nineteenth century in Figs 5.6–7 may be distorted by lower growth rates earlier, with depressed population levels in 1811 serving to accentuate later population trends, at least on paper. Certainly there is nothing to indicate from the work of Nesta Evans and others that there was an economic upturn in East Anglia at this

[48] J. D. Marshall and J. K. Walton, *The Lake Counties from 1830 to the Mid-twentieth century* (Manchester, 1981), pp. 18–35; also Marshall, 'Cumbrian Towns', pp. 197–200.

time. The agricultural depression after the French wars affected the corn-growing counties badly. William Cobbett observed that 'distress pervades all ranks and degrees'. At the same time, the deindustrialisation of the earlier period was not reversed. The proportion of the region's labour force engaged in agricultural trades was high. Transport innovation was slow to make an impact with only modest amounts of railway track laid by 1852. Not surprisingly, migration and emigration from the region were low, completing the scenario of economic retardation and isolation. In 1811 only 28.7 per cent of Suffolk's population was resident in towns – with 67.8 per cent in small towns. Four decades later in 1851 the picture was not dramatically different: only a third of Suffolk's population was urbanised and nearly half of these townspeople lived in settlements of under 5,000 inhabitants.[49]

Despite a marginally better performance in Table 5.6, most of the evidence points to the accelerating problems of the small towns of the South-West. As Figs 5.6–7 show, from Dorset and Hampshire to Gloucestershire, Somerset and Devon there were few fast-growth centres and a multiplicity of low-growth towns. This is true at the level of both major and minor small towns. In the eighteenth century there are some signs of decline in Devon (Figs 5.4–5), but other areas in the region were doing better, helped by the continuing success of the textile industry. After 1815, however, the West Country's cloth industry was in mounting, albeit not continuous, difficulty. To compete against Yorkshire mills, West Country producers needed to move from water to steam-power, but coal supplies were difficult and prices high – not least because of the slow development of canals and later railways. In Gloucestershire the number of mills fell from 137 about 1820 to 77 in 1841.[50] The region was sliding into an economic cul-de-sac with widespread agrarian poverty, as in Dorset, compounding depressed demand for urban manufactures.[51]

Figures 5.6–7 help to confirm that even within more overtly dynamic regions there was increasing urban polarisation. In Yorkshire, the North and East Ridings found economic prosperity and growth increasingly

---

[49] Evans, *East Anglian Linen Industry*, ch. 6; S. Wheeler *et al.*, 'Suffolk 1750–1850: An Analysis of Data Obtained from Contemporary Trade Directories' (Certificate dissertation, Centre for Urban History, Leicester Univ., 1991); L. Faire *et al.*, 'Report on Occupational and Economic Diversity in the County of Norfolk 1784–1854' (Certificate dissertation, Centre for Urban History, Leicester Univ., 1991); W. Cobbett, *Rural Rides*, vol. II (1912), p. 226; D. Baines, *Migration in a Mature Economy 1861–1900* (Cambridge, 1985), pp. 230–4.

[50] J. de Lacy Mann, *The Cloth Industry in the West of England from 1640 to 1880* (Oxford, 1971), pp. 123–93; also J. Tann, 'The employment of power in the West-of-England wool textile industry, 1790–1840', in Harte and Ponting, *Textile History and Economic History*, ch. 8; A. J. Randall, 'Work, culture and resistance to machinery in the West of England woollen industry', in Hudson, *Regions and Industries*, pp. 175–98.

[51] K. Snell, *Annals of the Labouring Poor* (Cambridge, 1985), esp. chs 1–4.

5.6 English small towns: absolute decline and low growth 1811–1851

elusive goals. The problems of particular North Riding towns were noted above, while Noble's work on Eastern Yorkshire has suggested a considerable degree of stagnation, particularly for the lesser centres dependent on agriculture.[52] Growth was heavily concentrated in the West Riding as large-scale industrialisation, increasingly factory-based, took command of the regional economy, sustained by major railway development in the 1840s. In much of the West Midlands region, such as Staffordshire, where there were now a number of very large towns, small centres continued to expand on their coat-tails. Even in this region, however, the Shropshire small

[52] See above, pp. 102–3; Noble, 'Growth and development of Country Towns', esp. pp. 157–67.

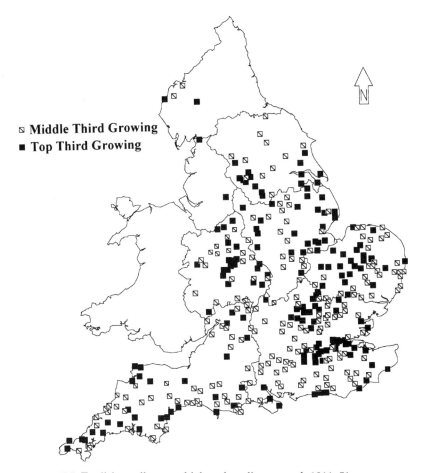

5.7 English small towns: high and medium growth 1811–51

towns, especially those near the border with Wales, were doing less well. Though a growing proportion of the demographic expansion of more dynamic small towns was due to natural population increase, immigration continued to play a significant role. It is no coincidence that both the industrialising West Midland counties and the West Riding were in close proximity to areas like Shropshire and the North and East Ridings, many of whose small towns were stagnant or declining.[53] Overall there are strong

[53] D. T. Jenkins and K. G. Ponting, *The British Wool Textile Industry 1770–1914* (1982), esp. chs 2–5; D. Gregory, *Regional Transformation and Industrial Revolution: A Geography of the Yorkshire Woollen Industry* (1982), esp. ch. 5; H. Pollins, *Britain's Railways* (Newton Abbot, 1951), p. 42; G. J. Barnsby, *Social Conditions in the Black Country 1800–1900*

indications of a process of regional concentration taking place during the first half of the nineteenth century, following the earlier phase of regional differentiation.

In the South-East the Home Counties, once the heartland of small-town prosperity, saw important new developments. In the area near to the metropolis, increasingly penetrated by commuters, one sees marked expansion. Already the metropolis is starting to cannibalise its hinterland, especially Surrey. But further afield in the region the picture was more variegated. One or two of the north Essex clothing towns revived as centres for low-cost silk manufacture, as the industry moved out of high-cost London. In Bedfordshire, the hat-making industry at Luton benefited from a similar infusion of London capital as firms moved out of the metropolis. In Buckinghamshire, certain niche industries such as furniture-making prospered, but generally urban industry suffered from the accelerating power of factory-based production. From the 1840s the railways made increasingly available to the capital cheap supplies of foodstuffs from all parts of the kingdom, not just the south-east. Agrarian poverty was widespread in the Victorian south-east.[54] This had a serious knock-on effect on small town economies at a time when the gentry no longer frequented them as fashionable social centres. Here the regional and local variations articulated in Figs 5.6–7 are a more illuminating indicator of the uncertain, clouded future of many English small towns than the national data.

VI

There are not only lies, damned lies and statistics, but the latter also give a deceptive air of security to their falsehoods. Certainly one can only reiterate how fragile are the sources and so the calculations which have underpinned this analysis. Nonetheless, despite the problems of documentation, a number of the findings appear persuasive. One of the most important is the growing regionality in the experience of English small towns. This was particularly marked in the eighteenth and early nineteenth centuries as England's urban system moved away from the lopsided, rather fragmented and localised pattern of the earlier period, more typical of the peripheral

(Wolverhampton, 1980), pp. 1–5; Lewis, 'Small Towns of Shropshire', ch. 16; Baines, *Migration*, pp. 230–4.
[54] R. C. W. Cox, 'The Old Centre of Croydon: Victorian Decay and Redevelopment', in Everitt, *Perspectives*, pp. 186–8; Raven, 'North Essex Towns'; S. Forster *et al.*, 'Bonnets, Beer and Bricks; an occupational study of Bedfordshire 1770–1850' (Small Towns project paper, Centre for Urban History, Leicester Univ., 1993); M. Reed, *The Buckinghamshire Landscape* (1979), pp. 226–43; K. Fitch *et al.*, 'An Investigation into the Occupational Structure of Buckinghamshire Towns 1780–1850' (Small Towns project paper, Centre for Urban History, Leicester Univ., 1993).

countries of Europe, to a more integrated, rank-sized ordered network on the model of the more advanced core European regions. In this period there were notable gainers, particularly the bigger small-towns and those in the industrialising regions, which frequently outgrew their small town status. Many small towns clearly did participate in the accelerating urban growth from the later seventeenth century. But substantial numbers of losers are also evident, very small or marginal places which by the nineteenth century had often disappeared from the urban map. Alongside the Banburys of England one must not forget the Billesdons and Hallatons.

As we have indicated, there was a mosaic of factors helping to determine these trends. Economic specialisation was one, especially industrial specialisation. This was clearly important from the late seventeenth century – usually workshop-based with limited investment in new technology, and therefore vulnerable to growing factory-type competition from the industrialising regions in the nineteenth century. No less important was the economic impact of the metropolis. London's economic and demographic ascendancy by the eighteenth century had both a negative and a positive dimension, changing over time. Though stifling big-city growth in the Home Counties, metropolitan expansion seems to have generated heavy demand in the seventeenth and eighteenth centuries for foodstuffs and specialist products marketed or produced by the region's small towns. By the early nineteenth century the metropolitan effect appears more generally negative, at least in terms of small towns. High prices and labour costs in the south-east and agricultural specialisation appear to have accelerated the migration of industry away from the area; after the end of the French wars falling prices further deflated local demand. The direct impact of transport innovation is more problematical, not least because improvements in river, canal, road and later rail transport were both incremental and contradictory. Generally, it appears to have confirmed rather than caused discriminatory trends against regional networks and types of town.

Increasing agricultural specialisation may have had a beneficial effect on small towns in the seventeenth and eighteenth centuries but by the early nineteenth century dependence on the local agrarian economy probably stunted small-town expansion. One crude index of the state of regional demand is provided by the incidence of relieved paupers (as a percentage of the local population). In 1843 the South-West had the highest average rate of 12.8 per cent; the Home Counties 12.5 per cent; East Anglia 11.6 per cent – all areas with small towns in difficulty. In contrast, the West Midlands had 8.0 per cent and the Northern industrial counties 8.8 per cent.[55] On the other hand, as elsewhere in early modern Europe, the influx of landowners

---

[55] *Official Circulars of Public Documents . . . 1841–51* (reprinted, New York, 1970), vol. 3, p. 180.

into small towns played a dynamic part in their economic and cultural transformation during the eighteenth century. The scale of the impact is difficult to quantify but arguably the effect of landed consumption on small-town economies may have been larger than in big cities with greater internal demand. The retreat of the gentry after 1800 was equally decisive.

Such an analysis inevitably resolves more questions than it answers. The emphasis has been on the external factors determining small-town developments in the period. But we also need to recognise the importance of the local urban response to the opportunities and challenges which these developments created. Why do some towns respond more vigorously and effectively than others to short-term or structural problems? Size may be part of the story, but the elasticities of the economy, the attitude of the elite, the pattern of social and cultural institutions also doubtless had a vital influence and require further research.

6 The cultural role of small towns in England 1600–1800

Michael Reed

> Pas une ville, pas une villette qui n'ait ses villages, son lambeau de vie rurale annexée, qui n'impose à son 'plat pays' les commodités de son marché, l'usage de ses boutiques, de ses poids et mesures, de ses prêteurs d'argent, de ses hommes de loi, même de ses distractions. Il faut, pour être, qu'elle domine un empire, fût-il minuscule.[1]

This chapter is concerned with the *distractions* of the *villettes* of seventeenth- and eighteenth-century England. These *villettes*, or small towns, may be defined in rather crude terms as those places with under 5,000 inhabitants at the time of the 1801 census. The *distractions* to be considered here are those which may be called 'polite' in that they are concerned with cultural and leisure activities which are literacy-based rather than 'popular' ones such as the ceremonies surrounding the blessing of the salt pit at Nantwich on Ascension Day,[2] sword dancing at Knaresborough[3] or the Whit Monday Greenhill Bower procession in Lichfield.[4] However, these 'polite' activities form only one part of the cultural role of small towns. 'Culture' is a word of Protean meaning, but for the purposes of this chapter it may be said to have two facets. On the one hand it has a broad socio-economic dimension embracing the total assemblage of artefacts available to society at any one given period in time, and on the other it has a narrower meaning in that it is concerned with *distractions*, that is to say with leisure interests and intellectual activities.[5]

Many regional centres such as Exeter and county towns such as Shrewsbury[6]

Biographical information is taken from *The Dictionary of National Biography* and architectural information from *The Buildings of England* series, edited by Sir Nicholas Pevsner, unless otherwise indicated.

[1] F. Braudel, *Civilisation matérielle, économie et capitalisme*, tome 1, *Les Structures du quotidien: le possible et l'impossible* (Paris, 1979), pp. 423–4.

[2] J. Partridge, *Historical Account of the Town and Parish of Nantwich* (1774), p. 59.

[3] E. Hargrove, *History of Knaresborough* (1775), p. 85.

[4] *VCH Staffordshire*, vol. 14 (1990), 159.

[5] cf. R. M. Wiles, 'Provincial Culture in Early Georgian England', in P. Fritz and D. Williams, eds, *The Triumph of Culture: 18th Century Perspectives* (Toronto, 1972), p. 49.

[6] A. McInnes, 'The Emergence of a Leisure Town: Shrewsbury 1660–1760', *Past and Present*, no. 120 (1988), 53–87.

were, well before the end of the seventeenth century, exerting a role as cultural centres, in both meanings of the word. Local gentry were buying town houses to make use of the shops, to go to the play, to attend Quarter Sessions and Assizes and the social functions which were associated with these events, and to see and be seen at assemblies, balls and card parties. At the same time they made use of the growing numbers of professional men, especially lawyers and physicians, then beginning to congregate in such towns, and they very often sent their children to school there. The cultural role of towns at this level developed rapidly in the years after the Restoration and continued to grow and diversify during the course of the eighteenth century.[7] Many acquired a permanent theatre during this period, race meetings became established upon a quasi-permanent footing, and developments in printing and publishing meant that many had printers and booksellers by the early years of the eighteenth century as well as local and regional newspapers.

It is, however, equally clear that towns smaller than these centres were also of considerable cultural significance during these two centuries.[8] There may have been six or seven hundred small towns in seventeenth- and eighteenth-century England.[9] At the base of the pyramid it is often difficult to draw a line between a small town and a village since a significant proportion of small towns lost their markets through inanition during the course of the eighteenth century. Nevertheless, many places with five or six hundred inhabitants possessed what may be called quasi-urban functions in that their markets were replaced by shops, most had a resident clergyman and many had, from time to time, one or more resident schoolmasters, lawyers or physicians, a book club or a music society, and some even had town houses of the country gentry.[10] Taken together these features constitute the irreducible

[7] See *passim*, P. Borsay, *The English Urban Renaissance* (1989).

[8] P. J. Corfield, 'Small Towns, Large Implications: Social and Cultural Roles of Small Towns in England and Wales', *British Journal of Eighteenth Century Studies*, vol. 10 (1987), 125–38.

[9] See A. Everitt, 'The Marketing of Agricultural Produce', in J. Thirsk, ed., *Agrarian History of England and Wales*, vol. IV, *1500–1640* (1967), pp. 467–85, and J. A. Chartres, 'The Marketing of Agricultural Produce', in J. Thirsk, ed., *The Agrarian History of England and Wales*, Vol. V, Pt. ii, *1640–1750* (1985), pp. 409–20. For Gregory King's estimates of the numbers of towns at the end of the seventeenth century see D. V. Glass, 'Two Papers on Gregory King', in D. V. Glass and D. E. C. Eversley, eds, *Population in History* (1965), pp. 159–220, esp. p. 178.

[10] According to S. Shaw, *The History and Antiquities of Staffordshire*, vol. I (1798), p. 421, 'divers gentlemen had their houses in Tamworth', and *ibid.*, vol. 2 (1801), 163, the Levesons had a town house in Wolverhampton and *ibid.* p. 321, Walter Chetwynd had a seat in Rugeley. Sir Thomas Haggerston had a town house in Berwick-upon-Tweed, see A. M. C. Forster, ed., 'Selections from the Disbursement Books of Sir Thomas Haggerston, 1691–1709', *Surtees Society*, vol. 180 (1969), 6. The Earl of Shrewsbury built a four-storey house in Buxton in 1572, see J. T. Leach, 'Buxton and the Cavendish Family', *Derbyshire Archaeological Journal*, vol. 108 (1988), 54–65.

minimum foundations for the cultural function of a small town across both meanings of the term.

The *villettes* of seventeenth- and eighteenth-century England were not an homogeneous group of towns, nor does the dividing line of 5,000 inhabitants in 1801 have any real significance. It is simply a useful point at which to mark off one segment of that unbroken continuum of human settlement in seventeenth- and eighteenth-century England which stretched from an isolated farmhouse to London. This means that small towns fall into the same broad functional categories that can be recognised for their larger brethren.[11] There were small county towns, such as Bedford, Hertford, Huntingdon, Aylesbury and Guildford. Not all manufacturing towns were giants like Birmingham at the end of the eighteenth century. Thus Rotherham, Barnsley, Burnley, Chesterfield, Darlington and Warminster all had under 5,000 inhabitants in 1801, as did such port towns as Bideford, Barnstaple, Grimsby, Bridgwater and Hartlepool, and resort and spa towns like Bakewell, Matlock, Cheltenham, Harrogate, Margate, Lowestoft, Cromer and Eastbourne. In addition there were, of course, many market towns with well under 5,000 inhabitants, places such as Winslow and Wendover, Leighton Buzzard and Market Harborough. There were even cathedral cities with under 5,000 inhabitants, including Ely, Lichfield, Peterborough and Chichester. Unfortunately, however, the evidence upon which to base a discussion of the cultural role of small towns is uneven and fragmentary. One of the consequences of this is that classification of small towns in this manner does not yet appear to be reflected in their cultural role, and a further consequence is that it is impossible, at least at present, to recognise any marked regional differences in this role.

The development of the cultural role of towns depends upon economic prosperity.[12] This is as true for small towns as it is for any other. This economic prosperity may be based in any one or more of three fields: marketing, manufacturing and transport. Even the smallest of small towns finds its *modus vivendi* in the processing and exchange of the products of its hinterland,[13] its *empire minuscule*, but if some further manufacture can be added and if the town should also be on an important line of communication, whether road or river, then its prosperity is assured. Thus of Cirencester it was noted in 1779[14] that there was 'a great deal of travelling through this place' by stage coaches to London, Bath and Oxford, whilst a

[11] See P. Clark and P. Slack, *English Towns in Transition, 1500–1700* (1976), and P. J. Corfield, *The Impact of English Towns, 1700–1800* (1982).

[12] cf. C. P. Darcy, 'The Encouragement of the Fine Arts in Lancashire, 1760–1860', *Chetham Society*, 3rd Series, vol. 24 (1976), 12.

[13] cf. J. D. Marshall, 'The Rise and Transformation of the Cumbrian Market Town, 1660–1900', *Northern History*, vol. 19 (1983), 128–209.

[14] S. Rudder, *A New History of Gloucestershire* (1779), pp. 343–5.

'great number of heavy carriages that keep their regular stages' also passed through the town. At the same time there were two weekly markets and a thriving manufacture of heavy edged tools, especially leather curriers' knives. Of Cannock, however, a commentator wrote in 1798 that the market had declined and what was once a country town 'has now only the appearance of a good village'. Even the chalybeate spring was now little used.[15]

The economic prosperity of individual towns was, in its turn, based upon rising agricultural and industrial production and the attendant falling prices, together with rapid growth in overseas trade. Getting a living was, for an increasingly wide range of society, no longer the strenuous, obsessive task that it had once been. Rising incomes meant that increasing numbers of men and women had more and more money over and above that needed for food, clothing and shelter and this could be spent upon books, music, horse-racing, going to the theatre and rebuilding, or at least refacing, their houses in the latest fashion.

The economic role of shops, markets and fairs in sustaining the wealth upon which all cultural activities are based is obvious and needs no exploration here. But what may be called the cultural role of the artefacts to be found in such profusion in the shops and markets of even the smallest market town has scarcely been explored. A consumer society, based upon a wide range of personal choice, was emerging rapidly in the last half of the seventeenth century, as shopkeepers' probate inventories make abundantly clear. At his death in 1730 Matthew Clarke, of Winslow, shopkeeper, had Kendal cottons, Holland linens and Norwich stuffs in his shop. Benjamin Atfield, of Speenhamland, grocer, at his death in 1682, had French barley, Valencia almonds, pepper and coriander in his shop. John Davies, a Bewdley mercer who died in 1682, had kerseys, Taunton and Dutch serges, Scotch cloth, sugar, raisins and pepper, at 6d. the pound, in his shop. The buttons in the draper's shop of Thomas Newman of St Neots were priced at 8s. the gross in 1684.[16] At the same time travelling dealers driving carts laden with a wide range of goods, particularly cloth and haberdashery, were making regular rounds of country districts supplementing and complementing the shops of the nearest town.[17] The impact of this rapidly widening range of merchandise upon the mental horizons of town dwellers and countrymen alike must have been profound – literally and metaphorically a real eye-opener. It is in this sense that the economic and cultural functions of small towns may be seen as facets of a single and continuous process.

[15] Shaw, *History of Staffordshire*, vol. II (1801), p. 319.
[16] Public Record Office. PROB. 3 30/24, PROB. 4, 2630, 5391 and 4613. For an account of the growth of shops in Cheshire towns see I. Mitchell, 'The Development of Urban Retailing, 1700–1815', in P. Clark, ed., *The Transformation of English Provincial Towns* (1984), pp. 259–83.
[17] J. Beresford, ed., *The Diary of a Country Parson*, vol. II (1926), pp. 69, 72; vol. III (1927), pp. 225, 266, etc.

If the cultural role of towns of every size is dependent upon economic prosperity, then both of these factors rely in their turn upon the exchange of ideas and of artefacts, and this exchange is determined by communication technology. Any development in this technology will interact with economic and cultural activities in a most subtle and complex manner. Significant technical developments took place in three areas of the communications network which served England in the seventeenth and eighteenth centuries.

First of all the state of the roads undoubtedly improved during the course of the eighteenth century, slowly and irregularly, but improve it certainly did. Turnpike trustees contributed to this improvement in a thousand trivial but cumulatively very important ways.[18] Their surveyors had little real knowledge of road engineering much before the end of the eighteenth century, but they did reduce gradients, straighten roads and lay out new ones. Road surfaces did slowly improve, and the general introduction of signposts and milestones after 1720 must have made an enormous contribution to improving the speed and safety of travel. Roads were crowded with vehicles of every kind. The stage coach network expanded and contracted according to local and regional demands, but it was the carrier and his waggon who made up the backbone of the English transport network in the eighteenth century. Again and again contemporaries note that towns are much frequented by travellers, and innkeepers and shopkeepers prospered on the trade that they brought.

Secondly, as the roads improved so too did the postal system. More and more post roads were designated, and crossroads became increasingly numerous. William Stukeley describes how his father obtained a post to come to Holbeach from Spalding with the letters.[19] William Cowper relates, on the other hand, how a plan to bring letters daily to Olney 'dropped to the ground' and he had to remain content with his letters arriving only three times in the week.[20] Letters were still expensive to send, or at least to receive, but the penny post in London, started in 1682, was handling 951,000 items a year by 1702.[21] Letters were still not delivered to individual houses but had to be fetched from the nearest post office. Parson Woodforde, who lived at Weston Longville, some ten miles from Norwich, sent a manservant into Norwich every few days to collect his letters, together with the newspapers, including one printed in Ipswich, a further 40 miles away.[22]

---

[18] W. Albert, *The Turnpike Road System in England, 1663–1840* (1972), and E. Pawson, *Transport and Economy: The Turnpike Roads of Eighteenth Century Britain* (1977).

[19] W. C. Lukis, ed., 'The Family Memoirs of the Rev. William Stukeley', vol. I, *Surtees Society*, vol. 73 (1882), p. 6.

[20] J. King and C. Ryskamp, eds, *The Letters and Prose Works of William Cowper*, vol. III (1983), pp. 162–3.

[21] See H. Robinson, *The British Post Office: a History* (1948).

[22] Beresford, ed., *Diary*, vol. V (1931), pp. 90, 92, 238, etc.

The third communication system which showed technical improvements during the eighteenth century was the printing and publishing industry. Printing and bookselling make an obvious contribution to the cultural role of all towns, and printers and booksellers are recorded in 212 English towns outside London by 1775.[23] At the same time there were technical improvements in the quality of engraving and mezzotinting in the first part of the eighteenth century, improvements which made the reproduction of paintings and other works of art increasingly realistic, spreading knowledge of painting, architecture and sculpture far beyond the confines of the narrow circle of aristocratic or royal owners and those whom they would allow into their houses to look at their pictures.[24] William Stukeley writes that during his years as an undergraduate at Cambridge he learnt French and designed to learn Italian, 'for I had thought of travelling, especially to Rome', 'but my hopes were frustrate, and Imagination alone and Prints must supply the want of Real inspection'.[25] By the last quarter of the eighteenth century English print-makers and publishers dominated the European market. One example may serve to underline the importance of the improvements in this last communication network. John Dunthorne (1770–1844) was a plumber and glazier of East Bergholt. He spent all his leisure hours painting landscapes from nature. It was his encouragement which set his young neighbour, John Constable, some six years his junior, off upon his career as an artist, and it was Constable's copy, made in about 1795, from Sir Nicholas Dorigny's engravings of the Raphael cartoons, finished in 1719, which attracted the attention of Sir George Beaumont.[26]

All three of these fields fostered growth and change by improving the distribution of artefacts, ideas and knowledge across the whole range of cultural activities, whether by extending the range of goods to be found in shops or by making books, prints and engravings more readily available.

Shops and markets provide for the cultural role of small towns in the broader socio-economic sense. What may be called the cultural life of small towns more narrowly defined is that which is concerned with books and literature, history and antiquities, music and scientific enquiry. This is difficult to describe with precision since much of our knowledge of cultural relationships generally depends upon chance references in letters, diaries and newspapers, but it is clear that a number of strands of influence are at work. It is equally clear that each of these strands has its own dynamic,

[23] See H. R. Plomer *et al.*, eds, *Dictionaries of the Printers and Booksellers who were at work in England, Scotland and Ireland, 1557–1775* (reprinted in Compact Form in one volume, 1977).

[24] See J. Burke, *English Art, 1714–1800* (1976), pp. 177–80.

[25] Lukis, 'Family memoirs', vol. II (1882), p. 25.

[26] See R. B. Beckett, ed., 'John Constable's Correspondence', vol. II, *Suffolk Records Society*, vol. 6 (1964), pp. 1–2, 21–3.

developing and changing with the passage of time, whilst new ones are added in response to changes in society at large. First of all the role of the church and of its clergymen should not be underestimated. Almost every small town had an Anglican parish priest, although he might be only a perpetual curate or serve a chapel of ease. The religious controversies of the sixteenth and early seventeenth centuries bred a new tolerance from the last years of the seventeenth, and nonconformist sects appeared with membership transcending traditional parish boundaries. Most small towns had at least one nonconformist place of worship, erected during the course of the eighteenth century. Congregationalists, Presbyterians and Independents quarrelled among themselves, with splinter groups seceding, often to become Unitarians. Baptist and Quaker congregations seem to have been more stable, whilst from the last years of the eighteenth century Methodist places of worship appeared on the scene. The market towns of the Vale of York, for example, became circuit heads for the developing Methodist Connexion, beginning with Thirsk in 1774.[27] Churches, whether Anglican or nonconformist, could become focal points for political rivalries and social divisions, and these could serve both to reinforce membership of a congregation and to polarise divisions within the corporation.[28] The acid remarks to be found in response to some bishop's visitation questions show how deeply these divisions could run. At Wootton Bassett, it was said in 1783, 'the body corporate seldom come to church unless to qualify themselves for their respective offices in the corporation'.[29]

Among the clergy several became antiquaries and historians of the first importance. Dr Treadway Nash, for example, whose *Collections for a History of Worcestershire*, published 1781–2, is still of value, was vicar of St Peters, Droitwich, and John Hutchins became vicar of Milton Abbas and master of the school there. He moved to Wareham in 1744. The fire of 1762 which devastated that town almost destroyed his collections. They were saved only by the extraordinary exertions of his wife. His *History and Antiquities of the County of Dorset* was published shortly after his death in 1773. Others practised as physicians and developed a network of patients extending over a considerable distance. Occasionally a physician became a clergyman. William Stukeley trained as a physician but took Holy Orders in

---

[27] R. W. Unwin, 'Tradition and Transition: Market Towns of the Vale of York, 1660–1830', *Northern History*, vol. 17 (1981), 72–116, esp. p. 88.

[28] See J. M. Triffit, 'Believing and Belonging: Church Behaviour in Plymouth and Dartmouth, 1710–1730', in S. J. Wright, ed., *Parish, Church and People* (1988), pp. 179–202; Unwin, 'Tradition', pp. 86–96; and Marshall, 'Rise and transformation', pp. 188–93.

[29] M. Ransome, ed., 'Wiltshire Returns to the Bishop's Visitation Queries, 1783', *Wiltshire Records Society*, vol. 27 (1971), 244.

1729.[30] Many clergymen, like the John Hutchins just referred to, also served as schoolmasters. James Mayo, vicar of Avebury, in fact lived in Calne, having been nominated master of the school there at a salary of £50 per annum, which he was 'under an indispensable necessity of accepting', having a family of fourteen children.[31] The Rev. Joseph Greene was both curate and schoolmaster at Stratford-upon-Avon until his death in 1790 and fulfilled both functions admirably, whereas Thomas Prosser, rector of Birlingham, in Worcestershire, was also headmaster of Monmouth grammar school, thus depriving his parish of a resident priest.[32]

By the Restoration England was well endowed with schools of every kind, and the practice of taking boarders was well established. Many were provided by the founder with an endowment which, when converted into land, provided stability and income, the indispensable basis for any educational establishment before the days of state education. Without foundations of this kind, and sometimes even with, schools seem to have come and gone with astonishing rapidity. It was reported of Princes Risborough in 1709 that there were no schools in the town. In 1715 there were three small ones, two taught by dissenting women. In Stony Stratford in 1709 there was a public school, with 16 or 17 boys, recently endowed with the Rose and Crown inn. In 1712 there were six children taught in school. By 1715 there was said to be no school at present.[33] But the reputation, even of the best-found school, depended very much upon the personality and ability of the headmaster. He alone could give the school a social and fashionable *cachet*, and his death or departure could lead to a rapid decline. Thus by 1695 Lichfield grammar school was attracting the sons of the Staffordshire gentry and under John Hunter, who was headmaster between 1704 and 1741, with the enviable task of correcting the exercises of the young Samuel Johnson, it had a hundred boarders at a time. The same story is to be told for Tamworth grammar school, which had a high reputation under George Antrobus, headmaster between 1659 and 1708 and this continued under his successor, Dr Samuel Shaw, headmaster between 1708 and 1730. After Shaw's death, however, the school declined.[34] The contribution of schools to the cultural role of small towns is of the first importance, but the

[30] S. Piggott, *William Stukeley: An Eighteenth Century Antiquary* (revised edn, 1985), pp. 97–8.

[31] Ransome, ed., 'Wiltshire Returns', p. 29.

[32] See L. Fox, ed., 'Correspondence of the Rev. Joseph Greene, parson, schoolmaster and antiquary, 1717–1790', *Dugdale Society*, vol. 23 (1965), and M. Ransome, ed., 'The State of the Bishopric of Worcester, 1782–1808', *Worcestershire Historical Society*, New Series, vol. 6 (1968), pp. 9, 83.

[33] Christ Church College Oxford. Bishop Wake's Visitation MSS.

[34] *VCH Staffordshire*, vol. 6 (1979), 160–8. For two very contrasting schools at the end of the eighteenth century, at Bury St Edmunds and Reading, see Jane Fiske, ed., 'The Oakes Diaries', vol. I, *Suffolk Records Society*, vol. 32 (1990), p. 173.

long-term significance of an individual school depended upon the character and ability of the schoolmaster in charge at the moment. Small-town schools very rarely had the social standing to carry a nonentity for very long.

The role of well-endowed, and hence comparatively stable, schools in the transmission of cultural values cannot be exaggerated. Latin formed the basis of the curriculum in the great majority of these schools, and by concentrating almost exclusively upon the inculcation of classical languages and literature they sustained and reinforced the enormous prestige of classical civilisation. This in its turn underpinned the reception of classical architecture which was taking place during the seventeenth century. There was a growing understanding of the underlying principles of classical architecture, one of the consequences of the diaspora of the country gentry which the Civil War brought about. This was reinforced by the enormous influence of Sir Christopher Wren and the reaction against him led by the Earl of Burlington. As a result, when this movement came to full maturity early in the eighteenth century, the prestige of classical architecture all but overwhelmed the vernacular traditions. To share in this movement was to participate in a national, indeed in an international, cultural milieu, so that to have a classical doorway, complete with Tuscan pilasters and a Venetian window, was to be lifted, on however superficial a plane, out of a provincial, vernacular tradition into a classical, European one.[35]

The diffusion of classical architecture and hence of the values and attitudes of mind which it symbolises is one of the most striking features of the cultural life of the eighteenth century. It was by no means confined to country houses and is to be found in small towns as well as in large ones. Very few small towns are without some eighteenth-century building which, however hesitatingly or amateurishly done, shows some pretensions towards classical architecture. Some have little more than a façade to medieval or sixteenth-century buildings, some are more thoroughly rebuilt, often by private men of means, with the money to pay for the visible expression of their knowledge or their cultural pretensions, or both. At a public level this reception of classical architecture is expressed in the rebuilding of town halls, something which is taking place on a national scale in the eighteenth century. Even Queenborough, with only a few hundred inhabitants, rebuilt its Guildhall in 1793. There are several problems in the identification of this kind of corporate cultural activity, since it is clear that in a number of instances nineteenth-century town halls are but replacements of eighteenth-century ones. Thus Thame has had at least three, including the present one of 1888 and two earlier, one of which was a sixteenth-century timber-

[35] See P. Borsay, 'Culture, Status and the English Urban Landscape', *History*, vol. 67 (1952), 1–12.

framed building. That at Wootton-under-Edge of 1698 was rebuilt in 1872, and the seventeenth-century one at Coleford, in Gloucestershire, was rebuilt in 1866. Henley-on-Thames had a classical town hall built in 1790, but it has subsequently been demolished and parts rebuilt at Crazies Hill, in Berkshire, as part of a country house. Everywhere classical models and themes prevail. The town hall at Chesterfield, built in 1790, was designed by John Carr of York, one of the finest provincial architects and builders at work in the eighteenth century, and that at Abingdon was designed and built by Christopher Kempster in 1678–82. The Guildhall of 1743 at South Molton has open rusticated arcades to the ground floor and the late-seventeenth-century one at Faringdon has Tuscan columns. The town hall at Barnard Castle of 1747 is an octagon surrounded by Tuscan columns, whilst that of Bishop's Castle of about 1765 has a Venetian window. All of these themes and motifs have by this date become part of the small change of the provincial builder.

Some town halls were erected by the corporation, some by subscription and some received substantial donations from wealthy landowners anxious to reinforce their political standing in a town with two seats in Parliament at its disposal. Thus the town hall at Tewkesbury, rebuilt in 1785 to replace a timber-framed one of 1586, was the result of the liberality of Sir William Codrington.[36] Another, at Nantwich, was paid for in 1720 by the Prince of Wales in his capacity as Earl of Chester,[37] and that at Burton-on-Trent was built in 1772 at the expense of the Earl of Uxbridge.[38] At Chichester, however, the council chamber was built by subscription in 1733, the Duke of Somerset, then High Steward of the city, contributing a hundred guineas.[39]

Town halls served cultural and social purposes as well as administrative ones. Itinerant companies of players often performed in town halls if no theatre was available, and several town halls also had assembly rooms or ballrooms attached. Thus the first known performance of a play by Shakespeare at Stratford-upon-Avon, *Othello*, was given in the town hall in 1746.[40] This town hall, built in 1633, was replaced in 1757 and the new one had a ballroom measuring sixty feet by thirty in the upper chamber.[41] The town hall at Rotherham, a town of 3,070 inhabitants in 1801, was rebuilt in 1739–43 and housed both the grammar school and assemblies,[42] whilst the

---

[36] W. Dyde, *The History and Antiquities of Tewkesbury* (2nd edn. 1798), p. 85.

[37] Partridge, *Nantwich*, p. 82.

[38] Shaw, *History of Staffordshire*, vol. I (1798), p. 12.

[39] A. Hay, *The History of Chichester* (1804), p. 371.

[40] Fox, ed., 'Correspondence', pp. 14, 57, 164–5.

[41] R. B. Wheler, *The History and Antiquities of Stratford upon Avon* (1806), pp. 107–9.

[42] K. Grady, 'The Georgian Public Buildings of Leeds and the West Riding', *Thoresby Society*, vol. 62 (1989), 172.

town hall at Tewkesbury had a handsome ballroom on the principal storey.[43]

Several small towns witnessed schemes of improvement during the course of the eighteenth century. At Dorchester, for example, the West Walks were laid out and planted with trees upon the line of the old town walls. A Park Walk was planted in Shaftesbury in 1753 and at Bridgnorth the outer bailey of the castle was laid out as walks in 1786. Queen Anne's Walk, with a lavishly decorated colonnade of Tuscan columns, was built as an exchange in Barnstaple in 1708, and New Walk, on the south side of the Minster Pool, was laid out in Lichfield in 1772.[44] Elm trees were planted on the north and east walls of Chichester in 1701, 'for the accommodation of the citizens and the ornament of the city'.[45] Some of this work was done by big landowners. The Duke of Chandos planned Castle Street in Bridgwater in 1721, and the Duke of Devonshire began the development of Buxton as a spa from about 1780.[46] Sir Henry Slingsby laid out the Long Walk in Knaresborough in about 1739, thus making access to the Dropping Well easier for townsmen and visitors alike.[47] In other towns improvement was the work of local builders and master masons. The Bridgwater master builder, Benjamin Holloway, built a big house for himself at West Quay in about 1730, complete with Venetian windows and Tuscan columns, whilst the Castle estate scheme laid out in Wisbech from 1793 was the work of Joseph Medworth, a local charity schoolboy made good.[48]

The reception of classical architecture at a domestic, private level was well under way in many towns, both large and small, by the last quarter of the seventeenth century, leading to much building and rebuilding, with new building materials such as brick and tile replacing timber and thatch. It was almost always concerned with individual houses rather than with terraces, streets or squares, and it was obviously based on the material prosperity of individual merchants, tradesmen and professionals. Wymondham, in Norfolk, for example, has a number of large eighteenth-century houses. Caius House, Middleton Street, built in the early eighteenth century, is particularly fine, with seven bays and a three-bay pediment marked by giant pilasters. Wymondham was situated on the main London to Norwich post road and one of the first turnpike acts, passed in 1696, was for a stretch of the road leading south from the town. Crewkerne also prospered as a 'thorough-fare' town, and the evidence is to be seen in the Market Square today. Similarly, at Warminster, the large eighteenth-century houses in Church Street exude prosperity, based upon the eighteenth-century textile

[43] Dyde, *Tewkesbury*, p. 84.   [44] *VCH Staffordshire*, vol. 14 (1990), 163.
[45] Hay, *Chichester*, p. 364.
[46] Leach, 'Buxton'.   [47] Hargrove, *Knaresborough*, p. 86.
[48] *VCH Cambridgeshire*, vol. 4 (1953), pp. 246, 254.

industry. The same industry brought prosperity to Shepton Mallet which has a number of substantial surviving Georgian houses, although several are only façades to earlier buildings. Topsham flourished as the port for Exeter, and this shows in the splendid early Georgian brick houses of its residential suburb at Lympstone. In Stamford timber framing ceases to be used in building construction by the mid-seventeenth century and is gradually replaced by stone.[49] The town was clearly very prosperous as a market and 'thorough-fare' centre during the eighteenth century, and much rebuilding and refacing went on, but almost always upon a piecemeal scale, with very little attempt at overall street design. Some pairs of houses were built with imposing elevations, Nos 66–67 High Street (St Martins), for example, but they are exceptional. The Earls of Exeter were the principal landlords in the town, but it was not until the 1780s that the ninth Earl began to erect blocks of houses with uniform façades, especially in St Mary's Hill and St Mary's Street, but again these are exceptional. Much detail from published pattern books can be recognised: architraves from James Gibbs' *Rules for Drawing*, decorative door panels from Salmon's *Palladio Londiniensis* and keystones from Batty Langley's *Treasury of Designs*, for example. The contribution of the third communication network, namely printing and publishing, to the cultural life of small towns was very real. At the same time the influence of the building and rebuilding of country houses upon urban architecture, whether visually through their design and decoration or more practically through the skill and experience gained by the craftsmen who worked on them, is clearly of great significance. At Chipping Norton, for example, there are a number of houses of the 1720s, 1730s and 1740s revealing the influence of the Baroque of Blenheim Palace upon local builders.

In a number of small towns disastrous fires had a considerable impact upon the built townscape.[50] A fire at Wareham in 1762 led to much rebuilding in brick and in the classical style, for example in West Street, and the rebuilding of Blandford Forum after the disastrous fire of 1731 was almost entirely the work of the Bastard brothers, William and John, with classical themes used as a matter of course. John's own house is part of a block of three, with a central carriageway marked by Corinthian pilasters. It cost him £704 to build.[51] In no town, however, was there any replanning of streets upon a large scale after a fire and no attempt was made to impose any kind of visual or structural unity. Any change was almost always upon a limited scale. In Wareham, for example, where a local rebuilding Act was

---

[49] See Royal Commission on Historical Monuments, *The Town of Stamford* (1977).

[50] E. L. Jones, S. Porter and M. Turner, *A Gazetteer of English Urban Fire Disasters, 1500–1900*, Historical Geography Research Series, No. 13 (1984).

[51] Royal Commission on Historical Monuments, *Dorset*, Vol. 3, Central Part 1 (1970), pp. 16ff.

obtained following the fire of 1762, a notorious obstruction in the centre of the town called the Throng was never rebuilt, and in Blandford Forum the Guildhall was rebuilt on a new site away from its old position in the middle of the Market Place and a few streets were widened, but this was all.

Rebuilding and refacing in classical styles is an indirect consequence of the enormous prestige of classical civilisation generally and of the overwhelming attention paid to classical languages and literature in the educational system of the eighteenth century. It is an aspect of the cultural life of the eighteenth century which brings together both meanings of the word culture, combining literature and the world of artefacts. The interplay between the two meanings of culture is immensely subtle and in a number of respects it is in the schools of eighteenth-century England that they converge. It is apparent, however, that the educational system which brought these two themes together was not itself beyond change, and this in a number of directions.

First of all there is growing evidence of new demands being made of the educational system during the course of the eighteenth century, and this appears to be particularly characteristic of small towns.[52] Some old grammar schools began to provide instruction in geography, history, mathematics and modern languages, whilst new, private, often boarding, schools appeared which gave instruction only in these 'modern' subjects. The Free School founded in Chichester in 1702 was said to pay 'a particular regard to navigation'.[53] The importance of education for business and trade was becoming increasingly recognised.

Secondly, even after the Toleration Act, dissenters were barred from the two English universities, and so, in order to provide for the education of nonconformist ministers, a number of societies were formed to fund their training.[54] These included the Presbyterian Fund, originally founded in 1689, and the Congregational Fund Board, founded in 1695. There were several more established in the eighteenth century. A number of dissenting academies were established in small towns, at Alcester, Bridgnorth, Bridgwater, Dartmouth, Daventry, Newport Pagnell, Rotherham, Stratford-upon-Avon and Tewkesbury. This last had about a hundred students in twelve years, including Thomas Secker, later archbishop of Canterbury. Academies often had only one tutor and no more than a handful of students at any one time. That at Northampton moved to Daventry in 1752, upon the death of Philip Doddridge. It provided a five-year course in languages and mathematics, with French and geography as optional subjects. In all it took 274 students (including Joseph Priestley), 44 of whom had bursaries

---

[52] See Unwin, 'Tradition', pp. 96–113.   [53] Hay, *Chichester*, p. 392.
[54] See H. McLachlan, *English Education under the Test Acts* (1931), *passim*.

from the Presbyterian Fund, before it moved back to Northampton in 1789.

Thirdly there was a growing movement for the establishment of charity schools, particularly under the auspices of the Society for Promoting Christian Knowledge, founded in 1698. These charity schools were established in order to teach sound Christian doctrine and to provide a basic education for 'those whom nature or failure had determined to the plough, the oar and other handicrafts'.[55] Tewkesbury charity school, for example, founded in 1719, taught reading, writing and arithmetic to 15 boys,[56] and the charity school at Wilton, supported by a settled endowment, taught reading, writing and arithmetic to 20 boys, each of whom received a new coat, waistcoat, breeches, stockings, shoes and a hat every year, together with £5 towards apprenticeship.[57] In the first 35 years of its existence the Society established some 1,500 schools and not the least of its achievements was to do something for the education of girls.

Charity school children were expected to sing in the parish church and this provides another point of contact between the two meanings of culture. It is clear that music played an important part in the life of towns in the seventeenth and eighteenth centuries. When Thomas Baskerville stayed at the Angel inn in Towcester during the reign of Charles II he records sending for the town music, but they did not come until the morning, 'when we did not care for them'.[58] He also wrote of the good singing and bell ringing at Cirencester. The 'town music' was almost certainly provided by the town waits, who were medieval in origin. Most towns, large and small, employed them on a more or less regular basis and they appear in town records up until the end of the eighteenth century.[59] Originally they patrolled the streets at night, playing a musical instrument, usually a hautboy, to show that they were performing their duties. But they were paid only a modest fee and so certainly from the end of the sixteenth century they appeared at inns to play for anyone who would pay. Pepys mentions music in inns on several occasions, that at the White Hart in Marlborough pleasing him because of its 'innocence', for which he paid 3s., whilst that at Huntingdon was better than that at Cambridge. He also describes how on one occasion Charles II compelled the fiddlers of Thetford to sing all the bawdy songs they could think of.[60]

[55] See W. H. G. Armytage, *Four Hundred Years of English Education* (1964), p. 40.

[56] Dyde, *Tewkesbury*, p. 86.

[57] Ransome, ed., 'Wiltshire Returns', p. 234.

[58] Royal Commission on Historical Manuscripts (HMC), *Portland MSS*, vol. II (1893), pp. 263ff. Parson Woodforde records hearing the New Singers of Castle Cary in 1768, see Beresford, ed., *Diary*, vol. I (1924), p. 82.

[59] See, e.g., J. Simpson, 'The Stamford Waits', *The Reliquary*, vol. 26 (1885), pp. 1–6.

[60] R. Latham and W. Matthews, eds, *The Diary of Samuel Pepys*, vols. VIII (1974), p. 474, IX (1976), pp. 241, 336.

Town waits provide one form of public music in towns, churches another. Voluntary parish church choirs are known by 1686, that at Romney forming itself into a religious society of young men by 1700, and a similar society and choir was in existence at Epworth by 1702. These choirs were often joined by the charity school children to sing the psalms, led by the parish clerk and accompanied by the organ. *A Collection of Psalms etc. sung by the charity children of Chichester* was published in 1761.[61] Church choirs and organists could provide the nucleus around which private music clubs would form, and many church organists made a genuine contribution to cultural life. George Guest, for example, who was organist at Wisbech, composed and published a variety of music, as did Dr John Alcock, organist at Lichfield. Music clubs were very numerous and were to be found in rural settings as well as urban ones.[62] They also often organised public concerts. Dedham had a music society by 1739 and the organist there, Joseph Gibbs, published two sets of compositions. There was a Philharmonic Society at Swaffham, and monthly subscription concerts were being organised by 1745. At Debenham the music society met monthly to perform works by Handel. Other societies are known at Wymondham, Walsingham, Saxmundham, Woodbridge, Sudbury, Hadleigh, Chelmsford and Matlock. The Chichester assembly rooms, erected in 1781–2, were used for assemblies and concerts every fortnight during the winter months, the band being assisted by a lately erected organ.[63] The Derbyshire Mineral Music Society is recorded in 1776, as well as the Fakenham Musical Society.[64] That at Lichfield was founded in 1739 and public concerts were taking place in the town from the 1740s.[65] There were two music clubs at Stamford in 1746 and the Truro Philharmonic Society was established in 1797.[66]

A number of small towns acquired purpose-built theatres, particularly during the last half of the eighteenth century. In the absence of theatres, plays were often performed by companies of itinerant players in inns or other public buildings, although in Blackpool in 1798, admittedly then 'only

---

[61] N. Temperley, *The Music of the English Parish Church*, vol. I (1979), pp. 142–3, and see K. H. MacDermott, *Sussex Church Music in the Past* (1922), p. 70. Other places for which special psalmodies and hymnbooks were published include Dunstable (c. 1780), Chesterfield (1799), Totnes (1797), Lyme Regis (1796), Romney (1724), Kendal (1757) and Stourbridge (1780). See K. H. MacDermott, *The Old Church Gallery Minstrels* (1948), Appendix 2, pp. 72–3.

[62] See S. Sadie, 'Concert Life in Eighteenth Century England', *Proceedings of the Royal Musical Association*, vol. 85 (1958–9), pp. 17–30.

[63] Hay, *Chichester*, p. 372.

[64] See the list of subscribers to C. Burney, *A General History of Music* (1776). Other subscribers included musical societies in Halifax, Manchester and Nottingham, the Pamphlet Club at Chester and the Literary Society at King's Lynn.

[65] *VCH Staffordshire*, vol. 14 (1990), 164.

[66] Lukis, ed., 'Family memoirs', vol. I (1882), p. 385, and N. Pevsner, *The Buildings of England: Cornwall* (1951), p. 212.

rising into existence',[67] the threshing floor of a barn was used. These companies often developed more or less regular circuits. Thus one based in Norwich put on plays in North Walsham, Aylsham, Holt and Woodbridge in 1727 and in Dereham and Beccles in 1749. A company based in Canterbury visited Deal, Sandwich, Margate, Romney, Rye and Tenterden in 1730 and put on a play in a large barn behind the Six Bells inn in Sittingbourne in 1771.[68] A barn was used in Sandwich in 1762, and Mr Watson, manager of the Cheltenham company of players, built a theatre in Hereford and gave occasional performances in Tewkesbury.[69] Dramatic performances in Banbury inns are known from the 1740s,[70] and Parson Woodforde saw performances of *Hamlet* and *Richard III* mounted by strolling players in the Court House in Castle Cary in 1770, and a performance of *Cato* in the Market House in Abingdon in 1774.[71] In his *The Theatric Tourist*, published in 1805, James Winston produced 'a genuine collection of correct views . . . of all the Provincial theatres in Great Britain'. He included coloured aquatints of 24 theatres, not only in Bath, Exeter, Liverpool and Birmingham but also in Andover, Margate, Newbury and Grantham. The surviving manuscript of his book is much more informative.[72] It gives details of 274 theatres throughout the British Isles, including ones at Alnwick, Bewdley, Bridgnorth, Bungay, Cirencester, Leek, Lydd, Nantwich, St Neots, Shepton Mallet, Honiton, Spalding and Wincanton. That at Faversham, he records, was a wooden one brought from Margate. The theatre at Lichfield was said in 1795 to be a newly erected building with a stucco front, a spacious interior and a neatly decorated stage. It was owned by a Society of Gentlemen.[73]

An even more popular form of entertainment was provided by balls and assemblies.[74] Thus Bruton has Georgian assembly rooms, Henley-on-Thames has late-eighteenth-century ones, and those of Chichester date from 1781. Sturminster Newton acquired assembly rooms at the very end of the eighteenth century, whilst those at East Dereham were built in 1756, complete with three Roman Doric columns at the main entrance. Parson Woodforde records monthly assemblies here in 1781, and rather later Alfred

[67] W. Hutton, *A Description of Blackpool* (1789), p. 37.
[68] S. Rosenfeld, *Strolling Players and Drama in the Provinces, 1660–1765* (1939, 1970 New York reprint), pp. 61–2, 221, 260.
[69] Dyde, *Tewkesbury*, p. 81 and J. Price, *An Historical Account of the City of Hereford* (1796), p. 73. Mr Watson subscribed to Dyde's book.
[70] *VCH Oxfordshire*, vol. 10 (1972), 14.
[71] Beresford, ed., *Diary*, vol. I (1924), pp. 100–33.
[72] C. B. Hogan, 'The Manuscript of Winston's *Theatric Tourist*', *Theatre Notebook*, vol. 1 (1945–7), 86–90.
[73] J. Jackson, *History of the City and Cathedral of Lichfield* (1795), p. 42.
[74] There is a rather disparaging account of assemblies and public balls in N. Scarfe, ed., 'A Frenchman's Year in Suffolk', *Suffolk Records Society*, vol. 30 (1988), 42–4.

Tennyson was a frequent and vigorous dancer in the assembly rooms at Horncastle before going up to Cambridge.[75] William Stukeley wrote of Grantham in 1747 that 'we have a monthly assembly for dancing among the fair sex, and a weekly meeting for conversation among the gentlemen'.[76]

Gentlemen's societies, whether political, debating or social, were widespread over eighteenth-century England.[77] The best-known survivor is that at Spalding,[78] but Maurice Johnson, who founded the Spalding society, was also closely involved with another at Peterborough, founded in 1730, 'for the improvement of Literature and promoting of Friendship and good neighbourhood'. It had a wide membership but attendance at meetings was always small. Discussion ranged over a wide variety of scientific and philosophical subjects, including a report of a lunar eclipse at King's Lynn and an account of 'the doctrine of fluxions according to Sir Isaac Newton . . . set forth in a plain and accurate manner'.[79] Other societies were not quite so strenuous. The Club, or Civil Society, attended by John Salusbury of Leighton Buzzard, met regularly in inns in the town at the choice of individual members. If attendance was small, and the presence of thirteen members was said to make 'a pretty full club', then they drank punch and wine in addition to beer. The Club met fairly frequently: in June 1758 it met on the 7th, 8th, 15th, 21st, 28th and 29th of the month.[80] Most of these clubs imposed fines for absence from their meetings, the proceeds going into club funds. The Bear Club, however, founded in Devizes in 1756 and meeting in the inn of that name, used this money to provide basic education for six boys in the town. By 1775 the number of boys provided for had risen to 16, and in 1783 they were receiving a coat, waistcoat and breeches every year, with some money, derived from subscriptions, donations and bequests, going towards apprenticeship expenses. By about 1848 the Club trustees had acquired their own school building. This finally closed in 1875.[81]

More specialised clubs were those composed of perhaps ten or a dozen

---

[75] Beresford, ed., *Diary*, vol. I (1924), p. 300, H. Nicolson, *Tennyson* (1923, 1960 paperback reprint), p. 49.

[76] Lukis, ed., 'Family memoirs', vol. I (1882), p. 190.

[77] cf. J. Money, 'Taverns, Coffee Houses and Clubs', *Historical Journal*, vol. 14 (1971), 15–47.

[78] D. M. Owen, ed., 'The Minute Books of the Spalding Gentlemen's Society, 1712–1755', *Lincoln Record Society*, vol. 73 (1981).

[79] H. J. J. Winter, 'Scientific Notes from the early Minutes of the Peterborough Society, 1730–1745', *Isis*, vol. 31 (1939), 51–9. Metereological observations are recorded in the minutes of the Brazen-nose Society at Stamford, see Lukis, ed., 'Family memoirs', vol. I (1882), p. 427, n. 12.

[80] J. Godber, ed., 'The Diary of John Salusbury of Leighton Buzzard', in 'Some Bedfordshire Diaries', *Bedfordshire Historical Records Society*, vol. 40 (1960), 46–94, esp. p. 65.

[81] *VCH Wiltshire*, vol. 10 (1975), 302–3, 305; Ransome, ed., 'Wiltshire Returns' pp. 85–6.

people who met, usually once a month and often in an inn, to subscribe to buy books which members were then at liberty to borrow.[82] In some clubs the books thus accumulated were sold off by auction at the end of each year. In others they were retained, so that they became in effect proprietary or subscription libraries.[83] Such societies were very numerous.[84] Taunton, with 5,794 inhabitants in 1801, had four book societies in 1791, one of which, recently established, was confined to ladies.[85] There was another ladies' book club in Penzance in 1770.[86] Perhaps the best-known is the Botesdale Book Club. With between eleven and fifteen members, it bought 454 books in 12 years, although average attendance at the monthly meetings was quite low and only a small handful of members borrowed books at all regularly. It subscribed to Martin's *History of Thetford*, published in 1779, together with book clubs and societies at Bungay, Diss and Eye and the Thetford Royal George book society.[87] The Huntingdon book club, founded in 1742, held its monthly meeting on the Tuesday before the full moon at the George inn, where dinner was to be on the table at 3 o'clock. This club accumulated a library over the years, and by 1790 had had a total of 218 members.[88] Other book clubs are known in Bamborough, Beccles, Dover, Lichfield, Repton, Tamworth, Braintree, Boston, Spilsby and Sedbergh, as well as Appleby and Dalton-in-Furness. The book society at Sandwich subscribed to Hasted's *History of Kent* (1778), as well as to Burney's *General History of Music* (1776), whilst the book society at Bungay subscribed to Burney, to Martin and to Gillingswater's *History of Lowestoft* (1790), giving it a life of at least fourteen years. The longest-lasting book club, however, seems to be that at Clavering. Founded in 1786 it did not come to an end until 1932.[89] The other side of the coin is revealed in the accounts of the Cirencester bookseller Timothy Stevens.[90] He supplied 561

---

[82] Cf. P. Kaufman, 'English Book Clubs and their Social Import', in his *Libraries and their Users* (1969), pp. 36–64.

[83] F. Beckwith, 'The Eighteenth Century Proprietary Library in England, *Journal of Documentation*, vol. 3 (1947), 81–98.

[84] See J. Lackington, *Memoirs of the First Forty-Five Years of the Life of James Lackington* (1792), pp. 387–8, and C. E. Whiting, ed., 'The Diary of Arthur Jessop', in 'Two Yorkshire Diaries', *Yorkshire Archaeological Society, Record Series*, vol. 117 (1952), pp. 25, 59, 76, 77, etc.

[85] J. Toulmin, *The History of the Town of Taunton* (1791), p. 187.

[86] Kaufman, *English Book Clubs*, p. 39.

[87] Kaufman, *English Book Clubs*, pp. 46–8, and the subscription list to S. Denne, *The History and Antiquities of Rochester* (1772). For some account of the book club at Beccles see M. Ellwood, 'Library Provision in a Small Market Town, 1700–1929', *Library History*, vol. 5 (1979–81), 48–54.

[88] Kaufman, *English Book Clubs*, pp. 48–51.

[89] P. Kaufman, 'A Bookseller's Record of Eighteenth Century Book Clubs', *The Library*, 5th Ser., vol. 15 (1960), 278–87.

[90] Kaufman, 'Bookseller's Record'.

titles to three book clubs, at Cirencester, Fairford and Bibury, including 56 to the club at Cirencester in 1791 alone. Only the Fairford book club, however, bought any novels, and then only *The Mysteries of Udolpho* in 1794. The impact of these clubs is difficult to measure, but writing of Tewkesbury in 1798 William Dyde said, 'that which above all evinces the superior taste and good sense of the town and neighbourhood is the establishment of a Reading Society; a certain criterion of elegant refinement'.[91]

There were yet even more specialised societies. Lichfield had a Society of Gardeners by 1769.[92] Faversham Farmers' Club dates from before 1750,[93] whilst that at Boston was certainly in existence by 1819.[94] On the other hand, there do not appear to have been any entomological societies, often called Aurelian Clubs, outside London before 1800.[95]

Attorneys and physicians lie at the dividing line between economic and cultural roles, since their services had an economic value as well as an intellectual component. They often, but not always, formed part of the social elite of small towns, but were by no means possessed of a monopoly of either intellectual interests or attainments. Some physicians, apothecaries and surgeons became men of wealth, building houses in the classical style to suit their position in society. Thus the fine house at 203 High Street Lewes was built in 1735 for Dr John Snashall, and the subtle interplay between cultural, social and economic roles is well summed up in Thomas Baskerville's comments upon Bury St Edmunds during the reign of Charles II. It is because the gentry do much frequent there, he wrote, that there are five physicians, that the apothecaries' shops are large and full of good drugs and the milliners' shops full of rich wares.[96]

The interaction between the professions in the intellectual life of small towns in eighteenth-century England is illustrated in the career of Thomas Martin.[97] He was the son of the rector of Thetford, who was also the master of the school there. Thomas attended this school and then was apprenticed as an attorney to his brother. In due course he went to live at

---

[91] Dyde, *Tewkesbury* p. 81.
[92] *VCH Staffordshire*, vol. 14 (1990), 164. William Stukeley describes how he erected a botanic club at Boston in 1710, 'to go out simpling once a week with the apothecaries'. Lukis, ed., 'Family memoirs', vol. I (1882), p. 122.
[93] H. S. A. Fox, 'Local Farmers' Associations and the circulation of agricultural information in nineteenth century England', in H. S. A. Fox and R. A. Butlin, eds., *Change in the Countryside; Essays on Rural England, 1500–1900* (1979), p. 58, n. 25.
[94] Lincolnshire County Archives, Boston Borough Archives, 12/7.
[95] See E. B. Ford, *Butterflies* (1945, 1990 reprint), p. 26.
[96] HMC, *Portland MSS*, vol. II (1893), p. 265.
[97] There are some very acid comments about him in Lukis, ed., 'Family memoirs', vol. I (1882), where, p. 388, he is described as 'very communicative, but at the same time very indolent', and p. 407, where, it is said, 'nothing can fix his thoughts or stay his motions but a bottle of old nog'.

Palgrave, where he practised as an attorney. He married as his second wife the widow of the antiquary Peter le Neve. He wrote a history of Thetford, which a chemist of Diss and a bookseller of Harleston unsuccessfully tried to publish. It eventually appeared in 1779, the year after his death.

The study of the antiquities and history of small towns rather than large ones develops only very slowly before 1800. The earliest history of a small town was *The Survey and Antiquitie of the Towne of Stamford*, by Richard Butcher, published in 1646. By 1800 histories of Harwich, Richmond (Yorks), Ripon, Bideford, Dunwich, Evesham, Thetford, Leominster, Lewes, Nantwich and Sandwich had appeared. The authors of these works came from varied backgrounds and their works are of very uneven quality. Samuel Dale, who died in 1739, was a distinguished physician who practised in Braintree. His principal work is *Pharmacologia*, of 1693, the first comprehensive survey of the subject, but almost as important is his appendix to Silas Taylor's *History and Antiquities of Harwich and Dovercourt*, published in 1730, and a comprehensive account of the natural history of the area. William Boys was a surgeon of Sandwich who was as much interested in antiquarian studies as in his medical practice. His *Collections for an History of Sandwich* was published in 1792 'at much pecuniary loss'. Guidebooks also begin to appear by the end of the eighteenth century, to Cromer, for example, and to Blackpool.

Many small towns also had booksellers and printers on an irregular basis.[98] Some were specialist booksellers, but others, like Abraham Dent of Kirby Stephen, sold books as part of the general merchandise in a very miscellaneous stock,[99] and Henry Purefoy, of Shalstone, in Buckinghamshire, bought his books in the 1730s through a Brackley bookseller who was also a baker.[100] Michael Johnson, of Lichfield,[101] was apprenticed to a London bookseller and returned to set up in Lichfield as bookseller, binder and stationer. He had stalls from time to time in the markets of the surrounding towns, including Uttoxeter, where his famous son once refused to serve, and then, fifty years later, stood there in the rain for an hour as penance for his ungraciousness. Michael Johnson found it increasingly difficult to sustain his business, and when he died he was worth little more than £60, of which his son received £20.

Many booksellers were also printers and some of the more enterprising published newspapers. By 1760 newspapers had appeared in 11 small towns, including Stamford, established in 1710, St Ives in 1717 and

---

[98] Plomer, *Dictionaries*.   [99] See T. S. Willan, *An Eighteenth Century Shopkeeper* (1970).
[100] L. G. Mitchell, ed., *The Purefoy Letters, 1735–1753* (1973), pp. 166–7.
[101] See Walter Jackson Bate, *Samuel Johnson* (1978), p. 129.

Cirencester in 1718, although only a small proportion of these news-papers lasted for more than a year or two.[102] Booksellers often owned circulating libraries. One of the earliest known is that of George Barton, a bookseller of Huntingdon who also had branches in Peterborough, St Ives and St Neots. He, like Abraham Dent, sold a wide range of merchandise in his shops, and also let out books to read by the week, according to an advertisement in the *St Ives Postboy* in 1718.[103] Other booksellers acted as agents for newspapers. Thus the *York Mercury* was sold in Thirsk, Northallerton, Malton, Ripon, Richmond, Wetherby, Selby, Skipton, Yarm, Knaresborough and Settle.[104] John Cheney, printer of Banbury, followed yet another occupation. He kept the Unicorn inn up to the time of his death in 1808.[105]

Printers and booksellers also made a significant contribution to the publi-cation of histories of small towns during the eighteenth century. The histories of Tewkesbury of 1790 and Stockton-on-Tees of 1796 were printed in their home towns and John Price's *History of Leominster* was printed in Ludlow in 1795. William Harrod was the son of a printer and bookseller of Market Harborough, a man who was also master of the free school there. He set up as a printer successively in Stamford, Mansfield and then Market Harborough, and he wrote and published histories of all three of these towns, Stamford in 1785, Mansfield in 1786 and Market Harbo-rough in 1808.

It is particularly difficult to find comprehensive material relating to the cultural role of small towns and the anecdotal evidence is fragmentary and uneven, factors which make the Posse Comitatus for Buckinghamshire in 1798 particularly valuable.[106] Here are lists of the male inhabitants aged between 16 and 60, together with a note of their occupations, for the 14 places which may rank as small towns (see Table 6.1).

Similar listings survive for other small towns, although none on a county-wide scale. Two may be summarised here. Brampton in Cumberland, had (in 1794) 1,951 inhabitants, including a chemist and druggist, a fiddlemaker, two musicians, three surgeons and apothecaries, an attorney and two clergy-

---

[102] See G. A. Cranfield, *The Development of the Provincial Newspaper, 1700–1760* (1962), and R. M. Wiles, *Freshest Advices* (Ohio, 1965), esp. Appendices B and C, pp. 373ff.

[103] P. Kaufman, *Libraries and their Users* (1960), Plate 17.

[104] Wiles, *Freshest Advices*, p. 511.

[105] *VCH Oxfordshire*, vol. 10 (1972), p. 65.

[106] I. F. W. Beckett, ed., 'The Buckinghamshire Posse Comitatus', 1798, *Buckinghamshire Record Society*, vol. 22 (1985). The material for Buckinghamshire towns is considered in more detail in M. Reed, 'Decline and Recovery in a Provincial Urban Network: Bucking-hamshire Towns, 1350–1800', in M. Reed, ed., *English Towns in Decline 1350–1800*, Centre for Urban History, University of Leicester, Working Papers No. 1 (1986).

Table 6.1. *Cultural role of Buckinghamshire small towns 1798*

	Attorney	Physician	Surgeon	Book-seller	Printer	School-master
Aylesbury	4	1	2	1	1	2
Princes Risborough	1		2			1
Wendover						2
Brill	1 apothecary					
Buckingham	1		3		1	2
	1 bookbinder	1 dancing master				
Amersham	2		5			2
Chesham	1					2
Beaconsfield	3		1			1
Winslow	2		3			2
Marlow	3		2			4
	1 dancing master	1 limner				
High Wycombe	2		4		1	1
Newport Pagnell	3		4		1	9
	1 quack doctor					
Olney	1 bookbinder					2
Stony Stratford	4		2			2
	1 musician					

men.[107] At Harleston, in Norfolk, in 1789, there were 1,344 inhabitants, including three surgeons, three attorneys, a bookseller and the rector.[108]

The cultural role of small towns has up to this point been studied through an assemblage of anecdotal evidence and although this may illustrate the diversity of their cultural world it also indicates how intermittent and particularistic was the role of any one centre. In order to study this cultural role in action we need to examine the records of some of the families who made use of the facilities of small towns.

The Earls and Dukes of Rutland have lived at Belvoir Castle in Leicestershire since 1528. Their household accounts for the early seventeenth century reveal the interaction of regional and local cultural centres.[109] In October 1592 payments were made to John Mathewe of Nottingham for new painting of divers pictures and hanging them in the long gallery. In May 1594 three psalm books were bought at Newark fair 'for my yong masters', and in 1607 physicians were sent for from Newark and Notting-

---

[107] W. Hutchinson, *The History of the County of Cumberland*, vol. I (1794, 1974 reprint), pp. 130–1. See also D. J. W. Mawson, 'Brampton in the 1790s', *Transactions of the Cumberland and Westmorland Antiquarian and Archaeological Society*, 2nd. Ser., vol. 73 (1973), 299–316.

[108] A. Young, *A General View of the Agriculture of Norfolk* (1804, 1969 reprint), p. 111.

[109] See, HMC, *Rutland MSS*, vol. 4 (1905).

ham. Indeed physicians came quite frequently from Newark, save in November 1614 when it was found necessary to send all the way to Newport Pagnell for one. The waits of Grantham played at the castle during the New Year festivities of January 1608 and a Grantham bearward brought his bears to be baited in January of 1610. A Nottingham craftsman mended a cithern and a lute in December 1617, and the choristers of Southwell minster sang at the funeral of Roger Earl of Rutland at Bottisford church in July 1612. Another Nottingham craftsman mended the organ in 1664.

The Harpur family was established at Calke in south Derbyshire by the beginning of the seventeenth century. Sir John Harpur succeeded to the title in 1681, when he was little more than a year old. The long and prudent management of his estates by his trustees left him with a substantial landed estate and an income of between £4,000 and £5,000 a year when he came of age. The family had no pretensions to notoriety, political importance or intellectual distinction. It is from the detailed, day-to-day account books kept by their stewards that a picture of the cultural role of small towns in the life of a country gentleman of considerable means in the first half of the eighteenth century can be drawn.[110] Sir John Harpur bought a London house, 19 St James's Place, in February 1705 for £930 and spent several months there each year, usually in the first part of the year, from January to May, but this could vary from one year to the next.

In the first decade of the eighteenth century Sir John was rebuilding his house at Calke. Payments for the work are scattered through the steward's accounts in a random manner so that it is difficult to arrive at firm date for the building, an exact cost, or to discover who was responsible for designing it. The actual building contractor, however, was a Mr Gilks of Burton-upon-Trent. Stone was quarried locally, bricks were made from clay found on the estate and timber was felled in the park. In all of this there is nothing unusual. All great country houses were built by contractors, often closely supervised by their owners, many of whom prided themselves upon their undoubtedly wide and genuine knowledge of the principles of 'polite', that is to say classical, architecture, whilst the actual building materials were produced locally, not least because of the costs of transport. For the furnishings and fittings it was a different matter. Sir John ordered his marble chimney pieces from London, the carriage of three of them cost him £2 1s. in September of 1701. Glass for the windows also came from London, 1,700 squares of it in March 1703 and a further 1,200 in February 1704. The carriers' network was clearly both extensive and reliable in early eighteenth-century England.

---

[110] Derbyshire County Record Office, Harpur-Crewe MSS. D 2375 M 277/3–11, a series of account books from 1701 to 1752.

In June 1702 he paid Mr London £2 3s. for his garden draught, and bought his seeds, trees and plants in London. In March of 1713 he paid Mr London £14 2s. for 5,500 hornbeam sets to send to Calke. In 1727 he paid Mr Gibbs for designing the garden steps and subscribed two guineas to his book on architecture. He also bought his wine in London. One of the first things he did upon his arrival in London each year was to go down to Wapping to taste and choose his wine. He was buying Burgundy and Champagne in 1708. By 1735, however, he was buying plants and seeds locally, 400 asparagus plants, Scots pine and yew trees from Melbourne in Derbyshire, yew trees and horse chestnuts from Newark, and his wine was coming from King's Lynn. In all of this Sir John and his family reveal themselves as rich and fashionable, enjoying a wide circle of friends and taking full advantage of everything which a rapidly developing consumer society could offer, making little distinction between London, provincial capitals and small towns when it came to seeking out what was needed. He subscribed to bowling greens in Ashby-de-la-Zouch and in Derby, where he also went to the play and where his daughter went to the assembly rooms. He subscribed to the *Stamford Mercury* newspaper and to a Gentlemen's Club in Tamworth. He went to race meetings in Guildford and Newmarket, Lichfield and Grantham. Ease and convenience of access appear to have been the overriding consideration.

Sir John sent his sons to school in Tamworth. The eldest, Henry, was entered under Dr Shaw in October 1716. He was then eight, and Dr Shaw had been headmaster of Tamworth Grammar School since 1708. He and the previous headmaster had given the school a good reputation, and it was frequented by the sons of the local gentry, a number of whom boarded there, including the young Henry Harpur. A year's board and tuition, together with board for his servant, amounted to between £25 and £30 a year. By September 1715 two of the boys were there, together with a servant, Mrs Betty, and the bill came to £52 for the year. Both dancing and singing lessons were extra. By 1725 a manservant was also being maintained there, and a horse for the boys to ride. Books to be sent to Tamworth were bought from Mr Johnson of Lichfield in December of 1728. In 1730 Dr Shaw died, and Sir John gave ten guineas towards his funeral expenses.

Sir John Harpur does not appear to have sent his daughters away to school. Nevertheless there are payments for lessons on the spinet, and payments to writing masters. In May 1726 Mr Phebush was paid for teaching Miss Harpur. He was probably John Christopher Pepusch (1667–1752), a German musician settled in London since about 1697 and chiefly remembered today as the arranger of the music for *The Beggar's Opera*. Mr Basano was also paid for giving lessons on the spinet, and in 1741 he was paid, not only for tuning the instrument but also for 'collecting and drawing out' Sir John's pedigree. Local musicians and ringers played a large part in the life of the family when it was at Calke. Waits from Derby, Ashby and Uttoxeter were employed from time to time to play country dances, especially at Christmas and New Year, at birthdays and weddings. Ringers in parish churches in the region were also paid on special occasions. When Sir John came of age in 1701 the bells were rung in twenty towns and villages in the neighbourhood of Calke.

The final personal record to be studied is the well-known diary of John Woodforde, lasting from 1758 until 1802.[111] His unselfconscious entries reveal village and small-town life within the orbit of a regional centre, since he lived for the greater part of his career at Weston Longville, about ten miles north-west of Norwich. He visited that city from time to time, especially at the beginning of each year, in order to pay his tradesmen, including his wine merchant, tailor, breeches maker, upholsterer, iron-monger, builder, brazier, coal merchant and tea merchant. At the same time he usually took the opportunity of going to a play. Norwich had a theatre at this time, but Woodforde also saw strolling players perform in the court house at Castle Cary, in Somerset, where his brother lived. He also bought goods from travelling pedlars and other tradesmen who called from time to time with carts laden with linens, cottons, laces and handkerchiefs, clearly in large quantities, since on one occasion he bought 25 yards of Holland for shirts. From other dealers he bought fish, wooden clocks, barometers, pottery and earthenware, and occasionally books. He also shopped at Odham Green, and shopkeepers from Reepham and Wymondham called occasionally to take orders. On a visit to Salisbury in 1786 he attended the Music Meeting. He travelled fairly frequently, and made great use of the stage coach and carriers' networks. It was through the medium of prints that he came to know something of the work of his nephew Samuel, since he was able to buy two prints of his pictures in a shop in Norwich in June 1787. His nephew's expenses to go to Italy to study painting had been paid by Richard Hoare of Stourhead.

All three of these examples demonstrate that the cultural functions of small towns were very real, but they also show that the functions of individual towns were by no means discrete. Instead they interlocked with other towns, large and small, at local, regional and indeed national levels. Individuals made use of them to suit their own changing needs over an area which grew ever wider as transport technology slowly improved and as the range of facilities available in small towns expanded, with the result that it is impossible to set precise limts to the *empire minuscule* of even the smallest of small towns.

---

[111] J. Beresford, ed., *The Diary of a Country Parson*, 5 vols. (1924–1931).

How may the cultural role of small towns between 1600 and 1800 best be characterised? The two meanings given to the phrase 'cultural role' clearly interact in a most subtle and complex manner. The broader socio-economic meaning finds expression through the shops which no eighteenth-century town, however small, was without, and secondly through the rebuilding following classical themes which is so striking a feature of eighteenth-century cultural life. Shops and their contents, houses with Tuscan columns and Venetian windows are, it is suggested, significant parts of the total range of artefacts available to seventeenth- and eighteenth-century society. They are to be found everywhere, and make a permanent contribution to the cultural role of every small town.

It is more difficult to be so precise about the narrower meaning given to 'cultural role'. It was clearly much more particularistic and very much more dependent upon the inclinations of individuals (William Stukeley was obviously a very 'clubbable' man) as well as upon changes in fashion, taste and intellectual preoccupations. This narrower cultural role finds expression through a number of formal institutions, including the church, however defined, through schools, theatres, clubs and societies, as well as through the professions, whether attorneys or physicians, printers or booksellers. It is clear that most small towns saw a slow accumulation of cultural activities over time, a process which appears to accelerate during the course of the eighteenth century. A crude outline chronology may be suggested. The church and schools were in place by 1600. Important structural changes take place in both institutions during the course of the seventeenth and eighteenth centuries. The professions are also in place by 1600 but the number of practitioners expands rapidly during the period. Theatres, clubs and societies, however, are essentially of the eighteenth century.

At present neither regional nor functional variations in the distribution of these activities can be detected. But the range of cultural activities is likely to be a function of population size, so that it may be possible in due course to construct scalograms setting cultural function against population size at different points in time in much the same way as has been done for the occupational structure of East Anglian towns.[112] It is also very likely that future research will show a close correlation between economic prosperity and cultural function, since basically this chapter has been concerned to describe some of the ways in which seventeenth- and eighteenth-century townspeople spent their disposable incomes.

It has not proved possible in this essay to find room to consider every aspect of the cultural role of small towns. Friendly societies,[113] town

---

[112] J. Patten, *English Towns, 1500–1700* (1978), pp. 273, 283.
[113] See Marshall, 'Rise and transformation', pp. 185–7. For Friendly societies in Devizes see *VCH Wiltshire*, vol. 10 (1975), 300.

libraries,[114] Freemasons' lodges,[115] Sunday schools[116] and circulating libraries[117] have been omitted, although they were undoubtedly to be found in small towns, especially from the second half of the eighteenth century. Town libraries are known from the early seventeenth century, circulating libraries and Freemasons' lodges appear to date from the early eighteenth century, and Friendly societies and Sunday schools from the last half of that century, but unfortunately knowledge about their diffusion remains very patchy and uneven. It is probably true to say, however, that only Chichester[118] among the small towns considered in this chapter developed any kind of role as a centre for painting in the same way that York[119] did early in the eighteenth century or Norwich[120] in the second half of that century.

That the cultural role of small towns in the seventeenth and eighteenth centuries was varied and wide-ranging must now be apparent. That it was sometimes trivial and often lacking in the depth and stability that a sustained tradition could bring to regional and metropolitan centres must equally be apparent. Its significance is equally difficult to evaluate. On the one hand there is the remark of William Stukeley: 'in my situation at Stamford there was not one person, clergy or lay, that had any taste or love of learning or ingenuity, so that I was as much dead in converse as in a coffin',[121] and on the other the comment of James Lackington, who wrote of circulating libraries that 'from those repositories many thousand families have been cheaply supplied with books, by which the taste for reading has become much more general'.[122] These are but assertions based upon personal experience, qualitative judgements upon a range of human activity which lies beyond quantification. To claim some cultural significance for the presence of two or three successful shopkeepers, a clergyman, physician or attorney with a taste for conversation, an interest in antiquities and with wives and daughters fond of dancing may seem to be both presumptuous and unwarranted, but it must also be apparent that life could be interesting, sometimes exciting and often stimulating for many of those who actually lived in the small towns of seventeenth- and eighteenth-century England.

---

[114] There was a town library in the south choir of St Mary, Stamford. R. Butcher, *The Survey and Antiquitie of the Towne of Stamford* (1646), p. 35.

[115] On Freemasonry in Marlborough see *VCH Wiltshire*, vol. 12 (1983), 204–5. The ubiquitous William Stukeley set up a lodge of Freemasons in Grantham in 1726. See Lukis, ed., 'Family memoirs', vol. I (1882), p. 123.

[116] See Unwin, 'Tradition', p. 103.

[117] Cromer in 1806 had a 'small circulating library consisting of a few novels'. E. Bartell, *Cromer Considered as a Watering Place* (2nd edn, 1806), p. 23.

[118] See Hay, *Chichester*, p. 532, and B. Stewart, *The Smith Brothers of Chichester* (1986).

[119] H. Honour, 'York Virtuosi', *Apollo*, vol. 65 (1957), 143.

[120] A. W. Moore, *The Norwich School of Artists* (1985).

[121] Lukis, ed., 'Family memoirs', vol. I (1882), p. 109.

[122] Lackington, *James Lackington*, p. 388.

7   Small towns in early modern Ireland

Raymond Gillespie

Those who drew up schemes for the reformation of Ireland in the sixteenth century may have disagreed on the approach to and implementation of reform programmes but most agreed on one point. Ireland lacked a sufficient urban base from which reform could proceed. Consequently almost all plans for the reform of the government of Ireland included a provision for the creation of towns of all sizes. At the simplest level administrators saw towns functioning primarily as garrisons to protect the surrounding countryside. As the Earl of Surrey commented as early as 1521, 'as ever, as the countries shall fortune to be won, strong towns and fortresses must be builded upon the same'.[1] Throughout the sixteenth century official and unofficial plans to protect the borders of the limits of English settlement in Ireland included a strong urban dimension. The formal plantations of the midland counties of Leix and Offaly in 1556 had provision for the creation of garrison towns at Maryborough and Philipstown. These new towns were also to act as administrative centres for the two newly created counties. Similarly at the north-eastern tip of the English pale the town of Newry was created by Nicholas Bagenal in an attempt to reduce hostile incursions into the pale by native Irish from the north. Further west, the mid-sixteenth-century plantation of Roscommon created new settlements at the medieval centres of Roscommon castle and Boyle abbey.[2]

In the course of the sixteenth century plans for the political and economic reform of Ireland became increasingly sophisticated and the role envisaged for towns became more complex. The spread of the market economy, which was part of the reform package, created a new role for towns. Outside the pale, in the provinces of Ulster and Connacht, the Gaelic economy was not commercialised to any great extent. Surpluses were usually redistributed not through merchants at a price but rather through renders or 'cearts' –

---

[1] Constantia Maxwell (ed.), *Irish History from Contemporary Sources* (1923), p. 90.
[2] Vincent Carey, 'Gaelic reaction to Plantation', MA Thesis, St Patrick's College, Maynooth, 1985, pp. 21–2; Harold O'Sullivan, 'A 1575 Rent Roll with Contemporaneous Maps of the Bagenal Estate in the Carlingford District', *Louth Archaeological and Historical Journal*, vol. 21 (1985), 31–47.

food, livestock, hospitality or even gold – to the local lord, within a lordship system. In return, services such as the administration of justice were provided by the lord, and surpluses were further redistributed by hospitality offered by a lord to his freeholders and followers, thus creating a mutual bond of obligation. There was, of course, some trading with the outside world but it was limited and the only town created by a native Gaelic lord was the O'Reilly's town of Cavan. This particular creation was doubly significant since the O'Reillys went as far as to strike their own coinage.[3]

The destruction of the complex Gaelic lordship system was one of the main aims of the English reform programmes in Ireland because the system encouraged ties of obligation which appeared similar to those of the 'over-mighty lords' of England. The commercial system with which that of lordship was to be replaced was a network of markets. As one Dublin official put it in 1611, 'it is confessed necessary that all merchandise shall be sold only in set markets'. The rationale for this move was simple. Markets operated within a well-defined legal structure which ensured that property rights were protected. Markets also promoted specialisation which would play a part in generating wealth. This would benefit not only the settlers but the native Irish also. 'Markets increase commerce', it was noted, 'and procures one produce to be brought for sale for the buying of another, which tends that [he] that hath access to the market shall be more readily furnished with commodities wherein to employ his money and so the seller is furnished with money to buy'.[4]

Some contemporaries took this argument one stage further and contended that such growth was the best way to pacify the native Irish who would not jeopardise new-found wealth by rebellion.[5] Towns, large and small, were seen as centres of civility which would set the standard of behaviour required from the native Irish who would, when attending markets and other urban events, observe and learn by example. Thus the divisions which separated native and newcomer such as language, dress, and above all religion, could be eliminated and a 'commonwealth' created. As Edmund Spenser, poet and Munster settler, wrote

for nothing doth sooner cause civility in any country than many market towns, by reason that the people repairing often thither for their needs will daily see and learn civil manners . . . besides there is nothing doth more stay and strengthen the country

---

[3] Raymond Gillespie, *The Transformation of the Irish Economy, 1550–1700* (Dundalk, 1991), pp. 3–4, 22–3, 24–9.
[4] *Calendar of the Carew Manuscripts, 1603–24*, p. 205.
[5] For example, British Library [hereafter B. L.], Additional Ms 12490, f. 119; B. L., Additional Ms 39853, f. 12v.

than ... corporate towns ... and lastly there do nothing more enrich the country ... than many towns.[6]

This view was regularly echoed throughout the seventeenth century. A dissertation written in the early 1640s reflected on the significance of the creation of markets and fairs in the social changes: 'they had placed markets and fairs throughout the land whereby the dilligent may make use of their labours and whereby the commerce and intercourse would advantage and incorporate the people'. The writer also commented on the economic effect of towns, noting that in the early seventeenth century land in the pale was worth 6/– to 10/– an acre 'and near some towns of good habitation 15/– is offered'.[7]

Despite the importance attached by contemporaries to towns, both large and small, in the settlement of early modern Ireland, they have received little attention from historians. In part this is the consequence of an archival problem. Most of the evidence which survives for Ireland in the sixteenth and seventeenth centuries is from the perspective of the central government. Thus we know a good deal about the plans which were made for the buildings of towns as part of plantation schemes but we know much less about the reality of urban life. Few corporation books dating from before the eighteenth century have survived, and this scarcity of information makes the description of urban government and society in Ireland difficult. More seriously, the fragmentary nature of early modern estate collections for Ireland and the almost total absence of manorial court material limits our understanding of the workings of non-corporate towns.[8] However, the problem is not entirely an archival one. Much material does survive which would permit the identification of small towns and offer some insights into their workings although it is not easy to recognise the existence of viable small towns in, for example, poll tax listings or grants of market rights. English definitions of size and range of urban function are of little help here since we are comparing the mature economy of England, which had a complex and relatively developed urban network, with a society in which towns were only beginning to emerge and where commercial life was poorly developed. This chapter attempts to establish parameters for the definition of the small town in early modern Ireland, to identify these settlements from contemporary taxation returns and to explain how these small towns evolved during the early modern period.

In trying to find ways of locating small towns in the early modern Irish landscape one of the easiest of urban functions to identify is that of the

---

[6] Edmund Spenser, *A View of the Present State of Ireland*, ed. W. L. Renwick (Oxford, 1970), p. 165.

[7] B. L., Additional Ms 4777, f. 65v, 66v.

[8] For example, Brian O'Dalaigh (ed.), *Corporation Book of Ennis* (Dublin, 1990), pp. 349–61.

Table 7.1. *Grants of market rights in seventeenth-century Ireland**

	1600–19	1620–39	1640–59	1660–79	1680–99	Total
Ulster	76	75	0	18	10	179
Munster	95	34	1	16	10	156
Connacht	83	37	1	12	9	142
Leinster	70	52	1	46	30	199
Total	324	198	3	92	59	676

* These figures refer only to sites and multiple grants for one site are not included.
Source: Report of the commissioners appointed to enquire into the state of fairs and markets in Ireland, Parliamentary papers, [1674] H.C., 1852–3, lxi, appendix.

Table 7.2. *Survivals of seventeenth-century grants of market rights in Ireland to 1850*

	All markets		Survival to c. 1850	
	No.	Density*	No.	Density*
Ulster	179	30.48	64	83.94
Munster	156	38.22	33	186.33
Connacht	142	29.79	27	156.69
Leinster	199	24.38	47	131.12

* Density is expressed as thousand acres per market. Comparative figures for seventeenth-century England are 45.0, and Wales 100.0
Source: As Table 7.1

market. Grants of the right to hold markets were made in large numbers to settlers in seventeenth-century Ireland (Table 7.1).[9]

However, the granting of a market patent is not evidence of urban activity or even evidence that a market was ever held and there was a very large number of speculative grants. Many of these markets failed to establish a firm base and survive into the nineteenth century. There was a process of natural attrition. Had all the markets created in seventeenth-century Ireland survived, Ireland would have been almost twice as densely served by markets as was England. Taking only those markets granted patents in the seventeenth century which survived into the early nineteenth century

[9] Patrick O'Flanagan, 'Markets and Fairs in Ireland, 1600–1800: an Index of Economic Development and Regional Growth', *Journal of Historical Geography*, vol. 11 (1985), 364–78.

gives a density more in line with seventeenth-century Wales, which would seem more appropriate to the Irish situation (Table 7.2).[10]

While the creation and survival of market rights is not a direct measure of small town growth the pattern it reveals highlights the instability and, outside the pale, the fast growth of market centres in the previously undeveloped west and north of Ireland. While it was relatively easy to plan for towns in these regions, either as part of a formal plantation scheme or as part of informal settlements, it was more difficult to ensure that they developed in the longer term. It is hardly surprising that there was a high failure rate of newly founded towns. Many of the sites chosen were unsuitable for urban centres but it is significant that of all the sites of market grants which did not survive to the mid-nineteenth century, between 34 per cent in Ulster and 43 per cent in Munster had a fair on that site in the mid-nineteenth century. In many centres where it did not prove possible to establish a regular market a more seasonal fair, which did not require a permanent urban infrastructure, proved a practicable proposition.

While grants of market rights can provide evidence for a broad geographical outline and chronology of the foundation of small towns in seventeenth-century Ireland, they are fundamentally unsatisfactory because it is not clear from the market grants what the relative importance of the towns was or what size they attained. To resolve this problem it is necessary to examine taxation records to identify the small-town populations. The problem with this approach is that of specifying the range of population which constitutes a small town and so identifying such agglomerations in poll tax returns. English small towns, defined as having a population up to 2,500 at the end of the seventeenth century, have no exact parallel in Ireland. Since most towns outside Leinster and south Munster were new foundations, they took a considerable period of time to establish themselves and consequently most were regarded as little more than villages in English terms. Many contemporaries commented on the small scale of even the largest Irish towns. James Verdon, rector of East Dereham in Norfolk, travelling through Ireland in 1699, noted, 'In the cities and great towns as they call them, though I saw none bigger than Market Deerham nor none so good, except Dublin, the people are civilised, do like christians but in the country they are barbarous in all points.'[11] In other comparisons with their English counterparts small Irish towns did not fare well. In county Cavan, Belturbet was described in the 1630s as 'built as one of our ordinary market towns . . . in England'. Cavan, the county town, was half the size of Belturbet, and Kilmore, the seat of the bishop, 'but a mere

[10] Joan Thirsk (ed.), *The Agrarian History of England and Wales*, vol. IV (Cambridge, 1967), pp. 467–9.
[11] B. L., Additional Ms 41769, f. 40.

country village'.[12] Many areas were insufficiently developed to support an urban centre of any size. Thus, for example, the corporate town of St Johnston in county Donegal could muster only 37 poll tax payers in 1660. Similarly, in the relatively poor midland county of Longford, Granard had 44 tax payers and the Longford borough of St Johnston had 47.[13]

The problem of defining an appropriate urban size is compounded by the archival problem of a shortage of taxation or other population listings which would reveal urban clusters. Only one document from the seventeenth century provides an almost country-wide survey which would enable the identification of small town populations – the so-called '1659 census'. This document is not without its problems.[14] It records the number of people, at townland level, for most areas in the country. However, five counties, Mayo, Galway, Cavan, Tyrone and Wicklow, are missing, as are four baronies in county Cork, and for county Meath the figures for only three baronies have survived. Estimates of the overall population of the missing areas have been attempted. Estimation of the urban population in those areas is not possible, although other evidence would suggest it was small. In some areas, such as the Lagan valley in east Ulster, the data is aggregated to such a high level that it is not possible to identify the population of individual small towns.

The situation is further complicated by uncertainty about the nature of the document. It appears to be an abstract of the poll money returns for 1660. It therefore provides only a partial listing of the Irish population including only adults over 15 years but excluding married women. It is impossible to know what regional multipliers to apply to inflate the poll return to total population although a working estimate of 2.5 has been suggested. Here only the recorded taxable population will be referred to. All these limitations of the source mean that any calculations based on the return must be treated as rough approximations but they are the best we are likely to find.

One advantage of the '1659 census' is that the larger corporate towns are usually dealt with separately and this enables an upper limit to be set for the small-town population at 500 taxable persons. Twenty Irish towns had taxable populations of over 500 and all were large corporate towns. Adding in estimates for the missing counties the proportion of the taxable population living in such centres can be calculated at between 7.6 per cent and 9.6 per cent, as opposed to about 15 per cent in equivalent urban centres in late seventeenth-century England (Table 7.3).

---

[12] E. S. Shuckburgh (ed.), *Two Biographies of William Bedell* (Cambridge, 1902), p. 57.

[13] Seamus Pender (ed.), *A Census of Ireland c. 1659* (Dublin, 1939), pp. 50, 457, 459.

[14] Pender (ed.), *Census*. For a discussion of the problems and potentials of this document, W. J. Smyth, 'Society and Settlement in Seventeenth Century Ireland: the Evidence of the

Table 7.3. *Large urban populations in Ireland c. 1659*

	n	Urban pop.	Max. % urban	Min. % urban
Ulster	3	2,304	3.2	2.5
Munster	9	13,564	11.8	11.8
Connacht	1	1,075	4.5	1.7
Leinster	7	14,701	11.5	9.2
Total	20	31,644	9.6	7.6

Source: Seamus Pender (ed.), *A Census of Ireland c. 1659* (Dublin, 1939).

Most large Irish towns in 1659 tended to be port towns, reflecting the importance of international trade, especially exports of live cattle, sheep, wool and timber, in the early seventeenth-century economy.[15] The town of Dungarvan in county Cork is a case in point. Trade dominated the occupational structure of the town, and of the landholding townsmen in the town's liberties in 1641 there was one husbandman, five gentlemen, three untitled and sixteen merchants.[16]

Having estabished a somewhat arbitrary upper limit for the taxable population in small towns, an equally arbitrary lower limit of 120 taxable persons has been taken as the cut-off point below which urban settlements should be classed as villages. This lower limit has been selected since nucleations below 120 taxable persons rarely show evidence of other urban functions, such as holding grants of market rights. Ninety-five small town settlements have been identified in this category of 120 to 500 taxable persons (Table 7.4). In all but ten of these the grant of a market patent has been traced, and all had patents for fairs. Thirty-four were corporate towns. Again, including estimates for areas missing in the census return, the share of the taxable population living in these small towns was between 4.5 per cent and 5.6 per cent of the Irish taxable population. Thus the total Irish urban population was probably no more than 15.2 per cent and probably not less than 12.1 per cent of the total Irish population; lower than most contemporary European countries. The evidence of the size distribution of towns further confirms the impression gained from travellers' accounts that the small towns tended to be very small, about 60 per cent having under 200 taxable inhabitants (Table 7.5).

While the evidence of the taxation records provides a more detailed

"1659 Census"', in W. J. Smyth and Kevin Whelan, eds, *Common Ground: Essays on the Historical Geography of Ireland* (Cork, 1988), pp. 55–7.

[15] Gillespie, *Transformation*, pp. 33–5.

[16] R. C. Simington (ed), *The Civil Survey*, vol. IV (Dublin, 1942), pp. 40–5.

Table 7.4. *Small urban populations in Ireland c. 1659*

	n	Urban pop.	Max. % urban	Min. % urban
Ulster	18	3,773	5.3	4.1
Munster	31	6,457	4.9	4.9
Connacht	6	1,578	6.6	2.6
Leinster	40	7,971	6.2	5.0
Total	95	19,779	5.6	4.5

Source: As Table 7.3.

Table 7.5. *Distribution of small-town sizes in Ireland c. 1659: taxable inhabitants*

	120–99	200–99	300–99	400–500	Total
Ulster	12	2	3	1	18
Munster	19	9	1	2	31
Connacht	2	2	1	1	6
Leinster	24	10	4	2	40
Total	57	23	9	6	95

Source: As Table 7.3.

survey of the urban hierarchy and the place of small towns within it, the picture drawn is a static one. An understanding of how the urban hierarchy of the mid-seventeenth century evolved and how it was to develop can only be provided by case studies of individual towns and regions of the urban network. One indication of the divergent origins and patterns of development in the network of small towns in Ireland is the radically different ethnic composition of those towns in different regions. It is possible to examine the ethnic composition of the urban population as revealed in the 'census' which classified the population as either settler or native, the latter including both the Gaelic and Old English communities (Table 7.6).

The ethnic composition of the towns points to the differing urban histories of the different regions of Ireland. In Ulster, for instance, towns, and the associated commercial economy, were a relatively recent settler innovation by the middle of the seventeenth century and the native population was slow to adjust to such an innovation. It was not that they did not live in towns; they did not even live near them. By the 1660s 90 per cent of settlers in Ulster lived within a five-mile radius of a market town while the native

Table 7.6. *Ethnic composition of Irish small towns, c. 1659*

	Urban native per settler	Rural natives per settler
Ulster	0.83	1.82
Munster	6.11	14.48
Connacht	2.85	15.84
Leinster	4.13	8.71
Total	3.01	15.84

Source: As Table 7.3.

Irish tended to live away from such towns.[17] In Leinster, by contrast, many more native Irish lived in towns, which is a reflection of the relative antiquity of the small Leinster towns. The pattern of urbanisation in Leinster was well established before the arrival of New English settlers in the sixteenth century, most of the towns being medieval in origin.[18] Of the 15 incorporated towns of medieval origin which can be categorised as 'small' in 1659, nine were in south Leinster and a further four in north Leinster. This group of towns was an integral part of the Kildare and Ormond lordships in the sixteenth century and extended in a band across Leinster and into north Munster but they can be subdivided into four main groups.

First, there were the small towns surrounding Dublin, such as Swords, Tallaght and Lusk which were market towns and centres for the administration of the estates of the archbishop of Dublin. Likewise Crumlin was the centre of a royal manor. These were mainly agricultural settlements but there are indications of trades such as smiths, shoemakers and tanners operating in them.[19] To the north of these towns lay a second group of small agricultural and trading towns. Ratoath, for example, was the site of a Norman settlement and the motte was still a prominent feature in the seventeenth century. In 1641 there were 85 tenements in the town owned by 20 individuals of whom all but four lived elsewhere.[20] These towns also lay on the borders of the pale in the sixteenth century and so acted as intermediaries between the native Irish and the merchants of the towns of Dundalk and Drogheda who sent their agents, the 'grey merchants', to trade with the native Irish. On a more negative note they were also subject to regular attack,

---

[17] Philip Robinson, *The Plantation of Ulster* (Dublin, 1985), pp. 167–8.
[18] Art Cosgrove (ed.), *A New History of Ireland*, vol. II (Oxford, 1987), pp. 232–9.
[19] For example, Herbert Wood (ed.), *The Court Book of the Liberty of St Sepulchre* (Dublin, 1930), pp. 7, 37, 59.
[20] R. C. Simington (ed.), *Civil Survey*, vol. V (Dublin, 1940), pp. 106–7.

which explains the 13 castles or urban tower houses in the town of Athboy in 1641.[21]

To the south of Dublin lay the third group of towns, including Naas, Kildare, Athy and Maynooth, which in the early sixteenth century acted as frontier towns bordering the territory of the native Irish. Most were heavily fortified and were frequently attacked. Although this position changed with the end of the Nine Years War in 1603, which ensured that the king's writ ran throughout the whole country, the fact that many of these towns were still garrisoned in the late seventeenth century is a reminder of their perilous origins. Despite this many had grown into substantial settlements. One account of the burning of Naas in 1577 recorded that 140 thatched houses were destroyed, reckoned to accommodate 500 persons.[22] Naas was a particularly sophisticated urban community with a guild system in the 1580s which continued into the late seventeenth century. Naas also had a wide circle of local trading contacts. Kilkenny freemen, for instance, claimed in the late sixteenth century that they could trade in Naas without paying local tolls.[23] The losses by one Naas merchant in 1641 included debts owed to him from Dublin, Carlow, Leix and Kildare. By 1641 the Naas merchants were dealing in a wide range of luxury goods for local consumption. One merchant, John Murphy of Athy, claimed losses in the rebellion which included ribbons, silks and other goods valued at £160.[24] While the depositions taken after the 1641 rising indicate that there was a wide range of trades in these north Kildare towns, such as carriers, smiths, merchants, skinners, weavers and clothiers, most of the towns remained closely integrated into the agricultural community and most urban dwellers included livestock and grain among their lists of losses.[25]

The nature of these north Kildare towns changed over the sixteenth and seventeenth centuries. The sixteenth-century settlement of Leix and Offaly moved the new frontier garrisons towns further west and the extension of royal authority in the seventeenth century meant they were no longer frontier settlements. The new towns of the Leix and Offaly plantations, such as Maryborough and Philipstown, were initially garrison towns but commercial and industrial centres were also developed by landlords to take advantage of the natural resources on their estates. Ballynakill, for example, was a town associated with a landlord's castle and the iron works. One commentator of the early 1640s described it as 'a colony of English planted there by Sir [Thomas] Ridgeway . . . besides that the town since it had been

---

[21] Simington (ed.), *Civil Survey*, vol. V, p. 210.
[22] *Calendar of the Carew Manuscripts, 1575–88*, p. 110.
[23] Public Record Office of Ireland, Dublin, R. C. 6/1, ff. 114, 159, 249.
[24] Trinity College, Dublin [hereafter T. C. D.], Ms 813, f. 328.
[25] T. C. D., Ms 813, ff. 263, 281, 282, 290, 316, 328, 348, 362, 376–8.

planted was well inhabited, the iron mill there kept many lusty men at work'.[26] A similar urban settlement was created at Mountrath by Sir Charles Coote who relied on cloth working as the basis of the settlement. In 1641 Philip Sergeant of Mountrath described himself as 'overseer of his [Coote's] linen and fustian works' and included among his losses fustian, yarn and cloth worth £761.9.0. Another Mountrath deponent, Issac Sands, listed among his losses £560-worth of wool, dying stuff, woollen yarn, looms and tackle. Mountrath also had an iron works from the early 1640s into the eighteenth century.[27] Such landlord activity certainly gave a considerable stimulus to urban development and by 1709 Mountrath was described as 'a very pretty English planted town' while Maryborough with no landlord was 'a sad and dirty town though the county town'.[28]

The fourth group of small towns in this region were those closely tied into the regional capital of Kilkenny and to the large ports of Waterford, Wexford and New Ross in the south-east of the country. These tended to be located on the main rivers, the Barrow, the Nore and the Suir, for ease of communications with the main port towns. In the 1530s, for example, boats were navigating the rivers from New Ross as far north as Inisteague, Athy and Carlow. The scale of the trade was, however, fairly modest. One merchant robbed at Leighlin Bridge in 1537 lost a pipe of Spanish wine, 2 quarters of salt, 2 cwt of iron and a dicker of leather. Again a boat from Clonmel to Cashel was carrying cloth, silk, saffron and other merchandise valued at over £100.[29] However, some of these settlements were wealthy ones. From the deeds which survive for sixteenth-century Callan it appears the town had a goldsmith and a falconer as well as the more mundane occupations of glover, smith, merchant, shoemaker and yeoman in the mid-sixteenth century.[30]

The pattern of urbanisation in this area was of considerable antiquity and was little affected by seventeenth-century developments. Only one new town of significance arose as a result of more intensive exploitation of resources. Enniscorthy had been a garrisoned castle in the sixteenth century but by the 1630s one traveller noted that it had become the gathering point for timber being cut upstream and transported down the River Slaney to Wexford. The most wealthy men in the town were the timber merchants. Enniscorthy received a new lease of life in the 1650s when it was transformed into the centre of an important iron-making venture and it remained

---

[26] J. T. Gilbert (ed.), *A History of the Irish Confederation and the War in Ireland*, vol. I (Dublin, 1882), pp. 149–50.

[27] T. C. D., Ms 815, f. 90.   [28] T. C. D., Ms 885, f. 46v.

[29] H. J. Hore and James Graves, eds, *The Social State of the South Eastern Counties of Ireland in the Sixteenth Century* (Dublin, 1870), pp. 70, 203.

[30] Edmund Curtis (ed.), *Calendar of Ormond Deeds*, vol. V (Dublin, 1941), pp. 281–6.

an industrial centre for the rest of the century.[31] An interesting though somewhat abnormal outlier of this group was the town of Holycross in Tipperary, based around a Cistercian monastery which held a relic of the true cross. Although the monastery was dissolved in the early sixteenth century it remained an important pilgrimage centre into the late seventeenth century. While there is no record of a grant of market or fair, both were held at the site, according to a 1640s history of the monastery and the miracles worked by the relic.[32]

Further south and west, the band of Munster towns stretching from Rosscarbery and Timoleague to Sixmilebridge in Clare were largely the creation of the formal plantation of Munster in the late sixteenth and early seventeenth centuries and the more informal settlement of Clare by the main landowner, the fourth Earl of Thomond. Some of these towns were new creations. Sixmilebridge and Ennis in county Clare were both new creations of the seventeenth century, Sixmilebridge being settled by Dutch and English invited to the area by Thomond. The occupations of the urban inhabitants recorded in the leases which survive included a butcher, merchants, a tanner and a yeoman. Most tenants living in the town also received land in the surrounding countryside. The evidence of rents suggests that the town grew quickly and property was in demand. One house set at £10 in 1623 was reset at £20 in 1635, and another lease of 1623 when released in 1637 had increased from £9 to £26.[33] Certainly there were men of considerable wealth in the town such as the merchant James Vandeleur who listed his losses in 1641 at £1,863. His trade seems mainly to have been in livestock, grain, tanned hides and, to a lesser extent, timber.[34]

Other settlements in the south-west such as Adare, Cullen, Castlelyons, Lismore and Rosscarbery were all small towns of medieval origin which were revitalised in the early seventeenth century as a result of the increase in population. Some of these small towns were minor settlements such as Tracton, Timoleague and Rosscarbery. However others, most importantly Cappoquin and Lismore, became important regional centres due to the patronage of the Earl of Cork, the largest landowner in Munster. By the

---

[31] *Calendar of State Papers, Ireland, 1601–3*, pp. 524, 598; Sir William Brereton, *Travels in Holland and the United Provinces, England, Scotland and Ireland*, ed. E. Hawkins (Chetham Society, London, 1844), pp. 147, 151; *Calendar of State Papers, Ireland, 1660–2*, p. 674; H. F. Hore, 'A Choreographical Account of the South West part of the County of Wexford Written 1684', *Journal of the Royal Society of Antiquaries of Ireland*, vol. 5 (1858–9), 464–5; T. C. Barnard, 'An Anglo-Irish Industrial Enterprise: Iron Making at Enniscorthy, Co. Wexford', *Proceedings of the Royal Irish Academy*, vol. 85, sect. C (1985), 101–44.

[32] Denis Murphy (ed.), *Triumphalia Chronologica Monasterii Sanctae Crucis in Hiberniae* (Dublin, 1891), p. 125.

[33] Bernadette Cunningham, 'Political and Social Change in the Lordships of Clanricard and Thomond, 1569–1641' MA Thesis, University College, Galway, 1979, pp. 216–22.

[34] T. C. D., Ms 829, f. 61.

1640s Cappoquin, which had been an important centre for the timber and iron trade, had branched out into cloth with the aid of loans from the Earl of Cork. By 1640 Cappoquin could boast a range of trades including a butcher and pewterer.[35] Lismore had become an important centre for regional trade and one merchant, Christopher Croker, estimated his loss of shop goods at £200 in 1641. The scale of his business is suggested by the fact that he had debts owing to him of £2,200 in areas as far apart as Galway, Waterford and Tipperary.[36] One other element was important in Mitchelstown, Buttevant and Mallow – the garrison. It is difficult to quantify their importance but the army, when paid (which admittedly was irregularly), could bring a considerable economic boost to a town. At Lisburn, in Ulster, Sir George Rawdon estimated that in 1670 the garrison was worth between £1,400 and £1,500 a year to the town.[37]

By contrast to this pattern of confirmation or re-establishment of older settlements in Munster, the small towns of Ulster were an entirely new feature in the landscape.[38] Ulster had almost no towns in the sixteenth century other than the ecclesiastical centres of Armagh and Downpatrick, and the Lecale ports of Strangford, Ardglass and Carrickfergus. Some of the new towns of the early seventeenth century arose as a result of the requirements of the formal plantation scheme which required 14 corporate towns to be created, as well as a market town for each estate. Other towns, such as Donaghadee, developed as port towns to cater for newly arrived immigrants. For these reasons the towns were essentially colonial centres populated largely by settlers and in at least one case, that of Magherafelt, there was also a garrison in the town. These inland urban settlements were largely agricultural. In 1622, for example, Lurgan had 47 residents of whom roughly half described themselves as yeomen or husbandmen. Other towns were set up as trading centres. Lisburn, for example, was used by the landlord, Lord Conway, as a collecting point for cattle from his estate which could then be sold to merchants from Belfast. Similarly in the west of the province Strabane on the river Foyle became a port linked to Derry. This development was also encouraged by the local landlord, the Earl of Abercorn, who appears in the Derry port books during the second decade of the seventeenth century trading in his own name.

A second characteristic of these new towns was that they were the creation of landlords who used building leases as a way of encouraging tenants to

---

[35] T. C. D., Ms 820, ff. 54, 83, 84, 159, 170, 203.   [36] T. C. D., Ms 820, f. 39.

[37] *Calendar of State Papers, Ireland, 1669–70*, p. 228.

[38] Raymond Gillespie, 'The Small Towns of Ulster, 1600–1700', *Ulster Folklife*, vol. 36 (1990), 23–30; Raymond Gillespie, 'The Origins and Development of an Ulster Urban Network', *Irish Historical Studies*, vol. 24, no. 93 (May, 1984), 15–29; R. J. Hunter, 'Towns in the Ulster Plantation', *Studia Hibernica*, vol. 11 (1971), 40–56; Brooke Blades, 'English Villages in the Londonderry Plantation', *Post Medieval Archaeology*, vol. 20 (1986), 257–69.

settle in towns at minimal cost to themselves. At least in the early stages of their foundation, they showed few of the characteristics of towns but these either developed rapidly or else the settlement quickly failed. The success or failure of a newly created town was mainly in the hands of the local landlord. Freely available land at low rents often meant that some planned towns broke up before they became established. As one commentator observed in 1619, 'all the tenants do dwell dispersedly . . . and cannot dwell together in a village because they are bound every one to dwell upon his own lands'.[39] One way in which this problem could be overcome was to attract new functions to the newly established small towns which gave them a rationale for existence. Some landlords tried to attract the assize to the town as the Earl of Antrim tried to do at Oldstone, one of the towns on his estate. Few landlords had the influence to achieve this although Sir Henry Dillon did move the Connacht presidency court from its traditional location at Athlone on to his lands at Roscommon.[40]

This pattern of urban development was interrupted by the outbreak of war in 1641 which was to continue sporadically until 1652. The effect of this disruption was regional. The Cromwellian campaigns of 1649, for example, had a disastrous effect on almost everywhere they touched. Over 40 per cent of the tenancies in the small town of New Ross in county Wexford were still waste by 1654 following the Cromwellian siege. By contrast the nearby town of Fethard which was not attacked by the Cromwellians had only 5.6 per cent of its tenancies waste in the valuation of 1663.[41] At least some of the small towns, especially Naas, Trim and Maynooth, became garrison towns. As a result they grew rapidly on the profits of the army trading with the spoils of the surrounding countryside.[42] The problem of a garrison town was that it attracted the attention of opposing armies and Naas was burnt on at least one occasion. The effect of war was limited but often devastating in specific regions such as south-east Ireland. The 1650s, however, saw a new inflow of settlers into Ireland, many of whom were former soldiers and the process of rebuilding towns made considerable progress. Kells, in county Meath, for example, lay in ruins in 1654 but by the end of the 1650s had been largely rebuilt by its new proprietor.[43]

Throughout all of Ireland in the years after 1660 the small towns saw both dramatic expansion and a re-orientation of their priorities. These developments were the result of changes in the wider economy. First the nature of

---

[39] *Calendar of Carew Manuscripts, 1603–25*, pp. 410–11.
[40] *Calendar of State Papers, Ireland, 1647–60*, pp. 143, 245.
[41] R. C. Simington (ed.), *Civil Survey*, vol. IX (Dublin, 1953), pp. 234–50; H. F. Hore, *A History of the Town and County of Wexford*, vol. IV (1911), pp. 333–4.
[42] For example, National Library of Ireland, Dublin, Ms 2307, ff. 443.
[43] *Calendar of State Papers, Ireland, 1647–60*, p. 681.

the Irish economy altered, moving away from the export of unprocessed agricultural goods such as live cattle and sheep, wool, timber, hides and some grain. Trade began to be more orientated towards processed goods such as butter, barrelled beef and cloth. The explanation of the change is complex but the prohibition of live cattle exports to England in 1665 was at least part of the reason for the move. A diversification of the economy was thus required to maintain levels of income.[44] Most vulnerable to an economic depression were the towns, and landlords began to consider ways of expanding their role to generate new income and many chose to promote urban craft industries. One correspondent wrote to the Earl of Ormond in 1674 that the setting up of a cloth trade in Clonmel would be 'an employment for a great many idle poor people for they must spin most of the yarn and by degrees be taught the whole mystery'.[45] Small towns such as Cappoquin, Tallow and Youghal, which had all been involved in the timber trade, and to a lesser extent in wool, in the early part of the century, switched their priorities and became important centres of woollen production by the end of the seventeenth century. Cappoquin, in particular, was producing 40 pieces of serge a week.[46] In fact most of these towns had already been involved in the cloth trade since the sixteenth century but the new scheme called for a more systematic exploitation of the trade by importing new skills. In Munster part of the plan for the Earl of Orrery's new town at Charleville was that it would be a linen-weaving town. Plans were made to develop the cloth trade further in the south by bringing settlers to the larger towns of Clonmel, New Ross and Waterford.[47] Further north at Carlow 'very good sheep's grey frieze, not at all inferior to that of Kilkenny city' was made according to the report of Thomas Dineley in the 1680s.[48] Again at Chapelizod, near Dublin, Richard Lawrence was attempting to set up a cloth manufacture which failed only because his intended customers, the army, did not purchase enough cloth. In Ulster both Lurgan and Lisburn had by the 1680s become important centres of the linen trade with fine linens being woven in the towns.[49]

The second development which affected small Irish towns after 1660 was

[44] Gillespie, *Transformation*, pp. 41–3.

[45] Historial Manuscripts Commission, *Sixth report* (1878), p. 742.

[46] Historical Manuscripts Commission, *Reports on Salisbury Manuscripts*, vol. IV (1892), p. 464, Historical Manuscripts Commission, *House of Lords Manuscripts*, n. s. vol. III (1905), p. 108.

[47] Liam Irwin, 'The Role of the Presidency in the Economic Development of Munster, 1660–72', *Journal of the Cork Historical and Archaeological Society*, vol. 82 (1977), 102–14; Historical Manuscripts Commission, *Sixth Report*, pp. 742, 743.

[48] E. P. Shirley, ed. 'Extracts from the Journal of Thomas Dineley', *Journal of the Royal Society of Antiquaries of Ireland*, vol. 8 (1862–3), 41.

[49] Raymond Gillespie (ed.), *Settlement and Survival on an Ulster Estate: the Brownlow Leasebook, 1667–1711* (Belfast, 1988), pp. xxxv–xxxviii.

Table 7.7. *Index numbers of Irish custom farm rents*

	Ardee	Drogheda
1665/6	100	100
1666/7	130	109.2
1670/1	175	135.5
1671/2	182.5	111.8
1673/4	150.5	100
1674/5	185	111.8
1675/6	200	100
1677/8	180.5	104.1
1678/9	200	117.1
1679/80	215	128.9
1680/1	305	130.3
1682/3	310	109.2
1683/4	334	112.3

Source: Louth County Library, Corporation Book of Ardee; T. Gogarty (ed.), *Council Book of the Corporation of Drogheda* (Drogheda, 1915).

intimately related to the first. The production of manufactured goods required a more sophisticated marketing structure than the export of basic agricultural goods which had underlain the growth of the port towns in the early part of the century. This more complex marketing structure and the beginnings of a national market was reflected in the growth of Dublin as the principal Irish port. In 1616 Dublin accounted for 20 per cent of the country's customs which had risen to 30 per cent by the 1630s. In the late seventeenth century its share rose from 40 per cent in the 1660s to 50 per cent by the end of the century when nearly 9 per cent of the Irish population lived in Dublin.[50] For small towns which were also ports, such as Sligo, Dingle and Carlingford, this was a serious development as much trade previously handled by them now passed through a series of inland markets to Dublin, Belfast or Cork. Thus the decline of some ports was mirrored by the growth of smaller inland towns. A comparison of the trends of the rents of the gate customs of the port town Drogheda and the inland town of Ardee shows the trend clearly (Table 7.7).

Small towns associated with the larger ports expanded rapidly. At Naas, close to Dublin, it was noted in 1682 that it was 'the greatest throughfare in the kingdom and well situated for trade and a good market but having no manufacture or trade'. It was the profits of trade which sustained an increase in the numbers of freemen recorded for Naas from 95 in 1667 to 364 in 1683. The Williamite wars had an adverse effect on the town, the number

[50] Gillespie, *Transformation*, pp. 28–9.

of freemen falling to 219 in 1693. What is significant, however, is that over the period the ratio of non-resident to resident freemen increased dramatically so that by 1680 non-resident freemen outnumbered residents by 86 to 79. This seems to be a reflection of the increased importance of the Naas market as a trading centre for non-residents.[51]

The same pattern is true of Mullingar which increased in importance as a fair centre during the late seventeenth century. As it was described in 1682, 'all the houses here are ale houses, yet some of the richer sort drive at other trades also. They sell all sorts of commodities to the gentry abroad in the country and some besides have large farms abroad.'[52] In Ulster, Lisburn also experienced dramatic growth in the wake of the expansion of Belfast's trade. The link between the fate of the two towns was noted by George McCartney, one of the main Belfast merchants, writing to George Rawdon, the agent at Lisburn, 'if our town prosper your town of Lisburn certainly must, for one depends on the welfare of the other'.[53] It is important to remember that these small towns catered not only for exports but also for imports. The diversification of the Irish economy in the late seventeenth century together with falling agricultural prices produced a dramatic rise in disposable income and a rise in the consumption of luxuries such as tobacco. Such goods were usually supplied locally by men who deemed themselves merchants but in reality were shopkeepers dealing locally and issuing tokens. The evidence of the distribution of the surviving tokens reinforces the impression of the rise of the small inland town in the late seventeenth century at the expense of the older ports.[54]

By 1700 the pattern of small towns was well established and was not to be significantly modified in the eighteenth century. The slowdown and cessation of immigration into Ireland during the eighteenth century was one factor limiting the growth of these towns in the early part of the century. There were some exceptions to this generalisation. Portarlington, for instance, grew in the wake of a substantial Huguenot influx at the end of the seventeenth century.[55] It was not until the 1740s, when the economy of Ireland began to expand after the depression of the first three decades of the eighteenth century, that the process of the shaping of the small town

---

[51] 'A Descriptive Account of the County of Kildare in 1682 by Thomas Monk' *Journal of the Kildare Archaeological Society*, vol. 6 (1909–11), 342; T. C. D., Ms 2251.

[52] Henry Piers, 'A Choreographical description of the County of Westmeath [1682]', in Charles Vallency, *Collectanea de Rebus Hibernica*, vol. I (Dublin 1786), p. 78. For merchants coming from Lisburn for the Mullingar fair *Calendar of State Papers, Ireland, 1663–5*, pp. 587, 602.

[53] Raymond Gillespie, 'George Rawdon's Lisburn', *Lisburn Historical Society Journal*, vol. 8 (1991), 32–5; *Calendar of State Papers, Domestic, 1679–80*, pp. 456.

[54] Peter Seaby, *Coins and Tokens of Ireland* (1970), pp. 34–5.

[55] For the Portarlington scheme, *Calendar of State Papers, Ireland, 1666–9*, pp. 259–61.

network could begin again.[56] The new creations of the eighteenth century were unlike the settlements of the seventeenth century in that they tended to be more carefully planned, usually under the control of a landlord. This control meant that the physical appearance of the town was monitored and this in turn affected the sort of functions it fulfilled. There was an intensification of the marketing and craft functions which had first become prominent in the late seventeenth century with landlords often financing the building of market houses. Many landlords also saw their towns as social centres and incorporated in their market houses an assembly room, thus adding a new specialism to the range of functions performed by the small town.

The experience of the small town in early modern Ireland was a varied one. There were fewer of this type of town than in England and they were smaller than their English counterparts. In age and function they varied from the well-established medieval network of small towns in south Leinster to which little was added in the seventeenth century, to the totally new creations in Ulster in the plantation period. This was reflected in the differences between the relatively simple agricultural settlements of Ulster and the more sophisticated settlements of the south-east with complex trading patterns through Dublin and the major southern ports of Wexford and Waterford. The small towns of Munster represent a mid-point between these two extremes with a medieval network reinvigorated through the settlement of Munster in the late sixteenth and early seventeenth centuries and also the creation of some new towns. It was not until the late seventeenth century that this varied regional pattern began to be bonded into something approaching a national urban network as all towns had to meet the challenges presented by the reshaping of the economy and the growth of Dublin. Some rose to the occasion while others, such as the small port town of Carlingford, fell into decline and were preserved (to the present day) in their near-pristine late medieval form as they became too poor to rebuild. In the seventeenth century, as in the twentieth, the blessings of progress were mixed.

[56] L. M. Cullen, *The Emergence of Modern Ireland, 1600–1900* (1981), pp. 61–82; W. H. Crawford, 'The Evolution of Ulster Towns, 1760–1850', in Peter Roebuck, ed. *Plantation to Partition* (Belfast, 1981), pp. 140–56.

8 In search of the small town in early nineteenth-century France

Bernard Lepetit

We are all familiar with the idea of the small town: its insertion in a landscape, its particular relation to time, its specific flavour. Together these ineffable qualities form an image which is both evident and impalpable. Thus the notion of the 'small town' comes to take its place in the class of neglected questions: small towns exist, and it is enough to note their existence. The investigator who wishes to analyse them in a scientific fashion immediately finds himself confronted with questions linked to their identification and development: what are the demographic, social or economic principles that allow us to assign lower and upper limits to the category and to identify the places belonging to it? However, if we proceed in this fashion, once we have defined the criteria, we are still obviously left with relating them to the reality of small towns. And we forget the premise which allows the entire operation to take place: small towns exist, not only with a certain urban rank, but as distinctive urban centres possessing particular qualities. As a means of focusing attention on this reality, I wish to propose a different method, one that takes greater account of the ways in which the modalities of urban economic processes combine with the modalities of their analysis. My aim is to develop a new approach to the problem of the historicity of small towns.

1 A question that is only apparently simple

Maurice Agulhon gave research a new dimension in the early 1960s with his pioneering study of the 'villages' of Provence in the eighteenth century. In the minds of contemporaries – and in reality – these were entirely distinct from agricultural hamlets or any other form of settlement. Although the countryside's population was uniform as measured by activity (agriculture) and social status (farmers, *ménagers*, living-in farm labourers), the mark of a 'village', however small, was its upper caste – the bourgeoisie and officialdom; its middle caste – traders and artisans; and its working caste –

My thanks to Jeanne Chase who translated my paper (too full of 'Frenchness', I fear) and Rene Le Mée who made some of the calculations.

agricultural labourers. Villages thus had a differential social structure which might reasonably be called urban (after all, 'peasants are to be found in most cities'). A great deal besides social composition made them urban. They had tightly grouped buildings, often surrounded by ramparts; a municipal organisation marked by a hierarchy of administrative institutions and elected officials similar to, if smaller than, those of Marseille, Aix or Toulon; and a particular kind of social interaction. 'In the Mediterranean world of Lower Provence, every village was a town, a sort of city distinct from rural areas, one element in a network of urban civilization.'[1] In contrast, in the alpine world of Upper Provence, the mountain village was distinct from the town, part of the rural fabric. The principal merit of Agulhon's outstanding study lies in having redrawn the boundaries separating urban from rural in such a way that they can no longer be taken for granted. If the Provençal 'village' is part of an urban world, then what is a small town? The implicit definition, that it resembles bourgs (market centres) and villages in size, but other cities in the nature of its socio-economic activity, seems inadequate. Other kinds of combinations must be taken into account – including the built form and social organisation, morphological structures and economic functions. An adequate definition requires a sensitivity to the complexities of a seemingly simple question.

2   Regional differences and their origin

Maurice Agulhon's contrast between Upper and Lower Provence, between alpine and Mediterranean worlds, suggests another source of complexity – regional differences. I would like to address these first of all. My source is the tax census of people living in nucleated settlements in 1809.[2] A new tax on spirits had been imposed and the imperial administration decided to assemble information on the population of all communes larger than 2,000 inhabitants, of whom more than 1,000 lived in nucleated settlements. Information from the 1806 population census was used. One definition first of all: any commune having between 1,500 and 3,000 persons living in a nucleated settlement will be considered a small town and its total population will serve as the base of our calculations. The definition is arbitrary, but in line with contemporary practice (in 1821 the lower limit for a nucleated settlement ranked as a town in official publications was 1,500 persons). This definition does not avoid the problem at hand, since 3,000 inhabitants is a figure low enough to encompass an area taking in towns, bourgs and villages

[1] M. Agulhon, 'La notion de village en Basse-Provence vers la fin de l'Ancien Régime', *Actes du 90e congrès national des Sociétés savantes (Nice, 1965), Section d'Histoire moderne et contemporaine*, vol. I (Paris, 1966), pp. 277–301 (quotation p. 301).
[2] R. Le Mée, 'Population agglomérée, population éparse au début du XIXe siècle', *Annales de Démographie historique*, 1971, 455–510.

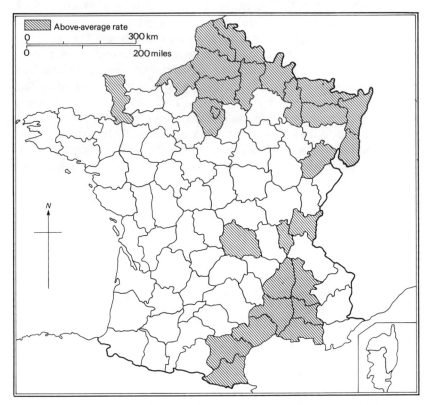

8.1 Rate of urbanisation in France: 1,500–3,000 inhabitants, 1809

alike. I measured the small-town share of the French population for each department, adjusting for differences in surface area. If small towns had been uniformly distributed, then all departments should have had the same proportion of that population. Deviations from the mean are best seen on a map (Fig. 8.1).

The regional deviations are, in fact, quite marked. The network of small towns is particularly dense in two regions: firstly, in the Mediterranean area, from Roussillon to Provence, and in the lower Rhône Valley (the northern limit of olive cultivation might well serve as a convenient benchmark); secondly, in north-eastern France, north of a line from Le Havre to Basle, where 15 of the 19 departments had a higher than average index. If the threshold were lowered to take in all the departments comprised in the first two quartiles of the distribution (43 departments), the group would be bounded by an extended line running from Rouen to Geneva. On the other

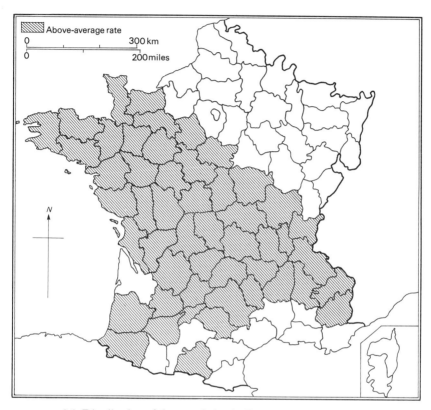

8.2 Distribution of the population in France, 1891

hand, the mountains, the west, the Loire Valley area and the Aquitaine Basin were clearly regions with few small towns.

A similar map indicates the distinction between regions of dispersed and concentrated settlement (Fig. 8.2). The 1891 census supplied figures for the share of dispersed population in each department, and since the physical pattern remained constant over a long period, the time lag between the censuses is unimportant. The second map is the photographic negative of the first. The geographical distribution of small towns bears the mark of environmental patterns.[3]

The result is interesting but scarcely surprising. So far, the only criterion for small towns has been size. But what is a small town? The definition is clearly multi-dimensional, including size, specific economic functions, a

---

[3] Ministère du Commerce, de l'Industrie, des Postes et Télégraphes. Office du travail. Statistique générale de la France. *Résultats statistiques du dénombrement de 1871* (Paris 1894).

certain type of society and forms of social interaction. The type of result obtained so far permits only one generalisation: where morphological configurations and socio-economic functions coincide, there a correspondence of size, function and society exists. It is, however, easy to see that the same form could have a variety of functions – in the form of industrial, university or administrative small towns. Is it possible to imagine the same economic function being carried out in other spatial contexts? In the early nineteenth century, that was the case for production and exchange. Industrial forms could be represented by the early concentrations of manufactories or the diffuse organisation of traditional proto-industry.[4] A portion of the rural population entered the networks of commerce by means of seasonal fairs, others through the dense network of open-air markets and shops.[5] Because the Revolution's uniform administrative apparatus was applied to regions with varying rates of urbanisation, it was uniform in appearance only, as the diversity of prefecture and sub-prefecture size demonstrates.[6]

It is clear, then, that any regional distribution constructed on the basis of one or other definition of a small town does not distinguish regions from one another so much as measuring what distinguishes each regional situation from the logic of the system of classification chosen. In other words, each map of the distribution of small towns indicates the degree of local pertinence to the 'small-town' model which oriented the choice of empirical criteria. It is to that point that I would like to turn now.

3   Criteria of definitions: a case study

I will start with a regional example. In his study of the small towns of the Lower Pyrenees in the middle of the nineteenth century, Jean-Pierre Jourdan put together an identification grid comprising twelve variables, distributed according to four criteria with differential weightings:[7] commercial functions – 30 index points (Category 1, fair; 2, markets; 3, shops); administrative functions – 40 points (Category 4, civil court; 5, sub-prefecture; 6, authority for social control; 7, fiscal authority; 8, mailing facilities and roads); service functions – 30 points (Category 9, physicians; 10, attorneys and public notaries; 11, schools); population functions – 50 points (Category 12, population in nucleated settlements). The grid represents a tacit model of the small town – Jourdan excluded agricultural activity and

---

[4] Statistique de la France. *Industrie* (4 vols, Paris, 1847).

[5] D. Margairaz, *Foires et marchés dans la France préindustrielle* (Paris, 1988).

[6] B. Lepetit, *Les villes dans la France moderne (1740–1840)* (Paris, 1988) (chapter 6).

[7] J-P. Jourdan, 'Petites villes et bourgs des Basses-Pyrénées au milieu du XIXe siècle', in P. Loupès and J-P. Poussou, eds, *Les petites villes du Moyen Age à nos jours* (Paris, 1987), pp. 227–54.

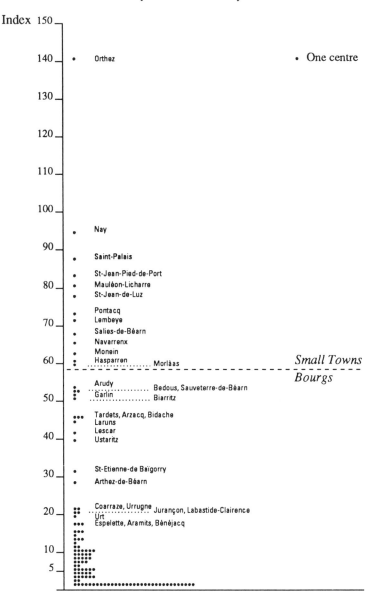

8.3 The hierarchy of small towns and bourgs in the Lower Pyrenees: mid-nineteenth century

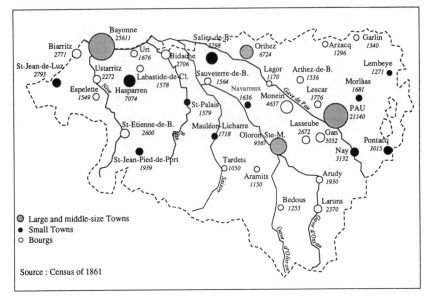

Map legend:

◎ Large and middle-size Towns
● Small Towns
○ Bourgs

Source : Census of 1861

8.4 Network of towns and bourgs in the Lower Pyrenees in 1861

industrial production. Since no justification is given for the weighting, the only explanation seems to be a concern for relative balance. It is certainly difficult to assign weights to the elements that make up this particular formula for the 'small town'. Jourdan's sources are the early nineteenth-century departmental directories, from which he derives a hierarchy (Fig. 8.3) and a map (Fig. 8.4) of the Lower Pyreneean urban network. The circularity of the operation is clear: the results are the product of pre-existing criteria whose pertinence has not been examined. The remainder of the study consists of a concentrated effort to break that circle, by comparing the initial results with community forms and the variety of ways local economic activity was organised. Neither the results nor their tautological character, however, interest me as much as the tensions they reveal among the different ways of catching glimpses of reality. The three-level hierarchy – small towns, bourgs, villages – is, in fact, not easily applicable to some local situations. Jourdan notes: 'Urt, Lagor, Cambo and Gan are ranked with simple villages on the graph. Knowing the terrain, however, would suggest grouping them with towns.' Further: 'Contemporaries themselves had difficulty distinguishing among those three realities. Letters from sub-prefects to the prefect at Pau continually use the term "town" for places which were only bourgs. Nor were travellers much more perceptive. Evidence from maps displays the same confusion.'[8] Who better than administrators and geographers would understand local realities? But, what they offer, it seems, are confused images: the 'small towns' of the Lower Pyrenees escaped the comprehension of those in the best position to see them.

What, then, can we conclude? Should a past society be described as it was perceived, or according to modern criteria? The past twenty years of social history demonstrate that the argument cannot be resolved.[9] So why not just use several commonplace ideas that lend themselves to statistical treatment?[10] Statistics, however, provide no objective measure of reality. They are as much the product of the conditions under which they were designed as they are of the object observed. The method of observation tends to confer a supplementary degree of existence to the object. On the other hand, whatever defies the observer's categories tends to be ignored or dismissed as beside the point. And thus the obstacles on the path of research are eliminated.

Instead of dismissing the inevitable difficulties as barriers in the way of definition and objective classification, we should admit them as part of the definition itself. Instead of beginning with a definition of the small town, we might consider when it was that the idea itself first appeared, and how it was that its contours were produced.[11]

4   The invention of an idea

The division of towns according to size appeared at a rather late date in France. In the Dauphiné and the south-west, for which there is abundant documentation, the 'small town' did not exist in the sixteenth or early seventeenth centuries. Here, there were only cities and towns distinguished by their special rights and by their walls which separated them from the countryside they dominated and claimed to represent.[12] Topographical surveys of France lend further support. These portraits of France proliferated from the mid-seventeenth to the mid-nineteenth centuries. Their authors took great pains with description, generally providing a label and a population figure for each locality treated, then a summary of their history, administrative functions, economic activity and architectural aspects. An image of the city shared by the enlightened elite of the time, makes for

---

[8] Jourdan, 'Petites villes', p. 237, for the two quotations.
[9] J-C. Perrot, 'Rapports sociaux et villes', *Annales ESC* (1968), 241–67.
[10] M. Volle, *Le métier de statisticien* (Paris, 1980).
[11] L. Boltanski, *Les cadres, la formation d'un groupe social* (Paris, 1982).
[12] P. Souriac, 'Les petites villes du Comminges au XVIe siècle', in Loupès and Poussou, *Les petites villes*, pp. 65–81, and R. Favier, 'Les petites villes dauphinoises face à leur environnement rural', *ibid.*, pp. 323–34.

interesting reading.[13] No mention of the 'small town' appears in Philippe Labbe's *Géographie Royale*, published in 1646, nor in Pierre Duval's *Géographie Française*, published in 1667. The distinction appeared only in 1718, in the six-volume *Description de la France*, published by Piganol de la Force, and which was used thereafter throughout the eighteenth century.

It is very difficult to apply the idea, however, even in the early nineteenth century, as the 1809 census of the population in nucleated settlements shows. The imperial administration wanted more than population figures from the prefects. It was working towards criteria for urban definition.

Therefore, Sir, you will kindly provide me with a statement concerning the communes of your department in the margin of which you will have indicated whether the commune has less than 1,000 inhabitants in its principal settlement, and, in the communes whose principal settlements are larger, what that number is, and also the number of houses the inhabitants occupy and if, among them, are to be found bourgeois, merchants, and persons living from land rents, and finally if that principal settlement may be regarded as a town, bourg or simply a village.

Although the three-tiered pyramid of the Parisian statistics offices left room for an additional distinction – 'small town' – it nevertheless proved inadequate to the task of understanding several local realities.

In the Cantal, Massif Central department, the prefect indicated that all principal settlements of communes were called towns. The prefect of Finistère in Brittany pointed to similar difficulties: 'Here, where farmers' houses are scattered about, a village may be a hamlet in which a single family lives, bourgs, the principal settlements of the communes, and towns, compact settlements that have markets or seasonal fairs.'[14] Dictionaries meant to bridge the gap between the French used in the Ile-de-France and the capital, and the languages of the peripheral world, provide further evidence of the pyramid's inadequacies. A French–Flemish dictionary of the mid-eighteenth century had no difficulty with the trilogy: 'ville', 'bourg' and 'village' had their equivalent in 'stadt', 'vlek', and 'dorp'. A French–Breton dictionary from the reign of Louis XV, on the other hand, struggled to find semantic equivalents. In Breton, town was 'bourch', but they also say 'guyc' if accompanied by the name of a parish, or also 'ploue'. Further along, one learns that 'guyc' means city whereas 'ploue' means country. As for 'kaer', it might mean city or village.[15]

In the circumstances, town, let alone small town, meant very little indeed. In economics as well, the language of the conqueror – Parisian centrality –

---

[13] B. Lepetit, 'L'évolution de la notion de ville d'après les tableaux et descriptions géographiques de la France (1650–1850)', *Urbi*, vol. 2 (December 1979), 99–107.

[14] Le Mée, 'Population agglomérée'.

[15] J. Desroches, *Dictionnaire français–flamand et flamand–français* (Antwerp, 1769); G. de Rostenem, *Dictionnaire français–celtique ou français–breton* (Rennes, 1762).

inserted itself between the observer and the reality by means of its categories. But we have to understand the reasons for such a taxonomy.

5   The identity of urban economic processes

A first hypothesis is that there was something in the hierarchy of settlements in the late pre-industrial period that necessitated a new category, 'small town'. Let us go back to the Lower Pyrenees to test it. Jean-Pierre Jourdan ended his study by comparing the characteristics of the small towns he had identified with bourgs lower in the hierarchy, according to three criteria: morphology; radius of economic influence; and occupational composition.[16] In theory, small towns should display urban spatial structures on a reduced scale. In fact, half of them resembled the numerous Basque bourgs, or even villages, quite closely. On the other hand, some bourgs, like Labastide-Clairence or Arudy, were incontestably urban in character. The spatial organisation of the small town and the bourg were virtually indistinguishable, as was the radius of economic influence over the countryside. Neither the demographic catchment area nor the radius of attraction for seasonal fairs, nor again the extent of the countryside from which notaries drew their rural customers, served to distinguish clearly the bourg from the small town. The only significant difference was occupational. Small towns had a greater range of artisan activity and more unusual artisan activity (a painter, a gilder and a calligrapher at Lembaye, which scarcely counted 1,000 inhabitants), but above all, a larger elite group. In the bourgs of the Lower Pyrenees, an average of six persons paid more than 200 francs in tax, but in the small towns, barely larger in population size, the average was 14. 'A relatively larger elite is the sociological mark of small towns.' Is that a general rule?

It is common knowledge that there is a threshold below which the survival of an animal species is no longer certain. This leads me to another hypothesis, and two observations. Firstly, I would suggest that social groups able to make a choice of residential location have limits below which the minimum conditions for satisfactory sociability disappear, or the social image of a place becomes definitively unacceptable. Below that threshold, a change of lifestyle occurs. The history of some areas of large cities is written in such change, the Halles at Paris, for instance.[17] Why not the history of urban systems? Secondly, small towns, especially administrative centres, stood above that threshold. The early nineteenth-century elite was

---

[16] Jourdan, 'Petites Villes'.
[17] F. Boudon, A. Chastel, H. Couzy and F. Hamon, *Système de l'architecture urbaine. Le quartier des Halles à Paris* (Paris, 1977).

particularly attracted by land and land rents, evidenced by the fact that the land tax accounted for three quarters of all direct taxation, as the electoral lists of the parliamentary monarchy amply demonstrate. The Revolution and political upheaval in the early nineteenth century made small towns attractive to the nobility, closer as they were to family domains and traditions. Many a noble became a provincial emigré within France. Furthermore, the urban bourgeoisie, even in small centres, and the relatively wealthy farmers, were the beneficiaries of the sales of property confiscated from the church and the nobility as a result of the Revolution. Thus landed proprietors were to be found at all levels of urban society.[18] As we have seen, the imperial census made the presence of land proprietors one criterion for the definition of a town. This elite developed its own form of satisfying social life, as the multiplication of learned societies and associations demonstrates. In 1827, the most complete of the trade directories listed some 256 learned societies, including groups for the propagation of knowledge, improvement, agriculture and trade, and arts and sciences. Civray, Florac and Barcelonnette, with fewer than 2,000 inhabitants, Lure, Gex and Trevous, with fewer than 3,000, and Bauge and Avesnes with scarcely more, all had their societies. For 1843, there is a semi-official listing of 1,928 associations (about the same as the number of communes with more than 2,000 inhabitants, including bourgs and villages); these had more than 120,000 members. Take, for instance, the literary circle at Parthenay, a town of some 4,300 inhabitants. Its charter was signed in 1846 by 56 founding members, among them the sub-prefect, the mayor and his assistant, two magistrates three public notaries, an advocate, two physicians, three pharmacists, a merchant, almost all the civil servants stationed in the town, and a fair number of landed proprietors. The annual dues were set at 25 francs, making the circle inaccessible to persons in modest circumstances, given that the average daily wage in the department at the time was 1 franc 60.[19] These leading people introduced elite consumption habits to small towns and in so doing gave a new dimension to the urban economy. Take Avesnes, a small sub-prefecture in the Nord department. Despite its mere 3,000 inhabitants, it had six households paying more than 1,000 francs in tax each year (as many as Tourcoing, a nearby industrial city of 20,000). The Avesnes directories listed four luxury shops, two high-fashion shops, four watch- and clock-makers, three jewellers, four pharmacists, three bookstores, one cafe, one hotel and one restaurant. Social and cultural

[18] A. J. Tudesq, *Les grands notables en France (1840–1849). Etude historique d'une psychologie sociale* (Bordeaux, 1964), includes many comments on the geography of elites.
[19] M. Agulhon, *Le cercle dans la France bourgeoise, 1810–1848. Etude d'une mutation de sociabilité* (Paris, 1977).

factors stimulated small towns to develop a consumer economy which pre-classical political economists took to be the motor of urban development.[20]

Thirdly, these characteristics served to distinguish small towns sharply from bourgs but not from the larger cities. Tax lists lead to three conclusions: most of the wealthy were urban residents; the absolute number of wealthy people increases with the size of a town, but the relative number remains stable; function, not size, distinguished towns by their ability to attract the rich. Whatever the size, it was the urban centre with administrative functions that had, proportionally, the largest number of influential people.[21] Size is not an explanatory variable of urban economic activity. The forms of demographic adjustment, notably the relative equilibrium of natural and migratory balance, are a different issue.

6   A community of fortunes at the start of the nineteenth century

The last observation highlights a specific sort of collision that occurs around the idea of 'small town'. Let us look at it from both ends of the spectrum. From below, there is no quantitative difference, in population terms, between large villages, bourgs and small towns – they are all uniformly small. There is, however, a qualitative socio-economic or socio-cultural difference which gives rise to differing behaviour and activity; hence the notion of the small town. From above, the difference between the small town and other towns is quantitative – fewer inhabitants in one place, more in another – and the only problem is one of defining the boundaries between them. Is there, however, any qualitative difference relating to socio-economic or socio-cultural activity? If not, or if there is only a difference of degree and not of kind, then size is not a criterion for distinguishing towns. There are no small, medium and large towns, just towns.

That, it seems to me, was the situation in France at the end of the pre-industrial period. Identical social and economic functions mean that the small town did not exist. Two arguments can be presented to support this idea: firstly, I will use Rene Le Mee's tables (Tables 8.1–8.4) showing urban growth by size-category between 1806 and 1851.[22] The tables include

---

[20] R. Cantillon, *Essai sur la nature du commerce en général* (London, 1755); E. de Condillac, *Le commerce et le gouvernement considérés relativement l'un à l'autre* (Paris, 1776).
[21] Lepetit, *Les Villes*, ch. 7.
[22] R. Le Mée, 'Les Villes de France et leur population de 1806 à 1851'. *Annales de Démographie Historique* (1989), 321–393, which provides on a departmental basis urban population figures according to enumerations of the early nineteenth century.

Table 8.1. *French towns of 2,000–2,999 inhabitants by region 1806–1851*

Regions	1806	1821	1831	1836	1841	1846	1851
Ile-de-France	17	7	13	15	12	13	13
Champagne-Ardennes	9	13	14	17	15	14	16
Picardie	14	19	20	20	21	24	24
Hte-Normandie	3	0	3	3	5	5	6
Centre	5	5	6	7	5	10	12
Nord	15	19	31	24	34	32	34
Lorraine	18	13	10	14	17	14	19
Alsace	15	(?9)	30	32	32	33	31
Franche-Comté	4	6	8	5	5	4	5
Basse-Normandie	6	1	4	3	5	5	6
Pays-de-la-Loire	7	7	4	4	3	3	3
Bretagne	3	3	3	3	3	3	6
Limousin	1	1	2	2	1	1	1
Auvergne	6	4	5	6	6	7	6
Poitou-Charentes	6	6	9	9	13	13	15
Aquitaine	3	0	4	3	1	2	6
Midi-Pyrénées	2	2	5	6	7	8	10
Bourgogne	9	10	11	8	11	13	13
Rhône-Alpes	8	5	10	12	9	9	10
Languedoc	16	16	16	17	19	19	26
Provence-Côte d'Azur-Corse	13	17	17	17	17	20	25
FRANCE	180	?163*	225	227	241	252	287

* Incomplete.

all towns in 1806 that the author considers as such (communes having more than 2,000 inhabitants in principal settlements).

Although the tables show stronger growth in towns of over 50,000 inhabitants, the conclusion is misleading. It stems from the small sample of towns analysed; from the fact that the calculations have been aggregated; from the 1841 change in the definition of population to be counted (from legal to *de facto* residence); from the fact that the largest towns were especially affected by the revolutionary crisis of the 1790s and from the doubling of the Parisian population in the first half of the nineteenth century. A variation analysis of the array of towns examined individually would show it to be deceptive. As for the towns with fewer than 50,000 inhabitants, growth variations are not strong enough to make small towns stand out. Taking those centres with fewer than 3,000 or fewer than 6,000 inhabitants, for example, there is no relation between town size and intensity of growth.[23]

[23] D. Pumain, *La dynamique des villes* (Paris, 1982), whose analysis begins with the census of 1831, confirms this result.

Table 8.2. *Population of French towns of 2,000–2,999 inhabitants by region 1806–1851*

Regions	1806	1821	1831	1836	1841	1846	1851
Ile-de-France	40,186	17,513	32,640	36,407	29,991	31,921	31,565
Champagne-Ardennes	22,044	31,412	33,323	42,355	38,275	35,786	40,692
Picardie	33,862	45,417	49,140	49,193	53,182	57,854	60,019
Hte-Normandie	7,526	0	7,510	8,088	12,337	12,238	14,894
Centre	13,481	13,783	15,858	18,461	13,786	25,255	31,409
Nord	35,221	45,361	75,603	60,749	86,271	79,550	84,969
Lorraine	47,088	33,335	24,518	34,758	41,225	34,695	47,267
Alsace	35,798	?21,575	71,991	78,726	76,725	81,628	76,009
Franche-Comté	10,362	15,404	22,353	13,437	13,281	10,479	12,799
Basse-Normandie	15,977	2,534	10,239	7,989	13,005	12,482	15,851
Pays-de-la-Loire	18,273	17,381	10,142	10,128	7,524	8,355	7,887
Bretagne	7,665	7,603	7,649	8,255	7,326	7,916	15,754
Limousin	2,646	2,875	5,264	5,487	2,493	2,504	2,490
Auvergne	15,834	10,568	13,421	14,644	14,372	17,674	15,496
Poitou-Charentes	14,538	15,390	23,290	23,612	33,396	33,438	38,144
Aquitaine	7,868	0	11,209	8,685	2,635	5,274	15,296
Midi-Pyrénées	5,191	5,407	13,398	16,128	18,448	21,136	27,017
Bourgogne	22,720	25,953	28,963	20,290	28,381	33,716	33,790
Rhône-Alpes	20,861	13,054	26,171	29,694	22,849	22,981	27,545
Languedoc	40,055	41,194	39,444	41,842	46,095	46,627	64,357
Provence-Côte d'Azur-Corse	34,295	45,142	43,489	42,856	41,920	52,622	66,829
FRANCE	451,491	?410,901	565,515	571,784	603,517	634,131	730,079

Towns were not differentiated by growth patterns any more than by social functions or economic mechanisms.

Could it be that small towns took on a distinctiveness at a later date? One place to begin is with the studies made by members of the Paris Statistical Society.[24] At the beginning of the twentieth century, 98 out of 400 sub-prefectures had fewer than 5,000 inhabitants. More numerous in rural departments, these were, clearly, true towns, as the age structures and occupational composition of their inhabitants show. From a nineteenth-century perspective, the change in demographic pattern appeared with the 1886 census. Although between 1836 and 1846 two thirds of the small towns showed net demographic growth (the average rate was 3.4 per cent), this dropped to 1 per cent between 1896 and 1906. Village populations declined, larger places increased in population, but the small sub-prefectures had the

[24] P. Meuriot, 'La petite ville française', *Journal de la Société de Statistique de Paris* (1908), 235–40, 245–53.

Table 8.3. *French towns of 3,000–4,999 inhabitants by region 1806–1851*

Regions	1806	1821	1831	1836	1841	1846	1851
Ile-de-France	9	13	17	18	21	21	20
Champagne-Ardennes	9	8	9	10	12	14	13
Picardie	10	10	11	12	13	18	16
Hte-Normandie	10	5	9	10	10	14	16
Centre	12	12	17	19	17	23	23
Nord	17	21	23	24	27	32	35
Lorraine	7	12	17	15	15	19	16
Alsace	19	13	23	23	23	26	29
Franche-Comté	5	5	4	6	7	7	8
Basse-Normandie	2	5	7	7	6	8	11
Pays-de-la-Loire	12	14	14	14	18	19	22
Bretagne	12	12	10	10	9	10	12
Limousin	3	4	6	6	6	7	8
Auvergne	11	9	12	12	13	12	13
Poitou-Charentes	6	6	8	8	8	10	11
Aquitaine	3	7	13	13	13	18	20
Midi-Pyrénées	14	15	19	20	24	25	28
Bourgogne	7	8	11	15	15	18	16
Rhône-Alpes	14	16	20	20	23	28	36
Languedoc	18	18	25	27	26	27	28
Provence-Côte d'Azur-Corse	22	22	29	30	31	31	25
FRANCE	222	235*	304	319	337	387	406

* Incomplete.

same population in 1906 as in 1876. In a period of increasing urbanisation, demographic stagnation was the hallmark of small towns. At that moment, and only then, did the small town become a particular category with a set of attributes that explain the specific direction it took. The development came at a late date, and therefore the hypothesis with which section 5 of this chapter opened is not substantiated. We must, therefore, discover another reason for the invention of the category 'small town' at the beginning of the eighteenth century.

7   Towns: from eternity to history

The explanation, I believe, is to be found in the general redefinition and reappraisal of towns at that time.[25] All definition proceeds by drawing boundaries. The ones relating to the definition of a town before the

[25] B. Lepetit, *Les villes*, ch. 2.

Table 8.4. *Population of French towns of 3,000–4,999 inhabitants by region 1806–1851*

Regions	1806	1821	1831	1836	1841	1846	1851
Ile-de-France	32,571	47,273	65,792	65,408	83,018	83,447	79,765
Champagne-Ardennes	33,621	30,986	32,874	37,400	44,461	52,193	48,296
Picardie	37,092	36,885	40,427	45,167	49,377	67,386	61,235
Hte-Normandie	38,495	19,587	33,012	36,033	35,852	50,090	58,093
Centre	45,045	48,210	67,935	76,062	66,353	88,828	88,929
Nord	61,693	76,863	85,426	89,147	100,222	117,753	127,362
Lorraine	27,144	42,073	61,214	54,791	55,739	70,538	60,771
Alsace	72,519	?	85,717	86,391	82,069	96,224	107,255
Franche-Comté	16,801	19,561	16,879	21,196	25,243	23,443	29,121
Basse-Normandie	6,927	37,243	25,235	26,629	22,562	30,484	42,549
Pays-de-la-Loire	47,142	54,743	53,422	53,074	66,695	71,580	82,490
Bretagne	47,923	50,484	42,518	40,498	37,830	40,457	49,773
Limousin	10,663	15,263	22,780	22,252	21,729	24,918	28,934
Auvergne	43,124	36,115	46,983	44,258	48,260	46,724	50,357
Poitou–Charentes	21,278	21,940	30,016	32,211	34,671	42,601	42,214
Aquitaine	11,773	24,766	49,920	50,598	48,715	67,712	78,760
Midi-Pyrénées	49,833	57,400	72,615	75,990	91,298	96,086	110,088
Bourgogne	26,374	32,197	41,260	54,514	57,823	67,998	60,510
Rhône-Alpes	53,277	58,557	79,866	76,807	90,430	105,216	134,802
Languedoc	67,478	66,184	93,035	100,680	97,121	102,249	109,181
Provence-Côte d'Azur-Corse	79,542	81,491	105,987	111,362	113,954	119,725	99,890
FRANCE	830,315	?	1,152,913	1,200,468	1,273,422	1,465,652	1,550,375

eighteenth century are particularly sharp. The town is a community of inhabitants distinguished from those in the environs by privileges granted to it. The surrounding wall, a key feature of collective representation, gave strong material and conceptual rigidity to the urban sense of space. By its evocation of the time-honoured image of the city, the wall represented both spatial and temporal fixity. The town's original characteristics (privileges, power to construct a wall) belonged to the past. Towns used history as a political weapon against incursions of royal power. Any material remains or local legends which signalled ties to a distant past conferred a special nobility on towns. This was a static vision of the universe. Immutable circumstances of town foundations were exclusive criteria (a community did or did not have privileges, or a wall, and so forth) and these furnished simple reference points. Reasoning was based on dissimilitude, on exclusion. Even if minuscule, a town was a town.

The new image of the town in the early eighteenth century was not as sharp. Novel elements of definition brought the town into the arena of variation and change. Making the type and intensity of economic activity one of the criteria of urban definition meant interpreting the town from the perspective of economic change. Trade might be prosperous or in decline, a town could grow wealthier or poorer. Time no longer stood still. The homology of functions exercised at various levels of the settlement hierarchy fixed continuity in space. As Robert de Hesseln's *Dictionnaire Universel* noted in 1771: 'There is an infinite number of small towns which resemble the larger in that they provide retail services to neighbouring villages, which in turn gives them the sort of advantages that most populated cities have with wholesale services.'

In the circumstances, only an empirical approach served to articulate these towns. Recourse to measurement and typology opened the door to reordering the urban world. Attempting to identify the town, one must try to understand what an episcopal, commercial, university or small town is. The essence of the town having vanished, various new forms of categorisation represent so many attempts to grasp at the variety of existence. The hierarchy of towns is thus the child of empirical knowledge. The entire history of statistical definition of the French urban population shows it to be a notion based on practice, not on concept.[26] This is an undertaking not without its own perils: there is the risk of confusing the category with reality, of accepting it without qualification.

---

[26] C. Lamarre, 'Aux origines de la définition statistique de la population urbaine en France', *Histoire et Mesure*, vol. 2 (1987), 57–71.

As any other, the category 'small town' has only problematical reality. Historical inquiry, therefore, should seek to identify when it appeared as an original socio-economic construct, distinguished by size, function and development, not only from villages and bourgs, but from larger urban centres as well. It is, however, not to be found in France at the close of the pre-industrial period. There were no small towns – only smaller ones.

9   Small towns in early modern Germany: the case of Hesse 1500–1800

Holger T. Gräf

'Un des charmes de l'Allemagne est bien son irréductible diversité et le foissonnement de ses contrastes.'[1] This comment of Etienne François, the former director of the *Mission Historique* in Germany, is also valid for German urban history and even for its present urban landscape. This diversity was essentially conditioned by unique historical developments, characterised by the territorialisation of the Holy Roman Empire from the late Middle Ages onwards, and by territorial state-building in the early modern period. In consequence territorial fragmentation produced a no less unique urban landscape, distinguished by an overcrowded urban network, a wide range of different types of towns and of the same functional types in relatively close proximity to each other but separated by territorial borders. Of course, as in Old Europe in general, the overwhelming part of towns in Germany were small, but they sometimes played a crucial role within a territory. It is especially important to study small towns in early modern Germany, for here, not only the character but also the limits of territorial state-building are intelligible and evident.

I

It is complicated but nonetheless necessary to define what is actually meant by a 'town' in general and a 'small town' in particular, in medieval and early modern Europe. Werner Sombart's classic demographic definition of a town as a settlement with more than 2,000 inhabitants is not very helpful since most towns in Old Europe were below this threshold.[2] Although Postan's argument that towns were non-feudal islands in a feudal sea has been

---

[1] I wish to thank Ute Lotz, New York and Dr Sarah Lewis-Higgins, Leicester for their help with the translation. I am especially indebted to Prof. Peter Clark for editorial help and advice. E. François, 'Immigration et société urbaine en Allemagne à l'époque moderne (XVIIe–XVIIIe siècles)', in M. Garden and Y. Lequin, eds, *Habiter de ville, XVe–XXe siècles* (Lyon, 1985), p. 37.

[2] W. Sombart, 'Der Begriff der Stadt und das Wesen der Städtebildung', *Archiv für Sozialwissenschaft und Sozialpolitik*, 25 (1907), 3.

Groups I = >10.000 (Großtadt/city)
    II = > 2.000 (Mittelstadt/medium-sized town)
   III = > 1.000 (ansehnlichw Kleinstadt/sizeable small town)
   IV = >   500 (mittlere Kleinstadt/medium-sized small town)
    V = >   200 (Kleine Kleinstadt/little small town)
   VI = <   200 (Zwergstadt/tiny small towns)
                (Categories after H. Ammann, 'Wie groß war die
                mittelalterliche Stadt?', in: *Studium Generale*
                9(1956), 504; Populationfigures from E. Keyser,
                Hessisches Städtebutch, Stuttgart, 1957)

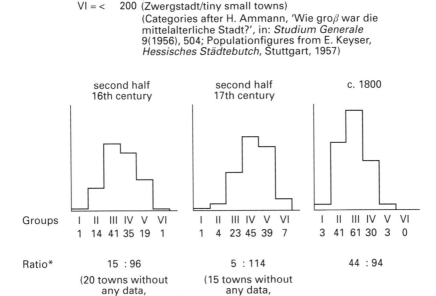

	second half 16th century	second half 17th century	c. 1800
Groups	I II III IV V VI	I II III IV V VI	I II III IV V VI
	1 14 41 35 19 1	1 4 23 45 39 7	3 41 61 30 3 0
Ratio*	15 : 96	5 : 114	44 : 94

Ratio*   15 : 96   5 : 114   44 : 94

     (20 towns without   (15 towns without
       any data,   any data,
  7 towns still to be found   4 towns still to
after the Thirty-Years-War)   be found)

*Ratio between bigger towns (groups I & II)
 and small-towns (groups III & VI)

9.1 Size categories of Hesse towns

subject to revision in recent years it seems appropriate to retain the legal definition of a town as a burgher community – at least for central Europe.[3]

Yet the problem of distinguishing small towns from other towns remains unsolved. A commonly used characteristic employed in the categorisation of urban forms is that of population size. Peter Clark has suggested 400–2,500 inhabitants for small towns in seventeenth- and eighteenth-century England.[4] This group, of approximately 700 towns, comprised the lowest

[3] M. M. Postan, *The Medieval Economy and Society* (Berkeley, 1975), p. 212.
[4] P. A. Clark, 'Demographic change in English small towns from the seventeenth to the early nineteenth century'. Paper given at the Conference 'Les petites villes en Europe Occidentale du XIIIᵉ au XIXᵉ siècle', Lille, 29–31 Jan. 1987, p. 3; P. A. Clark and P. Slack, eds, *Crisis and Order in English Towns, 1500–1700* (1972), p. 4.

level of the English three-tiered urban society. Above it were approximately 100 medium-sized towns, and seven or eight major cities, including London. The present study will employ the size categories proposed by Hector Ammann for the late Middle Ages. He defines small towns as those with fewer than 2,000 inhabitants. This group of small towns is further subdivided into 'tiny small towns' (< 200 inhabitants (category VI)); 'little small towns' (< 500 inhabitants (category V)); 'medium-sized small towns' (< 1,000 inhabitants (category IV)); and 'sizeable small towns' (< 2,000 inhabitants (category III)), (see Fig. 9.1). Category II comprises 'medium-sized towns' with 2,000–10,000 inhabitants and category I 'cities' above the threshold of 10,000 inhabitants.[5]

During the Middle Ages and the early modern period small towns played a crucial role in the German economic, social and political system.[6] Given the total number of approximately 3,000 to 4,000 towns in the Holy Roman Empire and the fact that towards the end of the fifteenth century 94.5 per cent of these towns had fewer than 2,000 inhabitants, one can say that small towns provided the most common experience of urban life.[7]

However, it is difficult to make any suggestions regarding the proportion of the population living in small towns, at least for the entire Empire. The only estimates available are for the end of the fifteenth century when almost two thirds of the urban population lived in small towns.[8] Given the fact that roughly 20 per cent of the total population lived in towns, one might suggest that 14 per cent of the population dwelt in small towns around 1500. At the other end of the urban spectrum, Jan de Vries has argued that 3.2 per cent lived in towns with more than 10,000 inhabitants.[9] Consequently, it is likely that of the total population of approximately 12.0 millions in 1500, 14.0 per cent lived in small towns with fewer than 2,000 inhabitants, 2.8 to 3.0 per cent in medium-sized towns with 2,000 to 10,000 inhabitants and 3.0 to 3.2 per cent in the large cities exceeding the threshold of 10,000 inhabitants. The overall level of the urban population rose from 20 per cent in 1500 to about 25–30 per cent around 1600.[10] Obviously the medium-sized towns

---

[5] H. Ammann, 'Wie groß war die mittelalterliche Stadt?', in C. Haase, ed., *Die Stadt des Mittelalters* (Darmstadt, 1969), vol. I, pp. 408–15, here p. 410.

[6] E. Keyser, ed., *Hessisches Städtebuch (Deutsches Städtebuch*, vol. IV, 1) (Stuttgart, 1957), p. 35.

[7] Ammann, *Stadt*, here p. 408; H. Stoob suggests 5,000 towns around 1450: H. Stoob, 'Stadtformen und städtisches Leben im späten Mittelalter', in H. Stoob, ed, *Die Stadt*, (Köln, 1979), pp. 148–94, here p. 194; see also E. Isenmann, *Die deutsche Stadt im Spätmittalalter 1250–1500* (Stuttgart, 1988), pp. 29–32.

[8] Isenmann, *Stadt*, p. 31.   [9] J. de Vries, *European Urbanization 1500–1800* (1984), p. 39.

[10] See K-O. Bull, 'Die württembergischen Steuerlisten von 1544/45 und ihre Bedeutung für die Sozial- und Wirtschaftsgeschichte', in *Voraussetzungen und Methoden geschichtlicher*

benefited most from this population increase. The rate of 25–30 per cent was regained at the end of *ancien régime* Europe after the recovery from the seventeenth-century crisis.[11]

Such estimates are of restricted value however, because towns in general as well as small towns were distributed very irregularly. Areas of high density were to be found along the Rhine and the Danube as well as in the fertile basins within, and north of, the German 'Mittelgebirge'. Fewer towns were situated in the low mountain ranges in altitudes over 300 metres, for instance, in the Black Forest, the Spessart and the Bavarian Forest. Nevertheless in some of these highland regions the territorial rulers founded or chartered towns due to military and political interests. These settlements lacked any demographic or economic dynamism. Exceptions were the so-called 'Bergstädte', late medieval and early modern mining towns, like those in the Harz Mountains and in upper Saxony.[12]

The visual appearance and the layout of small towns varied greatly. Most of them developed in the close neighbourhood of a castle and were walled. The existence of fortifications cannot be taken as a characteristically urban feature, however, as a considerable number of villages also had walls, and at the same time, many small towns lacked them.[13] What was apparently common to all small towns in Germany in this time was their modest architecture. The English traveller Fynes Moryson, gave the following description during his visit to Hesse: 'The houses were of timber and clay each one for the most part having a dunghill at the doore, more like a poore village, then a city; but such are the buildings in the cities in Hesse.'[14]

Any attempt to generalise about the small towns of Germany is thus inherently problematical. It is therefore necessary to restrict one's view to what may be considered a representative sample. There are three reasons for this. Firstly, one has to recognise the considerable historico-morphological heterogeneity of different regions. Occupation by the Romans gave regions along the river Rhine and in South-western Germany a developmental advantage of roughly one millennium compared with Northern Germany and the regions east of the river Elbe in respect of the spread of Christianity

---

Städteforschung (Köln, 1979), p. 103; F. Koerner, 'Die Bevölkerungszahl und -dichte in Mitteleuropa zum Beginn der Neuzeit', *Forschungen und Fortschritte*, vol. 33 (1959), 325–31.

[11] K. Gerteis, *Die deutschen Städte in der Frühen Neuzeit* (Darmstadt, 1986), p. 59.

[12] H. Dennert, *Kleine Chronik der Oberharzer Bergstädte* (Clausthal, 1954); H. Stoob, 'Frühneuzeitliche Städtetypen', in H. Stoob, ed., *Stadt*, pp. 195–228, here pp. 204–7.

[13] See W. Gerlach, 'Über den Marktflecken- und Stadtbegriff im späteren Mittelalter und in neuerer Zeit', in *Festgabe für G. Seeliger zum 60. Geburtstag* (Leipzig, 1920), pp. 141–59, esp. pp. 143 and 150–1.

[14] F. Moryson, *An Itinerary, Containing his Ten Yeeres Travell . . .*, 4 vols (Glasgow, 1907-8), vol. I, p. 72.

and the formation of an urban system.[15] These long-term developments were clearly significant for small towns. One cannot, therefore, group individual towns in different regions into just one category, since they differed widely in social, political and economic terms.[16] Secondly, the number of small towns and the size of a theoretically constructed network in the Empire are far too large to be dealt with in a single essay. Finally, there is a considerable lack of scholarly research on small towns in general, and the data are at present too incomplete to allow such an attempt.[17]

This study will therefore be restricted to a single region, namely the modern 'Bundesland' of Hesse. The region is especially interesting in terms of the 'small-town' phenomenon because it is situated between the main urban regions of medieval and early modern Germany, that is, the large and important Imperial cities in upper Germany and the Hanseatic League in the north, the old cathedral towns along the Rhine, and the urban region of Upper Saxony. Moreover, the enormous number of small princely territories which existed in Hesse throughout the early modern period resulted in a wide variety of towns within a small area.[18] Consequently one can

---

[15] On this problem see P. Moraw, *Von offener Verfassung zu gestalteter Verdichtung. Das Reich im späten Mittelalter 1250–1490* (Berlin, Frankfurt, 1989), pp. 24–5.

[16] For the 'eastern type' of small town characterised by small-scale craftsmen and farmers, only local market functions and a lack of political independence and identity, see: R. Barthel, *Strausberg* (in Brandenburg), (Strausberg, 1985). The 'western type', on the other hand, is described in H. Weizmann, *Wertheim und Miltenberg. Die Parallelen und divergierenden Entwicklungsphasen zweier Kleinstädte* (Würzburg, 1979). See also M. Terao, 'Rural Small Towns and Market Towns of Sachsen, Central Germany, at the Beginning of the Modern Age', *Keio Economic Studies*, 2 (1964), 51–89.

[17] A helpful manual is provided by E. Keyser, ed., *Deutsches Städtebuch*, 11 vols (Stuttgart, 1939–74). German research on urban history formerly concentrated on the Middle Ages and the sixteenth century. This has changed during recent years, at least for bigger towns, but is still true, to some extent, for small towns. Nevertheless, there are some studies of general interest, esp. by East German authors: K. Fritze, 'Charakter und Funktionen der Kleinstädte im Mittelalter', *Jahrbuch für Regionalgeschichte*, vol. 13 (1986), 7–23. On demography and migration: H. Böcker, 'Überlegungen zur demographischen Funktion vorpommerscher Kleinstädte im 13./14. Jahrhundert', *Jahrbuch für Regionalgeschichte*, vol. 15 (1988), 45–55; K. Vetter, 'Die sozialen Verhältnisse in brandenburgischen Mediatstädten im 17./18. Jahrhundert', *Zeitschrift für Geschichtswissenschaft*, vol. 18 (1970), 1061–7. On the relations between small town and hinterland: G. Wölfling, 'Die Beziehungen der Kleinstädte des oberen Werratales zu ihrer ländlichen Umgebung vom 15. bis zur Mitte des 16. Jahrhunderts', in W. Mägdefrau, ed., *Europäische Stadtgeschichte im Mittelalter und früher Neuzeit* (Weimar, 1979), pp. 259–85. In the wake of the fundamental study by H. H. Blotevogel, *Zentrale Orte und Raumbeziehung in Westfalen vor der Industrialisierung 1780–1850* (Münster, 1975), several studies using the central-place theory of Walter Christaller were carried out by historical geographers. See for example N. Toporowsky, *Zentrale Orte und zentralörtliche Beziehungen in der Nordeifel und in ihrem Bördenvorland vom Ende des 18. Jahrhunderts bis zur Gegenwart* (Köln, 1982). Unfortunately, they restrict themselves to the end of the eighteenth and the nineteenth centuries due to the poor sources earlier.

[18] A survey of the territorial development of Hesse during the early modern period is provided by V. Press, 'Hessen im Zeitalter der Landesteilung (1567–1655)', in W. Heinemeyer, ed.,

regard Hesse, at least north of the River Main, as a distinctive urban region dominated by small towns.[19]

The study is divided into four sections. Firstly, the geographical distribution of small towns, their linkage with the urban and economic network and their general development towards the end of the sixteenth century will be briefly described. The second section will examine the fundamental changes in the urban network due to the crisis of the seventeenth century.[20] The third will describe the reorganisation of the urban network and the recovery of individual towns. These changes occurred under new circumstances marked by the predominance of the territorial states. Finally, an attempt will be made to outline some general characteristics of the development of German small towns in order to relate the structural differences existing within this urban system to those of other European states at the beginning of the modern industrial age.

II

A close relationship can be observed between the occurrence of small towns in Hesse, and the region's geography and infrastructure.[21] The more substantial small towns in Hesse were situated on the western fringes of the Odenwald, in the plains of the river Rhine, further north in the fertile region of the Wetterau, and to the north-east in the valley of the river Kinzig through which ran one of the major trade routes between Frankfurt and Leipzig. Another chain of small towns was to be found along the river Lahn, which was navigable in this period.[22] Two further regions with a concentra-

Das Werden Hessens (Marburg, 1986), pp. 225–66, and F. Wolff, 'Grafen und Herren in Hessen vom 16. bis zum 18. Jahrhundert', *ibid.*, pp. 267–332.

[19] H. W. Struck, 'Die Entwicklung der Städte', in Keyser, *Städtebuch* (see note 6), pp. 31–48, here p. 31; P. Moraw, 'Das späte Mittelalter', in Heinemeyer, *Das Werden Hessens*, pp. 195–223, here pp. 199–200; H. Stoob, 'Die hochmittelalterliche Städtebildung im Okzident', in H. Stoob, *Die Stadt*, (note 7), p. 146.

[20] The first impact of the crisis became obvious in the 1590s when German towns were struck by economic and demographic problems and a wave of town revolts convulsing urban communities. See H. Schilling, 'The European crisis of the 1590s: the situation in German towns', in P. A. Clark, ed., *The Crisis of the 1590s* (1985), pp. 135–56. The research on the crisis of the seventeenth century is reviewed by H. G. Koenigsberger, 'Die Krise des 17. Jahrhunderts', *Zeitschrift für historisches Forschung*, vol. 9 (1982), 143–65.

[21] See the case study: A. Kulhavy-Bares, *Die oberhessischen Städte. Ihre Entwicklung aus der geschichtlichen und geographischen Lage* (Darmstadt, 1949); for the geographical basis see A. Pletsch, 'Das Werden Hessen Eine geographische Einführung', in Heinemeyer, *Das Werden Hessens* (note 18), pp. 3–41; for the economic background see H. Ammann, 'Der Hessische Raum in der mittelalterlichen Wirtschaft', *Hessisches Jahrbuch für Landesgeschichte*, vol. 8 (1958), 36–70, esp. p. 45 on towns.

[22] M. Eckoldt, 'Die Geschichte der Lahn als Wasserstraße', *Nassauische Annalen*, vol. 90 (1979), 98–123.

tion of small towns were located in the fertile basins of the Schwalm and around Kassel. Fewer towns, and towns of only marginal significance, were to be found in the hilly regions of the Vogelsberg, Taunus, the Westerwald, the Waldeck'sche Upland and the eastern fringes of Hesse towards the Thuringian Forest and the Rhön.

In the entire region of Hesse there were 138 towns in total,[23] many of which had been chartered during the Middle Ages. However, ten towns obtained their charters in the early modern period – mostly in connection with the settlement of French or Dutch refugees.[24] Only 15 of the Hesse towns had more than 2,000 inhabitants during the sixteenth century, including the largest city (category I), Frankfurt, which had almost 20,000 inhabitants at the end of the sixteenth century. The medium-sized towns with more than 2,000 inhabitants (category II) included Kassel, Homberg, Giessen, Alsfeld, Wetzlar and Darmstadt.[25] The largest group of communities comprised bigger and medium-sized small towns with 1,000 to 2,000 and 500 to 1,000 inhabitants, respectively (categories III and IV). For these categories see Figure 9.1.

All these towns had a certain significance as local market centres, as centres of textile production and/or as staging posts along the traditional overland highways connecting the important fair towns of Cologne, Frankfurt, Leipzig, Nuremberg and the Northern German Hanseatic cities.[26] Consequently, one has to emphasise the importance of the non-agricultural economy and of trade for even the smallest towns.[27] Although some of the little and tiny small towns (categories V and VI) may have been even smaller than the surrounding villages, they played an important role in the distribution of products emanating from all over the continent. And from the sixteenth century onwards they also supplied their hinterlands with overseas products. For example, spices from the East Indies were available

---

[23] This number corresponds to the towns listed in Keyser's *Städtebuch*, see note 6. The more recent and exhaustive *Geschichtlicher Atlas von Hessen*, ed. by the Hessisches Landesamt für geschichtliche Landeskunde Marburg (1960–74, 1984), lists many more towns. But because only the *Städtebuch* provides at least basic demographic data I have restricted my essay to this sample.

[24] For example, Dreieichenhain (1718), Friedrichsdorf (1686), Karlshafen (1699), Kelsterbach (1699) and Offenbach.

[25] The data on the population of the towns are provided by Keyser, *Städtebuch* (see note 6). In several cases only numbers of houses and/or burghers are given, from which the total population has to be estimated. The population figures are for example: Kassel 4,500 (1472), 5,300 (1585), 6,329 (1626), 12,289 (1723) and 17,625 (1795); Wetzlar 1,600 (1567), 2,800 (1617), 1,259 (1648), 3,000 (1695), and 5,000 (1800); Alsfeld 2,800 (1579), 1,120 (1648), 2,531 (1777) and 3,289 (1818).

[26] On the overland highways in Hesse see: W. Görich, 'Hessische Altstraßen', *Hessisches Jahrbuch für Landesgeschichte*, vol. 14 (1964), 328–44.

[27] Ammann, 'Stadt' (note 5), pp. 414–15.

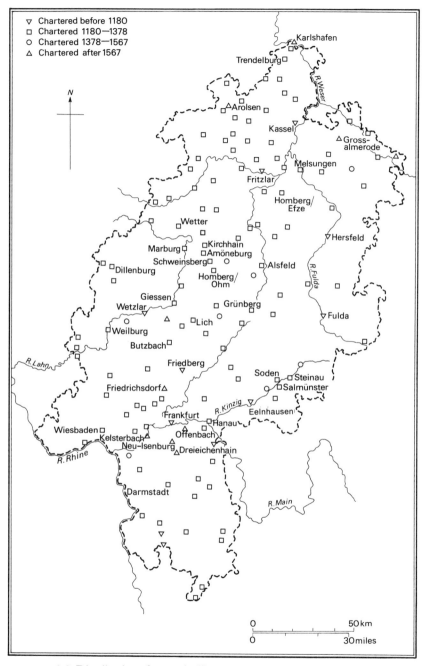

∇ Chartered before 1180
□ Chartered 1180–1378
○ Chartered 1378–1567
△ Chartered after 1567

9.2 Distribution of towns in Hesse

throughout the year in Trendelburg, a small town which had hardly more than 500 inhabitants in 1585.[28]

In general, however, most of the towns in categories V and VI fulfilled mainly administrative or military functions. They were located in close proximity to a castle and were in competition with the small towns of other territorial rulers. Examples of this are Soden, Hünfeld and Herbstein in the territory of the Imperial abbey (Reichsabtei) of Fulda, or the small towns in the valley of the river Ohm in the territories of the archbishopric of Mainz and the Landgraviate of Hesse (Fig. 9.2). When the political and military interests of the princely rulers diminished, these towns fell into decline.[29] This long-term development was accompanied by a far-reaching shift of economic initiative from the individual town to the territorial state; this became decisive in the second half of the early modern period.[30]

Preliminary estimates of the percentage of urban population in Hesse are necessarily rather vague. Of the estimated total population of approximately 400,000 in the region of the modern Bundesland of Hesse around 1580,[31] 4.0 per cent (16,000) lived in Frankfurt, the only city in Hesse at that time;[32] 9.0 per cent lived in the medium-sized towns with more than 2,000 inhabitants; 19.0 per cent lived in small towns with fewer than 2,000. Thus approximately 32.0 per cent of the population lived in towns, but it has to be remembered that many of these towns were only marginal. Hence the general picture of Germany given above has to be revised for Hesse. The great number of small towns and of medium-sized towns means that the proportion of urban dwellers is slightly higher than the overall German average.

This pattern changed towards the end of the early modern period. In 1800 approximately 1.2 million people lived in Hesse; 5.8 per cent (70,000) of the population lived in the three cities Frankfurt, Kassel and Hanau; 12.6 per

---

28 K. Krüger, 'Die deutsche Stadt im 16. Jahrhundert', *Zeitschrift für Stadtgeschichte, Stadtsoziologie une Denkmalpflege*, vol. 2 (1975), 31–47; here p. 34; L. Zimmerman, *Der Ökonomische Staat Landgraf Wilhelms IV.*, 2 vols (Marburg, 1933–4), vol. II, p. 93. On the linkage of small towns and even villages with international trade see J. Strieder, 'Die Frachtfuhrleute von Frammersbach in Antwerpen', in *Festgabe für G. Seeliger zum 60. Geburtstag* (Leipzig, 1920), pp. 160–7.

29 W. Görich, 'Straße, Burg und Stadt in Oberhessen', *Hessenland*, vol. 49 (1938), 145–50.

30 The impact of the absolutist prince's economic policies on towns is the subject of the anthology: V. Press, ed., *Städtewesen und Merkantilismus in Mitteleuropa* (Städteforschung vol. A/14), (Köln, 1983); see esp. the introductory chapter 'Der Merkantilismus und die Städte', by the editor, pp. 1–14 and chapter IV.

31 In this attempt we encounter poor sources and especially poor demographic data. If any data are available they are always restricted to a single territory. Some population figures are provided by K. E. Demandt, *Geschichte des Landes Hessen* (Kassel and Basle, 1972), pp. 240, 288, 415, 505 and 532.

32 H. Mauersberg, *Wirtschafts- und Sozialgeschichte zentraleuropäischer Städte in neuerer Zeit* (Göttingen, 1960), pp. 50–1.

cent (152,000) lived in the 41 medium-sized towns; and 8.7 per cent (104,500) in the remaining 94 small towns. This is a total of 27.1 per cent. The proportion of the urban population therefore decreased by 4.9 per cent in the period between 1600 and 1800. The fact that the rural population grew rapidly particularly during the eighteenth century, while many small towns in peripheral areas stagnated and struggled to recover from the massive casualties they had suffered during the Thirty Years War supports this argument. The figures clearly show that the overcrowded medieval urban network was rationalised by the crisis of the seventeenth century. Since the proportion of people living in cities and medium-sized towns rose by 1.8 per cent and 3.6 per cent, respectively, it would be misleading to speak of de-urbanisation. The urban network of the second half of the early modern period simply did not require so many towns as in the Middle Ages.

German history in the sixteenth century was characterised by two major developments: the growth of population and the Reformation. Throughout the century the population increased from 12.0 millions to 16.0 millions.[33] Much of this growth took place in towns. The city of Frankfurt doubled its population from 10,000 in 1520 to 20,000 inhabitants in 1605.[34] In 1502 Giessen was inhabited by 273 burghers and in 1608 by 591. Other medium-sized and especially small towns seem to have grown on a much smaller scale but the demographic data for the first half of the sixteenth century are not very reliable. In the small town of Haiger 98 houses were counted in 1447 and 134 in 1564, while the population of Herborn apparently stagnated with 285 houses registered in 1538 and 286 houses in 1606. The town of Butzbach even experienced a considerable decline in its population from 2,110 in 1497 to 1,685 in 1574. On the other hand, the population of Nauheim doubled in the forty years between 1580 and 1620 from 500 to 1,000 after the salt-works were revived in 1586. In Schwalbach the population also doubled, though over a longer period. Two hundred and forty people lived there in 1495 and 500 in 1587. In Wetter the population rose from 700 in 1502 to 1,100 in 1592. Though the picture for small towns is sketchy, one can conclude that demographic expansion during the sixteenth century resulted in the selected growth of some small towns, while others experienced population decrease.[35]

Undoubtedly 'the German Reformation was an urban event'.[36] German historiography has focused on the role of large urban communities in this

---

[33] De Vries, *Urbanization* (note 9), p. 36.
[34] All the following data are taken from Keyser, *Städtebuch*, (note 6).
[35] K. A. Eckhardt, *Politische Geschichte der Landschaft an der Werra und der Stadt Witzenhausen* (Marburg, 1928), pp. 102–9.
[36] A. G. Dickens, *The German Nation and Martin Luther* (1974), p. 182.

period.[37] However, the impact of the Reformation on small towns was also significant though it has to be stressed that, in contrast to the large Imperial cities, the small towns did not benefit directly from the reforms but indirectly, via the ruler, for as territorial towns they were subject to princely rule.

Church property was first seized by the territorial state. In Hesse this happened shortly after 1527.[38] In addition to church buildings, confiscated property comprised the monasteries, the landed church property within the boundaries of towns, the hospitals and, last but not least, the revenues from the different altars, which could be quite considerable. All in all, princely influence grew in the towns because of these developments. In Grünberg, for example, there existed before the Reformation four monasteries ranked amongst the most substantial buildings in the town.[39] The administration of the monasteries was transferred to the territorial ruler's financial officer (Rentmeister), who was nominated steward of the monasteries (Kloster-vogt). The revenues were used on the one hand for the compensation of the monks and nuns and on the other for the funding of hospitals, schools, the newly founded university in Marburg and payment of the Protestant preachers.[40] In the following decades part of church property was sold to private individuals, but at present it is impossible to assess the significance of these transactions for the property structure of the town. We merely know that two groups, rich burghers and officials, noble and non-noble, bought secularised real estate in the town.[41]

However, there is some evidence that in several towns conflicts concerning church property occurred between the burghers and the territorial administration. In Gudensberg, a small town situated between Kassel and Fritzlar, the church land comprising 159 gardens and almost 50 acres of arable land was leased to the burghers. The rent was paid to the minister. In the course of the sixteenth century several cases occurred in which the leaseholders tried to transform the land into freehold property. It is not necessary to discuss the arguments in detail, but the essential point is that all complaints about the land had to be made to the territorial authorities. Such matters were not to be discussed in the secular community or in the

---

[37] See B. Moeller, *Reichsstadt und Reformation* (Berlin, 1987) with a comprehensive discussion on the historiography since its first edition in 1962 which is translated by H. G. Midelfort Durham, NC, (1982).

[38] General reading on this subject: W. Heinemeyer, 'Das Zeitalter der Reformation', in Heinemeyer, *Das Werden Hessens* (note 18), pp. 225–66, here esp. pp. 234–41 with reference to the older literature.

[39] W. Küther, *Grünberg. Geschichte und Gesicht einer Stadt* (Giessen, 1972), pp. 238–43.

[40] Küther, *Grünberg*, pp. 242–3 and 277–82.

[41] The 'Rentmeister' was enfeoffed with the Franciscan monastery by the Landgrave in 1528 and some property was sold to the family of the Count of Riedesel later on. Küther, *Grünberg*, p. 241.

ecclesiastical parish.[42] As a result of the Reformation the ruler succeeded in further integrating the town into the territorial state and in extending his authority over the civic affairs of the town.[43]

While this did little to contribute to the independence of urban communities, the educational policy introduced by Protestant rulers was a distinct gain for all small towns. Until the Reformation, education in small towns was more or less monopolised by the church. Only a negligible minority of small towns had schools run by the urban community. For example, in Grünberg, which had a monastic school, there was also another school run by the town council and the church together.[44] Educational reform in small towns during the Reformation may have constituted an 'Educational Revolution'[45] similar to that suggested for England in the sixteenth and early seventeenth centuries.[46] In dozens of small towns territorial rulers founded or reformed elementary as well as grammar schools.[47] The latter were especially important for the smaller territories because here pupils were prepared for their studies in the universities outside the territory. This was the case in Büdingen in the Earldom of Isenburg (1601) and in Dillenburg in the Earldom of Nassau (1538). In Hungen, south-west of Giessen, the income from the altar was designated for the maintenance of the newly founded school by Landgrave Philip the Magnanimous in 1564. A similar case occurred in Grünberg in 1558. In this year the last altarist died and the Landgrave ordered that his income should be used for a second teacher.[48] In addition to the elementary and grammar schools, special schools for girls were founded, especially in the Calvinist Earldom of Nassau in the towns of Herborn (1589), Dillenburg (1590) and Weilburg (1614).[49] Moreover, the Counts of Hanau and Nassau established in Hanau (1607) and in Herborn (1584), respectively, so-called 'Hohe Landesschulen', institutions of the rank of universities but without the privilege of conferring doctoral degrees.[50] Both towns were only sizeable small towns with fewer than 2,000

---

[42] H. Brunner, *Gudensberg und die Grafschaft Maden* (Cassel, 1922), pp. 152–67, esp. 165.
[43] Survey by Gerteis, *Städte* (note 11), pp. 114–24.   [44] Küther, *Grünberg*, pp. 243–4.
[45] L. Stone, 'The Educational Revolution in England 1560–1640', *Past and Present*, 28 (1964), 41–80.
[46] On this field, see the chapter in Berg *et al.*, eds, *Handbuch der deutschen Bildungsgeschichte*, Bd. I: 15. bis 17. Jahrhundert (1992).
[47] See the case study by G. Menk, 'Territorialstaat und Schulwesen in der frühen Neuzeit. Eine Untersuchung zur religiösen Dynamik an den Grafschaften Nassau und Sayn', *Jahrbuch für westdeutsche Landesgeschichte*, vol. 9 (1983), 177–220; on the elementary schools see the provisional survey by G. Schormann, 'Zweite Reformation und Bildungswesen am Beispiel der Elementarschulen', in H. Schilling, ed., *Die reformierte Konfessionalisierung in Deutschland – Das Problem der 'Zweiten Reformation'* (Gütersloh, 1985), pp. 308–16.
[48] Küther, *Grünberg* (note 39), p. 244.   [49] Menk, 'Territorialstaat', p. 189.
[50] G. Menk, *Die Hohe Schule Herborn in ihrer Frühheit, 1584–1660. Ein Beitrag zum Hochschulwesen des deutschen Kalvinismus im Zeitalter der Gegenreformation* (Wiesbaden, 1981).

inhabitants during the second half of the sixteenth century, and Herborn did not exceed this threshold before the nineteenth century.

III

The urban hierarchy of the sixteenth century described above was radically altered during the first half of the seventeenth century. In general, one can say that very few towns were able to maintain a substantial population. The medium-sized towns in the Wetterau and in the southern parts of Hesse were badly affected by the crisis. Ten of them declined to small-town status and 91 of the 119 towns had barely 500 inhabitants at the end of the Thirty Years War. Formerly sizeable small towns, like Butzbach, decreased from about 1,800 inhabitants in 1600 to about 500 in 1650; another example is Friedberg where 300 burghers were taxed in 1617 but only 70 in 1647. Bensheim in the very south of Hesse was populated by approximately 3,000 people in 1618 but only by 1,016 in 1666. Nevertheless, it has to be stressed that this decrease in population was not always the result of continuous decline and did not affect all towns equally. An excellent example of this is the small town of Ortenberg.[51] Its population was struck by plague epidemics twice before the war in 1607/8 and 1612/13. Of the 110 burghers in 1600 only 96 remained in 1615.[52] However, the community recovered surprisingly quickly and since the town was hardly affected by the early stages of the war, its population grew constantly and reached a peak in 1634. During the increasingly violent military actions between the Swedish and Catholic forces in the region, the town was not only forced to support billeted soldiers, but was also subject to plundering, famine and the plague. In 1635, Ortenberg was overcrowded with villagers from its hinterland looking for shelter within the town walls; plague broke out and during the next few months half of the population died.[53] At the end of the war Ortenberg still had only half of its former population and was extensively in debt.[54] Since the town remained a condominium of the Counts of Hanau and of Stolberg, its economic and consequently its demographic recovery was very slow. Instead of taking necessary and reasonable steps towards economic recovery the two rulers of the town indulged in narrow-minded quarrels and petty jealousies, for instance over the so-called 'Fräuleinsteuer', a tax levied by the Count of Stolberg for the dowry of his daughter.[55]

---

[51] See H. Junker, *Die Stadt Ortenberg im Zeitalter des Dreißigjährigen Krieges* (Gießen, 1936).
[52] Junker, *Ortenberg*, pp. 46–7.   [53] Keyser, *Städtebuch* (note 6), p. 362.
[54] Junker, *Ortenberg*, pp. 83, 88.
[55] Junker, *Orgenberg*, p. 89.

IV

The trend of 'des républiques marchandes aux capitales politiques' identified by Etienne François in the cities in the Holy Roman Empire can also be recognised in small towns.[56] Recovery from the war and the crisis of the seventeenth century shows how essential the 'visible hand' of the territorial princes was for the further development of small towns.[57] This process led to the division of small towns into three groups during the late seventeenth and eighteenth centuries.

The first group of towns survived on the strength of their medieval past and experienced neither economic nor demographic growth. Butzbach, for example, was the same size in 1800 as in 1600, with approximately 1,800 inhabitants. Up to the end of the Thirty Years War Butzbach's production of linen and cloth and its dyeing industry were quite considerable. For a short time the mercers of Butzbach had their own warehouse in Frankfurt. However, during and after the war the textile industry suffered a decline and by the eighteenth century only two stocking-weavers remained in Butzbach.[58] Moreover, there is no evidence of specialisation in the urban economy, either in production or in trade or marketing. In Wetter, situated north of Marburg, where some 1,100 people lived in 1592 and only 50 more in 1800, the situation was similar: a prospering textile industry until the Thirty Years War, total impoverishment in the course of the seventeenth century and no growth until the twentieth century. However, it has to be emphasised that population decrease had already occurred in Wetter before the war. In 1617 only 700 people lived there. To some extent this may have been due to the changing fortunes of the grammar school, which had been famous but declined from the 1590s onwards. Of course all towns suffered severely from the plague and the war, not only those in this group. However, the essential point is that this first group of towns failed to develop a specialised function within the territorial state or a specialised economy.

[56] E. François, 'Des républiques marchandes aux capitales politiques', *Revue d'Histoire Moderne et Contemporaine*, vol. 25 (1978), 587–603.
[57] See Olaf Mörke's paper on 'Frühmoderner Territorialstaat und Stadtentwicklung in Deutschland (16.–18. Jahrhundert)' given at the Colloquium of the International Urban History Group, Leiden, 17–19 Nov. 1988: 'The fortunes of the city and the visible hand', Papers I (unpublished). The political and legal aspects are the subject of H. Schilling, 'Stadt und frühmoderner Territorialstaat ca. 1450–1650: Stadtrepublikanismus versus Fürstensouveränität – die politische Kultur des deutschen Stadtbürgertums in der Konfrontation mit dem frümodernen Staatsprinzip', in M. Stolleis, ed., *Verfassungs- und rechtsgeschichtliche Probleme der frühneuzeitlichen Stadt* (Städteforschung, vol. A/35), (Köln, 1991). See also H. T. Gräf, 'The impact of territorial state building on German small towns, c. 1500–1800', in P. Clark, ed., *Towns and Networks in Early Modern Europe* (Centre for Urban History, University of Leicester, Working Papers No. 4) (Leicester, 1990), pp. 56–67.
[58] E. Otto, 'Zur Geschichte des Gewerbes in Butzbach während des Mittelalters und der Reformationszeit', *Archiv für Hessische Geschichte*, New Series, vol. 1 (1894), 401–49.

Both were absolutely necessary for growth above the level achieved before the Thirty Years War.

The second group of towns succeeded in this respect. This group consisted of old towns which experienced a far-reaching transformation of their functions, either as the urban residence (Residenzstädte) of princely rulers with their growing bureaucratic administration, or as fortress towns.[59] Only about half of the pre-war population lived in Weilburg, the residential town of the Counts of Nassau, in 1650, but its population grew from 400 in 1650 to 1,500 in 1781 and to almost 2,000 in 1800. The Count's role in the rebuilding of the town was crucial. Through decree he forced the burghers to renovate the demolished houses in the town. Where owners failed to comply with his orders, the houses were sold. New burghers were attracted to Weilburg by the granting of unrestricted immigration and tax exemption for one year.[60] Recovery was at first modest, but from 1685 onwards Count Johann Wolfgang started to rebuild this small country town, transforming it into a modern residential town.[61] In the following years the old Renaissance palace was surrounded by new buildings. Opposite the palace the government building was erected between 1700 and 1703, followed by the record office, the mint, the financial department and the chancellery. On the periphery of the town a new prison and a post office were built.[62] In addition, court life required an impressive architectural framework which was provided by the indoor riding school, the Orangery and several extensions to the palace. In 1712 the town centre around the marketplace was rebuilt as well. The Count paid compensation to almost 40 burgher families and removed them to a new part of the town. The marketplace was then surrounded by Baroque houses. These princely activities obviously stimu-

---

[59] For general reading on fortress towns: H. Hermann and F. Irsigler, eds, *Beiträge zur Geschichte der frühneuzeitlichen Garnisons- und Festungsstadt* (Saarbrücken, 1983); on the rebuilding of towns as residential towns of the princely rulers after the Thirty Years War see H. Schilling, *Höfe und Allianzen. Deutschland 1648–1763* (Berlin, 1989), pp. 23–31; E. J. Greipl, *Macht und Pracht. Die Geschichte der Residenzen in Franken, Schwaben und Altbayern* (Regensburg, 1991). An interesting fact is that the rulers did not always build up their residential towns on the basis of existing towns. Well known are entirely new foundations, like Karlsruhe in Baden. It is less known that in some cases even simple villages were created as residences of a princely court, especially in south-western Germany where in the course of the seventeenth and eighteenth centuries the territorial borders changed several times through hereditary partition. See K. Stroebel, *Die Residenzorte in Hohenlohe. Ihre Entwicklung seit dem 18. Jahrhundert und ihre heutigen Funktionen aus geographischer Sicht* (Tübingen, 1982), pp. 7, 16–19. Examples in Hesse are the 'Residenzdörfer' Meerholz and Langenselbold in the Earldom of Isenburg. See G-W. Hanna, *Burgen und Schlösser im Kinzigtal* (Hanau, 1992), pp. 30–2 and 47–9.

[60] A. Kuhnigk, *Geschichte der Stadt Weilburg* (Wetzlar, 1972), p. 67.

[61] On Weilburg see the study by the geographer P. Janisch, *Weilburg/L., Der Funktionswandel einer ehemaligen Residenzstadt seit dem 18. Jahrhundert* (Giessen, 1982).

[62] Janisch, *Weilburg/L.*, pp. 55–7, esp. the contemporary map with the public buildings.

lated the town's economy. In 1756, 23 guilds with more than 120 masters were registered in Weilburg.[63]

The third group of towns, which developed in the early modern period, comprised newly founded towns and/or those in which the princely ruler had a special economic interest. The most prominent example in Hesse is the town of Hanau. Here the Count of Hanau, Philipp Ludwig, chartered a new town in 1597 just south of his medieval residence which had 1,600 inhabitants at that time. Until 1833 the new town kept its own privileges and urban administration. The new burghers were Calvinist immigrants from the Netherlands, who had been driven out of their first refuge in Frankfurt by the Lutheran council. The immigrants introduced the manufacture of jewellery and diamond cutting to Hanau, a trade which is still important there today. Moreover, the Netherlanders established significant business connections with Frankfurt and the Netherlands in the timber and wine trade from the Franconian upper Main area.[64] Although the town lost a considerable portion of its population during the Thirty Years War – especially during the 1630s when the town was besieged for almost a year – its economy saw a rapid recovery. Growth was so fast that by the middle of the eighteenth century there were already more than 10,000 people living in Hanau. Another completely new, but less successful, foundation was Karlshafen north of Kassel.[65] The establishment of this town was a function of the prince's mercantilist and fiscal interests. Landgrave Karl of Hesse-Kassel desired a port of his own on the Weser which he hoped would weaken the neighbouring Hanoverian harbour of Minden. Built by French Huguenots after 1699, Karlshafen had 600 inhabitants in 1745 and approximately 1,000 in 1800.

Economic interests alone could also result in urban growth.[66] Grossalmerode, for example, was already famous by the sixteenth century for its glass production though it was still only a village. The Landgrave supported this specialisation and the manufacture of pipes supplemented the town's economy. Finally in 1775 the town was chartered with urban privileges. Its population grew from 900 in 1700 to 1,500 in 1800.

The final example in this group is Steinau, world famous as a result of the

[63] Kuhnigk, *Geschichte*, p. 92.

[64] See the exhaustive study by H. Bott, *Gründung und Anfänge der Neustadt Hanau 1596–1620*, 2 vols, (Marburg, 1970); on the manufacturing of jewellery see L. Caspari, *Die Entwicklung des Hanauer Edelmetallgewerbes von seiner Entstehung im Jahre 1597 bis zum Jahre 1873* (Darmstadt, 1916); on the shipping trade see H. Fraeb, 'Beitrag zur Geschichte des Hanauer Mainverkehrswesens', *Hanauisches Magazin*, New Series, vol. 3 (1923/24).

[65] M. Zumstrull, 'Die Gründung von 'Hugenottenstädten' als wirtschaftspolitische Maßnahme eines merkantilistischen Landesherren – am Beispiel Kassel und Karlsfen', in Press, *Städtewesen* (note 30), pp. 156–221.

[66] On the important salt production see E. G. Franz, *Der Wiederaufbau Sooden-Allendorfs nach seiner Zerstörung im 30–jährigen Krieg* (Witzenhausen, 1954).

brothers Grimm, who were brought up in this small town. However, long before this, Steinau was well known for its tobacco and hop production.[67] Since more than 50,000 pounds of tobacco were weighed on the public scales annually during the second half of the seventeenth century, it seems probable that most inhabitants were engaged in the trade. Situated on an important trade route connecting Frankfurt and Leipzig, the tobacco and tobacco products of Steinau found a ready market in those cities. In the 1680s Steinau's planters and manufacturers benefited greatly from the expansion of the tobacco trade promoted by the economic policies of the Count of Hanau. For a short period of time even the Frankfurt tobacco market was outmatched.[68] In Hanau, a town which was at this time at least twice as large as Steinau and was one of the earliest centres of tobacco cultivation and manufacture in Germany, approximately 75,000 pounds of tobacco were weighed annually in 1682 and 1683.[69]

Most of the tobacco manufactured in Steinau was grown locally. A considerable portion of the tobacco was exported to Bremen, Hamburg, Nuremberg and even to Holland. There is some evidence that this tobacco was reimported into Germany as Virginia tobacco at a much higher price.[70] The increase of cheap imports and the criticism of tobacco cultivation, due to its damaging effects on the soil, led to a slow but steady decline of production in the Earldom of Hanau. Nevertheless, tobacco manufacture remained important throughout the eighteenth century and experienced a revival when imports from America ceased during the War of Independence. However, this high degree of specialisation was destroyed by the Napoleonic Wars, during which the tobacco markets in Frankfurt and Leipzig collapsed, not least because of the French Continental System. Manufacturers could not import tobacco, nor could domestic production be exported.[71] Without an awareness of the economic background one cannot understand the extraordinary demographic development of the town. Before the Thirty Years War more than 1,000 people lived in Steinau. At the end of the war it had about 400 people, and pre-war population levels had still not been reached in 1700 when only 800 inhabitants dwelt in the town. But during the eighteenth century, stimulated by the tobacco trade, the town's population grew at a rate of almost 250 per cent and reached well over 1,900 in 1795. The Napoleonic Wars made a substantial impact,

---

[67] Keyser, *Städtebuch* (see note 6), 411.
[68] K. Cramer, 'Entstehung und Entwicklung der Hanauer Tabakindustrie', PhD thesis (Frankfurt, 1925), pp. 76–7; A. Dietz, *Frankfurter Handelsgeschichte*, 4 vols (Frankfurt, 1925), vol. IV, 1, pp. 58, 59.
[69] R. Bernges, *Zur Geschichte des Hanauer Tabaks* (Hanau, 1922), p. 21.
[70] Bernges, *Geschichte*, p. 18.
[71] Cramer, *Entstehung*, pp. 103–5.

however, and the population fell to a mere 1,400 in 1815, a sharper decrease
than that experienced by any other small town in Hesse.

V

In discussing the developments of individual towns during the early modern
period there has been great emphasis on the impact of early modern state-
building. The state has been described as the most decisive force in urban
development up to the end of *ancien régime* Europe.[72] This has to be
qualified. Thus in Frankfurt, a large and important entrepôt and banking
metropolis of European rank, the impact of state building was less important – at least in the short term. But the smaller and the more marginal
towns were, the more important the 'state' became in their development.
The role of small towns in the urban network has been mentioned at least
implicitly. We must now examine whether the prominent role of the state
contributed to the unique form of the German urban network at its lowest
level.

To begin with, it has to be emphasised that from the Middle Ages
onwards the borderline between countryside and small towns, between the
rural and the urban sphere, was as fluid as in the rest of Europe.[73] One
cannot simply talk about an urban network superimposed on a rural area.
Non-urban settlements were also of importance within the urban network,
not only due to clusters of craftsmen but also because of the market, legal
and military functions they could offer.[74] However, these settlements were
only significant within the immediate rural neighbourhood, as were many of
the stagnating and marginal small towns. One can argue that settlements of
this order were not fully integrated into the urban system. Instead they

---

[72] The most prominent examples are the newly founded towns. Although these towns were
placed in an existing network, most of them succeeded because 'centrality was created by
the exercise of stately power', W. Leiser, 'Zentralorte als Strukturproblem der Markgraf-
schaft Baden', in E. Maschke and J. Sydow, eds, *Stadt und Umland* (Stuttgart, 1974),
pp. 1–19, here p. 19.

[73] Gerlach, 'Marktflecken- und Stadtbegriff', (note 13). See also Isenmann, *Stadt* (note 7),
pp. 19–25.

[74] For general reading on rural central places: K. Mittelhäußer, 'Flecken als ländliche
Zentralorte in der Zeit von 1650–1850', in D. Brosius and M. Last, eds, *Beiträge zur
niedersächsischen Landesgeschichte* (Hildesheim, 1984), pp. 263–84. Of comparative interest:
H. K. Roessingh, 'Village and hamlet in a sandy region of the Netherlands in the middle of
the 18th century', *Acta Historiae Neerlandica*, vol. 4 (1970), 105–29. In Hesse, for example,
the village of Fronhausen situated between Marburg and Giessen with a marketplace, a castle
and a court; see W. Schulze and H. Uhlig, eds, *Giessener Geographischer Exkursionsführer*, 3
vols. (Gießen, 1982), here vol. II, pp. 168–72; or the castle of Ronneburg 30 kilometres
north-east of Frankfurt in the Earldom of Isenburg with an archive, an apothecary, a
school and other central-places functions. P. Niess, *700 Jahre Ronneburg* (Rastatt, 1987),
pp. 22–4, 37.

constituted small town–hinterland units or 'local market systems' existing within the wider urban network.[75]

Towns with specialised functions acquired after the Thirty Years War figured in a wider network, though one which tended to be restricted by the territorial boundaries of the Holy Roman Empire.[76] It is obvious that from the first half of the seventeenth century German small towns were increasingly functioning in the territorial context only, whereas small towns in England, for example, advanced from having local functions to performing specialised functions within the developing national economy and nationwide urban system.[77] In Germany, moreover, urban developments and the process of urbanisation were affected not only by the rise of the territorial states but also by war. It is hardly surprising that there was virtually no continuity in the economic and industrial development of German towns in general and of Hessian small towns in particular. Emerging centres of nineteenth-century industrialisation bore little geographical reference to the old urban centres of the medieval and sixteenth-century economy.

During the second half of the early modern period, guilds in most of the formerly prosperous small towns found it difficult to adjust to new economic trends and shut themselves and the urban economy off from outside influences and innovations.[78] This can be observed in hundreds of cases; for instance, the small guild of bakers at Grünberg developed into an isolated body during the eighteenth century when entry fines for the sons of masters were abrogated while fees for outsiders were raised enormously.[79] It is self-evident that this is one of the reasons why Germany lacked a strong, liberal, economically active bourgeoisie, preparing society for the nineteenth century; instead, a hometown 'Bürgerschaft' was created, barricading themselves behind old-fashioned privileges.[80] The industrialising

---

[75] This seems to be generally valid of pre-industrial Europe as a whole and is exhaustively studied in England. See D. Fleming, 'A local market system: Melton Mowbray and the Wreake Valley, 1549–1720', PhD thesis, University of Leicester, 1980; J. Goodacre, 'Lutterworth in the sixteenth and seventeenth century: a market town and its area', PhD thesis, University of Leicester, 1977.

[76] See the concluding remarks of my article in: P. Clark, *Towns* (note 57).

[77] See forthcoming H. T. Gräf, 'Leicestershire small towns and pre-industrial urbanization', *Transactions of the Leicestershire Historical and Archeological Society* (1994).

[78] General reading: Mack Walker, *German Home Towns, Community, State, and General Estate, 1648–1871* (Ithaca, 1971), pp. 73–107. See also documents edited by M. Stürmer, *Herbst des alten Handwerks – Meister, Gesellen und Obrigkeit im 18. Jahrhundert* (München, 1986) which deals with the socio-economic and political problems resulting from the conflict between craftsmen's guilds, state economic policies and economic trends. See esp. pp. 28–35, 40–53, here §§26–33; 257–9.

[79] See the careful study by E. Kauss, 'Die Grünberger Bäckerzunft vom 16./17. Jahrhundert', *Mitteilungen des oberhessischen Geschichtsvereins*, vol. 29 (1930), 336–94.

[80] Walker, *Home Towns*, p. 4 *et passim*; H. Möller, *Fürstenstaat oder Bürgernation. Deutschland 1763–1815* (Berlin, 1989), pp. 185–7.

economy therefore had to establish an urban network and location system of its own.[81]

The trend towards social, economic and cultural petrifaction was not pursued by all settlements. Those towns which were subject to the mercantilist and absolutist politics of the princely rulers experienced quite a different pattern of development. They became 'stehende Heerlager der Kultur',[82] centres of a modern urban culture supported by the territorial elites, i.e. highly educated civil servants, professionals, entrepreneurs and also some sections of the aristocracy. Their one common characteristic was a rather close connection with the absolutist, bureaucratic state, and all broke the boundaries of the old hierarchical society. Their self-confidence was based on education and their service to the state. These people, constituting an enlightened bourgeoisie, were open to the influence of fashions, literature, art and architecture of national, if not European, standards. Compared with the closed 'medieval' town 'the absolutist town was in this respect an anti-town'.[83] This was especially so in the cases of residential towns and the newly created refugee towns. The extraordinary growth of Offenbach from a little town with fewer than 800 inhabitants in 1700 to one with almost 6,000 in 1790 and the emergence of this town as the leading industrial centre in Hesse during the nineteenth century supports this argument. In this case immigration policies complemented the Count of Isenburg's aim to counterbalance the overwhelming economic position of Frankfurt.[84]

Germany remained a politically and economically fragmented body until the second half of the nineteenth century. However small towns as distributors of modern urban culture became important forces in the functional integration of the supra-territorial urban network.[85] In this sense it is therefore legitimate to speak of the existence of one cultural nation in the eighteenth century.

The residential towns, even the smallest, were essential to the formation of this cultural nation.[86] For instance, Arolsen, the residence of the Counts

[81] Leiser, *Zentralorte* (note 72), p. 18.

[82] I.e. 'standing army camps of culture', a dictum by J. G. Herder, 'Ideen zur Philosophie der Menschheit' (1791), in *Sämtliche Werke*, vol. 14 (Berlin, 1909), p. 486.

[83] O. Borst, 'Kulturfunktionen der deutschen Stadt im 18. Jahrhundert', in Borst, *Babel oder Jerusalem? Sechs Kapitel Stadtgeschichte* (Stuttgart, 1984), pp. 355–92, here p. 362 (transl. H. T. Gräf).

[84] This growth is seen as the result of the mercantilist policies of Count Johann Philipp of Isenburg and the settlement of the Huguenots; Keyser, *Städtebuch* (note 6), pp. 355–6. For general reading on the importance of the refugees in economic development, H. Schilling, 'Innovation through migration: the settlements of Calvinistic Netherlanders in sixteenth and seventeenth century central and western Europe', *Histoire Sociale – Social History*, vol. 16 (1983), 7–33.

[85] W. Ribhegge, 'Europäische Urbanität 1500–1800', *Die Alte Stadt*, vol. 15 (1988), 53–67.

[86] W. Ribhegge, 'Europäische Urbanität', 62.

of Waldeck, with only about 800 inhabitants in the 1750s, had its own newspaper from 1769 onwards. Other sizeable small towns and even medium-sized towns, did not have newspapers of their own before the second third of the nineteenth century (Butzbach 1842, Fritzlar 1849, Melsungen 1869, Homberg/Efze 1869); and even the former Imperial town of Gelnhausen did not have its own newspaper until 1832.[87] Newspapers, however, are only one indicator of the shift from the old-fashioned corporate culture to a new, more refined cultural and social form. The establishment of reading societies, as well as music performances and even theatres, were a sign of an open-mindedness and desire for access to culture 'à la mode' in the small residence towns.[88] For example, Weilburg, a town of some 1,500 people, had a reading society with more than 160 members after 1791.[89] By the end of the century the cultural life of the town was also supplemented by a theatre.[90]

Another important aspect illustrating the division of the small towns into two groups in terms of socio-cultural development is urban architecture. In the residential towns and to a lesser degree in the refugee towns one finds fine stone buildings in the Baroque or classical style with French-style mansard roofs.[91] At the beginning of the eighteenth century German and Italian architects and artists cooperated to remodel Weilburg as a Baroque residential town. The Orangery, for instance, was one of the earliest in Germany adopting French and Dutch architectural details. In the other small towns, by contrast, the traditional half-timbered building forms executed by local craftsmen and described by Fynes Moryson at the end of the sixteenth century persisted for the next 250 years.[92] Attempts to copy

[87] All the data provided by Keyser, *Städtebuch* (note 6).

[88] See F. Marwinski, 'Lesen in Gesellschaft. Gelehrte und literarische Lesegesellschaften in Thüringen vom Anfang des 18. Jahrhunderts bis in die dreißiger Jahre des 19. Jahrhunderts', *Jahrbuch für Regionalgeschichte*, vol. 12 (1985), 116–40. On reading societies in the small residence towns of Schleiz and Greiz see *ibid.*, p. 129; D. Rouvel, *Zur Geschichte der Musik am fürstlichwaldeckischen Hofe zu Arolsen* (Regensburg, 1962).

[89] G. Fitjer, 'Die Weilburger Lesegesellschaft', in *300 Jahre Bibliothek des Gymnasiums zu Weilburg, 1685–1985* (s.l., 1985), pp. 71–9. More than half of the 160 members of this reading society were classified as members of the 'Civil-Staat', i.e. civil service, 74.

[90] F. Heymacher, 'Zur Geschichte des Weilburger Hoftheaters', *Heimatland (Weilburg)*, vol. 2 (1923); H. Lemacher, 'Zur Geschichte der Musik am Hofe zu Nassau-Weilburg', PhD thesis (Bonn, 1916).

[91] M. Vogt, *Die Ansiedlungen der französischen Glaubensflüchtlinge in Hessen nach 1685. – Ein Beitrag zur Problematik der sogenannten Hugenottenarchitektur* (Darmstadt and Marburg, 1990).

[92] Around 1800 in the Prussian state, for example, there were only 24,642 stone houses compared with 1,454,475 half-timbered houses; W. Sombart, *Die deutsche Volkswirtschaft im neunzehnten Jahrhundert und im Anfang des 20. Jahrhunderts* (Darmstadt, 1954), p. 14.

the Baroque style were made in some cases and elements of the Baroque style are to be found in half-timbered houses.[93]

All this would indicate that it is impossible to generalise in terms of de-urbanisation in seventeenth- and eighteenth-century Germany. Nor is it possible to talk of a simple demographic threshold below which there were only marginal or declining towns. Instead, the character of a town and its functions within the territory helped determine its development in the urban network of *ancien régime* Germany. At the same time, though some towns saw the development of a buoyant social and cultural sector, one would be mistaken in identifying the urban world as the 'melting-pot' of pre-industrial society.[94] Two distinct and separate spheres continued to exist in urban life, especially in residential towns: the aristocratic sphere which focused on the Court, and the bourgeois-urban sphere.[95] However, this could not prevent, especially in residential towns, the development of an increasingly homogeneous elite which advanced the 'Verbürgerlichung' of urban culture. Under this influence Germany became one of the leading, if not the leading cultural nation around 1800, though its social and political modernisation was inaugurated by forces from abroad.[96]

---

[93] G. Binding *et al.*, *Kleine Kunstgeschichte des deutschen Fachwerkbaus* (Darmstadt, 1989); A. Bernt, ed., *Das deutsche Bürgerhaus*, vol. V (Tübingen, 1965).
[94] R. Vierhaus, *Deutschland im Zeitalter des Absolutismus* (Göttingen, 1978), p. 71.
[95] R. Vierhaus, *Staaten und Stände, 1648–1763* (Berlin, 1984), p. 40.
[96] O. Borst, 'Kulturfunktionen' (note 83), p. 388.

10 Demography and hierarchy: the small towns and the urban network in sixteenth-century Flanders[1]

Peter Stabel

'There are a lot of very beautiful and famous towns in Flanders. Among them there are the three capital cities Ghent, Bruges and Ypres; after those come Lille, Douai and Tournai.[2] In this principality one can count a further 28 walled towns . . . and 30 open towns which are considered to have the same privileges as the closed towns, as some had had in the past town walls and are still very wealthy, densely populated and in all ways well off.' In these words the famous sixteenth-century observer Ludovico Guicciardini described the urban network of the county of Flanders. Although the Florentine writer centred most of his attention on the metropolis of the Habsburgian Netherlands, Antwerp, he still stressed the economic and political importance of Flanders and its towns during the second half of the century.[3]

As the organisation of the medieval representative bodies shows, Guicciardini's account was in many ways an exact description of the Flemish urban system. The convocation lists of the estates in the fourteenth and fifteenth centuries mention, besides the three capital cities Ghent, Bruges and Ypres, in the text often described as the three good cities ('bonnes villes'

---

[1] The paper deals only with the Flemish-speaking part of the former county: the actual Belgian provinces, Eastern and Western Flanders, the region of Zeeuws–Vlaanderen in the Netherlands and parts of the Département du Nord in France (the region of Dunkirk, Hondschoote, Cassel). Except for the larger urban centres and the towns in France, the towns' Dutch names are used. As the French versions are often better known abroad, the following checklist may be of some help:
Aalst = Alost, Dendermonde = Termonde, Geraardsbergen = Grammont, Kortrijk = Courtrai, Menen = Menin, Mesen = Messines, Nieuwpoort = Nieuport, Oostende = Ostend, Oudenaarde = Audenarde, Ronse = Renaix, Sluis = Ecluse, Veurne = Furnes, Waasten = Warneton.
[2] The city of Tournai was strictly not a part of the county. It was the residence of the bishop and formed a principality of its own. Until the reform in 1555, Tournai functioned as a diocese for the greater part of Flanders. Only small parts of the county belonged to other dioceses: the extreme north to the bishopric of Utrecht and the east to Cambrai.
[3] L. Guicciardini, *Descrittione di tutti i Paesi Bassi* (Antwerp, 1581). The author describes the Low Countries in the middle of the sixteenth century before the revolt and the religious troubles (French translation: P. Ciselet and M. Delcourt, *Belgique 1567. La description de tout le Pays-Bas par Messire Ludovico Guicciardini* (Brussels, 1943)).

or 'goede steden'), an impressive number of about 40 to 50 towns, which carry the epithet small towns ('petites villes' or 'cleene steden').[4] The demographic and economic reality of medieval Flanders in this way was translated into a fixed administrative organisation, which barely changed until the end of the eighteenth century, and which in its turn influenced the political and also the fiscal and economic customs of the county. The political dominance of the three big cities (the 'Members of Flanders') resulted in a division of the urban centres into two distinct and easily recognisable categories. Furthermore, the 'Members' succeeded in the course of the fourteenth century in dividing the county into their own zones of influence. Their efforts to form city-states were finally countered by the successful centralising policy of the Burgundian dukes.[5]

In contrast to the political supremacy of the three 'Members', the small towns had considerable demographic and economic importance. Half of the urban population of the county lived in the small towns. They were politically defined as a specific group. But were they in reality such a homogeneous group? When one looks at the urban population in the county, there was indeed an important gap between the capital cities and the other towns. No real middle-sized towns seemed to function in late medieval Flanders. But within the group of 'cleene steden' itself, there was a wide variety of settlements. There were very small towns with populations of less than 1,000. Other towns, however, could count up to 10,000 inhabitants. The question must be raised whether this demographic multiformity allows us to

[4] W. Prevenier, 'Representatief karakter van de Vlaamse parlementen der XIVe eeuw', *Handelingen van de Maatschappij voor Geschiedenis en Oudheidkunde Gent*, vol. 12 (1958), 242–62 and W. P. Blockmans, 'De samenstelling van de Staten in de Bourgondische landsheerlijkheden omstreeks 1464', *Standen en Landen*, vol. 47 (1968), 57–112. The Flemish representative bodies were almost exclusively dominated by the three capital cities, also called the Members of Flanders ('Leden van Vlaanderen'). In the course of the fifteenth century a fourth Member, the rural district around Bruges ('le Franc' or 'het Vrije') was added to this body. The other towns and districts in the county were in theory only represented by their capital city. For a complete survey of the administrative and representative organisations: W. P. Blockmans, *De Volksvertegenwoordiging in Vlaanderen in de overgang van middeleeuwen naar nieuwe tijden (1384–1506) (Popular representation in Flanders during the transition from Middle Ages to modern times)* (Brussels, 1978), with an extensive English summary, pp. 645–56.

[5] In 1384 Philip the Bold, the Valois Duke of Burgundy, who had married the daughter of Louis de Male, count of Flanders, succeeded his father-in-law. His successors, John the Fearless and Philip the Good, were able to extend their power to nearly all the principalities of the Low Countries (see the monographs by R. Vaughan: *Philip the Bold: the Formation of the Burgundian State* (1962), *John the Fearless: The Growth of Burgundian Power* (1966), *Philip the Good: The Apogee of the Burgundian State* (1970) and *Charles the Bold: The Last Valois Duke of Burgundy* (1973)). After the death of Charles the Bold in 1477, his daughter Mary of Burgundy inherited the Low Countries (Burgundy itself was taken by the king of France). She married Maximilian of Austria and the Netherlands became part of the Habsburgian possessions under his son Philip (1482–1506), Charles V (1506–55) and Philip II (1555–98).

use such a crude definition as 'small', in spite of the clear political significance.

Although there is a strong tradition of urban historiography on Flemish towns, hitherto the demographic features of the urban network at the beginning of the early modern period have been surprisingly neglected. Apart from some studies on the population size of the bigger cities, overall results have been disappointing. In a recent survey by P. Klep this hiatus is all the more striking.[6] For the calculation of the urban ratios in the Belgian provinces, this author used thresholds of 10,000 and 5,000 inhabitants. Needless to say, by using this method important parts of the urban system are left out. Taking only cities with more than 10,000 inhabitants leads to an urban ratio of 24 per cent in 1475. This ratio declines to a mere 15 per cent in the middle of the sixteenth century and to only 13 per cent in 1600. Including cities with more than 5,000 inhabitants gives a more stable picture: 33 per cent in 1475, declining to 24 per cent in the first half of the sixteenth century and 25 per cent in 1565.[7] The difference between the two figures reveals the demographic importance of towns of between 5,000 and 10,000 inhabitants. As we shall see, the number of small urban centres with fewer than 5,000 inhabitants is also very important, and urban ratios, which do not take them into account, are necessarily incorrect. The main problem, however, is one of calculating the size of the small towns, due to the lack of adequate sources. Yet the little quantitative evidence that does exist in many ways confirms the Guicciardini account.

Guicciardini's analysis, however, was made in the second half of the sixteenth century, when numerous changes in the economic and political life of the Netherlands had already taken place. These changes were already clearly visible at the end of the fifteenth century. A combination of political unrest and changing economic orientation had enormous consequences for the fundamental cohesion of the Flemish urban system. In this constellation, the vital role of small urban centres needs to be examined. In the first part of the following analysis, trends in the urban network as a whole will be compared to the experience of small towns. In the second part a more

[6] P. M. M. Klep, 'Population estimates of Belgium by Province (1375–1831)', in *Historiens et populations. Liber amicorum Etienne Hélin* (Brussels, 1991), pp. 485–507 and also his 'Urban decline in Brabant: the traditionalization of investments and labour (1374–1806)', in: H. Van der Wee, ed., *The Rise and Decline of Urban Industries in Italy and the Low Counties* (Leuven, 1988), p. 271. Klep made use of the population figures in J. De Vries, *European Urbanization 1500–1800* (1984) and P. Bairoch, J. Batou and P. Chèvre, *The Population of European Cities from 800 to 1850* (Geneva, 1988).

[7] Klep's urban ratio in 1475 is equal to that calculated by W. Prevenier, which is rather surprising as Prevenier used the complete sample of towns, including the population of important towns with fewer than 5,000 inhabitants (29 per cent of urban population). Using Klep's threshold the urban ratio in 1475 should be 24 per cent, which implies a very stable urban ratio in the fifteenth and sixteenth centuries.

detailed picture will be presented for several small towns in the southern part of the region. These towns show the varied ways in which urban centres responded to changing conditions. Demographic trends reveal the importance of these changes. But a major question remains: whether the shifts in economic activity influenced the structure and the balance of power inside the urban system of Flanders. How did the small towns react to the changes? Was there a typical response by the various categories of 'cleene steden', and how does their reaction differ from that of the capital cities and the countryside?

I   An urban system in change?

In the sixteenth century the Flemish urban system was in many ways still a medieval network. In the course of the twelfth and thirteenth centuries urbanisation in Flanders reached a level unrivalled elsewhere in Western Europe.[8] The late fifteenth and the first half of the sixteenth century, however, saw dramatic changes in economic relations inside the Netherlands. Commercial routes and industrial production shifted in a first phase eastward in favour of the Duchy of Brabant. More particularly there was the emergence of Antwerp as a new world market and the prosperity of the other Brabantine centres in Antwerp's shadow. In the first phase Mechelen, and later on a more important scale, Brussels developed as administrative centres for the central government and the Court in the Netherlands. Leuven profited from its university founded in 1425. The increasing power of the centralising government in the Burgundian Low Countries, which had begun in Flanders at the end of the fourteenth century but which had met with serious opposition from the powerful 'Members', created ideal conditions for luxury crafts in the Brabantine capital cities. Yet the big Flemish cities at this time also profited from investment by the dukes. In the sixteenth century, however, the government was increasingly based in the Duchy of Brabant. Only the county's central governing bodies were still located in the big Flemish cities, Lille in French Flanders (the 'Chambre des Comptes') and Ghent (the 'Council of Flanders'). Except for short periods in the fifteenth century, the small towns could never attract the governing bodies. But the flowering of the Brabantine capital cities cannot hide the fact that not all the towns flourished. There was even a clear

---

[8] The beginning of urbanisation in the county is described in A. Verhulst, 'The origin of towns in the Low Countries and the Pirenne thesis', *Past and Present*, 122 (1989), 3–33. No recent synthesis on urban expansion in the eleventh to thirteenth centuries exists. Most work has been done on the major urban centres Ghent, Bruges and Ypres (cf. the works of H. Pirenne, H. Van Werveke, F. Ganshof). On the evolution of the network in the later Middle Ages: W. Prevenier and W. P. Blockmans, *The Burgundian Netherlands* (Cambridge, 1983), pp. 12–47.

Table 10.1. *County of Flanders: demographic and fiscal hierarchies in the urban network*

	Population estimates 1469			Transport 1408		Transport 1517		100th penny tax total assessment	
	R	population	%	R	%	R	%	R	%
Ghent†	1	60,000	26.77	2	25.98	2	28.50	2	15.76
Bruges†	2	45,000	20.08	1	29.64	1	29.11	1	19.62
Ypres†	3	9,900	4.42	3	16.19	3	14.15	3	7.03
Sluis*	4	9,720	4.34	4	3.77	13	0.81	32	0.53
Kortrijk*	5	9,517	4.25	6	2.36	5	2.22	7	3.34
Oudenaarde*	6	7,290	3.25	8	1.41	6	2.19	5	3.94
Dunkirk*	7	6,885	3.07	12	0.94	4	2.43	11	2.22
Nieuwpoort*	8	5,670	2.53	?	–	7	1.42	18	1.25
Dendermonde*	9	5,062	2.26	8	1.41	10	1.01	14	2.00
Poperinge	10	4,050	1.81	5	2.83	8	1.38	4	5.58
Aalst*	11	3,962	1.77	15	0.80	9	1.18	6	3.53
Bergues*	12	3,847	1.72	12	0.94	12	0.98	17	1.36
Geraardsbergen*	13	3,817	1.70	11	1.21	18	0.61	31	0.58
Hulst	14	3,030	1.35	20	0.50	26	0.40	22	1.18
Hazebroek	15	2,566	1.14	?	–	18	0.61	45	0.26
Diksmuide	16	2,488	1.11	7	1.89	15	0.77	21	1.20
Veurne	17	2,484	1.11	16	0.75	22	0.57	15	1.97
Bailleul	18	2,380	1.06	?	–	40	0.20	20	1.22
Ronse	19	2,295	1.02	17	0.62	10	1.01	12	2.22
Merville	20	2,025	0.90	23	0.38	18	0.61	9	2.78
Eeklo	21	2,016	0.90	?	–	24	0.46	13	2.10
Ninove*	22	1,930	0.86	27	0.33	17	0.66	19	1.24
Damme*	23	1,930	0.86	14	0.85	40	0.20	33	0.44
Menen	24	1,710	0.76	32	0.20	13	0.81	8	3.02
Kaprijke	25	1,665	0.74	?	–	30	0.35	16	1.60
Wervik	26	1,575	0.70	19	0.55	15	0.77	10	2.43
Axel	27	1,543	0.69	35	0.17	30	0.35	30	0.64

Town									
Roeslare	28	1,516	0.68	26	0.37	34	0.29	24	1.00
Aardenburg*	29	1,448	0.65	18	0.57	38	0.24	29	0.64
Tielt	30	1,408	0.63	22	0.45	22	0.57	25	0.93
Estaires	31	1,350	0.60	?	–	51	0.04	42	0.28
Mesen	32	1,260	0.56	35	0.17	35	0.27	37	0.37
Oudenburg	33	1,197	0.53	21	0.47	40	0.20	35	0.43
Harelbeke	34	1,107	0.49	33	0.19	32	0.21	34	0.44
Biervliet*	35	1,053	0.47	23	0.38	40	0.20	48	0.16
Bourbourg*	36	965	0.43	23	0.38	36	0.25	36	0.38
Ostend	37	756	0.34	30	0.24	18	0.61	23	1.18
Oostburg	38	738	0.33	30	0.24	44	0.17	46	0.23
Gistel*	39	737	0.33	33	0.19	27	0.37	49	0.16
Blankenberge	40	711	0.32	37	0.14	25	0.45	43	0.27
Torhout*	41	702	0.31	28	0.28	44	0.17	40	0.29
Rupelmonde*	41	702	0.31	29	0.25	38	0.24	39	0.32
Deinze	43	684	0.31	37	0.14	29	0.36	27	0.69
Lo	44	661	0.29	39	0.12	27	0.37	47	0.20
Cassel	45	648	0.29	?	–	32	0.32	28	0.66
Lombardsijde	46	459	0.20	40	0.09	?	–	?	–
Gravelines*	47	439	0.20	40	0.09	36	0.25	44	0.26
Warneton	48	301	0.13	?	–	44	0.17	26	0.7
Iizendijke*	49	234	0.10	–	–	–	–	?	–
Monnikerede	50	225	0.10	42	0.08	53	0.02	51	0.0
Muide*	51	175	0.08	43	0.07	51	0.04	38	0.33
Mardijck*	52	166	0.07	45	0.02	50	0.05	41	0.28
Hoeke	53	135	0.06	44	0.03	48	0.08	50	0.13

Notes: The 1469 census is, though a remarkable survey of the population in Flanders, far from being complete. For a lot of towns the population size is not known. W. Prevenier has reconstructed some of these figures with the help of the average assessment in the 'Transport' of 1408 and 1517. He calculated the average number of hearths for every penny in the assessment for the towns whose population figure is known in the census. Using this average he extrapolated a hypothetical population size for the other towns. These towns are marked in the table with * (see: W. Prevenier, 'La démographie des villes', pp. 262–4). The population figures for the three capital cities (†) come from yet another source. The Ghent figure is derived from a fourteenth-century estimate of 64,000. In the course of the fifteenth century this number has obviously declined (*ibid.*, pp. 255–6). The figure for Bruges is an average between the number of households in 1437 and 1491 (*ibid.*, p. 270), while the figure for Ypres was calculated with data from 1412, 1431, 1437, 1491 and 1506 (see H. Pirenne, 'Les dénombrements de la population d'Ypres au XVe siècle (1412–1506)', in *Vierteljahrsschrift für Sozial- und Wirtschaftsgeschichte*, 1903).

tendency for a concentration of wealth and economic dynamics in Antwerp, at the expense of the other secondary urban centres.[9] How did these dramatic changes affect the urban network in the county of Flanders, which until well into the fifteenth century had been the economic core of the Burgundian Netherlands?

Because of the population census of 1469, carried out for fiscal purposes, the Flemish urban landscape in the second half of the fifteenth century is relatively well known (see Table 10.1). It is the only census which survives from before the end of the eighteenth century. Flanders was very densely populated with an average of nearly 79 inhabitants per square kilometre; over a third were townsmen.[10] The urban landscape in the Flemish-speaking part of the county was dominated by two big cities. Ghent, whose economy was based on the textile industry and river trade, mainly in grain, had a population of about 60,000, while the more commercial city of Bruges counted over 40,000 inhabitants.[11] A large gap separated both cities from 50 smaller towns. A rank size distribution shows the abnormal character of the urban system. There were no towns in the category 10–40,000 inhabitants.

[9] The evolution of urbanisation during the later Middle Ages and the early modern period within the Southern Netherlands is dealt with in H. Van der Wee, 'Industrial dynamics and the process of urbanization and de-urbanization in the Low Countries from the late Middle Ages to the eighteenth century. A synthesis', in H. Van der Wee, ed., *The Rise and Decline of Urban Industries in Italy and in the Low Countries (Late Middle Ages–Early Modern Times)* (Leuven, 1988), pp. 307–81. The negative effects of the rise of Antwerp on the Duchy of Brabant are described in: R. Van Uytven, 'In de schaduwen van Antwerpens groei: het Hageland in de zestiende eeuw', *Bijdragen tot de geschiedenis der Nederlanden*, vol. 57 (1970).

[10] W. Prevenier, 'La démographie des villes du comté de Flandre aux XIIIe et XIVe siècles. Etat de la question. Essai d'interprétation', *Revue du Nord*, vol. 65 (1983), 255–75. The census is (poorly) edited by J. De Smet, 'Le dénombrement des foyers en Flandre en 1469', *Bulletin de la Commission Royale d'Histoire*, vol. 99 (1935), 105–50. Among the other principalities in the Netherlands, only the county of Holland could rival Flanders. It had a population density of 66 inh/km² and already in the fifteenth century an extremely high urbanisation rate of 45 per cent. The duchy of Brabant (density of 40 inh/km² and an urbanisation rate of 31 per cent) had only the same level as the more rural county of Hainaut (W. Prevenier and W. P. Blockmans, *The Burgundian Netherlands*, pp. 391–2; unlike the poor sources in Flanders, the county of Hainaut and the duchy of Brabant have an impressive series of population censuses, edited by J. Cuvelier, *Les dénombrements des foyers en Brabant, 14e–16e siècles*, Comm. Roy. d'Histoire, Brussels, 1912 and M. A. Arnould, *Les dénombrements des foyers dans le comté de Hainaut*, Comm. Roy. d'Histoire, Brussels, 1956). In the late fifteenth and first half of the sixteenth century Brabant caught up very fast: in the first half of the century the level of urbanisation in the Duchy reached 41.5 per cent, in the third quarter 47 per cent (P. M. M. Klep, 'Urbanization in a pre-industrial economy. The case of Brabant, 1374–1930', *Revue Belge d'Histoire Contemporaine*, vol. 7 (1976), 155–7).

[11] There are only reliable figures for the fourteenth century (W. Prevenier, 'La démographie des villes', pp. 255–7): Ghent had c. 64,000 inhabitants and Bruges 46,000. In the middle of the sixteenth century Ghent had c. 50,000 and Bruges 35,000 inhabitants. At the end of the century these figures dropped to 31,000 and 30,000, respectively. In the middle of the seventeenth century Ghent recovered quickly to 46,000, while Bruges only slowly reached 34,000 (H. Van Werveke, *De curve van het Gentse bevolkingscijfer in de 17de en 18de eeuw* (Brussels, 1948)).

A small group of seven towns with a population from 5,000 to 10,000, was followed by 11 towns (2,000 to 5,000), 14 towns (1–2,000) and a numerous group of very small urban centres with fewer than 1,000 inhabitants.

The spatial distribution of the towns shows remarkable differences between coastal Flanders (the Bruges area) and inland Flanders (the Ghent region). In coastal Flanders, and in particular in the immediate surroundings of Bruges, the majority of towns had fewer than 1,000 inhabitants. They were mainly small fishing and trading ports or regional market places. The string of towns on the Zwin estuary (including Damme and Sluis) is remarkable. These formed a unique economic network with Bruges. As outports for the commercial capital, some of these towns in the fourteenth and fifteenth centuries developed economic functions of their own. In Damme, for instance, there was an important trade in cured herring and wine. The small ports, however, never escaped from the zealous control of Bruges and they were politically as well as economically subject to the domination of this city.[12] The towns in the west of the county (Dunkirk and surroundings) and in the neighbourhood of Ypres had somewhat larger populations which varied from 1,200 to 4,000. Most towns in this region had textile industries. The port of Dunkirk and the decaying industrial town of Ypres were the only exceptions with over 6,000 and 9,000 inhabitants, respectively.[13]

To the south-east, in inland Flanders, the morphology of the urban network differed considerably. The towns were not as numerous, but in general much larger than those in coastal Flanders. There existed an urban vacuum in a radius of 20 kilometres round Ghent. The only town in the immediate surroundings, Deinze, never experienced full-scale urban development during the middle ages and had no more than 700 inhabitants. It was one of the few dwarf towns in the Ghent region. Most towns in the region had populations which easily exceeded 1,000 inhabitants. Important industrial activity was omnipresent (mainly woollen cloth production) and

---

[12] The towns in the Zwin estuary have been studied by J. P. Sosson and B. Fossion (J. P. Sosson, 'Finances urbaines et travaux publics. A propos de Damme au 15e siècle', in *Actes du 45e Congrès de la Fédération des Cercles d'Archéologie et d'Histoire de Belgique*, part 3 (Comines, 1982), pp. 61–74 and B. Fossion, 'Bruges et les petites villes du Zwin. A propos des réseaux urbains', in *Le réseau urbain dans une perspective historique (1350–1850). Une approche statistique et dynamique. Actes du 15e colloque international. Spa 4–6 septembre 1990* (Brussels, 1992), pp. 327–39).

[13] In the twelfth and thirteenth centuries Ypres saw a spectacular economic expansion thanks to the production of cloth. In the period the city had 30–40,000 inhabitants. But as early as the fourteenth century the town economy was slumbering. In the beginning of the fifteenth century there were only 10,000 inhabitants left and this number declined further in the course of the fifteenth and sixteenth centuries (W. Prevenier, 'La démographie des villes', pp. 257–60, H. Pirenne, 'Le dénombrement de la population d'Ypres au XVe siècle (1412–1506)', in *Vierteljahrschrift für Sozial und Wirtschaftsgeschichte*, 1903, pp. 458–89).

practically all of these towns had an ideal geographical position, situated on the banks of the main rivers, the Leie (Lys), the Scheldt and the Dender.

In the sixteenth century there is no fiscal census comparable to that of 1469. Nevertheless, it is possible to establish the urban hierarchy from the fiscal assessment of the county: the so-called 'Transport' of Flanders (1517).[14] The purpose of the 1469 census was to adapt the assessment returns to reflect the real economic and demographic power of the different urban and rural areas. The enterprise failed. In 1517, however, the new assessment was more successful, though the political balance of power in the county only allowed limited revision. The new 'Transport' was, like its predecessors, a reflection not only of economic wealth, but also of the political realities (see Table 10.1). The taxation of the three big cities was disproportionate to their real fiscal capacity. But as their basis for political supremacy in the county depended on their power to collect taxes for the central authorities, they preferred to keep things as they were. During the course of the fifteenth, and more frequently in the sixteenth century they agreed to pay several 'aides' to the count, on condition that they received a significant reduction on their own original assessment. The countryside and the small towns in this way were victims, both of rising central taxation and of the monopolistic power of the 'Members'.[15] In spite of this imbalance in the assessments, the 'Transport' could not diverge too much from economic reality without causing permanent difficulties. Apart from the assessment of the big cities, the changes in 1517 do reflect real changes in economic and demographic relations in the region.

The revision of the 'Transport' in 1517 sheds lights on the dynamics of the urban network. Rising urban centres increased their contribution. This was especially true for the secondary industrial centres in the Ghent region and for the main fishing ports on the coast (Dunkirk, Ostend and to a lesser degree Nieuwpoort). The small market towns in the Bruges region lost rank, as did the towns in the east (Zeeuws–Vlaanderen proper). The economic system in the Zwin estuary had collapsed: thus the contribution of Sluis dropped from 3.77 per cent (fourth place in the county) to 0.81 per cent (13th).

---

[14] This type of tax assessment list dates back to the beginning of the fourteenth century. In a first phase, it was organised to pay the fine in the aftermath of the treaty of Athis-sur-Orge (1305), which temporarily ended the conflict of the county with the French kings (H. van Werveke, 'Les charges financières issues du traité d'Athis (1305)', *Revue du Nord*, vol. 32 (1950), 81–93). The tax became a permanent one and very soon it was used also as a guideline for the distribution of the direct taxation levied by the counts and dukes ('aides'). As economic, geographic or political developments affected the internal ranking inside the county, the 'Transport' lists were changed, as happened in 1408 and 1517 (cf. the unpublished dissertation by W. Buntinx).

[15] Examples of this policy in N. Maddens, *De beden in het graafschap Vlaanderen tijden de regering van keizer Karel V (1515–1550)*, Standen en Landen, 72 (Kortrijk-Heule, 1978), pp. 209–46.

The general tax on real estate and movable assets in 1569 gives a more reliable picture of the changes in the urban hierarchy. The tax was a turning point in fiscal practice. It was a direct measure of the distribution of wealth. Although essentially different from the 1469 census, whose sole purpose was to count the number of fiscal hearths, the hierarchy is now better defined than in the 'Transport' assessment.[16] At first sight the changes in the urban network are minimal. Bruges and Ghent were still predominant in the county. Population estimates indicate they had 35,000 and 45,000 inhabitants, respectively, which means a steady decline of their population since the fourteenth century, but continuing dominance in the urban hierarchy. The distance that separated the two capital cities from the smaller towns in the county, however, was clearly diminishing. Internal shifts had occurred. The port towns in coastal Flanders had lost ground due to a crisis in the fishing industry and changes in economic orientation, which in the long run had caused the decline of Bruges.[17] Industrial centres, however, were able to maintain and some even to strengthen their position. During the fifteenth and sixteenth centuries most of them were able to diversify their economic structure by attracting new industrial activities besides the traditional woollen cloth industry: for example, tapestries at Oudenaarde, linen at Kortrijk, Aalst, Eeklo and Tielt and brewing at Menen.

These towns directed most of their economic activity towards the rising Antwerp market. Typical in this respect is the spectacular rise of Hondschoote as a production centre for cheap cloth (the famous 'sayettes'). In the fifteenth century a mere village, Hondschoote grew in the first half of the sixteenth century into a town with more than 15,000 inhabitants. The settlement, however, never developed a real urban infrastructure. The decline of the industry at the end of the sixteenth century caused the collapse of the town itself.[18] Thanks to linen and tapestries the town of Oudenaarde, 25 kilometres west of Ghent, doubled the number of its inhabitants during the first half of the sixteenth century to 9,000. A similar

---

[16] The taxation met with fierce resistance from the representative bodies in the different principalities. The attempt to diminish the influence of the Estates in taxation matters ultimately failed. For the circumstances which led to the 100th penny taxation: J. Craeybeckx, 'La portée fiscale et politique du 100e denier du duc d'Albe', in *Acta Historica Bruxellensia, I, Recherches sur l'histoire des finances publiques en Belgique* (Brussels, 1967), pp. 342–74. For a basic first analysis of the tax list: M. A. Arnould, 'L'impôt sur le capital en Belgique au XVIe siècle', in *Le Hainaut économique* (1946).

[17] Much has already been said about the complex relationship between Antwerp and Bruges in the sixteenth century (a general introduction is W. Brulez, 'Bruges and Antwerp in the 15th and 16th centuries: an antithesis?', *Acta Historiae Neerlandicae. Studies on the History of the Netherlands*, vol. 6 (1973), 1–26. The classic general study on the rise of Antwerp as a new world market is: H. Van der Wee, *The Growth of the Antwerp Market and the European Economy* (The Hague, 1963)).

[18] E. Coornaert, *Un centre industriel d'autrefois. La draperie-sayetterie d'Hondschoote, XIVe–XVIIIe siècles* (Paris, 1930).

trend can be seen in the towns of Aalst, Eeklo, Menen and Kortrijk.[19] The very small local market towns (for example Deinze or Torhout) and the somewhat bigger administrative and market centres (Bailleul, Veurne, Bergues) held on to their positions. Traditional drapery towns like Geraardsbergen and Kaprijke, which did not succeed in making the changeover to the new industries, rapidly lost their importance, just like the towns in the eastern parts of coastal Flanders (such as Aardenburg and Biervliet).[20]

The end of the Middle Ages in Flanders is generally seen as the beginning of a long, slow process of de-urbanisation.[21] Though this was certainly the case from the end of the sixteenth century, when population figures dropped spectacularly in most towns, the sixteenth century itself shows a more differentiated picture. Of course the major towns lost much of their importance in favour of the Brabantine towns, as was clearly the case with Bruges. Many small regional market centres stagnated. But the industrial infrastructure of Ghent and the smaller towns in its region, which in the course of the fifteenth and sixteenth centuries saw dramatic changes, remained intact. Most of the small industrial towns knew how to diversify their production, adapting it to the new market situation. Population figures in these centres were maintained or rose, sometimes even doubled.

The last quarter of the sixteenth century saw an enormous crisis for the urban system in the Southern Netherlands in general and for the Flemish towns in particular. They suffered not only from the economic collapse, but they were also direct victims of the military conflict during the revolt. The depopulation of the countryside and the towns, especially in the west and the south of the county, was devastating. Massive emigration towards the Northern Netherlands, England and Germany added to the crisis. The demographic evidence is very striking: in the regions of Aalst, Oudenaarde and Veurne the total population dropped by 40 per cent and more. The bigger cities lost more than a quarter of their population. They recovered only partially in the last decades of the seventeenth century. The smaller towns suffered even more. The spectacular economic growth of the town of Oudenaarde, already slowing down in the third quarter of the sixteenth century, was brutally halted and people left the town on a massive scale. At

[19] At Kortrijk, population grew from over 5,400 in the middle of the fifteenth century to more than 6,700 in 1530 and more than 10,000 in 1570. The population of Aalst in 1469 can be estimated at 3,900. In 1572 there were almost 6,000 inhabitants. Other industrial towns in the Ghent region experienced similar growth rates.

[20] The decline of the small towns in the north of the present-day province of Zeeuws–Vlaanderen in the Netherlands during the late middle ages and the sixteenth century is described in M. Gottschalk, *Historische geografie van westelijk Zeeuws–Vlaanderen*, parts 1 and 2 (Dieren, 1955). Some of these towns were almost literally swallowed up by the sea.

[21] E. Thoen and A. Verhulst, 'Le réseau urbain et les campagnes dans l'ancien comté de Flandre (ca. 1350–1800)', *Storia della Città*, vol. 36 (1986), 53–60.

the beginning of the seventeenth century the town had no more than 4,000 inhabitants. The neighbouring town of Ronse suffered still more: declining from about 5,000 inhabitants in the third quarter to a mere 1,700 at the end of the sixteenth century. The towns in the Dender Basin, Dendermonde, Ninove and Geraardsbergen, lost half of their population. Some of the tiny towns in the Zwin estuary which had never developed an alternative economic activity, literally disappeared (Monnikerede) or reverted to mere villages (St Anna-ter-Muiden and Hoeke). Other towns, however, did better. Aalst even held on to its population size.[22] In the course of the seventeenth century most small towns partially recovered, some quite rapidly. The majority, however, had to wait until the middle of the eighteenth century and even the nineteenth century to regain their medieval or sixteenth-century size. No wonder that the level of urbanisation in Flanders dropped considerably: from 33 per cent to only 25 per cent in the first half of the seventeenth century.[23]

II   The demographic experience of the small towns in the urban network: internal and external dynamics

The preceding analysis of the development of the urban network has revealed divergent trends for small towns. In spite of their distinctive political status, small towns cannot be regarded as a homogeneous group. Rather, there was a wide variety of towns. Their reaction to the new circumstances was not only determined by their size, but also by a complex combination of geographical, economic, social and political variables. The economic and political changes in the sixteenth century had a different impact on the various types of small towns. The somewhat larger industrial small towns in the river basins (the Ghent region) could find new opportunities by channelling their textile production towards Antwerp. But some in the 'middle' group could not diversify their industries sufficiently, stagnated and lost rank. A comparison between the towns of Oudenaarde and Geraardsbergen is revealing. Both towns had an important woollen cloth industry in the late Middle Ages; they were both situated on the banks of a river leading to Antwerp and both had an important hinterland where linen and tapestries were manufactured. Although conditions for growth seemed to be identical, the evolution of both towns diverged. Oudenaarde became a big industrial success, while Geraardsbergen was unable to profit from the external growth possibilities and missed the important stimulus of the Antwerp network. Such dynamic changes were restricted to the top

---

[22] J. De Brouwer, *Demografische evolutie van het Land van Aalst 1570–1800* (Brussels, 1968).
[23] According to P. M. Klep ('Population estimates', p. 498) this proportion dropped still further until it reached 18.9 per cent in the middle of the eighteenth century.

group of smaller towns. The very small settlements seemed to have a more stable existence in the sixteenth century. The impact of export industries was never that important. Although there were a few successful towns (Eeklo, thanks to its linen industry, is a splendid example), the majority of very small towns tended to rely on their market function.

In other regions of Flanders the trends are not quite the same. This is obvious in coastal Flanders, where all small towns seem to have suffered. Most spectacular was the collapse of the Zwin network: as well as the important 'middle-sized' town of Sluis, the very small specialised port towns in the neighbourhood of Bruges all declined. But not only the Zwin towns experienced stagnation and decay. The industrial 'middle-sized' town of Diksmuide never recovered from the decline of its cloth production, which was focused on Bruges. The very small towns in the Bruges region were able to hang on, but never experienced growth. The towns of the third region, Western Flanders, show a much more differentiated evolution. Success and failure could be very close. The medieval market towns, like Bergues or Bailleul, stagnated. Other 'middle-sized' and small urban settlements, such as the port towns of Dunkirk and industrial centres, were successful due to massive investment from Antwerp and Bruges in the Scheldt trade network (Hondschoote, Merville). Again the very small settlements stayed where they had been in the fifteenth century.

It is difficult to give a comprehensive explanation for the different responses by the small towns. The new orientation towards Antwerp seems to be a key variable. The larger small towns which managed to abandon their traditional cloth-making and change their export production towards Antwerp were able to experience spectacular success. Towns which failed to establish this link stagnated. Most of the very small towns with fewer than 1,000 or 2,000 inhabitants did not have the opportunity to adapt and profit from the new economic order. Only a few, such as Hondschoote, could attract massive investment from the bigger cities and enjoy a short-lived economic boom. Was all this the consequence of a better-integrated urban network? Although the evidence is not certain enough to confirm or contradict such a statement, it seems that the sixteenth-century changes are not the result of better integration, but rather of a different economic orientation. Indeed the medieval Flemish urban system, with Bruges as a gateway to international trade, was an excellent example of a tightly integrated urban network, with big and small drapery towns directing their production towards Bruges and the international trade community which lived there (German Hansa, Italians and Iberians). The decline of the traditional woollen industries, the change in international trade and short-term political and military difficulties made Antwerp the new gateway for the economic network of the Southern Netherlands. Most Flemish towns were very flexible in adapating to the new situation, where they could. New industries appeared or became stronger, especially in the larger small towns in the Ghent region and in the smaller industrial centres of Western Flanders.

The demographic impact of the changes in the urban network of Flanders in the sixteenth century has received only limited attention. Population trends, as we have seen, are difficult to interpret. Demographic variables such as birth, marriage or death are even more obscure.[24] The analysis of these variables, however, is very important for our understanding of the changes in the urban systems. In the case of small urban centres, a series of questions needs to be considered. Do the characteristics of demographic performance vary according to the size of towns? In other words, was there specific city, middle-sized or small town behaviour? How does this compare to rural society? And last but not least, do the economic changes of the late fifteenth and the sixteenth centuries affect the demographic performance of small towns?

Answering these questions is not easy: until the end of the sixteenth and the beginning of the seventeenth century no parish registers can be used for family reconstitution. Instead historians must depend on a very hetero-geneous group of sources, among them wills and church accounts. Complete series are not only very scarce, but their value differs from place to place. Yet for a few towns in Southern Flanders (the Ghent region), evidence from probate inventories and church accounts does exist.[25] These towns are

---

[24] Research on early modern demography in the former county of Flanders has been mainly focused on the seventeenth and eighteenth centuries. And even for these centuries, studies about urban demography are not numerous. Research methods, in particular the use of parish registers, have been employed mostly on the countryside: see the work of, amongst others, C. Vandenbroeke, P. Deprez and D. Dalle. A brief survey of recent works on towns can be found in C. Vandenbroeke, 'Prospektus van het historisch-demografisch onderzoek in Vlaanderen', *Handelingen van het Genootschap voor Geschiedenis (Société d'Emulation)*, vol. 113 (1976), in the more general bibliography of the *Algemene Geschiedenis der Nederlanden* (parts 4 and 5) and in the current bibliography dealing with Belgian urban history (M. Ryckaert, *L'histoire urbaine en Belgique. Une bibliographie sélective*, Gentse stadshistorische reeks, parts 1–3 (Ghent, 1982–6)).

[25] Probate inventories have already been used for demographic purposes in: W. P. Blockmans, 'The social and economic effects of plague in the Low Countries, 1349–1500', *Revue Belge d'Histoire et de Philologie*, vol. 58 (1980), 835–63 and in a demographic study of the Flemish countryside by E. Thoen, *Landbouwekonomie en bevolking in Vlaanderen gedurende de late middeleeuwen en het begin van de moderne tijden. Testregio: de kasselrijen van Oudenaarde en Aalst*, Belgisch Centrum voor Landelijke Geschiedenis, 90 (Ghent, 1988), part 1, pp. 15–233 (English summary in: E. Aerts and H. Van der Wee, eds, *Recent Doctoral Research in Economic History, 10th International Economic Congress* (Leuven, 1990)). This chapter does not allow us to deal with methodological problems concerning the use of probate inventories and data from accounts. A short introduction can be found in E. Thoen, *Landbouwekonomie*, part 1, pp. 17–34. The inventories provide information about the family size (always at the moment of death of a parent), sex ratios, the number of married children and inheriting grandchildren, and the proportion of double or triple marriages and single parents. No

situated in the region where export industries adapted to the new economic shifts. Evidence from them is particularly useful in that it covers a wide variety of urban settlements: middle-sized industrial towns (Oudenaarde and Kortrijk: 6,000 to 10,000 inhabitants); small industrial towns (Menen or Ronse: 1,500 to 3,000); and very small market towns, some of them specialising in the linen and flax trade (Tielt with 1,500 inhabitants). Moreover, comparison with contemporaneous demographic behaviour in the countryside can be made for the same region. The sources allow us to pay attention to three demographic variables: household size, mortality and migration. In this way an attempt can be made to explain the process of demographic growth or stagnation in the different types of small towns in a particular region.

The first variable is the size of the average household. Sources do not allow us to make an exact calculation of the internal population movement, which is the result of the balance between births and deaths. But household size, at the moment of death of one of the parents, can act as a crude indicator of natality and nuptiality. As the proportion of extramarital births seems to be negligible,[26] the general trend of natality is determined by the length of the period of fertility within marriage. The age at marriage thus becomes the most important element in defining the birth rates. The trend is also influenced by mortality in general (death of one partner in the marriage) and the number of remarriages.

Evidence on family size in the probate inventories of Oudenaarde during the first half of the century is quite revealing[27] (see Table 10.2). In the first 20 years of the sixteenth century there was a slow rise in the average number of children recorded, from 2.65 to 3.32; the third decade witnessed a slight reduction. It was the beginning of a slow but steady decline, which seems to continue in the 1550s and 1560s.[28] There was also a minor difference in family size between the urban nucleus (inside the town walls) and the suburbs, where small tenants and textile workers lived. At the end of the fifteenth century the average number of children was lower in the latter.

---

indications about the age of the persons involved are, however, present: the sources therefore can only indicate certain trends, without giving the same details as the parish registers do in the following centuries.

[26] The percentage of inventories with illegitimate children in Oudenaarde is indeed very low: only 0.7 per cent of all recorded families.

[27] The probate inventories (kept in the town archives) are partially edited by P. Van Butsele. The inventories of Kortrijk and the towns in its jurisdiction can be found in the State Archives in Kortrijk (Old Town Archives).

[28] The evolution of the number of children in households with married children was slightly different. Here the growth continued throughout the first half of the century. This divergent tendency was caused by the difference in composition of the two types of families. The average age in families with married children of course was a lot higher, which also implies different mortality and nuptiality rates.

Table 10.2. *Average number of children per household in Flemish towns*

(1)	Oudenaarde town	Kortrijk	Menen	Tielt	Oudenaarde countryside
End 15th century	2.65	2.96	2.95	3.87	3.23
1500–1509	2.89				3.40
1510–1520	3.32	3.62	3.92	4.62	3.85
1520–1529	3.16				3.52
1530–1539	3.02	3.70	4.13	3.94	4.01
1540–1549	2.92				3.93
1550–1559		3.20	4.13	3.60	3.50

(2) Oudenaarde

	Within the town walls	Suburbs
End 15th century	2.85	2.17
1500–1509	2.97	3.13
1510–1519	3.33	3.41
1520–1529	3.37	3.00
1530–1539	3.32	3.56
1540–1549	2.97	2.86

Source: probate inventories.

The town, however, grew spectacularly in the course of the first quarter of the sixteenth century. The suburbs not only received many of the migrants, but also the average number of children outgrew the number within the town walls. In the middle of the century the trend was reversed. The proletarisation of the suburbs became an acute problem. The average number of children of the richer inhabitants in the town itself became higher than in the industrialised surroundings. A comparison with other towns reveals a similar pattern. In Kortrijk, a town of the same size, the average number of children rose from 3 at the beginning to 3.7 in the middle of the century.[29] Here, the decline in the number of children happened two decades later than in Oudenaarde. This correlates well with the population growth in general. Although the population size of Oude-

[29] The apparent higher average number of children in Kortrijk may be a result of differences in the source material. The number of probate inventories at Oudenaarde is much higher that at Kortrijk. It is probable that social selection in Kortrijk was stronger. Only the top layer and parts of the middle group in society needed to make the inventories. In Oudenaarde the barrier must have been lower; there is stronger representation of lower middle groups.

naarde kept growing during the whole of the first half of the sixteenth century, the peak of that growth is situated in the first three decades. In Kortrijk the growth peak occurs in the second quarter of the century. Similar growth patterns can also be seen in the much smaller towns of Menen and Tielt, in the neighbourhood of Kortrijk. In Menen the average number of children listed rose from 3 to 4.1; in this period the town flourished thanks to its cloth industry and its important breweries. The population grew from 1,900 in 1516 to more than 3,100 in 1548. The much more rural town of Tielt, which was also a centre for the linen trade, experienced an increase from 3.9 to 4.6 children per family in the first quarter of the sixteenth century. The subsequent fall in numbers of children in this small town was more marked. The average number of children declined to 3.6 in the middle of the sixteenth century, less than at the end of the fifteenth century, when the town was still recovering from the setbacks associated with the revolt of Flanders against Maximilian of Austria.

Of course, the change in the number of children recorded in the probate inventories cannot serve as a definitive indicator of the demographic pattern in a town. It is a product of the evolution of mortality and the marriage and natality patterns. Direct information about marriage patterns in the sixteenth century is very scarce. Church accounts of Saint Martin's parish in Kortrijk indicate yearly marriage rates of 13 per 1,000 at the end of the fifteenth century, 11.6 per 1,000 in the first quarter of the sixteenth century and less than 11.3 in the third quarter of that century.[30] One can assume that when marriages were numerous, the average age at marriage was lower and possibly the number of remarriages higher than in the case of declining numbers. The relatively high figures at the end of the fifteenth century came after a severe demographic and economic crisis following the uprising of the Flemish towns against Maximilian. During the first two decades of the sixteenth century the number of marriages fell, which implies a higher average age at marriage. In the period 1520–50 the trend was reversed: a more intensive marriage behaviour followed. This confirms the rise in the average number of children. The slow decline in the number of marriages in the third quarter of the century also corresponds with the fall in family size in the probate inventories.[31]

---

[30] Archives of Saint Martin's parish Kortrijk (State Archives Kortrijk), nos 64–71, church accounts of the sixteenth century.

[31] The same trend can be deduced from the proportion of married daughters in the probate inventories of the town of Oudenaarde. At the beginning of the sixteenth century nearly 28 per cent of the recorded families had married daughters. This proportion stagnated in the second quarter of the century. Towards 1550 the percentage dropped considerably (16 per cent). The proportion of families with married children inside the town walls is much lower than in the countryside: in 1530–9, 30 per cent against more than 50 per cent. This is in sharp contrast to the higher total number of children inside the walls. Did people marry and

Though there is a general trend in both very small and middle-sized towns – a fall in the average age at marriage at the beginning of the sixteenth century and an increase in the number of children, followed by a reversal of the trend towards the middle of the century – there are also substantial differences between the various types of towns. Household size is much larger in the very small towns. The average household size in the rural town of Tielt is nearly the same as that in the countryside. The strong connection of the town's economy with rural linen production may have caused this similar demographic behaviour. An exception was the small town of Menen: its average family size was similar to that of middle-sized towns at the beginning of the sixteenth century. There was also a similarity in the industrial structure, with the importance of cloth production. In contrast to the general trend, however, the number of children never really dropped in the first half of the century. Changes in the town's economy may help to explain this atypical evolution: the decline of cloth production was more than offset by the rise of brewing and an important increase in the number of richer inhabitants and rentiers.[32] The average number of children and consequently marriage behaviour depended not only on the size of the town. The difference in demographic behaviour between Tielt and Menen stresses the importance of the economic organisation of the small towns. Small industrial centres have a demographic experience similar to the middle-sized towns, while market towns much more closely resemble the countryside.

The second factor affecting demographic trends in the small towns was mortality. The population movement in the later Middle Ages and the early modern period was dominated by a succession of mortality crises. Extremely high mortality rates were recurrent. A simple count of the number of probate inventories of Oudenaarde or Kortrijk indicates the importance of crisis mortality. After a few crisis years in 1504 and 1506–7, hitting both towns hard,[33] the first three decades of the sixteenth century were less severe, though with mortality crises recurring, as in 1516 and 1517. The years 1530–50 were far more difficult, with high death rates in 1534–5 and 1540–2. This, however, was only the prelude to a disastrous period with the subsistence crisis of 1554–9, when the number of probate inventories almost tripled. The remainder of the third quarter of the sixteenth century was more stable (despite crises in 1564, 1571 and 1573). In

die sooner in the poorer quarters of the town? Until further research has been done, this question cannot be answered.

[32] The increase in the number of rentiers in Menen correlates with a marked growth in the probate inventories of the real property owned by burghers in the neighbouring countryside in the course of the sixteenth century (P. Stabel, 'The urban network in Flanders').

[33] During the mortality crisis of 1503 and 1504 in Kortrijk, there were 112 and 260 burials. In the previous and following years the average was only 40 to 50.

general, the trend in other small and secondary towns of Flanders was quite similar.[34]

However impressive the numbers of burials during mortality crises, their importance is often overstated. After a crisis, the population often recovered very quickly: mortality rates fell, people reacted by marrying earlier, and migration filled up the gaps. The very densely populated countryside, with mostly very small farms and important rural industries, was in this period a constant reservoir for prosperous towns in need of labour. Average mortality rates have more important consequences in the long run. Very few sixteenth-century mortality rates, however, can be found in contemporary sources. In the church accounts of the towns of Kortrijk and Hulst the number of burials is recorded.[35] In the small town of Hulst (2,500 inhabitants) the yearly general death rate in the first half of the sixteenth century was 44.5 per thousand. Behind this figure, however, was a clear divergence between the mortality of adults (39 per thousand) and children (54 per thousand). The impact of massive child mortality was a constant restraint on urban natural increase. The contemporary death rate of adults in Kortrijk was 35.5 per thousand.[36] As was the case with crisis mortality, there seems to be no significant difference between the small and the middle-sized town: Hulst and Kortrijk had important industrial sectors. No data have survived for the very small market towns. For the Flemish countryside in the fifteenth century, E. Thoen has calculated an adult death rate of 33 to 35 per thousand, which is slightly lower than in the town.[37] These death rates are an average. As we have seen, they hide the feverish course of death. The crisis mortality of the 1550s had disastrous short-term effects on urban populations. In Hulst the death rate rose to more than 75 per thousand (adults 65, children 90). In five years more than one third of the population was swept away. Again, children were the most vulnerable group in urban society.

With such heavy mortality, the only way in which the towns could experience growth was by way of immigration. This was certainly the case for Kortrijk, which grew from 7,000 to more than 10,000 inhabitants in the middle of the century. The town of Hulst, however, experienced stagnation,

---

[34] A similar death toll is to be found in 1516–17, in 1546 and in the 1550s.

[35] Town archives of Hulst (Netherlands), church accounts 1500–1600. The town specialised in the production of salt and textiles and also functioned as a market for local agriculture (cereals and dyestuffs). The trade in madder for the cloth production in Antwerp and the Flemish textile centres was an especially important element in the town economy (H. Van der Wee, *The Growth of the Antwerp Market*, part 2, p. 138).

[36] The figures in Kortrijk are less complete than those of Hulst. Burials of children and of people living from poor relief were delegated to an appointed grave digger. He gave part of his yearly income to the church, without specifying the number of burials. As there were different fees, an exact number cannot be reconstructed.

[37] E. Thoen, *Landbouwekonomie en bevolking*, p. 76.

in spite of a relatively developed economic infrastructure in the shadow of Antwerp, and could never outgrow its medieval size. It would be dangerous to use high mortality rates to prove the so-called urban graveyard effect. A lot of variables remain unknown. The impact of differential mortality between residents and migrants may have been important. Mortality seems to hit all Flemish urban centres, irrespective of size. There also seems to be only a minor difference between urban and rural society. The effects of death, however, are particularly felt in decaying towns. There, migration flows were inadequate to sustain quick recovery from crisis.

This brings us to the issue of migration. Although migration is seen by many as one of the key variables in urban demography, it is one of the most difficult to quantify, certainly for sixteenth-century Flemish towns. Its importance, however, cannot be doubted. Almost half of all surnames in a tax list of the town of Geraardsbergen in 1534 (3,000 inhabitants) belonged to newcomers compared with a similar list in the middle of the fifteenth century.[38] The only dynamic sources illustrating migration are the registers of new burgesses.[39] The best information again is to be found in the town of Oudenaarde. The immigrants ('poorters van versitte') became burghers after a stay of one year and a day in the town; this involved no costs.[40] In the second half of the fifteenth century the average annual number of entries was slightly over ten. In the course of the sixteenth century this figure rose rapidly: 18 to 20 in the first decades, 25 in the second quarter and more than 30 in the crisis years after the middle of the century. There is also a clear change in the origin of the migrants. In the fifteenth century most of them came from the surrounding countryside (a radius of 10 to 15 kilometres). The economic expansion attracted migrants from a much wider area (20–25 kilometres and more). There were also many newcomers from the neighbouring principalities of Brabant, Tournai and Hainaut and from the French-speaking parts of Flanders (Lille). Migrants even came from other drapery towns, attracted by the employment opportunities in the expanding

[38] Archives générales du royaume (Brussels), Chambre des Comptes, 45286–7.

[39] Registers with entries of new burghers survive for only a few towns. The accuracy of registration depended on the town administration. The city of Ghent for a very long time refused to keep registers. As the city was very powerful, it counted on obfuscation with regard to the number of its burghers and out-burghers in order to retain a strong grip on the county. In towns with effective registration, as was the case in Oudenaarde, many immigrants were not registered, because they did not feel the need to acquire the burghership, even when there were practically no costs involved: among these were temporary migrants, servants, beggars, refugees fleeing the war in the countryside, and many illiterate workers. The migrants who planned on staying in the town, on the other hand, had a lot to gain by registering. They were often the most important people for the local economy: skilled artisans or craftsmen and traders.

[40] The registers of new burghers are edited by: P. Van Butsele, *Poortersboeken van Oudenaarde. Het groot poortersboek van Oudenaarde of 'Poortersbouc der Stede en Caele van Audenaerde' (a° 1288–a° 1550)* (Handzame, 1977).

industry of tapestries, whereas inter-urban migration in the Middle Ages had rarely involved Oudenaarde. In other Flemish towns the registers of new burghers offer a different picture. In some towns, entry to the burghership could involve a relatively high income fee. It gradually became the privilege of an economic elite of craftsmen. This can be seen in the entries of the towns of Aalst or Kortrijk, where the number of newly registered burghers dropped during the sixteenth century. Nonetheless the population size of these towns increased.[41]

The figures for Oudenaarde are quite revealing, with the volume of migration very important. The evolution of the population size of the town is well known.[42] In 1504 the town counted more than 6,200 inhabitants; this rose to 7,646 in 1534 and to 8,467 in 1552. In the third quarter of the century it dropped a little (7,853 in 1571). At the start of the revolt against Philip II the population size collapsed: in 1619 the town had no more than 3,720 inhabitants. In the period 1504–24, when the town gained 1,433 inhabitants, more than 580 immigrants received the burghership. They were mostly craftsmen, (retailing) traders or merchants. In a less flourishing period of the town's history, the years 1552–71, when mortality was high and emigration rose, the population dropped by 600. Yet in the same period the town received 625 new burghers. The conclusion is tempting. The immigrants stimulated town growth in periods with normal mortality. In periods of high or extreme death rates they could fill up the gaps, and even in the case of economically flourishing towns allow some growth.[43]

Towns were by no means just reservoirs attracting migrants. Emigration too must have been very important. An analysis of the immigration figures of the bigger cities (Antwerp, Bruges, Ghent) indicates the function of the small towns as suppliers of trained labour to the bigger centres. Antwerp

---

[41] Town Arch. Kortrijk, poortersboeken. In the other towns information concerning the new burghers can only be found in the town accounts (Arch. Gén. Brussels, Chambre des Comptes: L. Gachard, *Inventaire des Archives de la Chambre des Comptes* (Brussels, 1931), part 5).

[42] A contemporary alderman, Joos Vandenbroucke, was very interested in collecting statistics. The figures are preserved in a chronicle of the history of the town by Bartolomeus De Rantere (1775–1831). Parts of his chronicle are edited by D. Tack and M. De Smet. The sixteenth century, however, is still to be studied in the manuscript (Town Archives Oudenaarde). The population figures have been published by L. Dhondt in an introduction to L. Robijn, *Historie van de Ketterije te Oudenaerde* (Oudenaarde, 1982).

[43] In this study E. Thoen (*Landbouwekonomie en bevolking*) tried to assess the impact of migration on urban growth. His figures, however, are quite incomplete (he used only the new burghers of the settlement on the left bank of the Scheldt river, without Pamele on the right bank: Oudenaarde was a typical 'double town', with two benches of aldermen and two distinct administrations). Pamele had a more marked industrial, proletarian character, while Oudenaarde was wealthier with more (retail) trade. The global figures therefore give a different picture from Thoen's. His hypothesis that the town in the course of the sixteenth century did not depend on immigration for its growth cannot be proven. The trend in the average household size only seems to suggest growing possibilities for natural increase.

alone attracted important numbers of migrants from the smaller Flemish towns: in the 1540s 20 from the nearby town of Dendermonde, 16 from Oudenaarde, nine from Kortrijk. In the following decades these figures doubled. At first sight such numbers seem unimportant, but as one can see from the registers of the small towns, the bigger cities almost exclusively attracted the dynamic forces as new burghers. This kind of 'brain drain' was also directed towards the big Flemish cities. Declining Bruges still managed to attract craftsmen and merchants from Oudenaarde and Kortrijk. Although exact numbers are missing, Ghent seems to have exercised a similar attractions.[44] Emigration, however, was not only directed towards the bigger cities; as the origin of the new burghers of Oudenaarde shows, inter-urban migration between small and secondary towns was important. Last but not least, there was the constant flow of temporary migration between town and countryside: seasonal labourers, servants and wanderers.

III   Conclusion

Because of the few studies so far on urban demography at the beginning of the early modern period, definite conclusions would be premature. However, the divergent demographic behaviour of the different types of the smaller urban centres suggests some major issues. The examples used in this paper come mainly from a specific part of the county, the region of Ghent, with its industrial river towns, in particular Oudenaarde and Kortrijk. Both towns belonged to the top layer of small towns, had similar administrative and market functions and also experienced similar growth in the course of the sixteenth century thanks to tapestries and expensive linen. Other sources deal with the smaller towns of Hulst and Menen and very small centres such as Tielt, which had clear rural characteristics. These towns showed similarities as well as dissimilarities in their demographic experience during the sixteenth century. The most striking example is the average family size. It was generally larger in the smaller centres than in the more urbanised towns. Moreover, nuptiality and natality patterns in the very small market centres resembled those in the countryside. In contrast, in the small industrial towns the pattern looked similar to that in the middle-sized towns. Whether there was also a parallel with the big Flemish cities remains to be discovered.

In the case of vital events, most significant is the impact of mortality. As the Hulst example shows, this was generally very high, even in normal periods. Moreover half of all recorded deaths were children. Combined with

[44] R. A. Parmentier, *Indices op de Brugsche poortersboeken 1418–1794* (Bruges, 1938), J. Van Roey, *Antwerpse poortersboeken 1533–1608* (s.d.) and J. Decavele, *Poorters – en buitenpoortersboeken van Gent (1477–1491, 1542–1796)* (Ghent, 1983).

the enormous impact of short-term crisis mortality, there was a serious constraint on natural increase. Nonetheless, in periods with stable mortality, the number of births seemed to be able to produce some natural increase. In the last decades of the fifteenth and the first decades of the sixteenth century, the average age at marriage was probably low. The number of children per family grew thanks to the extended period of fertility. This growth stagnated at a relatively high level in the second quarter of the century. Immigration into the successful secondary industrial centres steadily became more important, while these towns also expanded their area of recruitment. Some of the very small industrial towns seem to have enjoyed the same trend. The combination of natural increase and high immigration stimulated population growth. Industrial success and a linkage to the new economic system centred on Antwerp guaranteed expansion. In this way, it was not the size of a town that was a key factor in its demographic success, but its economic structure. The patterns of migration and household size of the small successful industrial centres are more like those of the middle-sized towns than of the small market towns. The latter towns and the old industrial centres that missed the link-up with Antwerp failed to attract comparable numbers of migrants. They stagnated by limiting activity to their central functions for the countryside. Some even experienced a significant reduction in their population size.

Emigration towards the bigger cities shifted in the first half of the century to the advantage of the big Brabantine cities (especially Antwerp). In the late 1540s and the 1550s the average family size dropped. The immediate effects on population size in the successful very small and secondary towns were compensated for by higher immigration from the countryside. But in the end the excessive death rates broke urban growth. The period of political instability in the 1570s, followed by an economic and military crisis, caused massive emigration, firstly to Antwerp, later on towards the Northern Netherlands, England and Germany. The textile centres lost the majority of their trained craftsmen and industry declined. Although the seventeenth century already saw signs of recovery, de-urbanisation was from the end of the sixteenth century the dominant theme. A lot of small towns could fall back on their market function for the industrialised countryside. But because of the decline of urban exports most Flemish towns had to wait until the eighteenth century to recover their late medieval or sixteenth-century size.

11 Domestic demand and urbanisation in the eighteenth century: demographic and functional evidence for small towns of Brabant

Bruno Blondé

1 Small towns in the Brabantine urban context

Brabant[1] in the eighteenth century was a densely populated region, forming (with the capital Brussels and some other important cities) the heart of the urban system of the Southern Netherlands during the early modern period. Moreover this region was highly urbanised. At the start of the eighteenth century 45 per cent of the population lived in urban settlements with at least 5,000 inhabitants compared to 'only' 16 per cent in England.[2] This figure decreased, however, to 31 per cent on the eve of the modern period (1806). The first half of the century was indeed characterised by steady de-urbanisation as measured by the urban share of the population. Absolute numbers show a similar trend. The total population living in settlements of at least 5,000 inhabitants dropped from 219,000 in 1709 to 169,000 in the mid-century (1755). During the second half of the century the Brabantine urban world managed to recover from these severe losses. In relative terms, however, the decline continued, though on a reduced scale.

Small towns in this highly urbanised region are – by European standards – not small at all. One Franco-British comparative research project on small towns used a lower limit of 1,000 and an upper limit of 5,000 inhabitants.[3] Even then agglomerations with a few hundred inhabitants could possess urban characteristics.[4] The size of small towns in Brabant was on average much greater, and varied between 2,000 and 10,000 inhabitants (see

---

[1] The region called Brabant, which I discuss in this chapter, covers only the Belgian part of the old duchy with the same name. It corresponds more or less to the present-day provinces of Brabant and Antwerp. The cities of Halle and Vilvoorde are not included in this research.

[2] P. Klep, *Bevolking en arbeid in transformatie. Een onderzoek in Brabant, 1700–1900* (Nijmegen, 1981), p. 81; P. Slack, 'Town and countryside in England (ca. 1500–1800)', *Storia della città. Rivista internazionale di storia urbana e territoriale*, vol. 36 (1986), 61.

[3] P. Clark, 'Les petites villes en Grande-Bretagne 1600–1850: problèmes de définition et grandes lignes de leur évolution', in J-P. Poussou and P. Loupès, eds., *Les petites villes du moyen-âge à nos jours* (Paris, 1987), p. 216.

[4] See, for example: H. Gräf, 'The impact of territorial state building on German small towns, c. 1500–1800', in P. Clark, ed., *Towns and Networks in Early Modern Europe* (Leicester, 1990), p. 57 quotes the example of Hatzfeld in Hesse with fewer than 200 inhabitants in 1600.

Table 11.1. *Population of eleven Brabantine cities (in thousands)*

	1709	1755	1784	1806
Brussels	78	60	75	74
Antwerp	70	46	51	60
Mechelen	25	19	20	20
Leuven	15	15	19	24
Lier	8	7	9.5	10
Turnhout	6.2	8.3	8.3	10
Diest	6	4.2	5.4	6
Tienen	5	5	6.3	7
Nijvel	5.5	5.3	6.4	7
Waver	2.2	2.7	4	4
Aarschot	2	2	2.3	3

Source: P. Klep, *Bevolking en arbeid in transformatie. Een onderzoek in Brabant, 1700–1900* (Nijmegen, 1981), pp. 341–54.

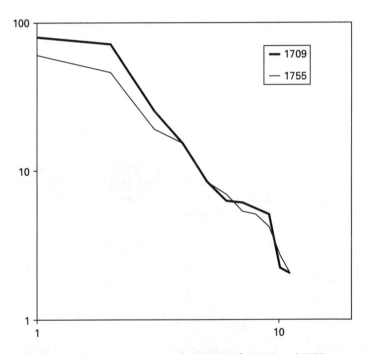

11.1 Towns in Brabant: rank size distribution for 1709 and 1755

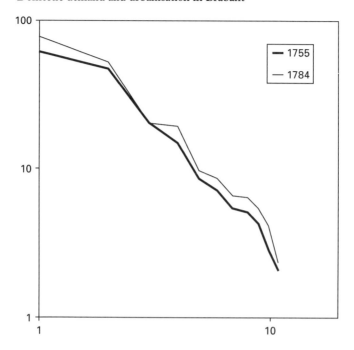

11.2 Towns in Brabant: rank size distribution for 1755 and 1784

Table 11.1). Identifying the lower limit, or making a distinction between predominantly rural and predominantly urban communities, is, of course, not a matter of population numbers alone. The village of Geel, for instance, counted 3,408 inhabitants in 1755, among whom were a handful of very specialised artisans and professions.[5] Yet, with more than two thirds of its population employed in agriculture, it was essentially a great village, exerting only a limited centrality for neighbouring villages. Tracing the upper limit on the other hand is more a matter of quantitative differences. Most small towns were walled, administered like big cities and *intra muros* agricultural activities remained small-scale, only occurring in the peripheral areas. Table 11.1 shows clearly the demographic ceiling for small towns. Mechelen and Leuven are far greater than the greatest Brabantine small towns and so *a fortiori* are Brussels and Antwerp.

Even though the Brabantine small town was comparatively big, a maximum of one fifth of the urban population lived in urban settlements

[5] J. Verbeemen, 'Steden der Antwerpse Kempen in 1755. Hun demografische en economische toestand', *Oudheid en Kunst*, vol. 38 (1955), 145–63.

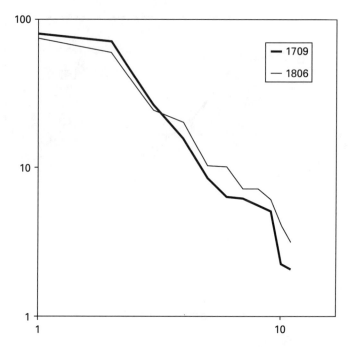

11.3 Towns in Brabant: rank size distribution for 1709 and 1806

with between 2,000 and 10,000 inhabitants. From the rank size distribution
we are able to describe the important changes which during the eighteenth
century occurred in the urban system of this region.[6] Between 1709 and
1755 the urban system shifted to a much more concave shape (Fig. 11.1).
Clearly the biggest urban centres suffered most from the de-urbanisation
process. During the second half of the century the urban world generally
recovered, with small towns showing the strongest growth (Fig. 11.2). In
1806 the urban space housed as many inhabitants as in 1709, but they were
no longer so heavily concentrated in the great cities (Fig. 11.3).[7] In the
following pages we will try to establish what factors determined this strong

---

[6] For our present purposes we do not attribute any explanatory value to the rank size rule
nor to the law of proportionate effect. As a descriptive tool, however, the rank size distribution has proved its merits. See J. De Vries, *European Urbanization, 1500–1800* (1984),
pp. 85–95 and more recently from the same author 'Problems in the measurement, description, and analysis of historical urbanization', in A. Van der Woude, A. Hayami and J. De
Vries, eds, *Urbanization in History. A Process of Dynamic Interactions* (Oxford, 1990),
pp. 48–53.

[7] This decentralisation process was a European-wide process; J. De Vries, *European Urbanization*, p. 101.

small-town performance and what distinguished small towns from the greater cities.

2   Explaining small town growth

2.1   *The export-industrial model*

Difficult urban conditions in the first half of the eighteenth century, and the slow recovery during the second half, are usually attributed to the fate of the urban export industries. An impressive synthesis and analysis of current research on this topic has been published by Herman van der Wee.[8] According to this model, the Brabantine urban decline after the turn of the century was mainly determined by the decline of urban export industries, which met increasing difficulties on foreign markets where state mercantilistic policies of import substitution rendered sales very difficult in the major European countries. More and more protectionist measures were promulgated. The Treaty of 1715, on the other hand, did not allow the Austrian Netherlands to develop an active tariff policy itself. Increasingly the metropolitan capitals of the nation states were setting the pace in international fashion and dominating upper-class consumption and trade. At the same time, falling agricultural prices and stable nominal wages stimulated the market for cheap standardised textiles, with the result that the centre of industrial gravity shifted towards the countryside.

The great Brabantine cities were severely hit by de-industrialisation. As we have already seen, the urban share of the population fell back dramatically. Employment in the urban production sectors collapsed. In 1650 the Antwerp textile industry employed 8,230 men; by 1738 this figure had fallen to 1,695.[9] The only trade resisting this decay, more or less successfully, was

---

[8] H. van der Wee, 'Industrial dynamics and the process of urbanization and de-urbanization in the Low Countries from the Middle Ages to the eighteenth century. A survey', in H. van der Wee, ed., *The Rise and Decline of Urban Industries in Italy and in the Low Countries (Late Middle Ages–Early Modern Times)* (Leuven, 1988), pp. 307–81. See also the interesting overview by A. Lottin and H. Soly, 'Aspects de l'histoire des villes des Pays-Bas méridionaux et de la Principauté de Liège (milieu du XVIIe siècle à la veille de la Révolution française', in J-P. Poussou *et al.*, *Etudes sur les villes en Europe Occidentale (milieu du XVIIe siècle à la veille de la Révolution Française*, vol. II (Paris, 1981), pp. 251–8. This paragraph is also strongly inspired by C. Lis and H. Soly, 'Living apart together: overheid en ondernemers in Brabant en Vlaanderen tijdens de tweede helft van de 18de eeuw', in *Arbeid in veelvoud. Een huldeboek voor Jan Craeybeckx en Etienne Scholliers* (Brussels, 1988), pp. 131–44 and from the same authors, 'Restructuring the urban textile industries in Brabant and Flanders during the second half of the eighteenth century', in E. Aerts and J. Munro, eds, *Textiles of the Low Countries in European Economic History* (10th International Economic History Congress, Proceedings, Session B-15), (Leuven, 1990), pp. 105–13.

[9] A. K. L. Thijs, *'Van "werkwinkel" tot "fabriek". De textielnijverheid te Antwerpen (einde 15de–begin 19de eeuw)* (Brussels, 1986), pp. 177–81.

lacemaking. By the mid-eighteenth century Antwerp employed 10,000 lace-workers, Brussels almost the same number, Mechelen 5,000 and the small towns of Lier and Nijvel 2,000 (perhaps 3,000) and 500, respectively. But, after the Peace of Aachen in 1748 the tide turned. The government of the Austrian Netherlands now started to follow a pragmatic *ad hoc* tariff policy. Due to population increase, labour became available at lower cost. New and expanding textile branches developed outside the old restrictive guild controls.

Cotton was without doubt one of the leading new sectors. Major cotton manufacturers emerged alongside cotton-printing and linen-bleaching firms. In Brabant Brussels, Antwerp and Mechelen were the most important production centres, but some small towns also benefited. In Vilvoorde a cotton-printing firm emerged; from 1762 flannels were produced in Tienen. Thanks to a detailed case study we can also follow the establishment and growth of 'De Heyder & Co.' at Lier.[10] In 1757 Peter Jacob de Heyder started in this small town a 'flannel' dyeing and weaving mill in a vertically integrated factory. A cotton-printing plant and a workshop for 'siamoises' followed. For several reasons de Heyder preferred the small town of Lier to Antwerp. In the latter strong resistance from some of the established guilds was a problem. Moreover the cost of living in the small town was considerably lower, hence also wages. For employment at Lier the firm was of great importance. In 1764 De Heyder & Co. employed about 350 labourers, nearly 14 per cent of the adult male population. In the industrial sector no alternative employment opportunities existed.

As we shall argue, however, this export-based theory may be more applicable to the larger urban centres than to small ones. The industrial export model indeed fails as a general explanatory model. The stagnation of small towns in the first half of the century was a general phenomenon (see Table 11.1). The same was also true for their rapid recovery during the second half of the century.[11] So far as we know, small towns such as Nijvel, Diest and Waver failed to acquire a significant export industry (except for female lace-working). Nevertheless, they grew at the same rate as, or faster than, bigger towns and cities such as Antwerp, Brussels, Leuven and Mechelen. We must therefore turn to other explanatory arguments such as the influence of the reduction in transport costs.

2.2   The transport-costs model

The structure of the transport network obviously played a key role in the

---

[10] C. Lis and H. Soly, *Een groot bedrijf in een kleine stad. De firma de Heyder en Co. te Lier, 1757–1834* (Lier, 1987).
[11] Even in small towns without export industries.

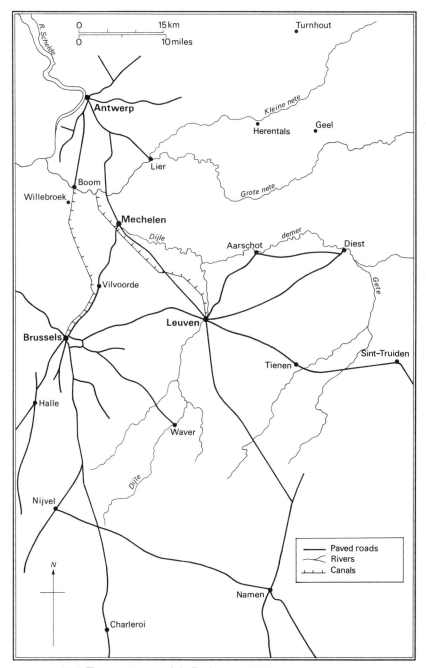

11.4 Transport network in Brabant c. 1780

spatial organisation of the Brabantine urban system. The Campine area (in the north-east) lacked navigable waterways (except for the small town of Lier which benefited from the river Nete). In the southern part of Brabant the incidence of urban settlements was greater, though here too no navigable rivers existed. The core area of the Brabantine urban world, however, was organised around an extensive river network. Here Brussels, Antwerp, Mechelen and Leuven emerged, assisted by a whole range of small towns including Zoutleeuw, Tienen, Diest, Aarschot, Vilvoorde and Lier.[12]

During the eighteenth century the transport system improved considerably. Under the supervision of the central government efforts were made to improve the navigability of the Demer, Dijle and Grote Nete.[13] More important, Leuven won government approval to dig a canal to the Rupel (near Mechelen) (Fig. 11.4).[14] Although the construction work ruined the Leuven municipal finances, the city profited greatly from the revival of transit trade to Luik.[15]

The expansion of the paved roads network was more spectacular. Before 1704 the old Duchy of Brabant counted only 94 kilometres of paved roads serving fragmented parts of the local market. By 1718 this figure had already risen to 208 kilometres and it expanded further to more than 500 kilometres by 1793.[16] We are still poorly informed about the economic consequences of the construction, maintenance and exploitation of these new roads for the regional economy.[17] Contemporaries as well as historians agree in their positive judgement of these infrastructural improvements. But this leaves unanswered the question of their impact on the *urban system*.[18] According to A. Lottin and H. Soly the construction of new roads benefited regions which

[12] See R. Van Uytven, 'Brabantse en Antwerpse centrale plaatsen (14de–19de eeuw)', in *Le réseau urbain en Belgique dans une perspective historique (1350–1850). Une approche statistique et dynamique* (Brussels, 1992), pp. 35–6.

[13] Y. Urbain, 'La formation du réseau des voies navigables en Belgique. Développements du système des voies d'eau et politique des transports sous l'Ancien Régime', *Bulletin de l'Institut des Recherches Economiques et Sociales*, vol. 10 (1939), 298–300.

[14] Map based on E. Lejour, 'De aanleg en het onderhoud der wegen in België door de locale besturen. De barrières en de tolrechten vanaf de middeleeuwen tot aan de revolutie van 1830', *Gemeentekrediet van België. Driemaandelijks tijdschrift*, vol. 9 (1955), 1–7.

[15] L. Van Buyten, 'Een laat initiatief: de Leuvense 'commerciekamer' (1789)', in F. Vanhemelrijck, ed., *Revolutie in Brabant, 1787–1793* (Brussels, 1990), pp. 209–14 and L. Van Buyten, *De Leuvense stadsfinanciën onder het Oostenrijks Regiem (1713–1794)*, vol. I (Leuven, 1982), pp. 105–43.

[16] L. Genicot, 'Etudes sur la construction des routes en Belgique', *Bulletin de l'Institut des Recherches Economiques et Sociales*, vol. 12 (1946), 584.

[17] An interesting case study has been written on the paved road from Leuven to Diest by G. Hanegreefs, 'De steenweg Diest–Leuven (1777–1797)', *Arca Lovaniensis*, vol. 9b (1980), 23–186. Compare J. De Vries, *Barges and Capitalism. Passenger Transportation in the Dutch Economy, 1632–1839* (Utrecht, 1981).

[18] See for France B. Lepetit, *Les villes dans la France moderne (1740–1840)* (Paris, 1988), pp. 280–322.

Table 11.2. *Number of paved direct intercity connections in Brabant*

From	By 1718	By 1748	By 1793
Brussels	4	6	9
Antwerp	2	2	3
Leuven	2	3	6
Mechelen	2	3	3
Lier	1	1	1
Tienen	1	2	2
Diest	0	0	2
Aarschot	0	0	2
Waver	0	0	1
Nijvel	0	0	4
Turnhout	0	0	0
Herentals	0	0	0

were already highly urbanised.[19] L. Van Buyten argues that it reinforced the commercial predominance of bigger centres *vis-à-vis* the small towns and the countryside.[20] Certainly, the greater Brabantine cities took the lead in the renewal of their transportation infrastructure. This can be seen in Table 11.2 which calculates the cumulative number of paved routes to other cities.[21] Only during the second half of the eighteenth century were the small towns integrated fully into the new commercial framework.[22]

Yet it is very difficult to establish a causal connection between the accessibility and connectivity of cities through paved roads or canals and their economic (or demographic) development. During the first half of the century the greater cities lost a big part of their population in spite of their initial advantage in the road construction boom. Furthermore, some roads turned out to be more successful than others.[23] And if Brussels, to quote one example only, succeeded in enlarging its hinterland to the south through a paved road to Waver,[24] the small town also shared in the advantages. Indeed

[19] A. Lottin et H. Soly, 'Aspects de l'histoire des villes', p. 230.
[20] L. Van Buyten, ' "Verlichting" en traditie. De Leuvense stadsfinanciën en hun economische grondslagen onder het Oostenrijks regiem (1713–1794)', (Unpublished PhD, K.U.L.), 3, p. 50.
[21] After 1763 the Brussels–Willebroek canal was extended thanks to the Antwerp–Boom road. From that time on this connection was also treated as a 'paved' intercity connection.
[22] E. Lejour, 'Création des chaussées dans l'ancien Brabant sous le règne de Marie-Thérèse (1740–1780)' (Unpublished PhD, U.L.B.), Brussels, 1925, p. 163.
[23] The paved Leuven–Diest road, for instance, was no great success. Hanegreefs, *De steenweg*, p. 182.
[24] The charter of 21 Jan. 1768 was motivated as follows '(. . .) *pour multiplier les voyes de communication entre cette ville [Brussels] et tous les cantons du Païs dont on tire les denrées et productions nécessaires pour l'usage et pour le commerce de ses habitants (. . .)*' Algemeen Rijksarchief Brussels (henceforth ARAB), *Rekenkamer*, 152, f. 203.

after the road's completion Waver started to function as a provisioning market centre for the capital. As a result, the town also gained importance as a central place.[25]

Although it remains difficult to measure the beneficial impact of transport innovations on urban growth, indirect evidence points in that direction. For small towns intercity connections (for interregional as well as local trade purposes) became essential to further economic growth, hence the eagerness with which they applied for authorisation by the central government to build roads.[26] Apart from the Campine towns (Turnhout and Herentals), all the small towns in Brabant benefited from the opening up of at least one paved road by the end of the early modern period. But other factors also were at work. As with the export-based model the general explanatory value of the transport-costs model is unsatisfactory. Transport improvements were, of course, a necessary but not a sufficient condition for economic growth.

2.3   The growth of the home market

In 1750 when the de-industrialisation movement reached its zenith, one third of the Brabantine population still lived in a town: but what sustained them? In order to answer this question we need to examine domestic demand factors. Paul Klep was the first to draw attention to the internal contradictions of the export-industrial model.[27] While per capita exports decreased during the second half of the eighteenth century, rent incomes per capita, he argued, rose and helped to compensate (albeit insufficiently) for losses in the export market. The conclusions of Klep were to a large extent based on econometric and demographic evidence. In this section it is necessary to test his findings against detailed historical data on urban functions.

If domestic demand indeed played a decisive role in the development of the Brabantine non-agrarian sector, then a well-integrated hierarchically structured urban network should have developed. To summarise the central-place theory,[28] the development of central places depends upon the

---

[25] See further below.
[26] There was one important exception. In 1735 the Estates of Brabant planned to extend the paved Leuven–Tienen road to Sint-Truiden via Zoutleeuw. The magistracy of the latter strongly resisted and finally the road avoided the small town. As a result Zoutleeuw was completely ruralised during the following decades.
[27] P. Klep, *Bevolking en arbeid*, pp. 249–64 and P. Klep, 'Urban decline in Brabant: the traditionalization of investments and labour (1374–1806)', in *The Rise and Decline*, pp. 281–4.
[28] W. Christaller, *Die zentralen Orte in Süddeutschland* (Jena, 1933).

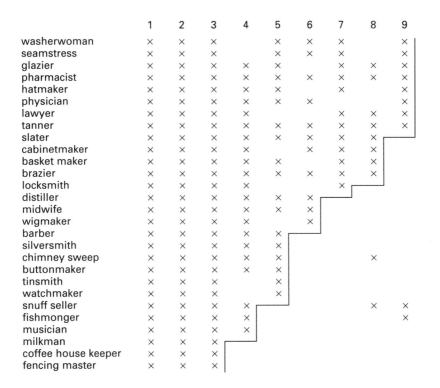

	1	2	3	4	5	6	7	8	9
washerwoman	×	×	×		×	×	×		×
seamstress	×	×	×		×	×	×		×
glazier	×	×	×	×	×		×	×	×
pharmacist	×	×	×	×	×	×	×	×	×
hatmaker	×	×	×	×	×		×		×
physician	×	×	×	×	×	×			×
lawyer	×	×	×	×			×	×	×
tanner	×	×	×	×	×	×	×	×	×
slater	×	×	×	×	×	×	×	×	
cabinetmaker	×	×	×	×		×	×	×	
basket maker	×	×	×	×	×		×	×	
brazier	×	×	×	×	×	×	×	×	
locksmith	×	×	×	×			×		
distiller	×	×	×	×	×	×			
midwife	×	×	×	×	×	×			
wigmaker	×	×	×	×		×			
barber	×	×	×	×	×				
silversmith	×	×	×	×	×				
chimney sweep	×	×	×	×	×			×	
buttonmaker	×	×	×	×	×				
tinsmith	×	×	×		×				
watchmaker	×	×	×		×				
snuff seller	×	×	×	×				×	×
fishmonger	×	×	×	×					×
musician	×	×	×	×					
milkman	×	×	×						
coffee house keeper	×	×	×						
fencing master	×	×	×						

Source: R. Van Uytven, 'Peiling naar de beroepsstructuur op het Brabantse platteland omstreeks 1755', in *Bijdragen tot de geschiedenis*, vol. 55 (1972), 172–203.

11.5 Presence–absence matrix of occupations in nine towns in Brabant in 1755 (see note 31).

consumption of goods and services in the central place. The supply of these goods and services (whose nature may be political, economic and cultural as well as administrative) is oriented towards the complementary region or hinterland. The *range* is the maximum distance consumers are prepared to travel to consume a certain central good. Within this range a *threshold demand* (a minimum level of consumption) should be present in order to make the supply of a central good or service profitable. The system of central places consists of a high number of central places of a lower order and a considerably smaller number of central places with a somewhat greater importance. Moreover, each centre of a higher order combines the

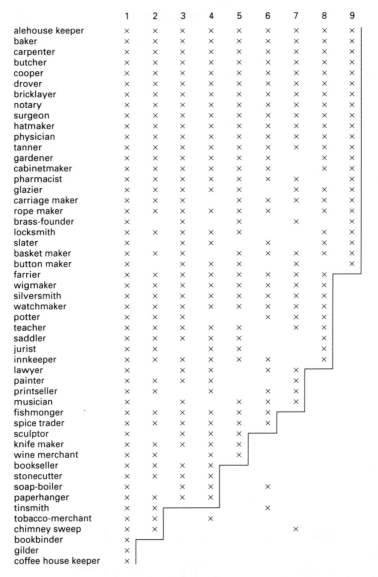

	1	2	3	4	5	6	7	8	9
alehouse keeper	×	×	×	×	×	×	×	×	×
baker	×	×	×	×	×	×	×	×	×
carpenter	×	×	×	×	×	×	×	×	×
butcher	×	×	×	×	×	×	×	×	×
cooper	×	×	×	×	×	×	×	×	×
drover	×	×	×	×	×	×	×	×	×
bricklayer	×	×	×	×	×	×	×	×	×
notary	×	×	×	×	×	×	×	×	×
surgeon	×	×	×	×	×	×	×	×	×
hatmaker	×	×	×	×	×	×	×	×	×
physician	×	×	×	×	×	×	×	×	×
tanner	×	×	×	×	×	×	×	×	×
gardener	×	×	×	×	×	×		×	×
cabinetmaker	×	×	×	×	×	×		×	×
pharmacist	×	×	×	×	×	×	×		×
glazier	×	×	×	×	×		×	×	×
carriage maker	×	×	×		×	×	×	×	×
rope maker	×	×	×	×	×	×		×	×
brass-founder	×		×		×		×		×
locksmith	×	×		×	×			×	×
slater	×		×	×		×		×	×
basket maker	×	×			×	×	×	×	×
button maker	×		×	×	×		×		×
farrier	×	×	×	×	×	×	×	×	
wigmaker	×	×	×	×	×	×	×	×	
silversmith	×	×	×	×	×	×	×	×	
watchmaker	×	×	×	×	×	×	×	×	
potter	×	×	×			×	×	×	
teacher	×	×	×	×	×		×	×	
saddler	×	×	×		×			×	
jurist	×	×		×	×			×	
innkeeper	×	×	×	×	×	×		×	
lawyer	×		×	×		×	×		
painter	×	×	×	×			×		
printseller	×	×		×		×	×		
musician	×		×		×	×	×		
fishmonger	×	×	×	×	×	×			
spice trader	×	×	×	×	×	×			
sculptor	×		×	×	×				
knife maker	×	×	×	×	×				
wine merchant	×	×		×	×				
bookseller	×	×	×	×					
stonecutter	×	×	×	×					
soap-boiler	×		×	×		×			
paperhanger	×	×	×	×					
tinsmith	×					×			
tobacco-merchant	×	×		×					
chimney sweep	×	×					×		
bookbinder	×								
gilder	×								
coffee house keeper	×								

Sources. 1. Leuven, ARAB, *Centrale administratie Dijledepartement*, 3637–3640; 2. Lier, Stadsarchief Lier, telling jaar IV; 3. Tienen, ARAB, *Dijledepartement*, 3721; 4. Nijvel, *Ibid*, 3664; 5. Waver, *Ibidem*, 3728; 6. Diest, M. Theys, *La population de Diest pendant les deux premiers tiers du XIXe siècle*, s.l., 1977, pp. 50–66; 7. Turnhout, Algemeen Rijksarchief Antwerpen (Henceforth ARAA), *Provinciaal Archief*, J174B; 8. Aarschot, ARAB, *Dijledepartement*, 3503; 9. Herentals, ARAA, *Provinciaal Archief*, J174A.

11.6 Presence–absence matrix of occupations in nine towns in Brabant in 1796 (see note 32).

specific functions linked with it, with the functions and goods provided by the centres of a lower order.

Here we will try to reconstruct the hierarchy of central places in order to show the regional differences in the Brabantine urban system. The approach will essentially be functional rather than demographic. Using two eighteenth-century censuses (1755 and 1796), we will attempt to reconstruct the occupational structure of late early modern Brabantine towns.[29]

Since the available data are incomplete it is necessary to use the technique of a presence–absence matrix as the basis of analysis.[30] There are obvious limitations to this method, not least the way that the numbers in particular trades are ignored, but we will return to this later. The presence–absence matrix for 1755 (Fig. 11.5) covers only a limited number of small towns.[31] Figure 11.5 shows the transition from the small town of Turnhout to the villages and towns of a lower hierarchical level. They offer such specialised functions as a glazier, a pharmacist, a lawyer and a physician. What distinguishes Turnhout, Diest and the other bigger cities from these settlements of a lower rank are, for instance, the presence of a barber, a silversmith, a chimney sweep, a buttonmaker, a tinsmith and a watchmaker. Below the level of Turnhout, settlements show the absence of a number of basic occupations; Hoogstraten, for instance, lacks a glazier, a lawyer, a hatmaker and a basketmaker. On the other hand Leuven, Antwerp and Brussels stand at the top of the hierarchy, offering highly specialised goods and services such as those of milkman, coffee-house keeper and fencing master.

The presence–absence matrix for 1796 (Fig. 11.6) reveals an equally interesting picture.[32] This matrix clearly illustrates the basic functional package provided by every central place by the end of the early modern period, such as a shoemaker, a surgeon, a hatter and a physician. Higher in the hierarchy the spectrum of goods and services becomes more extended, but there is a decline in the number of centres providing them. Musicians, tinsmiths, sculptors and booksellers only occur in centres of a higher order.

As already stated, the presence–absence matrix has the great disadvantage

[29] For a critical elaboration of these sources and the methodology used see my forthcoming dissertation.

[30] Occupational data available often relate to the heads of family only. So it is impossible to gather reliable employment data. For the technique, its use and limits, see, among many others, H. Carter, *An Introduction to Urban Historical Geography* (1983), pp. 85–91.

[31] 1 = Brussels, 2 = Antwerp, 3 = Leuven, 4 = Diest, 5 = Turnhout, 6 = Hoogstraten, 7 = Herentals, 8 = Geel, 9 = Meerhout. R. Van Uytven, 'Peiling naar de beroepsstructuur op het Brabantse platteland omstreeks 1755', in *Bijdragen tot de Geschiedenis*, 55 (1972), 172–203.

[32] 1 = Leuven, 2 = Lier, 3 = Tienen, 4 = Nijvel, 5 = Waver, 6 = Diest, 7 = Turnhout, 8 = Aarschot, 9 = Herentals.

Table 11.3. *Centrality index for eight Brabantine towns in 1796*

Leuven	41.46
Lier	14.27
Tienen	13.44
Nijvel	11.74
Waver	7.99
Turnhout	5.42
Aarschot	2.89
Herentals	2.80

of ignoring occupation numbers. A more accurate method of measuring centrality, therefore, has to be introduced. For small towns in 1796 an alternative method of measurement was tested.[33] Each function t (a bookseller, for example) received a location coefficient, c. This location coefficient equals the percentual value of one representative of this function t in the total number of functions t in the studied region. If the derived coefficient is multiplied then by the number of representatives per settlement, a centrality value is derived (the centrality given to a settlement by function t). If, finally, all centrality values (for all kinds of functions) are summed, a functional index is derived.[34] In Table 11.3 the centrality index for eight Brabantine towns in 1796 is calculated on the basis of the 1796

[33] H. Carter, *An Introduction*, p. 89 and H. Carter, *The Study of Urban Geography*, 3rd edn. (s.l., 1981), p. 85. This method was derived by Davies in 1967. W. Davies, 'Centrality and the central place hierarchy', in *Urban Studies*, vol. 4 (1967), 61–79. It has already been applied by J. Thomas, 'Foires et marchés, bourgs et villages dans le midi Toulousain au XIXe siècle', in Poussou and Loupès *Les petites villes*, pp. 165–89.

[34] Imagine a theoretical region with but two places and two different functions, namely bakers (n = 20) and surgeons (n = 1). The location coefficient for bakers is 5, since each baker represents 5 per cent of the total number of bakers. The location coefficient for surgeons is 100, since only one surgeon occurs in this hypothetical region. The centrality given to settlement A and B by bakers and surgeons must be summed, giving the centrality index (which in Table 11.3 is reduced to 100 for convenience of comparison).

Hypothetical region with two places, two functions and 21 representatives

Place	Number of		Centrality given by		Centrality index
	Bakers	Surgeon	Bakers	Surgeon	
A	15	1	75	100	175
B	5	0	25	0	25
Total	20	1	100	100	200

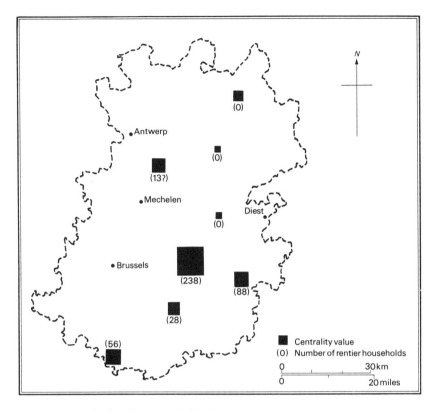

11.7 Brabantine central places in 1796

population census.[35] More than the presence–absence matrix this centrality index reveals the real centrality and attractiveness of regional centres for their surrounding countryside.

Two conclusions can be drawn from the projection of this centrality index on the Brabantine map (Figs. 11.7 and 11.8). First of all, and not surprisingly, the urban network does not correspond to the ideal 'Christaller

[35] The centrality index was calculated on the basis of more than 60 different occupations: lawyer, apothecary, baker, barber, sculptor, butcher, paperhanger, tinsmith, bookbinder, bookseller, surgeon, chocolate-seller, dancing-master, turner, printer, silversmith, physician, yeast-seller, glazier, trader, innkeeper, hatmaker, farrier, ironmonger, jurist, kettlemaker, tailor, buttonmaker, coffee-house keeper, coppersmith, grocer, cooper, tanner, slater, basketmaker, general shopkeeper, knifemaker, bricklayer, musician, notary, second-hand-shopkeeper, plasterer, potter, wigmaker, painter, shoemaker, schoolmaster, chimney-sweep, cabinetmaker, locksmith, stonecutter, tobacco merchant, carpenter, rope-maker, gardener, watchmaker, gilder, fishmonger, driver, carriagemaker, wine merchant, saddler, soapboiler.

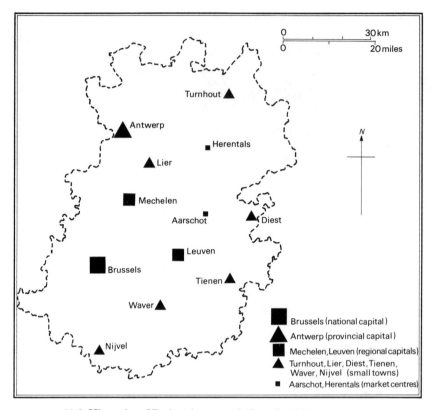

11.8 Hierarchy of Brabantine central places in 1796

network'. A variety of specific locational conditions is responsible for this variation. Moreover, the region falls – very roughly – into two urban systems. Below the line Antwerp, Lier, Aarschot and Diest, a well-established and structured urban system appears. Above this line only Turnhout and Herentals are located and they are relatively unimportant centres.

One should not forget that the urban network depicted here is based upon quantitative data only: the number of representatives of a certain function in a certain city. It ignores differences in turnover, income, wealth, expertise and quality. Diest, for example, housed during the whole eighteenth century some very highly specialised artisans, such as tinsmiths and silversmiths, but for important contracts foreign artisans had to be brought in.[36]

---

[36] M. Van der Eycken, 'Stadseconomie en conjunctuur te Diest (1490–1795)' (unpublished PhD, K.U.L.), Leuven, 1982, 390–1. Religious institutions almost always depended upon artisans from other Brabantine cities for sculptures.

Some differences in wealth and importance are reflected by official tax rates in the capitation of 1747.[37] Physicians and lawyers in the great cities had to pay 20 guilders while their colleagues in the small towns and in the countryside were assessed at only 12 guilders. The average tax rate of brewers in greater cities varied between 10 and 100 guilders, while brewers in small towns and in the countryside were forced to pay 16 guilders.[38]

Having said this, it is important to try and explain why in the north-east of the region no urban network developed, whereas in the north-west, in the middle and in the south, one finds a very well-structured urban system. In general the urban hierarchy is closely linked to the physical and economic productivity of the Brabantine agriculture.[39] In the 'southern' part more fertile soils and bigger farms guaranteed a market-oriented agriculture, aided by the relatively advanced transportation system.[40] In the north-east the opposite picture appears: the Campine area was composed of infertile sandy soils;[41] there was no established transport system, as we have already seen. Moreover the average size of farm in the Campine area was small. All these factors together determined the relatively weak development of the Campine towns.[42] In spite of size (8,300 inhabitants in 1784) Turnhout has a very low centrality value (5.42). This would suggest that domestic demand indeed played a decisive role in the structuring of the Brabantine urban system. The distribution of rentier households also illustrates the partial (but important) dependence of the Brabantine urban system on the

[37] *Instuction [sic] et Règlement pour la levée & collecte d'une Imposition capitale sur les Personnes, Chevaux & autres Bestiaux, Charrues, Cheminées & Redemption pour la Consomption du Thé qui sa fera de la part des Etats du Pays & Duché de Brabant pour la Subside de cette année 1747* (Brussels, 1747).

[38] The fact that Lier and Diest brewers – though small-town inhabitants – were taxed as if they lived in greater cities indicates that tax rates were based on different wealth levels. Indeed, in Diest as well as in Lier, a considerable beer-brewing industry existed in this period. Cf. E. Aerts, 'Bier, brouwers en brouwerijen in Lier. Institutionele, sociale en economische aspecten van een stedelijke industrie tijdens de late middeleeuwen en de nieuwe tijd (1400–1800)' (Unpublished PhD, K.U.L.), Leuven, 1988, *passim*, and for the social position of Lier brewers more especially pp. 519–32, and M. Vandereycken, *Stadseconomie en conjunctuur*, pp. 231–61.

[39] P. Klep, *Bevolking en arbeid*, pp. 28–31.

[40] See, among others, C. Vandenbroeke, *Agriculture et alimentation* (Belgisch Centrum voor Landelijke Geschiedenis, (no. 49), Ghent (Leuven, 1975), pp. 27–33.

[41] In 1800 more than two thirds of these sandy soils were still not cultivated. E. Vanhaute and G. Landuyt, 'Turnhout en de Turnhoutse Kempen op het einde van de achttiende eeuw. Een sociaal-economische schets', in H. De Kok, ed., *Turnhout den eersten troost der Staten*, *Taxandria. Jaarboek van de Koninklijke Kring van de Antwerpse Kempen*, vol. 61 (1989), 311–24.

[42] P. Klep, *Groeidynamiek en stagnatie in een agrarisch grensgebied. De economische ontwikkeling in de Noordantwerpse Kempen en de Baronie van Breda, 1750–1850* (Bijdragen tot de geschiedenis van het Zuiden van Nederland, dl. 26) (Tilburg, 1973), *passim* and especially pp. 186–7.

agricultural investments in the central and southern parts of the region (Fig. 11.8).[43]

What then were the dynamics of domestic demand, so important for the development of the urban system? Undoubtedly rental income played an important role in the consumption of relatively expensive and specialised urban goods and services.[44] An increase in wage income, on the other hand, tended in the first place to be spent on extra food and standardised low-quality products often produced in the countryside.[45] For Brabantine urban development the evolution of rental income may well have been of great importance. The first half of the century was in this respect an unfavourable one.[46] Grain prices dropped. Between 1709 and 1755 the agricultural sector went through a deep crisis, and incomes from capital investments stagnated or even declined. At the same time real wage incomes reached their peak.[47] In the second half of the century, the reverse was true. Population pressure forced grain prices and agricultural rents up,[48] while the real wages of labour deteriorated. The distribution of income between capital and labour began its long switch to capital.[49]

Significant in this respect was the increase of the number of rentier households in some towns. In 1755 15 rentier households resided in Tienen.[50] In 1796 this figure had risen to 88. The same happened in Waver

---

[43] Cf. L. Van Buyten, 'Grondbezit en grondwaarde', p. 104.

[44] This essentially goes back to Engel's law. Most important in this law is the decrease in the percentage of income spent on food as income rises. See: V. Van Rompuy and others, *Inleiding tot de economie* (Leuven, 1977), pp. 116–18; P. Klep, *Bevolking en arbeid*, pp. 239–40; P. M. Hohenberg and L. Hollen Lees, *The Making of Urban Europe, 1000–1950* (1985), pp. 111–20 and 343–4 and P. M. Hohenberg and L. Hollen Lees 'Urban decline and regional economies: Brabant, Castile, and Lombardy, 1550–1750', in *Comparative Studies in Society and History*, vol. 31 (1989), 450–5. P. Hohenberg, 'The city: agent or production of urbanization', in *Urbanization in History*, pp. 358–60.

[45] Contrast E. A. Wrigley, 'Urban growth and agricultural change: England and the Continent in the Early Modern Period', in Wrigley, *People, Cities and Wealth: The Transformation of Traditional Society* (Oxford, 1987), pp. 157–93, which includes an attempt to correlate real wage income changes with urban development. Also: E. A. Wrigley and R. S. Schofield, *The Population History of England, 1541–1871; A Reconstruction* (Cambridge, 1989), pp. 474–5.

[46] See P. M. Hohenberg and L. Hollen Lees, 'Urban decline', pp. 452–3.

[47] E. Scholliers, 'De materiële verschijningsvormen van de armoede voor de industriële revolutie. Omvang, evolutie en oorzaken', *Tijdschrift voor Geschiedenis*, vol. 88 (1975), 466.

[48] For example: F. De Wever, 'Pachtprijzen in Vlaanderen en Brabant in de 18de eeuw. Bijdrage tot de konjunktuurstudie', *Tijdschrift voor geschiedenis*, vol. 85 (1972), 180–204 and F. Daelemans, 'Pachten en welvaart op het platteland van Belgisch Brabant (15e–18e eeuw)', in *A. A. G. Bijdragen*, vol. 28 (Wageningen, 1986), pp. 165–83.

[49] P. Klep, 'Urban decline', p. 284.

[50] B-M. Dupuy, 'Description de l'économie des Pays-Bas Autrichiens', in P. Moureaux, ed., *La statistique industrielle dans les Pays-Bas autrichiens à l'époque de Marie-Thérèse. Documents et cartes*, vol. II (Brussels, 1974), p. 16 (written in 1751): 'La ville de Tirlemont n'est pas considérable, il n'y a qu'une seule paroisse qui contient environ 2,000 maisons et 10,000

where the number of rentier households rose from 0 to 28 at the end of the century. At least one third of these rentiers were immigrants (probably from the surrounding countryside). Detailed research on consumption patterns and material culture in Brabant still needs to be undertaken.[51] Nevertheless, the growth of the Brabantine cities in this period was clearly encouraged by an increase of 'domestic' luxury consumption, an increase which was stimulated by the growth of sociability among urban elites. The growing social gap between rich and poor within Brabantine society was articulated in the cultural field by an increasingly exclusive elite-culture.[52] Respectable people visited the opera and theatre, preferably by coach: they also met in coffee-houses, at balls and so on.[53] Brussels and the other bigger cities enjoyed a comparative advantage as far as socio-cultural attractivity was concerned. Less is known about the cultural life in Brabantine small towns. Yet, the growth of the rentier class there must have stimulated cultural expenditure. Documents concerning the 'emprunt forcé' of 1796 record 25 rentier households in Waver with an average capital of 47,108 French livres, 2.5 times the average capital of 'wealthy' tradesmen in the small town.[54] Both categories dominated local social life. They were probably responsible for the presence in the town of a specialised music shop, together with six musicians, one sculptor and two silversmiths.

The increasing incomes of the Brabantine abbeys confirm the favourable

habitants. Il peut y avoir 25 maisons vivant noblement sans faire aucun négoce, ni désservir aucun emploi.'

[51] For Ghent, H. Soly, C. Terryn, J. Van Ryckegem, I. Pisters and I. Bourgeois undertook the first systematic research, *Oostvlaamse Zanten*, vol. 63 (1988), 3–50; 71–98. Also: G. Staes, *Le cadre de vie des élites louvanistes (1750–1796)* (U.C.L., mémoire de licence inédit) (Louvain-la-Neuve, 1987) and A. De Wachter, *Le cadre de vie de la noblesse: quelques intérieurs bruxellois dans la seconde moitié du XVIIIe siècle* (U.C.L., mémoire de licence inédit) (Louvain-la-Neuve, 1984). Further systematic research is indispensable in order to uncover changing consumption patterns, the advance of manners in eighteenth-century bourgeois circles, the differentiation of consumption patterns over the urban hierarchy, etc. Cf. in this respect L. Weatherill, *Consumer Behaviour and Material Culture in Britain, 1660–1760* (1988); P. Benedict, 'French cities from the sixteenth century to the Revolution: an overview.', in P. Benedict, ed., *Cities and Social Change in Early Modern France* (1989), pp. 42–3 and J. R. Farr, 'Consumers, commerce and the craftsmen of Dijon: the changing social and economic structure of a provincial capital, 1450–1750', in Benedict (ed.), *Cities*, pp. 134–5, 143, 147.

[52] H. Soly, 'Social aspects of structural changes in the urban industries of eighteenth-century Brabant and Flanders', in *The Rise and Decline*, p. 251 and H. Soly, 'Economische en sociaal-culturele structuren: continuïteit en verandering', in J. Van der Stock, ed., *Stad in Vlaanderen. Cultuur en maatschappij, 1477–1787* (Brussels, 1991), p. 42.

[53] See among many others M. Van den Berg, 'De adel in de 18de eeuw: een "leisure class"?', in *De adel in het hertogdom Brabant* (Brussels, 1985), pp. 143–83.

[54] ARAB, *Dijledepartement*, no. 1372.

Table 11.4. *Selected occupations of heads of family at Tienen in 1755 and 1796*

	1755	1796
Pharmacist	4	5
Lawyer	3	13
Sculptor	0	1
Paperhanger	0	3
Tinsmith	1	4
Bookseller	0	1
Surgeon	7	14
Silversmith	1	3
Glazier	3	5
Spice seller	0	5
Basketmaker	1	4
Musician	4	2
Wigmaker	4	6
Locksmith	6	11

position of landowners in the late eighteenth century.[55] In the countryside, bigger farmers were also very well off.[56] Abbé Mann wrote in 1783:

Il n'y que ceux du Brabant-Wallon qui soient restés à leurs anciens principes, et qui ont conservé leur ancienne culture et les grandes fermes. Dans ce pays-là, les fermiers sont riches, bien logés, bien nourris, mangeant comme des patriarches à une table longue, le fermier et sa femme au bout de la table, avec leur bouteille de vin: ses enfants et les domestiques mangeant à la même table.[57]

The growth of the service sector in the countryside between Brussels and Antwerp shows that demographic growth was not synonymous with general impoverishment.[58]

Thus Table 11.4 shows how in Tienen the number of several specialist urban functions increased substantially between 1755 and 1796. At Waver, to give another example, growing diversification in retailing and specialised

[55] R. Van Uytven and J. De Puydt, 'De toestand der abdijen in de Oostenrijkse Nederlanden, inzonderheid der statenabdijen, in de tweede helft der 18de eeuw', *Bijdragen tot de geschiedenis*, vol. 48 (1965), 44–7.

[56] For example C. Billen, 'Een ingebeelde landbouwrevolutie?', in *Oostenrijks België, 1713–1794. De Zuidelijke Nederlanden onder de Oostenrijkse Habsburgers* (s.l., 1987), pp. 115–18.

[57] Abbé Mann, 'Mémoire sur la question: dans un pays fertile et bien peuplé, les grandes fermes sont-elles utiles ou nuisibles à l'état en général?', in *Mémoires de l'Académie impériale et royale des sciences et belles-lettres de Bruxelles*, Vol. IV (Brussels, 1783), p. 216.

[58] G. Leenders, 'De beroepsstructuur op het platteland tussen Antwerpen en Brussel (1702–1846)', in J. Craeybeckx and F. Daelemans, eds., *Bijdragen tot de geschiedenis van Vlaanderen en Brabant. Sociaal en economisch*, vol. I (Brussels, 1983), pp. 167–228.

services became noticeable.[59] In his study on the economy of Diest, M. Vandereycken drew similar conclusions. Diest developed further in the second half of the century as a beer-brewing city and a centre for the regional economy.[60]

Conclusions

Compared to small towns in other European countries Brabantine ones had quite large populations. They also proved to be a very dynamic part of the urban world throughout the eighteenth century. Three different models were discussed in order to explain this dynamism. The models were treated separately, and so artificially isolated. In reality however, they interacted with each other. So important sectors of the Brussels export trade in luxury products succeeded on the international scene due to a strong locally based market.[61] Transport improvements promoted export as well as transit trade, but also positively influenced agricultural productivity, hence the local market.[62]

The most dramatic shift in the urban system took place during the first half of the century under the pressure of de-industrialisation, which especially affected the bigger cities. In the decades after 1748 dynamic growth was to a large extent regionally based. As a result both the capital, Brussels, and the majority of small towns of the region grew vigorously between 1755 and 1784.[63] The expansion of the urban output of specialised goods and services was not only supported by a (rather weak) revival of trade and export industries, but also by an increase in agricultural incomes.

---

[59] J. Martin, *Histoire de la ville et franchise de Wavre en roman Pays de Brabant* (Wavre, 1977), pp. 270–3.

[60] M. Vandereycken, *Stadseconomie en conjunctuur*, pp. 575–8.

[61] See P. Moureaux, 'Le grand commerce à Brussels en 1771', in R. Mortier and H. Hasquin, eds, *Bruxelles au XVIIIe siècle* (Etudes sur le XVIIIe siècle) (Brussels, 1977), pp. 40–3.

[62] See E. A. Wrigley, 'Parasite or stimulus: the town in a pre-industrial economy', in P. Abrams and E. A. Wrigley, eds, *Towns in Societies: Essays in Economic History and Historical Sociology* (Cambridge, 1978), pp. 299–302.

[63] The decentralisation process without doubt parallels our findings on the expansion of the Brabantine home market. D. Morsa, 'L'urbanisation de l'espace belge (1500–1800)', in E. Aerts *et al.*, eds, *Studia Historica Oeconomica. Liber Amicorum Herman Van der Wee* (Leuven, 1993), p. 207. J. De Vries, *European Urbanization*, p. 215. Contrast Lees and Hohenberg, 'Urban decline', p. 38, who consider the evolution towards lognormality as typical for an increasingly integrated regional urban system.

12 The small towns of northern Italy in the seventeenth and eighteenth centuries: an overview

Peter Musgrave

The north Italian small town was, and is, an elusive beast. Everybody knows, and Jan de Vries has confirmed,[1] that the north Italian plain, from Piedmont, through Lombardy, Emilia and the Veneto to the northern boundaries of the Romagna, was one of, perhaps *the* chief centre of urbanisation in early modern Europe, even in the eighteenth century. Furthermore, northern Italian urbanisation is identified, in professional as well as popular eyes, with the glittering successes of its cities: Genoa, Turin, Milan, Bologna, Venice of the first rank, and innumerable cities of the second rank: Pavia, Mantua, Verona, Ravenna, Modena and many others. Of small towns and other urban centres little, if anything, is heard.

The reasons for this 'city-centred' view of north Italian urban history are many and varied. The contorted political history of northern Italy since the early nineteenth century, in particular foreign domination and then incorporation into the modern Italian national state, have produced a tendency to see History in terms of nation-building, or conversely, of the legitimisation of localism which belongs with the live political tradition of history in nineteenth-century France or the modern Third World rather than to the avowedly neutral 'scientific' tradition of modern Anglo-Saxon historiography. In this history of national or local self-image-making the cities, and above all the free communes, have offered an example either of the validity of a free and independent Italy or of the success of local as distinct from regional or national entities. Florence, Bologna, Venice and Milan have, in a sense, become symbols for the problems and aspirations of the new Italy and have, therefore, in the hands of a politically active academic profession become the inevitable and almost invariable centre of concern. The small town represents an Italy basically 'rural' and 'conservative' which does not fit at all comfortably with the carefully constructed national or local image.

The city-centred nature of modern historiography is, however, not merely the result of modern political and ideological preoccupations. The rising city-republics of the Middle Ages and the *Signorie* which followed

[1] J. de Vries, *European Urbanisation 1500–1800* (1984).

250

them were, in their relations with the areas which fell under their control, ruthless centralisers.[2] Although the political structure, and the basics of administrative structure remained nominally unchanged, the provincial and later regional centres effectively crushed all independence in the smaller urban centres which might, even remotely, pose a threat to the dominance of the city and its elite.[3] The smaller urban centres were left, in the eyes of the central state, as no more than more densely populated pieces of countryside, with no institutional or legal factor to distinguish them from the rural commune. Their privileges were suppressed and their economic role, in theory at least, limited and constrained to the advantage of the dominant city. The well-documented process by which, for instance, Venice brought the cities of the newly conquered Terra Ferma under control in the fifteenth century[4] is no more than a later, and less successful, repetition of the process by which these cities had themselves controlled their subordinate urban centres in the previous centuries.

The smaller urban centre then, had, and has, little role to play in the received picture of north Italian urbanisation; historians have concentrated on the city or alternatively and increasingly on the countryside,[5] heightening and re-emphasising the sharp implied distinction between the urbanised city and the rural remainder. It is, in fact, extremely difficult at present to disentangle the fate of the smaller urban centres from a mass of information which largely, sometimes almost actively, ignores their existence. This dismissal of the smaller urban centre produces a further problem for the historian of the small town. Northern Italy has one of the greatest stores of archival material from the Middle Ages and the early modern period anywhere in Europe; its administration was for centuries bureaucratic in its widest sense, while its society was one in which literacy, although by no means universal, was nevertheless very widespread. The material that is available for the history of the cities is immense and rich; on the other hand, that for the smaller urban centres, and indeed for the rural communes, is tiny. Frustratingly it is clear that both smaller urban and rural centres did, as late as the eighteenth century, possess considerable archives, many stretching back for long periods.[6] The general history of Italy's

[2] D. P. Waley. *The Italian City Republics*, second edition (1978).

[3] G. M. Varanini, *Il distretto Veronese nel Quattrocento: Vicariati del Comune di Verona e Vicariati Privati* (Verona, 1980).

[4] G. Cracco, *Società e Stato nel Medioevo Veneziano* (Florence, 1967).

[5] For instance P. J. Jones, *La Storia Economica*, in *Dalla Caduta del Impero Romano al Secolo XVIII*, Einaudi, ed., *Storia d'Italia*, Vol. II, Tom. ii (Turin, 1974) pp. 1469–811 and F. McArdle, *Altopascio: A Study in Tuscan Rural Society* (Cambridge, 1974).

[6] See, for instance, the Archive of the Commune of Negrar listed in Archivio Storico della Curia Vescovile Verona, Amministrazione Economica del Diocesi: Pievi: S. Giorgio: Stampa Secolo XVIII: *RR Signori Chierichi di S. Giorgio contra SS Avanzi Al Taglia* (Verona, 1772).

archival material, as distinct from her Archives, remains to be written, but it is clear that large-scale destruction of material took place in the nineteenth and twentieth centuries.[7] This is entirely comprehensible: warfare, from the 1790s to 1945, led inevitably to destruction, as did climatic and natural disaster. Furthermore, the growing poverty of northern Italy in the nineteenth and early twentieth centuries led to the use of archival material for utilitarian purposes – as fuel or, as in the 1930s, as salvage for recycling. In this destruction of material, the records of the historic cities suffered much less severe depredations; the city materials, often preserved in Archives themselves with histories going back to the Middle Ages were protected as national treasures, heroically defended by local historians and archivists.[8] The records of the smaller centres were unimportant and hence expendable. There are, therefore, great gaps in the records of the smaller centres and the reconstruction of their population, social structure and economies is peculiarly difficult.

Despite this conspiracy against the smaller urban centres, it is quite clear that the urban hierarchy was not suddenly truncated at the level of the cities, with a totally rural countryside around them. There was a complex pattern of smaller urban centres, not as many proportionally perhaps as in some other regions of Europe, but certainly dense, and interrelated with each other, as well as with their 'metropolitan' centres. Further, it is clear that in northern Italy, as elsewhere, there was a rank of even smaller 'rur-urban' centres, often with populations only slightly larger than purely 'rural' villages.

The identification of these second- and, in particular, third-ranking centres is not straightforward. Throughout northern Italy, the basic unit of administration and self-government, the *comune* or *comunità*, was common to both rural and urban areas: in terms of formal administration, there is little discernible differentiation between the smallest rural community and the largest of the second-ranking towns. Furthermore, communes, even the great city communes, tended to be mixed in the sense that an agrarian sector was, administratively, linked with an urban one; the existence of a large agricultural population and of relatively large areas of cultivated land within a commune, cannot be used as an indicator of necessarily 'non-urban' status. This was not merely a convenient linking of 'suburban' rural villages to an urban centre. It is clear that virtually every north Italian small town was also an agricultural centre with a resident population of farmers and agricultural labourers; equally, local agricultural land was a favourite home for the investment of urban wealth.

[7] See, for instance, G. Sancassani, *L'Archivio di Stato di Verona: gli Archivi Veronesi dal Medioevo ai giorni nostri* (Verona, 1961).

[8] Sancassani, *L'Archivio.*

The small town in Italy was, then, extremely difficult to specify or to locate in a formal sense. Nonetheless it is possible to be clear about the basic pattern of urbanisation and, to some extent at least, about the interrelationship between the levels. At the top, virtually in the stratosphere, were the great international centres – Genoa, Milan, Turin, Bologna, Venice – operating at least at the beginning of the period on a European and, indeed, a world stage. Beneath them, both in population and wealth terms on one hand and in political terms on the other, were what might be called the regional cities – Padua, Vicenza, Verona, Brescia, Mantua, Modena, Parma to name but a few. Subordinated in political and, to some extent, economic terms to the metropolitan cities, they still retained a great deal of their social and cultural independence. In particular in the territories of Venice in the Veneto and Lombardy, the subject cities remained in a very real sense independent of the social and even political control of the Imperial city.[9] Venice was willing, indeed keen, to leave the complexities of internal administration and internal taxation in the hands of the traditional ruling elites and traditional bureaucracies of the cities. If, in many ways, the Venetian land empire can perhaps be seen as an Imperial federation rather than an absolutist state, in which the subject cities retained greater independence and greater privileges than almost any other group of cities outside Germany, there was also a down-side to that equation. Again, in contradistinction to virtually every other European state or state system in the early modern period, the Veneto, in particular, saw very little integration of rural elites into a single national elite.[10] The nobilities of Venice and the Terra Ferma cities remained effectively separate, not merely institutionally but also socially, even in those areas like the Padovano or the Vicentino where relatively large numbers of Venetian noble families bought land and built houses. To a lesser extent the same was true of the individual nobilities of the regional centres which remained largely local in their interests and their loyalties. While there is less evidence for Lombardy, Emilia and Piedmont, it seems to be clear that there, too, a similar pattern of localism was the rule.

The smaller towns existed within a framework of essentially local urban contexts; the metropolitan significance of the great cities and their financial and commercial relationships can very easily conceal the fact that most of the smaller towns of Italy, as elsewhere in Europe, were of essentially local or at best regional significance, rather than being part of a wider-ranging European or world economy. It is possible to isolate two levels of small towns in northern Italy in the early modern period, although the line of

[9] See Joanne M. Ferraro, *Family and Public Life in Brescia, 1580–1650: The Foundations of power in the Venetian State* (Cambridge, 1993).
[10] Ferraro, *Family* and G. Borelli, *Un Patriziato della Terraferma Veneta: la Nobiltà Veronese nel Sei- e Settecento* (Verona, 1972).

distinction between them is never absolutely firm and clear. The example of the Territorio Veronese is used here in an illustrative way. Although Verona itself has a number of claims to be considered as a rather special case within the cities of the Terra Ferma, and although the position of the Veronese at the junction of a number of crucial regional and international trade routes does give a special twist to the position of some of the towns of the Territorio, it is sufficiently typical to be illustrative. Verona itself lies close to the centre of its Territorio, albeit near to the northern edge of its main centres of population. It was encircled by a series of small towns at a distance of something between 10 and 15 miles. Most of these towns – Caprino, Bussolengo, Pescantina, Villafranca, Isola della Scala, Legnago, Soave and S. Bonifacio – had populations of between 2,000 and 5,000 in the early 1630s, at their low point, although some, like Pescantina, had below 2,000.[11] In addition to this circle of small towns a number of other urban centres can be identified, some naval or military bases like Peschiera on Lake Garda or Cologna Veneta in the east of the Veronese, other communications centres like Valeggio sul Mincio at the most important crossing of the Mincio or Zevio, whose boatmen controlled navigation on the Adige below Verona.[12]

It is also possible to identify, albeit somewhat mistily, a further layer of even smaller centres with some urban functions, even in the sixteenth and seventeenth centuries. Centres like Negrar in the Valpolicella, Lazise and Malcesine on Lake Garda, Cerea in the plains are all very clearly essentially agricultural or fishing centres, but equally clearly they have a number of urban functions and urban occupations: retailing, administration, as the centres of Vicariates which were the basic unit of jurisdiction in the Veronese, professional groups, in particular notaries but also doctors and apothecaries.

It must be emphasised that it is only by a careful study of function that these smallest urban centres, and indeed some of the larger ones, can be distinguished from more purely rural and agricultural ones. Population certainly offers no infallible guide; the census of 1631, drawn up in the aftermath of the most serious outbreak of plague to affect northern Italy in the later sixteenth and seventeenth centuries, indicates quite clearly, for those centres for which information was collected and has survived, that the communes which included some, at least, of the urban centres had, both in 1630, before the plague, and after, lower total populations than communes

---

[11] Archivio di Stato di Verona (ASVR), Ufficio di Sanità, Registro 191.

[12] On Peschiera and Valeggio see the appropriate volumes of the series *Le Guide*, normally without author or date of publication, published by *Vita Veronese*. This series, and the equivalent series for other provinces, are the major present sources for the history of the small towns; they vary from the professionally highly competent to the merely antiquarian. On Zevio C. F. Zamboni, *La Navigazione sull'Adige in rapporto al commercio Veronese* (Verona, 1925).

like Colognola ai Colli which were made up of an aggregation of a number of scattered, relatively small, undoubtedly rural villages.[13]

There is some evidence to suggest that the pattern of urbanisation in the Veronese was typical in its form of much of the rest of northern Italy, with the exception of marginal and relatively undeveloped areas such as Friuli or the Val d'Aosta, where urban centres seem to have been very scattered. The Veronese may well have had a greater scattering of urbanised centres, and in that sense a less dominant central city than many or most other territories in northern Italy: in the Mantovano, the Milanese, the Torinese and the Dogado (the area around Venice directly controlled by the city), for instance, the attraction of the great metropolitan centre drew the wealth of the smaller centres inexorably to it. Elsewhere, in the Vicentino or the Pavese, for instance, and in Emilia in general, less complex, though no less prosperous, economies meant that smaller urban centres were less common. Obviously at the present stage of research any attempt at quantification of urban centres can only be very impressionistic, approximate and provisional, above all as regards the smallest centres. On that basis and in that spirit, it may be hazarded that northern Italy had perhaps 150 or 200 of the medium-range urban centres discussed above and perhaps two to three times that number of the smallest centres, although this latter figure almost certainly fluctuated during the period.

II

The continued existence of a complex pattern of urbanisation below the level of the 'regional' cities, then, is not in doubt. The social, economic and political relationship of the structure of small towns to their regional centres, has, however, many peculiarities which may even permit the idea of a separate 'north Italian' pattern of urbanisation. The history of the relationship between the small towns and their metropolitan centres had been, throughout the Middle Ages, one of jealousy and competition, a contest in which the smaller centres had been the losers, not merely in political but also in economic and social terms. As the political power of the regional cities had expanded, so they had increasingly monopolised, in theory as well as, in some cases, in practice, all the most important economic activities. The regional cities had become virtually the social centres of international or interregional trade within their provinces. Furthermore the power of the city guilds effectively established a monopoly of urban functions for the regional city which left the small towns with little more than

---

[13] On the Census of 1631 in the Veronese see P. J. Musgrave, *Land and Economy in Baroque Italy: Valpolicella 1630–1790* (Leicester, 1992), pp. 39–40.

purely local functions. This was not merely a question of the industrial concentration and monopolisation typified by the actions of the Venetian councils in limiting the most important and most profitable of the industrial activities of its empire for the island city and its near neighbours, and replicated on a smaller scale by all the major cities and regional centres of northern Italy. It was also a matter of the monopolisation of the commercial sector of the economy by traders and merchants from the regional centres to the almost total exclusion of the smaller centres. The external trade of virtually all of the north was, at least in theory, passed through the markets of its regional centres, and the small towns were, in a very real sense, no more than subordinates of the regional centre.[14]

The commercial and industrial subjection of the small towns of the north was paralleled by their political and administrative subordination. The centralisation of political and administrative functions in the hands of the ruling elites of the cities inevitably meant, in a society in which patronage and clientage networks were absolutely central, that the centre of political focus, and the centre for all those for whom politics in its widest sense was important, became the city and its councils. There was little patronage of much significance in the smaller towns, certainly little compared with the advantages to be gained in the city. Furthermore, in a society which was, and was increasingly, litigious, the concentration of real jurisdiction in the courts of the regional centres, and later in the courts of the dominating cities, inevitably pulled social, political and professional concern away from the smaller centres and towards the great cities.

The inescapable consequence of the concentration of economic, political and administrative power in the hands of the regional cities was that although wealth and social power might develop in the smaller town, the newly developing small-town elite was drawn towards the regional centre. There lay the opportunities for further wealth, for professional advancement and for enhanced social and political status. The regional cities, in effect, encouraged the drift of wealth and power from the small towns towards them. In all the major regional cities, the possession of citizenship conveyed considerable privileges, in terms of access to markets, to the law courts and above all in terms of taxation both direct and indirect.[15] In contrast to the firmly closed and exclusive councils and nobilities of the cities, citizenship was effectively open to migrants who were sufficiently wealthy to buy or rent houses and to pay taxes to the city; the effect of the purchase of citizenship was in reality to transfer the whole of the migrant's land, commercial and professional activities into the privi-

---

[14] See Richard Tilden Rapp, *Industry and Economic Decline in Seventeenth-Century Venice* (Cambridge, 1976).
[15] On the citizen class of Venice see F. C. Lane, *Venice, a Maritime Republic* (1973), pp. 151–2.

leged sector of the city.[16] The consequences for the small town could be very marked; the transfer of the residence and centre of activity of the develping elite of the small centres to the regional cities was a constant drain on the small centres' economic status and on their political role; furthermore the transfer of land and other activities to the taxation sphere of the city reduced the taxation base of the small town, without at the same time reducing the historically fixed tax demands of the city upon the smaller centre. For much of the sixteenth century and in particular in the difficult economic conditions of the last quarter of the century and the first decades of the seventeenth century, the small towns complained loudly to their Venetian or Spanish overlords of the dangerous burdens this was placing on their economies. By the 1620s the overlords were beginning to listen to these complaints and to bring pressure on the city councils to reduce the flow of land and taxation into city hands, in particular into the hands of newly citified groups from the small towns.

The advantages of the city were not, however, limited to this advantage of citizenship. All over Europe, the 'ladder' pattern of migration, of the relatively rich leaving the small towns for the more promising prospects of the city and being replaced by waves of new migrants from the countryside, often bringing new wealth deriving from agriculture to the town, was common and contributed greatly to the continuing vitality of the smaller towns. Not merely was it a question of the rich peasant becoming the new dweller in the small town, but in addition, the small town provided the first step on the professional ladder for many of their sons. The capture of all significant activity by the regional centres meant that the undoubted rural prosperity of the sixteenth century in northern Italy was not mirrored, as might have been expected, by growing prosperity for the smaller urban centres, but rather that wealth was almost entirely diverted to the regional cities. The smaller towns did experience some growing prosperity in the sixteenth century, but it was relatively minor compared with that of the greater centres.

Even if the relatively well-to-do rural dweller did wish to urbanise himself and his family, a further institutional barrier was placed in his way in the smaller towns. In the city, citizenship, as has been suggested above, was relatively easily obtained; residence and contribution through the taxation system were enough. 'Citizenship' in the smaller urban centres, as in the rural communes, was extremely difficult to attain. The Statutes of most urban and rural communes restricted membership of the citizen body – effectively defined in terms of members of the popular assembly, the *vicinia*,

---

[16] ASVR, Antichi Estimi Provvisori (AEP), Reg. 231, *Elenco de Particolari Forestieri che anno aquistado la cittadinanca dal 1633 in qua* and its inclosures.

and in terms of rights to use the communally owned pastures – to a group of families defined as *originari*. Just who these *originari* were is never entirely clear; the *originari* of any commune seem, in effect, to have been a self-defining and closed group, claiming, with greater or lesser probability, descent from the original settlers or original contractors to the Statutes. All outsiders, defined as *forestieri*, were excluded from any of the privileges or status of citizenship and from all, or most, communal offices.[17] Paradoxically, then, it was easier to gain citizenship of Verona or Padua than it was to obtain entry into the charmed circle of the smaller centres; furthermore, of course, the advantages of citizenship of a city were much greater than the very limited advantages in smaller centres.

The smaller centres, then, played a strange role in the urban geography of northern Italy in the sixteenth century and before; they were essentially local service centres of restricted importance. The geographical scatter of larger centres meant that few, if any, places or individuals in the region were more than a day's journey from the greater urban centres and their markets; consequently, the smaller centres were little more than small-scale suppliers, the markets of the greater cities being the essential sources of major purchases. This commercial domination of the region by the markets of the greater centres was intensified in times of difficulty, such as the later sixteenth century, by the action of the city authorities in subsidising the supply and price of grain in the city markets, often by commandeering food from the local markets where prices rose disproportionately. Equally, rather than playing the small town's common role as the first focus for the transfer of newly accumulated rural wealth into urban wealth, the small towns were largely bypassed by migrants who moved into the regional centres rather than to their local small town.

By the sixteenth century the policy of economic and political concentration followed, consciously or unconsciously by the cities had, in effect, reduced the small towns to a status which was little more than that of satellites of the city to which they were tied by close economic as well as political ties and which drew from them any developing elite almost as quickly as it emerged.

III

The north Italian small town was thus, by the end of the sixteenth century, linked very tightly into a clear urban structure which, in many ways, was much more interrelated and interlinked than that of much of the rest of

---

[17] L. Simeoni, *Comuni Rurali Veronesi: Valpolicella–Valpantena–Gardesana*, in *Studi su Verona nel Medioevo*, vol. IV (Verona, 1964).

Europe. Unlike many other areas of Europe, northern Italy did not see the development of vital small-town sectors in its urban structure before the end of the sixteenth century, but rather the opposite. Small towns which had been independent economically and in many cases also politically, had been pulled into a close dependence on their provincial centres. The revitalising force of new rural capital and new rural population was very largely directed towards the cities rather than towards the small towns. Education – professional and vocational as well as academic – was increasingly concentrated on the cities. The culture of northern Italy in the sixteenth century is essentially, and almost wholly, a culture of the cities and of their rural extension, the Villa, rather than of the small towns.[18]

The fate of the smaller towns was, then, in a way which distinguishes them very clearly from the situation elsewhere in Europe, deeply inter-linked with the fate of the greater cities. The economic, demographic and political crisis of the years between 1590 and 1650 might perhaps have been expected to involve the smaller centres in a crash as significant as the problems which all the greater centres of Italy suffered during this period and which continued to dog them through the later seventeenth century and well on into the eighteenth. In fact, although the evidence is vague and at times ambiguous, it seems reasonably clear that the seventeenth century saw something of a revival for the small towns of northern Italy.

The effects of the plague outbreaks of the later sixteenth and early seventeenth centuries were most strongly felt in the large centres rather than the small. As part of the process by which plague became essentially a disease of the larger cities, the outbreaks of this period, although they were pretty general, had their most general effects in the major cities; this pattern was most marked in the eastern Veneto and western Lombardy, while in the middle stretch of the north, from Milan to Vicenza, the very high levels of rural as well as urban fatalities masked a generally higher urban death rate, coupled with a low rate of recovery as migration from countryside to town slowed down as a consequence both of the higher levels of rural employment and of the decline of the urban economy. It is difficult to calculate a distribution of population between larger and smaller urban centres in the period after 1630, but such evidence as there is points to a greater proportion of the urbanised population of the north being in smaller centres than, almost certainly, at any period since the earlier Middle Ages. The greater importance of the lesser centres seems to have continued through the seventeenth century and on into the eighteenth.

It was not merely a demographic readjustment, however. Indeed, as

[18] D. Cosgrove, *The Palladian Landscape* (Leicester, 1992).

Domenico Sella has pointed out[19] for Lombardy, one of the central features of the economic crisis of the cities in the later sixteenth and seventeenth centuries was the loss of their economic and industrial bases to the countryside and to the smaller towns. Not merely did the cities lose population, they also lost the industry and commerce necessary to feed and employ that population. Industry, and with it commerce, moved away from the cities to the countryside and to the smaller towns which serviced the nearer countryside. By the middle–late seventeenth century it would probably not be an exaggeration to say that the cities had become essentially service centres for their rural and small-town hinterlands rather than being the economic arbiters of those hinterlands. In a very real sense a revolution had taken place in the urban hierarchy, a revolution in which the small towns had been the gainers.

This improving position of the smaller towns in the seventeenth century, stretching on into the early and middle years of the eighteenth, can be seen in a number of important ways. The evidence, such as it is, points to a growth in population in many, although perhaps not all, of the smaller towns, a growth which was more rapid either than the general growth in population or than that of the cities themselves. Many more migrants from the rural areas seem to have gone to the smaller towns than had been the case in the preceding century. The physical towns changed too, spreading out into their fields and also rebuilding their historic centres. Not merely were churches rebuilt and refurbished, very frequently by communal councils or confraternities, but in addition a great deal of private building was undertaken. There is very clear evidence during the seventeenth century not merely of the revival of small-town markets as distribution centres, but also of the development of permanent shops in the smaller towns. The developing retail sector was paralleled by a growth, more strictly a revival, of the professional sector, in particular by the expansion of the number of notaries operating in the smaller centres, paralleled by the growing concentration of notarial business in the cities in the hands of a few large companies of fashionable practitioners. A number of distinctive urban institutions such as guilds and the religious confraternities also expanded, both in numbers and in wealth. This growth was particularly evident in those smaller urban centres which succeeded in transforming themselves into new industrial centres, both for actual industrial production and as collection and distribution centres for the production of rural industry. Towns like Rovereto and Ala in the Trentino[20] expanded markedly in the course of the seven-

---

[19] Domenico Sella, *Crisis and Continuity: The Economy of Spanish Lombardy in the Seventeenth Century* (Cambridge, 1979).

[20] E. Ferrari, F. Sembianti, M. Tomasi and G. Sampredi, *I centri storici del Trentino* (Trento, 1981), pp. 126–39.

teenth century as a result of the transfer there from Venetian territory of the major centres of silk throwing; towns in Lombardy benefited in the same way from the decline and transfer of industry from Milan and the other larger centres.[21]

This revival of small towns was also expressed in a shift towards the small towns in formal political terms. Particularly in the Veneto, where the peculiar structure of Venetian rule led to a situation in which the dominant power sought a counterbalance for the power of the provincial cities in the support of the small towns and the countryside, the small towns regained and expanded their privileges *vis-à-vis* the declining greater towns. A series of decisions by the courts and councils in Venice in the course of the seventeenth century helped to reduce the attractiveness of the provincial cities and to strengthen the position of the smaller towns. The decisions of the courts were, strictly, specific to particular situations and particular provinces, but they were in effect used by the small towns of the whole of the Veneto to seek and to establish similar rights.

The first of these transfers was the decision to put a stop to the drift of land into the taxation registers of the cities and away from those of the communes. In the Veronese, which may be taken as typical, the courts ruled in 1633 against the process by which land in the possession of non-citizens of Verona (forming part of the tax base of an extra-urban commune) was removed from the communal tax base to that of the city if the land passed into the hands of a citizen of the city, or if the land's owner gained citizenship. A compromise was reached between the City and the representatives of the communes of the Territorio Veronese, rural as well as urban, under which all land that had passed into city hands, and therefore into the city *Estimo*, before 1633 should remain taxed under the city; but that after that date, the changed status of the owner would not affect where the land was taxed.[22] This compromise, which remained in place until the end of the Venetian Republic in 1797, effectively removed one of the major economic advantages of gaining citizenship. It also meant that many important landowners, including members of the city nobility, inevitably became more deeply involved, either directly or through their agents, in the politics of local communities, since it was those local communities which now decided important questions of taxation.

The second major change, which, in the Veronese, came rather later, at

[21] A. M. L. Trezzi, 'A case-study of the de-industrialisation of the city: the silk mills of the city and duchy of Milan from the seventeenth to the eighteenth century' in H. Van der Wee, ed., *The Rise and Decline of Urban Industries in Italy and the Low Countries* (Leuven, 1988), pp. 139–51.

[22] See *Transatione seguita tra la Magnifica Citta di Verona et il spetabile Territorio MDCXXXIII 27 Novembre in materia de stabili passati da distrittuali in cittadini e da cittadini in distrittuali dal 1575 per tutto l'anno 1633*, ASVR, Comune, Registro 798.

the end of the seventeenth century, was the opening of the citizenship of the rural (and smaller urban) communes to 'outsiders', who, as pointed out above, might have lived in the commune for many years or even gener-ations.[23] Not merely did this remove a long-felt injustice, it also made it much easier for the relatively well-to-do to enter the formal community and also strengthened the political status of the leaders of the smaller urban communes in their relationship both with the officials of the provincial cities and with the representatives of the dominating imperial power.

Perhaps of greater symbolic importance than either of these two develop-ments was the establishment of the rights of guilds to organise themselves in the smaller towns, reversing a basic element of the centralising policy of the medieval cities. In the Veronese, the key decision was again taken in the 1630s and concerned the control of river navigation on the Adige. The Adige was Verona's major transportation link, both with the Trentino and, more importantly, with Venice and the Adriatic.[24] The control of the navigation was, obviously, very central to the whole economy and to the whole question of economic and political power within the Territorio. Much of the shipping on the river was owned and operated by ship captains – *parons* – based at Pescantina, for the river above Verona, and at Zevio, for the river below the city. Although the *parons* dominated the trade they were forbidden by the Statutes of Verona either from establishing an *arte* (guild) or from making their monopoly of the trade legally effective. The decision of 1630 allowed, in effect, the establishment of a guild at both Pescantina and Zevio and the enforcement of those guilds' monopolies over the river trade.[25] The breaking of the city's monopoly of trade organisation was a major gain for the small towns, reversing as it did the situation in which the city sought to draw all economic power and influence to it.

The seventeenth century, then, saw not merely a period of growth for the small towns, but also a major realignment of the whole economy and society of northern Italy. By the middle of the eighteenth century it almost looked as if the balance had shifted decisively away from the historical cities and towards the smaller towns, reflecting a shift away from the industrial and international aspect of the medieval prosperity of northern Italy towards a more rural and agricultural-based prosperity.

IV

The middle and later eighteenth century, however, saw a decisive reversal of this process. In a formal sense the final blow came with the fall of the

[23] See ASVR, S. Fermo Maggiore, Processo 640.
[24] G. Borelli, *Una Città e il suo Fiume: Verona e l'Adige*, 2 vols (Verona, 1977).
[25] ASVR, Arte dei Burchieri, Processo 177.

Venetian Republic in 1797; as a result, the closed political and social world of the cities was blown open. No longer were migrants from the countryside and the small towns limited to a restricted role in the political and administrative life of the cities. They could, and did, become involved in the government of the city as well as of the province. Furthermore, the centralised and bureaucratic administrative structures set up in northern Italy, firstly by Napoleon and then by the Austrians, made the cities, even more than they had been, the vital centres of power and influence. In many ways, though, the decline of the influence and importance of the small towns had begun a half-century earlier.

The history of the small towns in the eighteenth century is not a simple one; much more than in the sixteenth and seventeenth centuries, the fate of towns cannot be fitted into a single pattern. For some of the more successful towns the eighteenth century saw a further extension of their development as independent centres, moving away from the tutelage of the traditional centres. For most, on the other hand, the later eighteenth century saw a decline from the position they had established in the relatively palmy days of the seventeenth. The most successful smaller towns were those such as Legnago or Rovereto which had succeeded in establishing an economic position clearly and definitely separate from that of their provincial city. Legnago became, in the course of the eighteenth century, a regional and international grain market of such importance that, by the 1760s and 1770s, the major grain purchasers and sellers of Verona, the provincial city, bought and sold their grain in Legnago in preference to the city. Its significance was such that not merely did Legnago change the place in which grain was traded, it also changed the fundamental pattern of grain trading in Verona, large-scale and relatively infrequent bulk purchases of grain replacing the older pattern of smaller-scale frequent purchases.[26] Rovereto became and continued to be the major centre of the north Italian silk-spinning and weaving industries, drawing production of raw silk to it from the Veronese, the Bresciano and the Vicentino as well as its own home production.[27] This was truly an industrial centre with an economic hinterland which stretched far beyond the confines of its province and certainly outstripped the economic power and influence of its provincial city, Trento. The development of these towns was not simply a matter of economic growth and the development of an associated service sector, but also the beginnings of a cultural role for the smaller town. In the seventeenth century and before, culture had largely been a matter of the city urban elites and of the nobilities in particular. In towns like Rovereto and Legnago in the eighteenth century there was the first stirring of a new small-town culture. The *Accademia degli*

[26] C. Boscagin, *Storia di Legnago* (Verona, 1966).   [27] See Ferrari *et al.*, *I centri storici*.

Agiati of Rovereto came to be famous in Italy and beyond, in particular for the liberalism of its views.[28] Legnago also developed the beginnings of a cultural life, giving the composer Salieri, a native of the town, his first opportunities.

The efflorescence of Legnago and Rovereto, and of a number of similar smaller towns across the north of Italy, was not matched by the fate of the great majority of the smaller towns, however. The later eighteenth century saw many of them sinking back from the relative prosperity of the seventeenth. Shops closed or became less specialised, the professional classes moved away, either to the outlying villages or, more usually, to the provincial cities. In many ways the end of the eighteenth century saw a drift of the new urban elites which had developed in the smaller towns during the seventeenth century towards the honeypot of the provincial cities which they were to take over so successfully and so completely in the nineteenth.

A small but significant centre like Pescantina provides a useful series of illustrations of this process. The seventeenth- and early-eighteenth century prosperity of the town and in particular of the *parons* had begun the process of creating a new urban elite who, through the *compagnia* of S. Nicolo of Bari, usurped many of the functions of the communal council. The *parons* built town houses for themselves, bought up land in the surrounding area and began to place their sons in the professions, in particular the church and the law. Many of them, too, began to expand their businesses. Few of the *parons* in the early seventeenth century had had more than a single boat and a single pair of draught horses. By the early eighteenth century a number had two or three boats and the requisite horses.

By the 1760s this picture of prosperity and urban development has gone into reverse. Few of the resident *parons* have any longer more than a single boat and many have only half shares or broken-down hulks. The great mass of the most prosperous families had moved to Verona, while still retaining the necessary foothold in Pescantina to allow them to retain the vital membership of the *arte* of Pescantina.[29] Similar patterns can clearly be seen in many other smaller towns.

Undoubtedly the later eighteenth century saw something of an economic, and above all commercial revival for the regional cities and, equally undoubtedly, growing competition from new and newly mechanised industries elsewhere in Europe weakened the industrial sectors of many of the

---

[28] On the *Accademia degli Agiati* of Rovereto see A. Stella, 'I Principiati Vescovili di Trento e Bressanone', in G. Galasso, ed., *Storia d'Italia*, Vol. XVII (Turin, 1979), pp. 556–7; on the Academies in general see: G. Torcellan, 'Un tema di ricerca: le accademie agrarie nel Settecento', *Rivista Storica Italiana*, vol. 2 (1964), 530–2.

[29] The discussion of Pescantina here and elsewhere in this paper is based on ASVR, AEP, Registri 603 & 604. For the company of S. Nicolo see ASVR, Compagnie Ecclesiastiche di Provincia: S. Nicolo di Pescantina.

smaller centres. Increased imports of manufactured goods, and of Asiatic goods and American sugar perhaps above all, meant that the larger centres again became more crucial centres of distribution than they had been in the relatively local market structures of the seventeenth century. The middle and later eighteenth centry saw a cultural revival in the provincial cities, with the foundation of academies, of musical societies and groups of anti-quaries, for instance. This revival of the provincial centres inevitably led to the growing concentration of the wealthier and more ambitious sectors of society in them and consequently to a reduction of the social and cultural as well as the economic functions of the smaller centres, decline which even the establishment of state schools and *licei* in the nineteenth century did nothing to reverse.

In the course of the middle and later eighteenth century, then, the provincial cities had regained the attractiveness to the elites of smaller towns which they had lost in the preceding century. In part this was a consequence of the process which can be seen throughout northern Italy in the eighteenth century in which elites, both rural and urban, which had developed through economic activity, broadly defined, in the relative pros-perity of the seventeenth century, gradually diverted their wealth into land and into professionalisation. In a sense, this process had been going on continually from the Middle Ages onwards. After all, many of the most important city families traced their origins to farmers and traders in the hinterland. Equally, even in the Middle Ages, and certainly in the sixteenth and seventeenth centuries, there had been no single route from rural wealth to city settlement; by no means all rural families stopped off, as it were, in the small towns on their way to the city. Rural wealth had always been haemorrhaging into the cities, and important rural and small-town families had constantly moved to the city. What was different was that in the eighteenth century few new men came up to replace them. This failure of north Italian society in the later eighteenth century to regenerate a leader-ship group in the countryside and, by extension, in the small town is, in many ways, much more significant as a cause of decline of the north Italian small town than was any real economic shift between the small town and the city.

The causes of this failure are many. One striking feature of the pre-eighteenth-century north Italian economy had been its ability, shared perhaps only by England, to generate a continuous supply of rising families. Above all, rural Italy seemed to possess the flexibility and vitality to provide opportunities for large numbers of new men to establish themselves. As in England that flexibility lay, above all, in a combination of a post-feudal pattern of agrarian relations and a lively and mixed economy. On the one hand the north Italian economy was sufficiently buoyant to make economic progress for individuals possible, while, on the other, the greater variety of economic activity – commercial agriculture, rural industry and production of industrial raw materials, small- (and not so small)-scale commerce, professional employment – made economic progress more secure and less involved with the dangers of risk. In an age in which catastrophe was an ever-present possibility in perception as in reality, economic strategies had to be aligned above all to provide the greatest level of security of income, and hence of food, possible. Risk and progress came only second. The favoured north Italian economy allowed individuals and families to spread risks and hence to engage in economic advancement without the full dangers of over-commitment to boom and slump in a single activity. In this process, of course, the small towns, as well as being a major beneficiary, particularly in the seventeenth century as the recipients of upwardly mobile migrants, were also a major contributor, providing a market relatively close at hand for production, a potential market for professional services and so forth.

The seventeenth-century prosperity of the smaller towns coincides with perhaps the last period of this flexibility. In many ways the disasters of the late sixteenth and early seventeenth centuries had, in an almost Malthusian way, created the conditions in which economic flexibility and economic opportunity would be at its height. The population collapse, in countryside as well as in town, relieved pressure on resources: throughout northern Italy the early seventeenth century saw a decline in the area of land cultivated, a growing shortage of agricultural labour. At the same time, although total population had fallen, the growing forced reliance of Italy on its own supplies of food, following the disappearance, or at least reduction, of imported supplies, meant a buoyant market for agriculture. The loss of skilled labour in the towns, above all, gave a further and decisive push to the movement of industry out of the cities into the small towns and the countryside and hence the development of industrial employment as part of the economic package of a family. Greater rural and small-town prosperity meant more employment for professional men outside the provincial centres.

The prosperity of the later seventeenth and earlier eighteenth centuries, of course, contained within itself the seed of its own destruction. Growing population and growing pressure on land coupled with the undeniable evidence of ecological degradation – deforestation, erosion and some water-logging[30] – meant that living standards and incomes fell. Furthermore increased competition in industrial markets meant declining opportunities for industrial employment and declining rural opportunities for the pro-

---

[30] See E. Turri, *Dietro il Paessagio: Caprino e il Monte Baldo; ricerche su un territorio comunale* (Verona, 1982).

fessionals. The balance clearly shifted back to the provincial cities, not now as manufacturing centres, or even in reality as commercial centres, but above all as administrative, judicial and patronage centres. In the later eighteenth century most small towns which had not succeeded in creating some special and clear urban niche for themselves were again unable to compete with the attractions of the cities.

This was not, however, a single-sided problem. On the one hand the provincial centres were again beginning to attract and to hold rural elites, to drain the smaller towns of their professional and commercial functions in particular; on the other hand the small towns faced a new and severe form of competition in their own backyards. The distinction between town and village in northern Italy had never been, as argued earlier, an especially clear one. Town and village had never been differentiated constitutionally or legally. It is worth indicating that in the seventeenth- and eighteenth-century dialects of the Veneto there is no vocabulary which allows any clear distinction between 'town' and 'village', any more strictly than there is any clear way of distinguishing between 'town' and 'city'. The eighteenth century saw, even more than before, a blurring of such distinctions as existed. As small towns became less prosperous, so their economies became increasingly dominated by agriculture and by directly agriculturally based activities. At the same time there is considerable and general evidence of the 'urbanisation' of the small centres of settlement, if that is not too grandiose a term for what was going on. From all across northern Italy there is clear evidence that the second half of the eighteenth century saw a spread of what may be conceived of as basically urban functions to a whole range of smaller centres. The towns' effective monopoly of retailing was under attack, partially as a result of the establishment of permanent shops, usually general stores but in some cases rather more specialised retailers, in many villages. Some villages also, albeit illegally, established what were effectively periodic markets and fairs.[31]

The professions too began to establish themselves outside the urban centres. As so often the best indicator of this transfer of professional activity is provided by the location and activity of practising notaries. The notariate is one of the least studied and least understood of the professions in Italy, but its combination of private and public function made it crucial to the whole structure of what were essentially bureaucratic, literate and litigious societies. Notaries could be found formally in practice over the whole of the region from a very early period. By the later Middle Ages all towns and many villages had a notary in residence. This picture of a wide-ranging profession at an early date is, however, misleading. By the sixteenth century

---

[31] See for instance ASVR, Comune, Processo 9786.

a clear distinction needed to be drawn between those notaries, the minority of those matriculated in the Notarial Colleges of the cities, who were engaged in practice on a professional scale and those, matriculated and licensed, perhaps practising on a small scale for whom, like so many English gentlemen of the same period matriculated at the Inns of Court, a legal training was no more than part of a proper education. In the sixteenth and seventeenth centuries the great mass of practising notaries were to be found in the cities and the smaller urban centres; certainly the greatest bulk of registered documents were drawn up by urban notaries. At some point around the middle of the eighteenth century this pattern begins to change, at least temporarily. The growing population and the growing litigation caused by the increasing number of conflicts between a more overcrowded population, led to a major increase in the volume of notarial work, in part because of the growing volume of transactions, contracts and so forth, but also in part because of the growing desire to have agreements which had previously been ratified by private contract (*scrittura privata*) formally registered. That increase in business led in part to the expansion of notarial firms and also, particularly in the cities, to their specialising in specific types of work. The expanding demand for notarial registration also led to an expansion in the numbers of matriculations and to an expansion in the numbers of practising notaries. Strikingly, many of these new notaries came from relatively well-to-do rural families. Small-town families are markedly under-represented. Furthermore the later eighteenth century saw many of these new notaries setting up, not in the smaller towns, but in the villages, frequently their own home villages, and from their family houses. It is clear from the volume of material they recorded that a great deal of local legal business was diverted to them rather than going to the notaries of the smaller towns. In many smaller towns, indeed, it is clear that the number of notaries was static or falling and also that many of the small-town notaries at this period went off to the provincial cities to try their luck at more specialised forms of legal activity.[32]

V

By the time of the great political changes of the last decade of the eighteenth century and the first two decades of the nineteenth, political changes which were profoundly important socially and economically as well as on a constitutional and diplomatic level, the small towns of northern Italy had fallen back very sharply in the competition with both the provincial cities and the

---

[32] See G. Sancassani, *Documenti sul Notariato Veronese durante il Dominio Veneto* (Verona n.d.) and ASVR, Collegio dei Notai, Matricole 1, 2, 3.

countryside. The provincial cities had recovered much of the ground which they had lost in the seventeenth century and were to be the real gainers from the new political and social structure of the Napoleonic and post-Napoleonic world. At the same time the distinction between the small town and the village, which had never been clear and decisive in population terms, was also blunting in functional terms. It is much more difficult in nineteenth-century Italy than it had been two centuries earlier to be sure just where the small town ended and the countryside of villages began.

In a culture and society in which the distinction between urban and rural is especially strong, this blurring of the lines is of greater interest merely than that of historical curiosity. Italian society and Italian culture were and remain much more aware of the distinction, even the conflict, between town and countryside. Consistently, in literature and in art, and through into the twentieth century, the urban is identified with the progressive, the developed, the educated and the good while the rural is backward, primitive, dangerous and evil. The very concept of the *villeggiatura*, of a residence in the countryside as much forced by the discomforts of city life in the summer as a source of pleasure, largely a transfer to a rural setting of town life and town activity, as carefully separated from the life of the countryside as possible, suggests clearly that the urban and the rural did not mix and that that separation was also in some senses at least a matter of quasi-moral judgement. This clear separation between town and country, and the general acceptance of the superiority of the urban life as the only civilised life, has played a role – a major one – in the drift of population from the countryside into the towns throughout the recent history of northern Italy. Its origins lie in the distant past, but it was strengthened and intensified by the relative revival of the major centres in the eighteenth century, even before the decisive boost it was to receive from the Napoleonic administrative system and the centralisation of education, litigation and patronage in the cities in the nineteenth and twentieth centuries.

In this process of the re-emphasising of the status of the cities, the small towns were, and remain, a major loser. The growing conflation of small town and countryside in the eighteenth century meant that the small towns no longer had, as they had during their seventeenth-century revival, anything distinctively different to offer but were in a sense, and were perceived as being, merely part of the backward and uncultured *mondo contadino*. In that sense, as in so many others, the eighteenth century was a decisive period for the small towns of northern Italy. Not merely did it determine that the small towns were likely to remain small and to be only very partial participants in any economic development in the nineteenth century, which was largely to be concentrated in the major cities, but also that, in the great and widening cultural division between town and countryside, the small towns would decisively fall into the camp of the countryside rather than into that of the urban sector. In the end, in northern Italy, as in the centre and the south, the great distinction was to be that between the greater cities and the countryside, including the smaller towns, rather than between a wider urban sector and the 'true' countryside.

13   Cities, towns and small towns in Castile, 1500–1800

Juan E. Gelabert

The Spanish word *villa* has the same meaning as the English word 'town'[1] and like it implies a degree of self-government based on specific charters of privilege. Indeed, in the case of Spain this characteristic seems to be the essence of these communities of inhabitants regardless of population size. Thus Madrid, to take the most extreme example, has long had exactly the same 'town' status as minor centres like Villacastín, Rueda or Bujalance. The point to be stressed in the present context is that the number of towns with jurisdictional autonomy increased significantly in the course of the sixteenth and seventeenth centuries at the same time as the country's cities and larger towns underwent demographic collapse. By 1800 not only had the total number of towns risen sharply but the population of Spain – and in particular that of Castile – was concentrated in urban centres that were smaller than in the sixteenth century. While this was in part a consequence of demographic change, it also stemmed from changes in the jurisdictional status of the communities of inhabitants.

This chapter will explore the factors behind the increase in the number of towns in the sixteenth and seventeenth centuries, an increase observed in other Mediterranean countries (Italy, France) and which was closely related to attempts by villages to shake off the tutelage of cities or large towns and obtain jurisdictional autonomy. By 1537 the financial administration of the Crown of Castile had realised that sizeable sums could be raised by selling the privileges of exemption which authorised these bids for autonomy. The result was a wave of town creations over a hundred years or more, and thus, in jurisdictional terms at least, a large increase in the number of towns between the dates mentioned above.

The distribution of the Spanish population between urban and rural settlement was also profoundly modified. Broadly speaking, centres with fewer than 10,000 inhabitants accounted for a larger share of the population in 1800 than in 1600. Behind this lay the fact that the large Castilian cities

Translated by Ian Williams and Godfrey Rogers
[1] 'In senses later than OE times it is the equiv. of L. *villa*', *The Oxford Dictionary of English Etymology*, 1979.

271

had been especially badly hit by the economic crisis of the seventeenth century. Unable to provide employment for those flocking in from the countryside, the cities became subject to the familiar 'graveyard' effect. When general demographic recovery began around 1700 they were still unable to attract newcomers: the countryside had weathered the seventeenth-century crisis relatively well and there was nothing to make moving into the cities more attractive.

By 1800 a large number of centres existed which had acquired the title of 'town' as a consequence of changes in juridical status. At the same time, however, the total urban population in cities or towns over 10,000 inhabitants had fallen considerably. This raises the old question of how to define the urbanisation process, the problem here being not so much over selection of a particular quantitative limit, such as 10,000 or 5,000 inhabitants, as over the choice between a quantitative or juridical criterion. That said, it does seem that the larger its population, the larger the number of urban attributes a centre possessed, self-government included. On the other hand, even when they enjoyed self-government, these 'towns' were characterised by a limited division of labour and a high proportion of employment in the agricultural and related sectors. This forms a paradox not only for historians but also for contemporaries.

Although calculation is difficult, probably over half (60 per cent has been suggested) of the settlements in the Kingdom of Castile were mere villages at the start of the sixteenth century. Two centuries later more than three quarters of these settlements – little information is available on new centres – had been officially converted into towns. A hundred years later, however, under the Bourbon dynasty, the proportion reached in 1700 had hardly altered. The calculations made by Helen Nader record 146 sales of privileges to create *villas* in the 180 years up to 1700, while the 100 years of Bourbon rule saw the creation of only 48 new *villas* (37 of them in 1789). In other words, whereas in the sixteenth and seventeenth centuries a new *villa* was created almost every year, in the eighteenth century the rate fell to just one every two years, and if 1789 is excluded only 11 appeared between 1700 and 1758, that is, one every six years.[2]

The figures given by Nader, though not complete, show clearly the importance of the process of *villa* creation between 1500 and 1700, a phenomenon that helped shape the urban and political landscape of Castile in ways still visible today yet which has received little attention from historians. According to the so-called census of the Count of Floridablanca, in 1787, at the end of the process outlined above, Spain had 145 cities, 4,572

---

2 *Liberty in Absolutist Spain: The Habsburg Sale of Towns, 1516–1700* (Baltimore–London, 1990), p. 3 and Appendix, chs. 3 and 4.

towns and 14,605 villages, hamlets and farms.[3] The differences in jurisdictional status between a city and a town appear in practice to have been nil. The title of city had an essentially honorific significance and was granted by the king in return for some special show of loyalty or service.[4] It was also sometimes justified by ancient precedents dating from Roman times (*civitas*) and more commonly in the Mediterranean world by the existence of an episcopal see, as in England. Thus when William Cecil, Lord Roos was describing Alcalá de Henares in 1610–11, he observed that: 'although it is not a city in our sense of the word for it is not an episcopal see, it is, however, much more beautiful than many other cities besides having a university, where the study of theology is said to flourish greatly'.[5] There is evidence that larger settlements were more likely to be cities and, conversely, smaller ones towns. However, just as Madrid was always merely a 'town', so Chinchilla and Calahorra boasted 'city' status with a mere 641 and 812 households, respectively, in 1591.

The imbalance in the city/town relationship that existed beween the Kingdom of Castile and the Kingdom of Aragón (Valencia, Aragón, Mallorca, Catalonia) may be the clearest proof of the honorific character (*honore decoratur*) of the title of city. In 1787, 38 of Spain's 145 cities were in the territories of Valencia, Aragón, Mallorca and Catalonia, which also had 720 *villas*; in Castile, however, the proportion was approximately half, with 138 cities to 3,852 *villas*. The first and most obvious reason for this inflation in city titles is that it accompanied the parallel inflation of personal honours known to have favoured the subjects of Catalonia far more than their Castilian counterparts. In both cases we are dealing with a mechanism for purchasing loyalties, some individual, others collective, and which reflected 'the crown's desire to appease the notoriously quarrelsome and stubborn' political system peculiar to the non-Castilian peninsular territories.[6]

---

[3] *Censo Español* . . . (Madrid, 1787). Facsimile edition (Madrid, 1987), published by the Instituto Nacional de Estadística.

[4] Arcos de la Frontera changed from town to city on 5 December 1472 by a charter granted by Henry IV. The reasons invoked in the charter were: 'the many good and loyal services you have performed for me and continue to perform, in the war against the Moors, enemies of our Holy Faith, and notably in the taking of the town of Cardela . . .', *Privilegios Reales y Viejos Documentos*, vol. XII, Arcos de la Frontera, 1–VIII (Madrid, 1975).

[5] Patricia Shaw Fairman, *España vista por los ingleses del siglo XVII* (Madrid, 1981), p. 100.

[6] James S. Amelang, 'The Purchase of Nobility in Castile, 1552–1700. A Comment', *Journal of European Economic History*, vol. 11 (1982), 219–26. Amelang's article is a comment on I. A. A. Thompson's, 'The Purchase of Nobility in Castile, 1552–1700', *Journal of European Economic History*, vol. 8 (1979), 313–60. The case of the Kingdom of Navarre provides further proof, since it had nine cities and 154 towns; a similar proportion to that of Valencia where there were nine and 161, respectively. For one of the Basque Provinces, Guipúzcoa, the process of town-building can be followed in Pablo Fernández Albaladejo, *La crisis del Antiguo Régimen en Guipúzcoa, 1766–1833. Cambio económico e historia* (Madrid, 1975),

Second, examination of the rate at which the privileges converting villages into towns were sold reveals that sales were concentrated in the years around the great financial crises suffered by the Habsburg kings. In the year of the first bankruptcy (1557) of Philip II's reign, more privileges were sold than in any other year in the sixteenth century; the same thing occurred in 1627 under Philip IV (according to the data given by Helen Nader). In short, after 1537, sale of privileges granting villages self-government (*privilegios de villazgo*) was used as a remedy for the government's financial difficulties. The restricted fiscal powers enjoyed by the Habsburg monarchs outside Castile meant that sales of privileges were mainly concentrated here, in the heart of the Empire, and affected other Kingdoms and provinces to a far lesser extent. Villages seeking town status began from a situation of jurisdictional dependence on a *villa* (town) or city, on the seigneurial estate (*señorío*) of some great lord, or on monasteries, cathedrals or Military Orders. Demands for autonomy had to be justified, and in the Mediterranean countries the usual reason given was abuse of jurisdictional power by superior lords, towns or cities. In the first half of the fifteenth century, Pistoia, a dependency of Florence, complained about its position under 'the rule of the city and its leaders'.[7] Similarly, in the last years of the *ancien régime*, Du Pont de Nemours' *Mémoire sur les municipalités*, commissioned by Turgot for Louis XVI, described French towns as 'very tyrannical with their neighbouring villages'.[8] Concerning Castile, the dependent villages of the city of Salamanca, for example, protested to the Royal Council of the Catholic Kings in 1492 that the taxes they paid to the municipal council – as a result of the city's autonomous fiscal power – were higher than those demanded by the Crown. In 1532 the villages in the *señorío* of Segovia denounced the procedures whereby the municipal authorities (*regidores*) were able to force the villagers to pay considerably more than the city dwellers.[9] When Gerónimo Castillo de Bovadilla, a connoisseur of the Castilian urban political system, published his *Política* in 1597 he was well aware of the abuses arising from jurisdictional control and recommended that:

---

pp. 148–55. The original sources for these sales are at the AGS (Archivo General de Simancas), CJH (Consejo y Juntas de Hacienda), 671, 1608–15.

[7] Giorgio Chittolini, *La Formazione dello Stato Regionale e le Instituzioni del Contado* (Turin, 1979), xx.

[8] Quoted by Charles Petit-Dutaillis, *Les communes françaises. Caractères et évolution dés origines au XVIIIe siècle*, p. 255 of the Spanish translation (Mexico, 1959).

[9] Clara Isabel López Benito, 'Usurpaciones de bienes concejiles en Salamanca durante el reinado de los Reyes Católicos', *Studia Historica*, vol. 1 (1983), 169–83; and Miguel Santamaría Lancho, 'Del concejo y su término a la comunidad de ciudad y tierra: surgimiento y transformación del señorío urbano de Segovia', *Studia Historica*, vol. 3 (1985), 83–116. For the general context see Angus Mackay, 'Ciudad y campo en la Europa medieval', *Studia Historica*, vol. 2 (1984), 27–53.

Just as it pertains to the duty of the Good Judge to prevent the high and mighty from oppressing and mistreating the lowly and weak, so he must ensure that the city and its dwellers shall not harm or oppress, either the villages under its jurisdiction, or their inhabitants, and that these shall honour and respect their city, as is fitting, because it is the natural order of things that the head shall guide and govern well and with fair treatment, and shall defend and maintain its whole body, and all its members, and that these shall obey, so that the whole may be conserved in the being and order that God gave it.

It was wrong, however, to disrupt the natural order of things: there had to be those who gave orders and also those who obeyed; but it was no less true that, because of specific circumstances (distance from the city or town, civic abuses), villages could ask to be freed from an undesirable tutelage. Immediately afterwards, however, the author proclaimed what to his mind was the main reason for the creation of towns. This was 'the needs of the Kings and that it was necessary for them to make use of this project (*arbitrio*) to satisfy such needs, as is written into the contracts of the privileges of these towns'.[10]

And this was in effect what happened. Although *villas* had been created during the Trastámara period (1369–1516), after 1537 Charles V, beset by pressing financial needs,[11] decided to sell certain villages located in the territory of the Military Orders (incorporated into the Crown in 1523) and to detach 'for an agreed price some villages from the cities and towns under whose jurisdiction they fell'.[12] In the case of the Military Orders, incorporation into the Crown in 1523 had simply granted the Kings of Spain the role of administrators of their patrimony; for any part of it to be sold required prior authorisation from the Pope. This is what Clement VII gave in two papal bulls dated 28 September and 12 October 1529 and which also imposed a limit on the sums Charles V could obtain from such transactions.[13]

But if this first set of sales got the Emperor out of trouble at home with minimal political cost (the negotiations in Rome with Clement VII had been a different matter), the announcement that villages could purchase their jurisdictional autonomy was a serious cause of concern to the cities and towns who saw themselves as victims of the manoeuvre. Relations between

---

[10] There is a facsimile edition, Madrid, 1978, with an introductory study by Benjamín González Alonso, of the 1704 Antwerp edition; both quotations appear in vol. II, pp. 628ff and 631–1.

[11] Ramón Carande, *Los caminos del oro y de la plata (deuda exterior y tesoros ultramarinos)*, vol. III of his *Carlos V y sus banqueros* (Madrid, 1967), p. 147.

[12] Comments on the Cortes' meeting at Valladolid made by Pedro Girón in his *Crónica del Emperador Carlos V* (Madrid, 1964), p. 110; ed. by Juan Sánchez Montes, with a foreword by Peter Rassow.

[13] Nader, *Liberty*, pp. 100–1; see also Alonso María Guilarte, *El régimen señorial en el siglo XVI*, 2nd edn (Valladolid, 1987), pp. 64ff.

King and Kingdom were already not particularly good, and in the following year (1538) the *Cortes*, assembled this time in Toledo, was the scene of turbulent sessions in which the high nobility – the grandees – attempted to form a united opposition front with the representatives of the cities (*procuradores*) against certain financial measures proposed by the King and his Council of Finance.[14]

Although the extraordinary meeting of the estates failed to grant the Emperor what he had specifically sought, the *procuradores* and the Crown did manage to reach agreement over several financial matters and over the sale of the *privilegios de villazgo*. The seventeen cities and one town (Madrid) with representation in the *Cortes* obtained favourable treatment through a royal writ (*cédula*) issued the following year by the King and the Council of Castile. Given that the sale of privileges had been under way since 1537 and had aroused high hopes of liberation in the villages (and enthusiasm among the members of the Council of Finance), only minor amendments could be made to the original decision. Charles accepted that the cities could prevent the liberation of their dependent villages by paying a sum equal to or higher than the latter had offered. It was also agreed, in return for large sums of money, that during the King's reign cities could purchase the privilege of not being deprived of the villages which formed part of their *señorio*.

Cities took up both options. Córdoba, Toledo and Seville, for example, preferred the second, which was more expensive but safer. Soria, on the other hand, paid 4,000 ducats to avoid losing Noviercas.[15] When the Council of Finance drew up a list in 1555 of all the new towns that had appeared since 1537, they totalled 73;[16] and with the exception of Cuenca (3,536 households in 1561, 3,095 in 1591) and Guadalajara (1,900 in 1591) – fairly large cities by Castilian standards – the new towns had come from the *señorio* of old medium-size towns such as Mérida (1,213 households in 1591), Trujillo (1,580), Huete (1,340) and Almagro (1,789).[17]

Creation of new towns from formerly dependent villages was thus partially contained in the first half of the sixteenth century thanks to the privileges the larger cities of Castile had extracted from Charles V. Taking advantage of the Emperor's financial difficulties, they offered him a form of

---

[14] The politics of these crucial years has been portrayed by Charles David Hendricks, *Charles V and the 'Cortes' of Castile. Politics in Renaissance Spain* (Ann Arbor, 1985), pp. 231ff.

[15] Carande, *Los caminos*, p. 208.

[16] 'Memorial de los lugares que se hizieron villas desde el año pasado de DXXXXVII hasta fin de noviembre de DLV', AGS (Archivo General de Simancas), Mercedes y Privilegios (MP), 251.

[17] Data extracted from Annie Molinié-Bertrand, *Au siècle d'or l'Espagne et ses hommes. La population du Royaume de Castille au XVIᵉ siècle* (Paris, 1985).

financial help that safeguarded the integrity of their jurisdictional space. Most, moreover, were in a healthy financial position at this time and purchase of privileges to prevent creation of new towns did not impose an unacceptable burden on municipal treasuries. The new towns which emerged between 1537 and 1555 did so in fact from the jurisdiction of lesser towns without the political and economic power enjoyed by the main centres.[18] Even here, however, it was legally doubtful how far the King could act against the integrity of the urban jurisdictional space. In 1552, when Philip II was in Castile as regent, the Emperor harassed him from the Low Countries with constant demands for money, urging his son to adopt the sale of *privilegios de villazgo* as a financial expedient. Philip's reply was discouraging.[19] Besides reminding his father that in 1539 he had promised not to pursue creation of new towns, Philip pointed out that if such action proved unavoidable it could only be: 'with great justification and restraint, owing to experience of the lawsuits and disputes between villages and head-towns caused by the villages having become towns in earlier years', and added that 'some people doubt whether money can be obtained from these jurisdictions, for if they are to be granted it has to be done for reasons of good government and according to justice, which should be stated so as not to do anything against conscience'. Three years later, the Royal Council of Castile wrote to the Emperor in terms similar to those used by his son in 1552.[20] The members began their letter by transcribing the 1539 writ – lest the Emperor should have forgotten what had been agreed. Next they became spokesmen for the towns and cities likely to become victims of the procedure, stating quite bluntly that 'the terms of Your Majesty's writ must be upheld for the towns and cities' for two reasons: first, the King should keep his word given in the contracts with the cities of the Kingdom; second, what had been agreed in Toledo on 30 March 1539 was a contract. It was, therefore, a strict question of justice on which the Royal Council was bound to find in favour of the towns and cities. More generally, there was the fact that this was certainly not the last occasion on which the King would have to seek financial help from the Kingdom. The Kingdom had always received rewards (*mercedes*) for such help, but if the King now failed to honour those granted in 1539 the Kingdom would have little reason to trust his word in future. Only one exception to the agreed terms could be admitted, and it was precisely the one advocated by Gerónimo Castillo de

---

[18] In the list published by Nader, *Liberty*, Appendix A, ch. 3, only 21 new towns appear, and only seven of these came from royal towns (Huete and Guadalajara), the rest belonging to seigneurial lands of the Military Orders or the Archbishopric of Toledo.

[19] *Corpus documental de Carlos V*, ed. by Manuel Fernández Alvarez, vol. III (1548–54) (Salamanca, 1977), p. 504.

[20] *Corpus documental de Carlos V*, vol. IV (1554–58).

Bovadilla; in the interest of the 'good government' of a village the King could grant it autonomous jurisdiction and separate it from its head-town, though in this case it should be made absolutely clear that the corresponding privilege could not then be granted through a financial transaction.

This insistence of the Kingdom on respect for what had been agreed in 1539 was a direct response to attempts by the Council of Finance to extend sales of *privilegios de villazgo*; on this point the list published by Helen Nader leaves no doubt.[21] Sales of privileges did continue during Philip II's reign though it is difficult to establish either their rate or total number. Arguably the King did not feel bound by the contract signed by his father in 1539; and his financial difficulties were in any case greater. Piecemeal information points to an acceleration of sales in the second half of the century. In 1565, Alcalá de Henares was said to have lost 15 of its 24 dependent villages since 1537.[22] The city of Seville – in spite of the privilege purchased from Charles V in 1539 – suffered a progressive loss of its dependent villages, and, out of a total of between 56 and 65,[23] had lost control over 44 by 1600.[24] The policy of putting more and more *privilegios de villazgo* up for sale continued in the seventeenth century. In the province of Guipúzcoa, for example, only Legazpi had obtained town status when the Crown offered the opportunity in 1608; but in 1615, even through the per capita price of exemption had risen from 20 to 25 ducats, 30 villages were prepared to pay for it.[25] For a city like Guadalajara, the systematic amputation of its jurisdictional space was dramatic. It had lost 24 out of 28 villages by 1636, and when in that year Don Carlos Ibarra sought to buy one of those that remained, it was the Council of Finance itself which said no![26]

Moves by villages to obtain exemption, encouraged by the Council of Finance, were resisted by the towns and cities as best they could. Each summons of the *Cortes* was the occasion to demand that the King put an end to sales of *privilegios de villazgo*. The contracts signed with the King

---

[21] See Nader, *Liberty*, Appendix A, ch. 3.   [22] AGS, MP, 252.

[23] Both figures appear in the 'Noticia de los pueblos de la Tierra de Sevilla . . .', Archivo Municipal de Sevilla, section 11, vol. 56, doc. 41.

[24] I. A. A. Thompson, 'The impact of war', in Peter Clark, ed., *The European Crisis of the 1590s: Essays in Comparative History* (1985), pp. 261–83. An account of the money collected by the Royal Treasury through these sales during Philip II's reign can be seen in Modesto Ulloa, *La Hacienda Real de Castilla en el reinado de Felipe II*, 3rd edn (Madrid, 1986), pp. 670–2.

[25] See above note 6.

[26] Antonio Domínguez Ortiz, 'Ventas y exenciones de lugares durante el reinado de Felipe IV', *Anuario de Historia del Derecho Español*, vol. 34 (1964), 163–207. Córdoba's losses in the sixteenth and seventeenth centuries can be followed in José Ignacio Fortea Pérez, *Córdoba en el siglo XVI. Las bases demográficas y económicas de una expansión urbana* (Córdoba, 1981), pp. 98ff.

between 1590 and 1664 (the so-called *escrituras del servicio de millones*)[27] made financial help from the Kingdom subject to a number of conditions, among which was usually one that the Council of Finance should not create any more exempted towns.[28] As the seventeenth century progressed, however, the option of avoiding such losses by outbidding the villages became harder. Seville's municipal treasury, for example, was bankrupt in 1602, as was Valladolid's in 1642.[29] Compared with their prosperous position during most of the sixteenth century, the seventeenth century saw municipal treasuries in Castile fall into an appalling state.[30] Nonetheless, when the whole Kingdom in the *Cortes* acceded to a request for financial help from the Crown, both sides signed a contract and the Kingdom made general conditions favourable to the cities and *villas* summoned to the *Cortes*. Moreover, when the King sought help from a particular city, it could draw up its own contract with specific conditions. For the city in question this was a golden opportunity to try to repair completely or in part the prejudice caused to it by the creation of exempted towns. Seville and Córdoba had such an opportunity in 1629.[31] In return for a grant of 500,000 ducats, Seville demanded fulfilment of what had been agreed with Charles V in 1539, namely that exempted towns such as El Garrobo, Bormujos, Gerena and Burguillos should return to its jurisdiction. The conditions made by Córdoba when granting Philip IV 200,000 ducats over sixteen years had a similar punitive purpose, with the city stipulating that in order

---

[27] I. A. A. Thompson, 'Crown and "Cortes" in Castile, 1590–1665', *Parliaments, Estates and Representation*, vol. 2 (1982), 29–45; Charles Jago, 'Habsburg absolutism and the Cortes of Castile', *American Historical Review*, vol. 86 (1981), 307–26; Pablo Fernández Albadalejo, 'Monarquía, Cortes y "cuestión constitucional" en Castilla durante la Edad Moderna', *Revista de las Cortes Generales*, vol. 1 (1984), 11–34.

[28] *Escrituras, Acuerdos, Administraciones, y Súplicas de los Servicios* . . . (Madrid, 1734).

[29] For Seville there is much eighteenth-century local information on the subject, such as the *Noticias de las causas que originaron los empeños de Sevilla y atrasos de sus Propios y rentas, formación de su concurso y nombramiento del señor Juez para conocer su desempeño* (undated but certainly eighteenth century), Archivo Municipal de Sevilla, section 11, vol. 21, doc. no. 1; and *Noticia de los Propios de Sevilla, ibid.*, vol. 56, doc. no. 41. See also José Ignacio Martínez Ruiz, 'Donativos y empréstitos sevillanos a la hacienda real (siglos XVI–XVII)'. *Revista de Historia Económica*, vol. 2 (1984), 233–44. For Valladolid, Adriano Gutiérrez Alonso, *Estudio sobre la decadencia de Castilla. La ciudad de Valladolid en el siglo XVII* (Valladolid, 1989).

[30] There is no good history of municipal finances in Castile during the Old Regime, but see the preliminary study by Bartolomé Yun Casalilla to the modern edition (Valladolid, 1990) of the *Estado de la bolsa de Valladolid. Examen de sus tributos, de cargas y medios de su extinción, de su gobierno y reforma*, written in 1777 by José Ruiz de Celada. For a similar pattern in Southern Italy, see Francesco Caracciolo, *Sud, debbiti e gabelle. Gravami, potere e società nel Mezzogiorno in età moderna* (Naples, s.d.).

[31] *Escriptvura del Servicio de los doscientos mil dvcados, con que la muy noble, y muy leal Ciudad de Cordoua, por si, y las villas de su juridición, sirue a Su Magestad, por via de Donativo este año de MDCXXIX* (printed), AGS, Consejo y Juntas de Hacienda (CJH), 672; *ibid.*, for Seville's loan.

to raise the sum it be allowed to sell off the common lands of its exempted towns. When the latter discovered the agreement their former head-town was about to reach with the Council of Finance, they held a meeting at Nuestra Señora de Piedras Santas and addressed a strong protest to the Council and to the city of Córdoba. They were convinced that the latter was taking revenge on its old dependent villages by trying 'to place on the seven [exempted] towns the greater part of the burden' of the aid to the King.

Although I have been concerned above with moves to create new towns from the dependent villages of royal cities or towns, it is worth noting that throughout this period a parallel change was occurring in the domains of the high aristocracy of Castile whereby the seigneurial lords allowed, albeit for reasons different from those of the King, small villages in their domains to obtain town status.[32] This process displays certain similarities of chronology and form with that responsible for creation of new towns in Sicily (90 *licentia populandi* were granted between 1590 and 1650 under the initiative of the Sicilian *baronaggio*).[33]

To sum up, by the middle of the eighteenth century, at the time of the Catastro of the Marquis de la Ensenada, there were provinces where the proportion of population living in exempted towns ranged from 12.44 per cent (Salamanca) to 30.11 per cent (Segovia), with intermediate levels in Toledo (13.62 per cent), Soria (19.03 per cent) and Avila (16.74 per cent).[34] Most of these new towns having appeared in the sixteenth and seventeenth centuries, this period witnessed an extensive disintegration and redefinition of jurisdictional space, a development which had major economic and demographic consequences.

These conflicts between villages and the cities and towns, with the former fighting for 'liberation' and the latter to conserve authority, were of course over more than just a change of title. The fierce resistance put up by the head-towns to this kind of 'dismemberment' suggests they regarded their very existence as inconceivable without the dependent villages in their territory. All cities and towns exercised control over their surrounding lands,[35] so any village that obtained town status then faced the difficult task of building up its own *tierra* (land), something that again could typically only be achieved at the expense of the head-town. For their part, towns and cities needed to retain jurisdictional and political control over their land at

---

[32] Numerous examples in Nader, *Liberty*, ch. 2.
[33] See Timothy B. Davies, 'Village-building in Sicily: an aristocratic remedy for the crisis of the 1590s', in Clark, *European Crisis*, pp. 191–208. Also Francesco Benigno, *Una casa, una terra. Ricerche su Paceco, paese nuovo della Sicilia nel Sei et Settecento* (Catania, n.d.).
[34] See my 'Il declino della rete urbana nella Castiglia dei secoli XVI–XVIII', *Cheiron*, vol. 11 (1989–90), 9–45.
[35] See Giorgio Chitolini, 'Quasi-Città. Borghi e terre in area lombarda nel tardo medioevo', *Società e Storia*, vol. 47 (1990), 3–26.

Table 13.1. *Demographic patterns in Córdoba province 1530–1591*

	Number of settlements by number of households		
	Up to 500	500–1,500	Over 1,500
1530	26 (67%)	11 (28%)	2 (5%)
1591	18 (46%)	12 (31%)	9 (23%)

Source: Fortea Pérez, *Córdoba en el siglo XVI*, p. 96.

all costs. As the city of Córdoba argued concerning the exemption of Hornachuelos (1599), such moves were to be avoided: 'for with them the authority and strength to serve Your Majesty are diminished'.[36] This authority of the towns in Guipúzcoa was translated into numbers of votes, quotas of political participation in the *Juntas* of the Province; the power of established towns was thus necessarily reduced as new ones were created. This explains the determination of cities with a vote in the *Cortes* to prevent, in return for large sums of money, any increase in the number of towns with the same prerogative.[37]

The demographic result of this process of town creation was that the distribution of the Castilian population between 1600 and 1800 showed a marked tendency to cluster in smaller centres. By contrast, during the sixteenth century (1530–91) population growth had been accompanied by a trend towards concentration in large centres. Thus while overall population growth was in the order of 40 per cent, in a sample of 40 towns and cities in Castile it reached 75 per cent.[38] The changes in the province of Córdoba are shown in Table 13.1.

Between 1500 and 1600 the rate of urbanisation in Spain rose from 6.1 per cent to 11.4 per cent. Yet in 1700 – after the demographic crisis of the seventeenth century – it had fallen to 9 per cent, and it would fall back even further to 8.6 per cent in 1750; in 1800 it was still lower (11.1 per cent) than in 1600.[39]

A sample of ten Castilian provinces contained 658,825 households in 1591, 546,018 in 1750 and 750,081 in 1827. The urbanisation rate for centres over 1,250 households (about 5,000 inhabitants) fell from 11.94 per

[36] AGS, CJH, 386.
[37] I. A. A. Thompson, 'Cortes y ciudades: tipología de los procuradores (extracción social, representatividad)', *Las Cortes de Castilla y León en la Edad Moderna* (Valladolid, 1989), pp. 191–248.
[38] David Ringrose, 'Il mutamento dei sistemi urbani: concetti generali e il caso spagnolo', *Cheiron*, vol. 11 (1989–90), 47–74.
[39] Jan de Vries, *European Urbanization, 1500–1800* (1984), p. 39.

Table 13.2. *Urbanisation rates in Old Castile (towns with more than 1,250 households)*

Province	1591	1750	1827
Avila	7.27	5.22	0.00
Soria	3.27	0.00	0.00
Segovia	13.02	7.17	6.47
Burgos	4.23	3.75	9.28
Salamanca	9.68	9.43	6.53
Total	7.49	5.11	4.45

Sources: see those for the appendix.

cent in 1591 to 9.54 per cent in 1750. Whereas overall population declined by 17.13 per cent, the figure was as high as 33.79 per cent for centres with more than 5,000 inhabitants. By 1827 the general population had increased by 16.28 per cent over its late sixteenth-century level and by 40.30 per cent compared to 1750. Yet over the whole period the urbanisation rate was virtually stable, going just from 11.94 per cent to 11.96 per cent. Thus there were hardly any more people living in urban centres over 5,000 inhabitants in 1827 than two and a quarter centuries earlier. But this apparent stability of the urbanisation rate in fact masks sharp differences between areas within Castile. The urban centres of Old Castile (provinces of Avila, Salamanca, Soria, Segovia and Burgos) experienced a spectacular decline, with Burgos being the only province subsequently to break from this trend, as can be seen in the 1827 data, as a direct result of Santander's growth after 1750 (see Table 13.2).

In New Castile (provinces of Cuenca, Guadalajara and Toledo), Extremadura and La Mancha, the fall in the urbanisation rate is also apparent between 1591 and 1750; from then until 1827, however, the recovery in certain provinces was more than enough (see Table 13.3) to push the overall rate slightly above its 1591 level.

Table 13.4 shows how the size of population evolved in Tierra de Campos between 1591 and 1752.

Eighteenth-century demographic recovery hardly affected the urban centres of Castile, and especially not those – with the notable exception of Madrid[40] – which had been the largest in 1591. This was because of another factor which played a part in redistributing the Spanish, and more precisely

---

[40] David R. Ringrose, *Madrid and the Spanish Economy, 1560–1850* (Berkeley, Los Angeles, 1983); Maria F. Carbajo Isla, *La población de la villa de Madrid desde finales del siglo XVI hasta mediados del siglo XIX* (Madrid, 1987).

Table 13.3. *Urbanisation rates in New Castile (towns with more than 1,250 households)*

Province	1591	1750	1827
Cuenca	9.00	5.34	14.30
Guadalajara	8.83	5.13	4.88
Toledo	22.12	15.95	18.12
La Mancha	25.54	28.81	31.21
Extremadura	16.88	14.56	25.61
Total	16.47	13.95	18.82

Sources: see those for the appendix.

Table 13.4. *Demographic patterns in Tierra de Campos*

	Number of settlements by size (number of households)			
	1–50	51–300	301–400	400+
1591	19 (4%)	45 (36%)	4 (9%)	13 (51%)
1752	29 (6%)	63 (49%)	6 (14%)	6 (31%)

Source: Bartolomé Yun Casalilla, *Sobre la transición al capitalismo en Castilla. Economica y sociedad en Tierra de Campos (1500–1830)* (Salamanca, 1987), p. 438.

Castilian, population, namely the persistent demographic crisis affecting most of the large cities of Castile after the last quarter of the sixteenth century. Even by the start of the nineteenth century, the urban network in Castile had not recovered the level reached at the end of the sixteenth century. Among the largest cities, Toledo, for example, shrank from 12,142 households in 1571 to 10,933 in 1591 and to 4,889 in 1639.[41] Seville, the most populous centre in Spain at that time, had 25,886 households in 1588, 24,301 in 1597, around 20,000 in 1638 and 16,081 in 1693; not until well into the nineteenth century did the city recover its size of the golden years of the sixteenth century.[42] Valladolid reached 60,000–70,000 inhabitants during

[41] The most comprehensive demographic databank for sixteenth-century Castile is Annie Molinié-Bertrand's book quoted above. For Toledo's demographic history see also Michael Weisser, 'The decline of Castile revisited: the case of Toledo', *The Journal of European Economic History*, vol. 2 (1973), 614–40; Linda Martz, *Poverty and Welfare in Habsburg Spain; The example of Toledo* (Cambridge, 1983); Julio Porres and Linda Martz, *Toledo y los toledanos en 1561* (Toledo, 1961); Julián Montemayor, 'Tolède en 1639', *Mélanges de la Casa de Velázquez*, vol. 18 (1982), 135–63.

[42] Jean Sentaurens, 'Séville dans la seconde moitié du XVIe siècle: population et structures sociales. Le recensement de 1561', *Bulletin Hispanique*, vol. 72 (1989), 3–15.

the brief period (1601–5) at the start of the seventeenth century when the Duke of Lerma, Philip IV's favourite, transferred the Kingdom's capital there from Madrid where it had been established in 1560. But thereafter the city's decline was spectacular; by 1631 it had just 5,400 households, or 20,770 inhabitants, and had to wait until 1900 to reach 68,789 inhabitants again.[43] Burgos is another case worth mentioning: the so-called 'head of Castile', seat of the merchant community's Consulate after 1494 and the leading centre of trade between Castile and northern Europe, had 4,280 households in 1560, 2,665 households in 1591, 6,294 inhabitants (some 1,500 households) in 1631, and fewer than 1,000 households a decade later.[44] Ciudad Real reached 2,049 households in 1591, had 1,340 in 1631 and roughly 1,200 in 1751.[45] Cuenca, a major textile centre with a significant tertiary sector (seat of an Inquisition court) never recovered its demographic level of the second half of the sixteenth century; by the nineteenth century it was a 'ghost of its former self and had become a sleepy provincial capital'.[46]

It is clear that the social and economic difficulties which befell Castile from 1600 onwards tended to have a greater impact on daily life in the more populous centres than in centres of lesser rank, a situation which seems to have been typical of a broader Mediterranean context.[47] The growth of Castilian cities in the sixteenth century had been dependent on heavy migratory movements from the surrounding countryside, but after 1600 this influx was substantially reduced and remained so for a long time afterwards.[48] Population movements of this kind were likely to be influenced by decisions about living conditions, real or supposed, and Helen Nader has observed that 'the general perception was that being a seigneurial town was

[43] Bartolomé Bennassar, *Valladolid au Siècle d'Or. Une ville de Castille et sa campagne au XVIᵉ siècle* (Paris, 1967); Gutiérrez Alonso, *Estudio sobre*, pp. 89 and ff. I would like to thank Prof. Emiliano Fernández de Pinedo for allowing me to consult his unpublished study of the 1631 census data.

[44] Paul J. Hiltpold, *Burgos in the Reign of Philip II: The Ayuntamiento, Economic Crisis and Social Control, 1550–1600*, University Microfilms International, Ann Arbor (MI), 1985.

[45] Carla Rahn Philips, *Ciudad Real, 1550–1750: Growth, Crisis, and Readjustment in the Spanish Economy* (Cambridge, Mass., 1979).

[46] David Sven Reher, *Town and Country in Pre-industrial Spain. Cuenca, 1550–1870* (Cambridge, 1990), p. 15.

[47] Domenico Sella, *L'economia lombarda durante la dominazione spagnola* (Bologna, 1982), ch. 6; Luigi Faccini, *La Lombardia fra '600 e '700. Riconversione economica e mutamenti sociali* (Milan, 1988), ch. 5.

[48] On this controversial question see Alan Sharlin, 'Natural decrease in early modern cities: a reconsideration', *Past and Present*, vol. 79 (1978), 126–38; De Vries, *European Urbanization*, pp. 180 and ff; Alfred Perrenoud, 'Croissance ou déclin. Les mécanismes du non-renouvellement des populations urbaines', *Histoire, Economie et Société*, vol. 4 (1982), 581–601; Peter Clark, 'Migration in England during the late-seventeenth and early-eighteenth centuries', in Peter Clark and David Souden, eds., *Migration and Society in Early Modern England* (1987), pp. 213–52.

preferable to being a village or a city but worse than being a royal town'.[49] Let us examine the bases for this view.

From the second half of the sixteenth century, the large cities and towns of Castile, royal towns for the most part, experienced a progressive decline involving a loss of the industrial, financial and mercantile functions on which their former splendour had been based. Of the 37 Castilian cities which appear in de Vries' list of European centres in 1600, seven have in fact 'disappeared' from it (level 0) by 1800. Six of these had been centres of industrial (Segovia, Cuenca, Avila) or mercantile and financial activity (Medina del Campo, Medina de Rioseco, Villalón) in the sixteenth century. Burgos, the heart of the wool export trade in the sixteenth century, had fallen to below 10,000 inhabitants in 1750, though by 1827 it had recovered to reach 2,368 households, approximately its size in 1591 after two decades of population decline. Toledo is another important case of urban, industrial and demographic decline which had not been reversed by the middle of the nineteenth century. Around 1750 it had 4,872 lay households (or 17,187 inhabitants, this latter figure including the ecclesiastical population) and 15,797 lay inhabitants in 1857, close to, or perhaps slightly lower than the mid-seventeenth-century figure.[50] Toledo lost much of its industrial production (silks, woollens, linens) in the course of the seventeenth century, as did Segovia, Cuenca and many other cities or towns with the same specialisation. Segovia's textile output, for instance, vast in both quality and quantity, was 16,197 pieces of 40 *varas* each between 1579 and 1584 (i.e. some 647,880 *varas*), yet in the best years of the eighteenth century (1780–89) its looms produced only a third of that quantity.[51] According to contemporary estimates – accepted by a present-day historian – the textile sector in Cuenca had been reduced to 7 per cent of its 1600 level by 1617.[52]

Turning to the financial sector characteristic of Medina del Campo, Medina de Rioseco, Villalón and even Seville, by 1567 the fairs at Medina de Rioseco and Villalón had already been transferred to Medina del Campo and all banking activity was concentrated here *de iure* until 1602. Activity at the fairs was disrupted by the vicissitudes of royal finances and by the establishment of Madrid as the capital of the Kingdom. The fairs at Medina del Campo continued to thrive as long as Burgos prospered, and as long as the King honoured his credit commitments, did not sequester treasure sent from the Indies to private individuals and authorised the export of bullion

[49] Nader, *Liberty*, p. 154.
[50] Laura Santolaya Heredero, 'La ciudad de Toledo en el siglo XVIII', *I Congreso de Historia de Castilla-La Mancha*, vol. VIII (2) (Ciudad Real, 1988), pp. 267–74.
[51] Angel García Sanz, *Desarrollo y crisis del Antiquo Régimen en Castilla la Vieja. Económica y sociedad en tierras de Segovia, 1500–1814* (Madrid, 1977), pp. 205–41.
[52] Reher, *Town and Country*, p. 31.

from Castile. While these conditions lasted, Medina del Campo, favoured by its position halfway between Burgos and Valladolid, the *de facto* capital of the Kingdom, functioned well.[53] From the 1560s, however, a series of events tipped the balance against Medina del Campo. Once Madrid had become the capital businessmen found it more convenient to go to the fairs set up for this very reason in Alcalá de Henares and moved in 1599 to Guadalajara.[54] The fairs in the north of Castile dwindled to a fraction of the their former importance; in 1602 they were moved to Burgos with the express aim of helping to arrest that city's decline. Here they remained until 1604 though Burgos did not recover its prosperity.[55] One can imagine the impact on the economic activity of Seville, when, in 1601, the city's last surviving bank failed (56 had collapsed at one fell swoop in 1567).[56] Shortly afterwards the secular upward trend in trade with the Indies was reversed and there began Seville's fall from greatness.

Establishing why industrial activity declined in the cities is not easy. What seems to have happened is a parallel 'industrialisation' of the country-side and a 'ruralisation' of the cities. In the case of Toledo, for example, the eighteenth century saw the total industrial output for the small *villas* of its *tierra* equal and even surpass that of their head-town. During the sixteenth century, Orgaz, Ajofrín and Sonseca, like many others, had worked for Toledo merchants; in 1623 and 1624 they requested and obtained their own ordinances for the manufacture of light low-quality woollens aimed at a large market of lower-class consumers. Toledo made a similar move but without the same success.[57] Thus, whereas the city produced 144,300 *varas* of woollens in 1786, the figure for Ajofrín was 164,900, for Consuegra 192,080 and for Madridejos 272,000 in 1719 (the only available data). Annual production of woollens at Cuenca, one of the most important industrial centres in the sixteenth century, ranged between 20,000 and 30,000 *varas* in the second half of the eighteenth century, the same as at Mota del Cuervo in 1787, and only a third of that at Iniesta (95,000) at the same time.[58] The reasons for this displacement of the textile industry from

[53] Henri Lapeyre, *Une famille de marchands: les Ruiz. Contribution à l'étude du commerce entre la France et l'Espagne au temps de Philippe II* (Paris, 1955), pp. 477ff.

[54] Felipe Ruiz Martín, 'La banca en España hasta 1782', *El Banco de España. Una historia económica* (Madrid, 1970), pp. 43ff.

[55] Manuel Basas Fernández, *El consulado de Burgos en el siglo XVI* (Madrid, 1963), pp. 419–20.

[56] Eufemio Lorenzo Sanz, *Comercio de España con América en la época de Felipe II*, 2 vols., 2nd edn (Valladolid, 1986), vol. I, p. 199.

[57] Julián Montemayor, 'Tolède entre fortune et déclin (1530–1640)', unpublished thesis, University of Toulouse, 1991, pp. 334ff.

[58] Mariano García Ruipérez, 'La industria textil en Castilla–La Mancha durante el siglo XVIII', *I Congreso de Historia de Castilla–La Mancha*, vol. 8 (2), *Conflictos sociales y evolución económica en la Edad Moderna* (Ciudad Real, 1988), pp. 351–97.

cities to small towns and villages, which was not of course unique to Castile, are varied and complex.[59] In the case of Toledo, for example, it has been suggested that the greater rigidity of its guild organisation may be among the main causes.[60] What is certain is that with its new towns the countryside was to be in a stronger position than the traditional urban world to weather economic depression in the seventeenth century. And the long-term demographic consequences were such that economic recovery, when it came, was more dynamic in the countryside.

It may also be noted that the cities experienced an increase in the share of their population employed in the agricultural sector. The population of Ciudad Real engaged in agriculture was only 10.4 per cent in 1550, but had risen to half (49.5 per cent) or perhaps more (68.0 per cent) by 1750.[61] Cuenca provides another example of the decline in industrial activity being paralleled by an increase in agriculture. In 1561, 58 per cent of its heads of household were in the industrial category and only 9.6 per cent in agriculture; after 1700 and up to the middle of the nineteenth century, however, percentages for agriculture ranged between 21.8 and 37.6, while those for the industrial sector fell to 36.8 in 1700 and to 20.1 in 1856.[62] Likewise, the industrial population of Palencia, which had varied between 57.0 per cent and 54.9 per cent in the years 1530–1622, represented only a quarter of the inhabitants in 1751.[63]

The differences in living conditions between the urban and rural worlds and between seigneurial and royal towns were fairly accurately perceived by contemporaries and helped to determine migratory movements. We have already seen how large cities ceased to be attractive to migrants in the course of the seventeenth century. What remains to be seen is whether within the countryside a similarly uneven appeal was working to the detriment of the royal towns and in favour of the seigneurial centres.

For a group of 20 towns in Extremadura whose demographic evolution (birth data) can be traced from 1574 to 1834, recent research has found that 'up to 1700 the most dynamic demographic performance was characteristic of the seigneurial centres. The upward trend of the sixteenth century continued here till the end of the 1580s and the downward movement was

[59] Herman van der Wee, 'Industrial dynamics and the process of urbanization in the Low countries from the Late Middle Ages to the eighteenth century. A Synthesis', in Herman Van der Wee, ed., *The Rise and Decline of Urban Industries in Italy and in the Low Countries (Late Middle Ages–Early Modern Times)* (Leuven, 1989), pp. 307–81.

[60] Montemayor, 'Tolède entre fortune et déclin', ch. 7.

[61] Phillips, *Ciudad Real*, pp. 126–8.

[62] Reher, *Town and Country*, p. 27.

[63] Guillermo Herrero Martínez de Azcoitia, 'La poblacion palentina en los siglos XVI y XVII', *Publicaciones de la Institucion Tello Téllez de Meneses* (Palencia, 1961), p. 68; Alberto Marcos Martín, *Economica, sociedad, pobreza en Castilla: Palencia, 1500–1814*, 2 vols (Palencia, 1985), vol. I, p. 58.

rather smaller than that recorded for the royal or Military Order centres'.[64] The greater demographic dynamism of the settlements on seigneurial lands was often still apparent even in the middle of the eighteenth century. This was the case in the Province of Salamanca; and of the population increases of more than 50 per cent (1751–1827) in the Provinces of Burgos, Soria, Segovia and Avila, 73 occurred in seigneurial settlements as against 37 in *realengo* settlements. By the same token, of the 88 deserted villages in the Province of Avila in the second half of the eighteenth century, 81 were situated on royal lands.[65]

The explanation for these differences can be traced to the time when the new exempted towns were created, although it is valid for both old and new seigneurial towns. New exempted towns removed from the jurisdiction of royal cities or towns had to pay for the privilege, whereas in the case of seigneurial towns it is not certain that the lords either had the juridical power to grant autonomy or, assuming they did, if they could charge for the privilege. On this point, Gerónimo Castillo de Bovadilla wrote that 'although in his lands a King may separate a village (*aldea*) from the jurisdiction of the head-town and give it its own jurisdiction, the lords cannot do the same in their lands. And thus it was decided in the Council [of Castile] in this year of [15]92 against Don Pedro Lasso de Castilla that he had so done to a village in his lands.'[66] The inhabitants of seigneurial lands might consider themselves relatively well off and with nothing to gain from a specific *privilegio de villazgo*. Many lords gave their vassals a more than adequate protection, certainly compared with that provided by cities and towns in the exercise of their *señorio*.[67]

By contrast, when the inhabitants of a dependent village of a royal city or town decided its position would be improved by exemption they had to purchase the privilege, and it was here that their problems began. The commonest means of paying – in cash, of course – the sum demanded by the Council of Finance for exemption involved contracting a *censo* or long-term loan. In order to make the annual repayments the village resorted to measures (*arbitrios*) such as selling off common lands or imposition of *sisas* (excises) on consumer goods. In all such cases the community required the authorisation of the Council of Castile to impose these extraordinary forms of taxation. It seems likely that the progressive deterioration in general economic conditions between the sixteenth and seventeenth centuries

---

[64] Enrique Llopis Agelán *et al.*, 'El movimiento de la población extremeña durante el Antiguo Régimen', unpublished paper to the *IV Congreso de la Asociación de Historia Económica* (Alicante, 1989).

[65] See Gelabert, 'Il declino', for references.   [66] *Política*, I, p. 484f.

[67] For an account of the reasons why economic conditions from the sixteenth to the seventeenth century favoured inhabitants of seigneurial lands, see my 'Il declino', p. 32ff.

affected the ability of exempted towns to escape these forms of indebtedness.[68] And the later a village decided to buy its *privilegio de villazgo*, the less likely it was to succeed.

Imposition of these forms of extraordinary taxation created a vicious circle from which it was difficult to break out. The combination of decreasing agricultural production, declining population and increasing royal taxation, meant gradually diminishing yields from the original tax measures (*arbitrios*), thereby forcing the community to ask the Council of Castile for an extension on its loan or for imposition of new taxes, though the expedient chosen made little difference in the long-run. One of the arguments used by head-towns to prevent their villages gaining autonomy was precisely that they would fall into an irreversible spiral of debt, 'spending and offering what they have not got, using *arbitrios* to raise the sum they have granted, and it is for this reason that the villages are finished and spent'.[69] There is no doubt that to make acquisition of the *privilegio de villazgo* more attractive to the community, the 'coqs de village' who promoted the idea painted a rosy picture of the financial future by minimising the length of time the *arbitrios* would be in force. The reality was generally more sombre, not least because administration of the extraordinary taxation was seldom efficient and not always equitable.

The frequent extensions and progressive fall in living standards were likely to result in some residents abandoning the community and settling elsewhere. This outcome could be invoked by the new authorities of a town to justify to the Council of Castile the low yield of the proposed *arbitrios* and to request further extensions. In truth, however, it is hard to reach even a rough assessment of the economic situation of the exempted towns or of small towns in general.

Mention can be made of two exempted small towns that were geographically close but whose experience was diametrically opposed. The first is Rueda, a centre dependent on Medina del Campo, which obtained its privilege of exemption on 21 May 1636. In 1571 it had 225 households, 251 in 1591, 179 in 1610, 347 around 1630, and 249 in 1636 when it achieved the category of *villa*. It paid 6,640 ducats for the title and cleared the debt completely after 25 years.[70] The second town, Villacastín, presents an entirely different picture. It had 888 households in 1591, of which the majority were *pecheros* (tax-payers); around 1530 there were 706 tax-payers of a total of some 732. When in 1627 it bought its privilege to free itself from Segovia, the population had fallen to 525, and the price it had to pay amounted to 21,000 ducats. Three years later 548 residents still lived in

[68] Nader, *Liberty*, p. 172.   [69] *Escrituras*, f. 128.
[70] Félix J. Martínez Llorente, *Rueda: de aldea a villa. El privilegio de villazgo de 1636* (Valladolid, 1988).

Villacastín; however, in 1751 and by now a new town, its population was only half what it had been in 1591.[71]

Villacastín's decision to purchase its autonomy from Segovia at a cost of 21,000 ducats, almost certainly borrowed, was economically unsound. As a dependent centre, it had lived in the shadow of its head-city, reproducing on a small scale Segovia's industrial activity. Its heyday must have been the first half of the sixteenth century, up to 1565. From this date the parish registers show a continuous fall in the annual number of baptisms, the ten-yearly average reaching its lowest point in 1631–40 (with the low point for marriages in 1621–30). What is known of the demographic history of Villacastín confirms the existence of rapid out-migration around this period. Even on the threshold of the nineteenth century (1787), the town's population had not recovered to half its 1591 level. Industrial activity, meanwhile, had disappeared from the urban economy and the inhabitants depended for their livelihood on agriculture and stock-farming.[72]

The misfortune of Villacastín well illustrates the dramatic conjunction of negative factors that overtook many Castilian cities and towns in the seventeenth century. Rueda, on the other hand, is a significant example of how the seventeenth-century recession could be weathered without excessive hardship thanks to specific forms of agricultural activity. The prosperity of Rueda was based on the expansion of its vineyards following the decline in the better-quality wines from the *tierra* of Medina del Campo, demand for which slumped when that town lost its commercial and financial importance. From the 249 households it had when it was separated from Medina del Campo, Rueda rose to 268 in 1684, and by the middle of the eighteenth century had doubled this figure.[73]

The development of the agro-villes, particularly in Andalusia but also in New Castile and Extremadura, confirms this picture. South of the Tagus, more than in any other part of Castile, the high urbanisation levels of the end of the sixteenth century were maintained and even exceeded between 1750 and 1800. Over the same period, profound changes occurred in the distribution of the population. In New Castile, for example, Cuenca had reached 6,007 households in 1591 and was the only large centre in its province; by 1827 there were five small towns grouping together 10,327 households while the capital had only 1,775 (see Appendix). A similar development was observed in the nearby region of La Mancha, where the

---

[71] J. L. Bermejo Cabrero, 'Villacastín, de aldea a villa', *Estudios Segovianos*, vol. 24 (1972), 105–18.

[72] García Sanz, *Desarrolo y crisis*, pp. 56ff. Vicente Pérez Moreda, *Las crisis de mortalidad en la España interio (siglos XVI–XIX)* (Madrid, 1980), pp. 225ff. Figures for earlier and later decades were 257 (1601–10), 213 (1611–20) and 104 (1641–50).

[73] Alain Huets de Lemps, *Vignobles et vins du Nord-Ouest de L'Espagne*, 2 vols (Bordeaux, 1967), vol. I, pp. 325ff.

number of small towns rose from four to 17 and their total households from 7,328 to 32,486; and in Extremadura, where the small towns increased from 11 to 20 and the number of households went up from 19,401 to 36,101.

Information for Andalusia is less accurate. Nevertheless, the population figures collected by de Vries and by Bairoch indicate that it was this southern-most area of Castile that contributed most to maintaining overall levels of urbanisation. Cities such as Granada and Córdoba, though important in the sixteenth century, had lost much of their greatness by the eighteenth century. Seville, too, as we have seen, lost its privileged role though its decline was largely offset by the growth of Cádiz. Also on the Mediter-ranean coast Málaga grew enormously. But there can be no doubt that if levels of urbanisation were maintained and even raised it was thanks to former small towns such as Ubeda, Ronda, Osuna and Jerez de la Frontera which shared many of the characteristics of their counterparts in Extrema-dura and New Castile. What they had in common was agriculture. In the eighteenth century, this became the economic activity that provided a boost to the country as a whole and in particular to certain areas of Andalusia and New Castile around Madrid, the former exploiting the revival of trade with the Americas, the latter supplying the capital with grain, oil and wines. Available data on the evolution of trade between Spain and the Indies in the eighteenth century show that almost half the tonnage (45.6 per cent) trans-ported from Cádiz to the Americas in the years 1720–51 consisted of agricultural products, notably wine, vinegar, oil and spirits, all typical products of the Andalusian agriculture of the hinterland of Cádiz and neighbouring areas. The correlation between the development of wine and oil production, as indicated by tithe data, and export figures is evident, and clearly increased during the eighteenth century. Production of wine and spirits from San Lúcar de Barrameda, Puerto de Santa María and Jerez de la Frontera helps to account for the exceptional demographic growth regis-tered by small towns in Lower Andalusia.[74]

It is important to note that in terms of population size these communities were authentic urban centres even though they lacked some of the other attributes of urban society.[75] Jerez de la Frontera, for example, was already a city in the sixteenth century, with 6,271 households in 1587 and 5,084 in 1591, figures which stand comparison with some of the most important cities of northern Castile. Where it differed from them, however, was the fact that in 1598 half (52.74 per cent) of its inhabitants for which occu-

[74] Antonio García-Baquero González, *Cádiz y el Atlántico (1717–1778)*, 2 vols (Seville, 1976), vol. II, pp. 303ff.

[75] For a comparison of settlement sizes at the end of the sixteenth century and the middle of the eighteenth century, see Pierre Ponsot, *Atlas de Historia Económica de la Baja Andalucía (siglos XVI–XIX)* (Seville, 1986), pp. 133–4.

pations are recorded belonged to the agricultural sector, and a large proportion of the men and women for whom no occupation is recorded were also probably casual or day-labourers. This is consistent with the share agricultural activities are known to have had in overall urban wealth, 98 per cent of which derived from this sector.[76] In such conditions, the label 'agricultural cities' cannot be considered a contradiction in terms.

The fragmentation of the urban network between the sixteenth and eighteenth centuries was accompanied by a splitting up of the market space and a multiplication of periodical marketplaces; 153 of the latter were granted licences by the crown between 1753 and 1808.[77] As was the case with the new towns, the sale of the right to hold a weekly market undermined the integrity of the economic space formerly controlled by the old market centres; it comes as no surprise that established towns and cities viewed the creation of new marketplaces with hostility.

Finally, at the same time as rural industry, flourishing agriculture and local markets were helping to create a new type of human settlement, particularly in New Castile and Andalusia, the great majority of the large sixteenth-century towns were being relegated to the category of minor centres. The functions that had made them powerful in the Late Middle Ages and during the sixteenth century were lost; their importance now depended almost exclusively on their ability to retain the institutional apparatus of which they were the seat: royal or seigneurial courts, religious institutions, military installations, universities, cathedral chapters. Historians given to viewing trade and industry as the main motors of urban activity have frequently overlooked or underestimated the contribution of tertiary activities to the vitality of the city. Yet as Josiah Cox Russell has suggested, in demographic terms, the presence of a bishop is 'worth' about half a dozen merchants.[78] It is noteworthy that when Philip III decided to move the capital of the Kingdom from Madrid to Valladolid in 1601, to transfer the High Royal Court (*Chancillería*) from Valladolid to Medina del Campo and, finally, to move the fairs from Medina to Burgos, the city council of Burgos argued that the fairs were not enough to bring about the city's desired recovery and that, given the choice, their preference would be to receive the *Chancillería*, the University of Valladolid or the Council of Finance. In other words, for the Burgalese authorities the solidity of such

---

[76] Francisco Javier Vela Santamaría and Alberto Marcos Martín, 'Las grandes ciudades campesinas de Andalucía occidental en el siglo XVI. El caso de Jeréz de la Frontera', *Andalucía Moderna (siglos XVI–XVII)*, Actas del I Congresso de Historia de Andalucía (Córdoba, 1978), vol. II, pp. 403–17.

[77] Gonzalo Anes, *Las crisis agrarias en la España moderna* (Madrid, 1970), pp. 321–5.

[78] *Medieval Regions and their Cities* (Newton Abbot, 1972), p. 35. Figures for Cuenca's tertiary sector range from 32.4 per cent (1561) to 45 per cent (1800), Reher, *Town and Country*, p. 27.

institutions was worth more than a transient prosperity conditional on economic circumstance.[79]

Other examples from the critical period around 1600 can be found. Toledo also argued desperately for an *Audiencia* or *Chancillería* in 1621 as a remedy for its ruin and depopulation. Similarly, Soria made an attempt to have the Cathedral chapter of Burgo de Osma transferred there.[80] In cities like Salamanca, Valladolid and Alcalá de Henares the only demographic group which continued to grow up to the end of the first third of the seventeenth century was the university population.[81] For some of the old Castilian cities stable institutions like these constituted a core around which some of the traditional forms of city life survived until 1800.

By the end of the eighteenth century the distribution of Spain's urban population was quite unlike what it had been in the sixteenth century. What draws one's attention, firstly, is the dynamism of urban centres along the Mediterranean coast from Barcelona to Cádiz. Catalonia and Valencia had both been spared the effects of the seventeenth-century economic crisis which so crippled urban centres in Castile. In the area of the Straits of Gibraltar, Seville's commercial decline and the removal of the Indies monopoly to Cádiz caused economic activity related to the American trade to shift towards Eastern Andalusia when commerce revived towards the end of the seventeenth century. And this shift accelerated when direct trade with the Indies was opened up for cities such as Alicante, Barcelona, Cádiz, Cartagena, Málaga and Seville in 1765, and later extended to Almeria, Palma de Mallorca and Los Alfaques. Finally, in 1778 free trade was authorised from any Spanish port.

In the interior, meanwhile, the functions characteristic of the different urban systems of the sixteenth century (Old Castile, New Castile, Guadalquivir Valley) had tended either, as in the case of industry, to move out into the towns and villages of the countryside, or, in the case of commerce and finance, to become concentrated in Madrid. During the eighteenth century the old interior towns of Castile were the impotent spectators of a sustained population growth that favoured the small towns and villages. Some observers were already blaming Madrid for this state of affairs. One enlightened clergyman wrote from Jaen in the mid-eighteenth century:

After all, the stomach and heart of this body politic is the Court, into which flows all the blood from the other limbs. Yet it does not flow out again in the same proportion. And for their part the poor cities and other inhabitants have nowhere else to resort to. Though they may enjoy a fertile soil, they are marching steadfastly to their ruin.[82]

[79] Basas Fernández, *El consulado de Burgos*, p. 421.
[80] Montemayor, 'Tolède entre fortune et déclin', p. 421.
[81] Richard L. Kagan, *Students and Society in Early Modern Spain* (Baltimore, 1974), ch. 9.
[82] Miguel Avilés Fernández, 'Jaen en el siglo XVIII, visto por el clérigo ilustrado D. José Martínez de Mazos', *Espacio, Tiempo y forma*, vol. 2 (1989), 219–42.

Appendix

Summarised here is demographic information on total household numbers in each of ten Castilian provinces in 1591, 1752 and 1827, the number of 'small' towns (more than 1,250 households), and total population of these settlements.

| | Households | 'Small' towns | |
		Number	Population
Avila			
1591	38,829	1	2,826
1752	23,925	1	1,250
1827	32,113	0	
Soria			
	39,014	1	1,279
	38,832	0	
	47,349	0	
Segovia			
	42,600	1	5,548
	34,854	1	2,502
	43,226	1	2,800
Cuenca			
	66,733	3	6,007
	61,636	2	3,292
	72,204	5	10,327
Guadalajara			
	38,657	2	3,417
	25,333	1	1,300
	34,361	1	1,680
Burgos			
	98,008	2	4,155
	96,304	2	3,614
	124,062	4	11,253
Toledo			
	125,212	10	27,700
	78,656	6	12,553
	97,502	10	17,670
Salamanca			
	66,193	2	6,412
	42,414	1	4,000
	54,261	1	3,545
La Mancha			
	28,684	4	7,328
	43,298	8	12,475
	104,064	17	32,486
Extremadura			
	114,895	11	19,401
	100,768	9	14,679
	140,939	20	36,101

Sources: For 1591, Molinié-Bertrand, *Au Siècle d'or l'Espagne, passim.* For 1752 and 1827, Miguel Artola, ed., *La España del Antiguo Régimen* (Salamanca, 1966) (for Salamanca), 1967 (Old Castile) and 1971 (New Castile and Extremadura).

Select bibliography

Andressen, L. T., *Moss bys historie*, vol. I (Moss, 1984).

Authén-Blom, G., ed., *Urbaniseringsprosessen i Norden. Del 2. De anlagte steder pa 1600–1700 tallet* (Oslo, 1977).

Autour de la ville en Hainault. Mélanges d'archéologie et d'histoire urbaines offerts à Jean Duqnoille et à René Sansen (Etudes et documents du cercle royal d'histoire et d'archéologie d'Ath et de la région et musées athois, vol. VII, 1986).

Bairoch, P. *La population des villes européennes* (Geneva, 1988).

Balogh, S. *et al.*, eds, *Balassagyarmat története* (Balassagyarmat, 1977).

Benda, G., ed., *A keszthelyi uradalom 1850 elötti hagyatéki és vagyonösszeírásai 1. Keszthely 1711–1820. Fontes Musei Ethnographiae*, vol. I (Budapest, 1988).

Benda, G., 'A lakásfelszereltség változásai Keszthelyen 1790–1848', in L. Novak and L. Selmeczi, eds, *Építészet az Alföldön* (Az Arany János Múzeum Közleményei, vol. VI) (Nagykörös, 1989).

Benda, G. and Kiraly, F., 'Iparosok egy kisváros társadalmában', in Peter Nagybákay and Gábor Németh, eds, *VI. Kézmûvestörténeti Szimpózium, Veszprém 1988, november 15–16* (Veszprém, 1989).

Benedict, P., ed., *Cities and Social Change in Early Modern France* (1989).

Bennassar, B., *Valladolid au Siècle d'Or. Une ville de Castille et sa campagne au XVIe siècle* (Paris, 1967).

Beriac, F., 'Petites villes ou bourgs? Le cas du Gers', in J-P. Poussou and P. Loupès, eds, *Les petites villes du moyen âge à nos jours* (Paris, 1987).

Biziere, J. M., 'Petites villes et micro-ports: l'exemple du Danemark au XVIIIe siècle', in J-P. Poussou and P. Loupès, eds, *Les petites villes du moyen âge à nos jours* (Paris, 1987).

Blades, B., 'English villages in the Londonderry plantation', in *Post Medieval Archaeology*, vol. 20 (1986).

Blotevogel, H. H., *Zentrale Orte und Raumbeziehungen in Westfalen vor der Industrialisierung (1780–1850)* (Münster, 1975).

Bogucka, M. 'Le réseau urbain et les campagnes en Pologne (1500–1800)', *Storia della Città*, vol. 36 (1986).

Bogucka, M., 'The network and functions of small towns in Poland in early modern times', in A. Maczak und C. Smout, eds, *Gründung und Bedeutung kleinerer Städte im nördlichen Europa der frühen Neuzeit* (Wiesbaden, 1991).

Boscagin, C., *Storia di Legnago* (Verona, 1966).

Brown, J., *In the Shadow of Florence: Provincial Society in Renaissance Pescia* (Oxford, 1982).

Buyck, R., *De magistraat van Eeklo. Bijdrage tot de sociaal-economische geschiedenis van de 18e eeuw* (Brussels, 1982).

Calonge Matellanes, M. P. *et al.*, *La España del Antiguo Régimen, vol. III (Castilla la Vieja)*, ed. by M. Artola (Salamanca, 1967).

Clark, P., ed., *Country towns in pre-industrial England* (Leicester, 1981).

Clark, P., 'Small towns in Early Modern England' in *Storia Urbana* (Florence) forthcoming.

Clark, P. and Slack, P., *English Towns in Transition 1500–1700* (Oxford, 1976).

Coornaert, E., *Un centre industriel d'autrefois. La draperie-sayetterie d'Hondschoote, XIVe–XVIII siècles* (Paris, 1930).

Corfield, P. J., *The Impact of English Towns 1700–180* (Oxford, 1982).

Corfield, P. J., 'Small towns, large implications: social and cultural roles of small towns in England and Wales', *British Journal of Eighteenth Century Studies*, vol. 10 (1987).

Cosgrove, D., *The Palladian Landscape* (Leicester, 1992).

Couturier, M., *Recherches sur les structures sociales de Châteaudun* (Paris, 1969).

Crawford, W. H., 'The evolution of Ulster towns, 1750–1850', in P. Roebuck, ed., *Plantation to Partition* (Belfast, 1981).

De Vries, J., *European Urbanisation 1500–1800* (London, 1984).

Duby, G., ed., *Histoire de la France urbaine* (Paris, 5 vols, 1981–5).

Dupeux, G., *Atlas historique de l'urbanisation de la France (1811–1975)* (Paris, 1981).

Eliassen, F-E., 'Norske byer, 1500–1800: Identifikasjon, avgrensning, funksjoner', *Heimen*, vol. 24 (1987).

Eliassen, F-E., 'Den førindustrielle byen', *Marital bys historie*, vol. 1 (1994).

Eliassen, F-E., 'The Urbanization of the Periphery. Landowners and Small Towns in Early Modern Norway and Northern Europe', *Acta Poloniae Historica*, vol. 70 (1994).

Enceintes urbaines en Hainaut (Brussels, 1983).

Ericsson, B., 'The foundation and function of small towns in Sweden in the Early Modern Period', in A. Maczak and C. Smout, eds, *Gründung und Bedeutung kleinerer Städte im nördlichen Europa der frühen Neuzeit* (Wiesbaden, 1991).

Ericsson, B. *et al.*, *Stadsadministratlon i Norden pa 1700-talet. Det nordiska forskning-sprojektet Centralmakt och lokalsamhälle – beslutsprocess pa 1700-talet*, vol. I (Oslo, 1982).

Everitt, A., 'The Bainburys of England', *Urban History Yearbook 1974* (Leicester, 1974).

Everitt, A., 'The market towns', in P. Clark, ed., *The Early Modern Town* (1976).

Favier, R., 'Les petites villes dauphinoises face à leur environnement rural: emprise foncière, financière et humaine', in J-P. Poussou and P. Loupès, eds, *Les petites villes du moyen âge à nos jours* (Paris, 1987).

Favier, R., 'Economic change, demographic growth and the fate of Dauphiné's small towns', in P. Benedict, ed., *Cities and Social Change in Early Modern France* (1989).

Ferrari, E., Sembianti, F., Tomasi, M. and Sampredi, G., *I Centri Storici del Trentino* (Trento, 1981).

Ferraro, J. M., *Family and Public Life in Brescia, 1580–1650: the Foundations of power in the Venetian State* (Cambridge, 1993).

Fladby, R., 'The urbanization of Norway in the early modern period', in A. Maczak und C. Smout, eds, *Gründung und Bedeutung kleinerer Städte im nördlichen Europa der frühen Neuzeit* (Wiesbaden, 1991).

Fortea Perez, J. I., *Córdoba en el siglo XVI Las bases demográficas y económicas de une expansión urbana* (Córdoba, 1981).

Fritzell, Y., 'Yrkesfördelningen 1753–1805 enligt Tabellverket: de särskilda städerna', *Statistisk tidskrift*, vol. 4 (1983).

Gaspar, J., 'Le réseau urbain et la campagne au Portugal (XIIe–XVIIe siècles)', *Storia della Città*, vol. 36 (1986).

Gerteis, K., *Die deutschen Städte in der frühen Neuzeit. Zur Vorgeschichte der bürgerlichen Welt* (Darmstadt, 1986).

Gillespie, R., 'The origins and development of an Ulster urban network', *Irish Historical Studies*, vol. 24 (1984).

Gillespie, R., 'The small towns of Ulster, 1600–1700', *Ulster Folklife*, vol. 36 (1990).

Greipl, E. J., *Macht und Pracht. Die Geschichte der residenzen in Franken, Schwaben und Altbayern* (Regensburg, 1991).

Guerin-Pace, F., *Le système urbain français XIX–XXèmes siècles* (Paris, 1993).

Guignet, P., 'Le genèse des petites villes du bassin minièr du Valenciennois au XVIIIe siècle', *Revue du Nord*, vol. 70 (1988).

Guignet, P., 'Contribution à l'étude des réseaux urbains des Hainaut français et belge au XVIIIe siècle', *Annales de démographie historique* (1992).

Hahn, H-W., *Altständisches Bürgertum zwischen Berharrung und Wandel. Wetzlar 1689–1870* (München, 1991).

Head, A-L., 'Contrastes ruraux et urbains en Suisse de 1600 au début du XIXe siècle', in L. Mottu-Weber and D. Zumkeller, eds, *Mélanges d'Histoire Economique offerts au Professeur A-M. Piuz* (Geneva, 1989).

Heckscher, E., 'Den ekonomiska innebörden av 1500- och 1600-talens svenska stadsgrundningar', *Historisk tidskrift* (1923).

Hilton, R. H., 'Medieval market towns and simple commodity production', *Past and Present*, no. 109 (1985).

Hohenberg, P. and Lees, L., *The Making of Urban Europe 1000–1950* (Cambridge, Mass., 1985).

Horváth, F., ed., *Sárvár monográfiája* (Szombathely, 1978).

Huetz de Lemps-Emine, M-C., 'Villes et petites villes en Nouvelle Castille à la fin du XVIIIe siècle et au début du XIXe siècle' in J-P. Poussou and P. Loupès, eds, *Les Petites villes du moyen âge à nos jours* (Paris, 1987).

Hufton, O., *Bayeux in the late 18th Century* (Oxford, 1967).

Hunter, R. J., 'Towns in the Ulster Plantation', *Studia Hibernica*, vol. 11 (1971).

Jorgensen, J., 'The economic condition of Zealand provincial towns in the 18th century', *Scandinavian Economic History Review*, vol. 19 (1971).

Jourdan, J. P., 'Petites villes et bourgs des Basses Pyrénées au milieu du XIXe siècle' in J-P. Poussou and P. Loupès, eds, *Les petites villes du moyen âge à nos jours* (Paris, 1987).

Kanyar, J., ed., *Kaposvár. Várostörténeti tanulmányok* (Kaposvár, 1975).

Kiessling, R., *Die Stadt und ihr Umland. Umlandpolitik, Bürgerbesitz und Wirtschaftsgefüge in Ostschwaben vom 14. bis ins 16. Jahrhundert* (Köln, 1989).

Klep, P., *Bevolking en arbeid in transformatie. Een onderzoek in Brabant 1700–1900* (Nijmegen, 1981).

Klep, P., 'Population estimates of Belgium by province (1375–1831)', in *Historiens et populations. Liber amicorum Etienne Hélin* (Brussels, 1991).

Kuntar, L. and Szabó, L., eds, *Szentgotthárd. Helytörténeti, müvelôdéstörténeti, helyismereti tanulmányok* (Szombathely, 1981).

Laborie, J-P., *Les petites villes* (Paris, 1979).

Lachiver, M., *La population de Meulan du XVIIe au XIXe siècle* (Paris, 1969).

Lamarre-Tainturier, C., 'Administrations et petites villes en Bourgogne à la fin du XVIIIe siècle', in J-P. Poussou and P. Loupès, eds, *Les Petites villes du moyen âge à nos jours* (Paris, 1987).

Langton, J., *Geographical Change and Industrial Revolution: Coalmining in South West Lancashire 1590–1799* (Cambridge, 1979).

Lepetit, B ., *Les villes dans la France moderne (1740–1840)* (Paris, 1988). Translated in English as *The Pre-Industrial Urban System: France 1740–1840* (Cambridge, 1994).

Lewerenz, T., *Die Größenentwicklung der Kleinstädte in Ost- und Westpreußen bis zum Ende des 18. Jahrhunderts* (Marburg, 1976).

Lis, C. and Soly, H., *Een groot bedrijf in een kleine stad. De firma de Heyder en Co. te Lier, 1757–1834* (Lier, 1987).

Lottin, A., 'Un chantier de recherche – les petites villes du Nord/Pas de Calais (1750–1850)', *Revue du Nord*, vol. 70 (1988).

Marcos Gonzalez, M. D., *La España del Antiguo Régimen*, vol. VI (Castilla la Nueva and Extremadura), ed. by M. Artola (Salamanca, 1971).

Marshall, J., 'The rise and transformation of the Cumbrian Market Town, 1600–1900', *Northern History*, vol. 19 (1983).

Martin, J., *Histoire de la ville et franchise de Wavre en Roman Pays de Brabant* (Wavre, 1977).

Mateos, M. D., *La España del Antiguo Régimen*, vol. 0 (Salamanca), ed. by M. Artola (Salamanca, 1966).

Matsson, P., ed., 'Symposiet "Städers-uppkomst och liv" 17–19 September 1985, Landsarkivet i Härnösand 50 ar 1935–1985', vols I and II, in *Arkiv i Norrland*, 7–8 (Härnösand, 1986).

Meyer, J., *Etudes sur les villes en Europe Occidentale*, vol. 1 (Paris, 1983).

Millward, R., 'The Cumbrian town between 1600 and 1800', in C. Chalklin and M. A. Havinden, eds, *Rural Change and Urban Growth 1500–1800* (1974).

Molinié-Bertrand, A., *Au Siècle d'Or l'Espagne et ses hommes. La population du Royaume de Castille au XVIe siècle* (Paris, 1985).

Molinier, A., 'Villes Languedociennes (XVe–XVIe siècles)', in J-P. Poussou and P. Loupès, eds, *Les petites villes du moyen âge à nos jours* (Paris, 1987).

Mörke, O., *Die Ruhe im Sturm. Die katholische Landstadt Mindelheim unter der Herrschaft der Frundsberg im Zeitalter der Reformation* (Augsburg, 1991).

Morsa, D., 'Les petites villes dans la principauté de Liège à la fin du XVIIIe siècle. Premières approches', *Histoire et Mesure*, vol. 2 (1987).

Morsa, D., 'Distribution empiriques, distributions parétiennes et distributions log-normales: réponse à M. Marc Barbut', *Histoire et Mesure*, vol. 3 (1988).

Musgrave, P. J., *Land and Economy in Baroque Italy: Valpolicella 1630–1790* (Leicester, 1992).

Nader, H., *Liberty in Absolutist Spain: The Habsburg Sale of Towns, 1516–1700* (Baltimore, 1990).

Nagy, Z., 'Körmend kézmûves társadalmának vázlata a 18–19. században összeirasok és matrikulák adatai alapján', in P. Nagybákay and G. Németh, eds, *VI.*

Kézmüvestörténeti Szimpózium, Veszprém 1988, november 15–16 (Veszprém, 1989).

Nières, C., 'Les villes en Bretagne: 12, 40 ou 80', *Revue du Nord*, vol. 70 (1988).

Nilsson, L., *Privilegiesystem under upplösning. Administrativt tätortsbildande i Sverige 1620–1865* (Studier i stads- och kommunhistoria, vol. IV) (Stockholm, 1989).

Noble, M., 'Growth and development in a regional urban system: the country towns of Eastern Yorkshire, 1700–1850', *Urban History Yearbook 1987* (Leicester, 1987).

Norborg, L. A., 'Krona och stad i Sverige under äldre vasatid. Nagra sy punkter', *Historisk tidskrift* (1963).

O'Flanagan, P., 'Three hundred years of urban life: villages and towns in County Cork, 1600–1901', in P. O'Flanagan and C. G. Buttimer, eds, *Cork: History and Society* (Dublin, 1993).

Owen, D. M., ed., 'The Minute Books of the Spalding Gentlemen's Society, 1712–1755', *Lincoln Record Society*, vol. 73 (1981).

Patten, J., 'Village and town: an occupational study', *Agricultural History Review*, vol. 20 (1972).

Peeters, J. P., 'De-industrialization in the small and medium-sized towns in Brabant at the end of the Middle Ages', in H. van der Wee, ed., *The Rise and Decline of Urban Industries in Italy and the Low Countries* (Leuven, 1988).

Plessix, R., 'Les petites villes d'Anjou, du Maine et du Perche', in J-P. Poussou and P. Loupès, eds, *Les Petites villes du moyen âge à nos jours* (Paris, 1987).

Poussou, J-P. *et al.*, *Etudes sur les villes en Europe Occidentale*: vol. II (Paris, 1983).

Poussou, J-P. and Loupès, P., *Les Petites villes du moyen age à nos jours* (Paris, 1987).

Prevenier, W., 'La démographie des villes du comté de Flandre aux XIIIe et XIVe siècles. Etat de la question. Essai d'interprétation', *Revue du Nord*, vol. 65 (1983).

Pumain, D., *La dynamique des villes* (Paris, 1982).

Rapp, R. T., *Industry and Economic Decline in Seventeenth Century Venice* (Cambridge, Mass., 1976).

Reed, M., 'Decline and recovery in a provincial urban network: Buckinghamshire Towns 1350–1800', in M. Reed, ed., *English Towns in Decline 1350–1800* (Leicester, 1986).

Le réseau urbain en Belgique dans une perspective historique (1350–1850). Une approche statistique et dynamique (Brussels, 1992).

Robinson, P., 'Urbanisation in North West Ulster', *Irish Geography*, vol. 15 (1982).

Rosser, G., 'Communities of parish and guild in the late Middle Ages', in S. Wright, ed., *Parish, Church and People* (1988).

Salomon, N., *La campagne de Nouvelle Castille à la fin du XVIe siècle d'après les Relaciones Topograficas* (Paris, 1964).

Schilling, H., 'Die Stadt in der frühen Neuzeit', in *Enzyklopädie deutscher Geschichte*, vol. XXIV (München, 1993).

Sella, D., *Crisis and Continuity: the Economy of Spanish Lombardy in the Seventeenth Century* (Cambridge, Mass., 1979).

Simms, A. and Fagan, P., 'Villages in County Dublin: their origins and inheritance', in F. H. A. Aalen and K. Whelan, eds, *Dublin City and County* (Dublin, 1992).

Sogner, B., 'De "anlagte" byer i Norge', in G. A. Blom, ed., *Urbaniseringsprosessen i Norden*, vol. II (Trondheim, 1977).

Stabel, P., 'Décadence ou survie? Economies urbaines et industries textiles dans les petites villes drapières de la Flandre orientale (14e–16e siècles)', in M. Boone and W. Prevenier, eds, *Drapery Production in the Late Medieval Low Countires: Markets and Strategies for Survival (14th–16th centuries)* (Leuven, 1993).

Stadin, K., *Smàstäder, smàborgare och stora samhällsförändringar. Borgarnas sociala struktur i Arboga. Enköping och Västervik under perioden efter 1680, Studia Historica Upsaliensia*, vol. CV (Uppsala, 1979).

Stroebel, K., *Die Residenzörte in Hohenlohe. Ihre Entwicklung seit dem 18. Jahrhundert und ihre heutigen Funktionen aus geographischer Sicht* (Tübingen, 1982).

Sundberg, H. G., *Den svenska stapelstadsrätten. En undersökning av institutets utveckling och nuvarande innehall* (Stockholm, 1927).

Svalastoga K., *Byer i emning. Porsgrunn, Brevik og Langesund 1660–1740* (Oslo, 1943).

Terao, M., 'Rural small towns and market towns of Sachsen, Central Germany at the beginning of the modern age', *Keio Economic Studies*, vol. 2 (1964).

Terrier, D., 'Capacité d'attraction et hiérarchie des petites villes de Flandre Maritime', *Revue du Nord*, vol. 70 (1988).

Thoen, E. and Verhulst, A., 'Le réseau urbain et les campagnes dans l'ancien comté de Flandre (ca. 1350–1800)', *Storia della Città*, vol. 36 (1986).

Tommila, P., ed., *Stadsväsendets historia i Finland* (Kunnallispaino Vanda, 1987).

Torras, J., 'The old and the new marketing networks and textile growth in 18th century Spain', in M. Berg, ed., *Markets and Manufacture in Early Industrial Europe* (1991).

Turri, E., *Dietro il Paessagio: Caprino e il Monte Baldo: ricerche su un territorio comunale* (Verona, 1982).

Underdown, D., *Fire from Heaven: Life in an English Town in the Seventeenth Century* (1992).

Unwin, R. W., 'Tradition and Transition, Market Towns of the Vale of York, 1660–1830', *Northern History*, vol. 17 (1981).

Van der Wee, H., ed., *The Rise and Decline of Urban Industries in Italy and in the Low Countries* (late middle ages- early modern times) (Leuven, 1988).

Walker, M., *German Home Towns–Community, State and General Estate, 1648–1871* (Ithaca, 1971).

Walton, J., *The English Seaside Resort: a Social History 1750–1914* (Leicester, 1983).

Weedon, R. and Milne, A., eds, *Aspects of English Small Towns in the Eighteenth and Nineteenth Centuries* (Leicester, 1993).

Whyte, I. D., 'The function and social structure of Scottish burghs of barony in the 17th and 18th centuries', in A. Maczak and C. Smout, eds, *Gründung und Bedeutung kleinerer Städte im nördlichen Europa der frühen Neuzeit* (Wiesbaden, 1991).

Wyrobisz, A., 'Townships in the Grand Duchy of Lithuania during the agrarian and urban reform . . .' in A. Maczak and C. Smout, eds., *Gründung und Bedeutung kleinerer Städte im nördlichen Europa der frühen Neuzeit* (Wiesbaden, 1991).

Yun Casalilla, B., *Sobre la transición al capitalismo en Castilla. Economia y sociedad en Tierra de Campos (1500–1830)* (Salamanca, 1987).

Zamboni, C. F., *La Navigazione sull'Adige in rapporto al commercio Veronese* (Verona, 1925).

Zschunke, P., *Konfession und Alltag in Oppenheim, Beiträge zur Geschichte von Bevölkerung und Gesellschaft einer gemischtkonfessionellen Kleinstadt in der Frühen Neuzeit* (Wiesbaden, 1984).

Zylbergeld, L., 'Les villes en Hainaut dès origines à la fin du XVIème siècle', *Albums de Croij, V: Comté de Hainaut*, vol. II (Brussels, 1987).

Index